REVIEW FOR THE PRAXIS* ELEMENTARY EDUCATION CONTENT KNOWLEDGE EXAMINATION

By
COMEX SYSTEMS, INC.
STAFF

comex systems, inc.
5 Cold Hill Rd. South
Suite 24
Mendham, NJ 07945

© Copyright 2002

Published by

comex systems, inc.
5 Cold Hill Rd. South, Suite 24
Mendham, NJ 07945

ISBN 1-56030-156-2

INTRODUCTION

The Praxis Elementary Education Content Knowledge Examination is the most common exam required by states for teacher certification in elementary education. Requirements vary from state to state, so consult with your state department of education to determine the requirements for certification.

Breakdown of the Examination

The Elementary Education Content Knowledge Examination tests four main areas:

Language Arts Reading
Mathematics
Social Studies
Science

The content of each area is:

Language Arts Reading

30%   Understanding Literature

5%   Structure & Organization

30%   Literacy acquisition & Reading Instruction

25%   Language in Writing

10%   Communication Skills

Mathematics

31%   Number Sense & Numeration

23%   Algebraic Concepts

23%   Informal Geometry and Measurement

23%   Data Organization and Interpretation

Social Studies

15%   Geography

10%   World History

25%   United States History

20%   Political Science

15%   Anthropology, Sociology, & Psychology

15%   Economics

Science

25%   Earth Science

25%   Life Science

25%   Physical Science

5%   Science as Inquiry

10%   Science in Personal and Social Perspectives

5%   History and Nature of Science

5%   Unifying Processes

Format of the Test

The test is designed to test the prospective teacher's knowledge of basic concepts in the four areas to insure that he or she will be equipped to apply that knowledge in the classroom. The exam is two hours in length. Each subject has 30 questions and you have 30 minutes to complete it.

The questions are all multiple choice, and each one has four answers. There is no penalty for wrong answers; do not leave any answers blank.

Bring a calculator to the exam. The Elementary Content Knowledge Exam currently allows you to us a non-programmable calculator.

How to Use This Book

This book is designed to provide an overview of the background material that will be tested in each subject. The questions in each section will assist you in assessing your basic knowledge.

Additional Information

For the most up to date information about the Elementary Education Content Knowledge Examination contact:

Educational Testing Service (ETS)
PO Box 6081
Princeton, NJ 08541-6051
609-771-7395
www.ets.org\praxis

PART I
LANGUAGE ARTS

Language Arts

The Language Arts section will test your content knowledge in several general areas: fields of linguistics such as phonemics and semantics that are relevant to reading instruction; elements of grammar and syntax; the various forms of written discourse and the stages of the writing process; and the forms and devices of fictional literature.

Chapter 1: GRAMMAR AND SYNTAX

Grammar focuses primarily on words as its fundamental units and how words are combined into larger units such as phrases, clauses and sentences.

Parts of Speech

Words fall into eight classes: nouns, pronouns, verbs, adjectives, adverbs, prepositions, conjunctions, and interjections.

Key Point

> **Nouns** are words that name or denote a person, place, thing, quality or idea.

There are several classifications of nouns:

1. common nouns
2. proper nouns
3. concrete nouns
4. abstract nouns
5. collective nouns.

a) **Common nouns name general, not specific, persons, places or things.**

Examples: ball, card, tree

b) **Proper nouns name particular persons, places or things.**

Examples: Mike, Statue of Liberty, Mr. Smith

c) **Concrete nouns name words that can be perceived by the senses.**

Examples: bike, desk, radio

d) **Abstract nouns name words that are theoretical and not particular or tangible.**

Examples: pain, happiness, joy

e)   **Collective nouns name words that are characterized by a group or a collection.**

Examples: people, crowd, team

Key Point

> ***Pronouns*** are words that assume the functions of nouns in a sentence.

Types of Pronouns	Definition/Function	Examples
Personal		Singular: I, you, he, she, it, me, you, him, her, it Plural: We, you, they, us, you, them
Possessive	Show ownership	(S): My, mine, your, yours, his, her, hers, its (P): Our, ours, your, yours, their, theirs
Reflexive	Refer back to the antecedent	(S): myself, yourself, himself, herself, itself (P): ourselves, yourselves, themselves
Intensive	Emphasize the antecedent	(S): myself, yourself, himself, herself, itself (P): ourselves, yourselves, themselves
Relative	Introduce subordinate clauses	who, which, what, that, whom, whose
Interrogative	Asks a question	who, whom, whose, which, what
Demonstrative	Points out / refers to a specific noun	this, that, these, those
Indefinite	Does not point out / refer to specific nouns	all, anybody, both, each, either, everyone, few, many, most, neither, none, one, several, some, somebody

Key Point

> ***Adjectives*** are words used to describe a noun or a pronoun. Some helpful hints for recognizing and properly using adjectives are as follows:

♦ Typically, adjectives appear before the nouns they modify.

Example: That was an <u>interesting</u> play.

♦ "A", "an" and "the" are called *articles*, and are considered adjectives.

♦ There are several words that can be used either as a pronoun or as an adjective.

Examples: I enjoyed <u>that</u>. (pronoun)
             I enjoyed <u>that</u> movie. (adjective)

♦ Adjectives that follow linking verbs and that complete the subject of a sentence are called *predicate adjectives*.

Example: The play <u>was</u> boring. ("boring" modifies "play" and "was" is the linking verb).

♦ Adjectives can be stated in one of three forms of comparison: the positive, the comparative or the superlative.

Examples:

Positive	Comparative	Superlative
Strong	Stronger	Strongest
Fast	Faster	Fastest
Slow	Slower	Slowest

Key Point

> ***Verbs*** are words that denote or express action or occurrence. Walk, yell, build, happen and seem are all examples of verbs.

There are several different types of verbs:

1. action verbs
2. mental action verbs
3. state of being verbs
4. transitive verbs
5. intransitive verbs

(a) ***Action verbs* denote activities that can be seen.**

Example: Steve <u>runs</u>.

(b) ***Mental action verbs* denote activities that take place in the mind.**

Example: Lisa <u>thinks</u> about hitting a homerun.

(c) ***State of being verbs* indicate that something exists.**

Example: Steve <u>is</u> the best hitter on the team.

(d) ***Transitive verbs* are action verbs that take an object.**

Example: Steve <u>threw</u> the ball.

(e) ***Intransitive verbs* show an action without taking an object.**

Example: Steve <u>ran</u>.

In order to accurately indicate the time relationship of the action in a sentence, the verb(s) can change form. These forms are called *tense*. There are six tenses:

TENSE	EXAMPLE
Present	I <u>run</u>.
Past	I <u>ran</u> yesterday.
Future	I <u>will run</u> tomorrow.
Present Perfect	I <u>have run</u> very quickly.
Past Perfect	I <u>had run</u> before I ate lunch.
Future Perfect	I <u>will have run</u> before dinner.

Adverbs are words used to modify or describe verbs, adjectives or other adverbs.

Some helpful hints for properly identifying and using adverbs:

- Adverbs can be used to answer questions (how, where, when, to what extent?)

Example: Betty ate <u>quickly</u>.

- Adverbs can be used to ask questions (when, where, why, how?)

Example: <u>Where</u> is my mitt?

- Adverbs that modify verbs typically follow the word they modify.

Example: Susan talked <u>quietly</u>.

- Adverbs that modify adjectives typically precede the word they modify.

Example: That car is <u>very</u> fast.

- Like adjectives, adverbs can be stated in one of three forms of comparison: the positive, the comparative or the superlative.

Example:

Positive	Comparative	Superlative
slowly	slower	slowest
loudly	louder	loudest

Prepositions are relation or function words that connect a noun or pronoun to another element of a sentence, such as a noun or a verb.

Examples: The car <u>in</u> the driveway is blue.   (noun to noun)
Tina sleeps <u>in</u> a bed. (verb to noun)

Common prepositions include: at, above, around, after, between, beyond, below, down, during, for, in, inside, near, on, onto, over, through, throughout, under, until and with.

Key Point

> ***Conjunctions*** are words used to connect words, phrases, clauses or sentences.

There are three types of conjunctions:

1. coordinating conjunctions
2. subordinating conjunctions
3. correlative conjunctions

(a) ***Coordinating conjunctions*** **connect words, phrases, clauses and sentences which are of equal importance.**

Examples: and, but, for, nor, or

(b) ***Subordinating conjunctions*** **connect complete thoughts that are not of equal importance.**

Examples: after, although, as much as, because, since, unless

(c) ***Correlative conjunctions*** **connect words, phrases, clauses and sentences of equal importance, and are always used in pairs.**

Examples: either...or, neither...nor, both...and, not only...but also, and whether...or.

Key Point

> ***Interjections*** are words that express emotion, but have no real grammatical relationship to other words in the sentence.

Examples: Ouch!, Stop!, Hurry!...

Phrases

Phrases come after words in the grammatical hierarchy: besides prepositional phrases, which have already been mentioned, there are phrases corresponding to the other parts of speech. Phrases cannot function on their own; sentences and some types of clauses can. That is, phrases do not express a complete thought.

Key Point

> An important kind of phrase is a verbal phrase, of which there are three main types: **infinitive**, **gerund**, and **participle**.

Infinitive: is the tenseless form of a verb and always begins with *to*: to be, to speak, to love, etc. It can function like a noun (To err is human), like an adjective (He wants books to read), or like an adverb (Those tickets were hard to get).

Gerund: is formed from the present participle of a verb and always ends with –*ing*. It functions like a noun (Jogging is good for you; I don't like sweating).

Participle: is formed from either the present or past participles of a verb and it functions like an adjective (The gathered flowers smell nice).

Clauses

Clauses are of two main types: independent and dependent (sometimes called principal and subordinate). A clause contains a subject and a verb. Independent clauses can stand on their own as sentences, while dependent clauses cannot because they do not express a complete thought. A special type of dependent clause is a **relative clause**, which starts with a relative pronoun:

The tree ***that is on the corner***.

The song ***which was playing last night***.

The man ***who went insane last year***.

Clauses can also be categorized according to their meaning, that is, according to semantic aspects. Here are some of the more important ones:

- Condition: I would have come ***if*** *you had called*.
- Temporal: I'll let you know ***before*** *I leave*.
- Comparative: She's much nicer ***than*** *I thought*.
- Cause: He missed the test ***because*** *he overslept*.

Sentences

Sentences express a complete thought; they start with a capital letter and end with a period, question mark, or exclamation point. There are four types: simple, compound, complex, and compound-complex.

- Simple: a sentence with only one (independent) clause.

   Mario ate the pizza.

   Ravaged by hunger, Mario ate the whole pizza in five minutes.

- Compound: two or more independent clauses joined by a coordinating conjunction.

   John went to the store, or he went to the movies.

8

- Complex: has one independent clause and one or more dependent clauses.

    She left despite the fact that I apologized.

- Compound-complex: two or more independent and one or more dependent.

    The man slept, and the woman wept as the opera came to an end.

A sentence can also be categorized by its mood or use:

- **Declarative** sentences make statements of fact or give information. The declarative use of sentences has much in common with the **indicative** mood:

    John went to the store.

    Water freezes at 32 degrees Fahrenheit.

- **Interrogative** sentences ask a question and begin with an interrogative pronoun. (who, what, when, where, how):

    Who is the President of Albania?

    How were you able to do it?

- **Imperative** sentences issue a command. These come under the **imperative** mood:

    Finish your homework!

    Clean your room!

- **Exclamative** sentences express emotion or feeling, or make an evaluation:

    What a lovely gift!

    How wonderful you must feel!

The third mood in English, beside the indicative and imperative, is the **subjunctive** mood. The subjunctive is not as important in English as in some Romance languages (like French and Italian). Its main (optional) use in English is for counterfactual statements such as: *If I **were** a bird, I would fly far away* or *If I **had** the chance, I would go to Tahiti.*

The same word may fall into several word classes: for example, *that* can be used as a pronoun (That is the man!) or as an adjective (That man is a beast!). So it is useful to be aware of the various ways that words actually function in sentences and how they relate to one another. In other words, it is good to be aware of **syntax**. Some of the more important of these functions are subject, predicate, direct object, and indirect object.

The **subject** of a sentence performs the action expressed by the verb, although in a sentence such as *Bruno is tall*, Bruno (the subject) doesn't seem to be performing anything; in this sentence "tall" is referred to as a **predicate adjective**. In a sentence such as *Bruno is president*, "president" is referred to as a *predicate nominative*. The predicate is everything in a sentence besides the subject; it is usually identified with the verb. The direct object receives the action of the verb.

The standard syntax (word order) in an English declarative sentence is subject-verb-direct object. For example:

Nancy wrote a letter.

Sometimes the direct object can be a clause:

Mary noticed *that the table had been moved.*

Frank drank *what he thought was an espresso.*

Betty likes *to play draw poker.*

If there is an indirect object involved, it is placed after the verb and before the direct object:

*Nancy wrote **me** a letter.*

If there is only a subject and a verb, then the verb is being used *intransitively*:

The snow melted.

That is, a transitive verb requires a direct object, while an intransitive verb does not. However, most verbs in English can be used either transitively or intransitively.

To change a declarative sentence into an interrogative can be accomplished by inverting the order of the subject and verb:

***There is** a fly in the ointment.*

***Is there** a fly in the ointment?*

Finally, the active **voice** can be changed to passive by switching the subject and direct object, adding the preposition *by,* and changing the verb accordingly:

Active: Maria ***ate*** the cake.

Passive: The cake ***was eaten*** by Maria.

The active voice indicates that the subject performs the action, while in the passive voice the subject is acted upon by someone or something.

Verbs generally express action with a reference to time. That is, verbs have **tense** and **aspect**. The tenses are past, present, and future, while the aspect may be simple, perfect, progressive, or perfect-progressive:

- Simple present: I speak.
- Simple past: I spoke.
- Simple future: I will speak.
- Perfect present: I have spoken.
- Perfect past: I had spoken.
- Perfect future: I will have spoken.
- Progressive present: I am speaking.
- Progressive past: I was speaking.
- Progressive future: I will be speaking
- Perfect-progressive present: I have been speaking.
- Perfect-progressive past: I had been speaking.
- Perfect-progressive future: I will have been speaking.

Subject-Verb Agreement

Agreement of subject and verb is a key element in English grammar and composition. There are a number of special rules in the area of subject/verb agreement that you will review in this section.

A VERB AND ITS SUBJECT MUST AGREE IN NUMBER

Key Point

Agreeing in number means that if the subject is singular, the verb must also be singular. If the subject is plural, the verb must be plural.

Remember that singular means one <u>single</u> thing and that plural means <u>two</u> <u>or</u> <u>more</u> things.

EXAMPLE: The dog walks down the street.

In this sentence the subject <u>dog</u> is singular and so is the verb <u>walks</u>. Most verbs ending in a single <u>s</u> are singular.

EXAMPLE: The dogs walk down the street.

In this sentence the subject <u>dogs</u> is plural and so is the verb <u>walk</u>.

Now, try some sample questions.

DIRECTIONS: Underline the correct verb in the following sentences.

1.   The chair (is, are) broken.

2.   The chairs (is, are) broken.

3.   The singer (sing, sings) her latest song.

4.   The singers (sing, sings) their latest song.

5.   The phone (was, were) ringing.

6.   The phones (was, were) ringing.

7.   The lady (enter, enters) the room.

8.   The ladies (enter, enters) the room.

9.   The child (has, have) the toy.

10.   Both children (has, have) the toy.

Answers

1.   <u>Is</u> agrees with the singular subject <u>chair</u>.

2.   <u>Are</u> agrees with the plural subject <u>chairs</u>.

3.   <u>Sings</u> agrees with the singular subject <u>singer</u>.

4.   <u>Sing</u> agrees with the plural subject <u>singers</u>.

5.   <u>Was</u> agrees with the singular subject <u>phone</u>.

6.   <u>Were</u> agrees with the plural subject <u>phones</u>.

7.   <u>Enters</u> agrees with the singular subject <u>lady</u>.

8.   <u>Enter</u> agrees with the plural subject <u>ladies</u>.

9.   <u>Has</u> agrees with the singular subject <u>child</u>.

10.   <u>Have</u> agrees with the plural subject <u>children</u>.

Phrases Between Subjects And Verbs

Sometimes choosing the correct verb is complicated by the introduction of a prepositional phrase which is placed between the subject and verb. It is important to determine the correct subject before you choose the verb.

Most people will correctly say *"The pipes are clogged."* but, some people might have problems with *"The pipes in the bathroom is/are clogged."*

In the second sentence the subject is <u>pipes</u> and the correct verb is <u>are</u>. But some people might mistakenly think that the noun <u>bathroom</u> is the subject and so select the verb <u>is</u>. The noun <u>bathroom</u> is the object of the preposition <u>in</u>, and this prepositional phrase is an adjective phrase modifying the subject <u>pipes</u>. If you have problems deciding which word is the subject, cross out the prepositional phrase.

EXAMPLE: The pipes in the bathroom is/are clogged.

Practice this skill in the following exercise.

DIRECTIONS: Underline the correct verb in the following sentences.

1.   The house beyond the hills (is, are) vacant.

2.   The homes at the top of the hill (is, are) vacant.

3.   This box of pencils (is, are) full.

4.   These three boxes of chocolate (has, have) been opened.

5.   The announcer of the show (wear, wears) a microphone.

6.   The girls in the bus (ride, rides) to school.

7.   His uncles with their families (take, takes) vacation every year.

8.   Employees of the company (seem, seems) to want a raise.

9.   The appeal of the song (is, are) worldwide.

10.   Her dresses with the buttons (is, are) at the cleaners.

ANSWERS

1.   **<u>Is</u>** agrees with the singular subject **<u>house</u>**.

2.   **<u>Are</u>** agrees with the plural subject **<u>homes</u>**.

3.   **<u>Is</u>** agrees with the singular subject **<u>box</u>**.

4.   **<u>Have</u>** agrees with the plural subject **<u>boxes</u>**.

5.   **<u>Wears</u>** agrees with the singular subject **<u>announcer</u>**.

6.   **<u>Ride</u>** agrees with the plural subject **<u>girls</u>**.

7.   **<u>Take</u>** agrees with the plural subject **<u>uncles</u>**.

8.   **<u>Seem</u>** agrees with the plural subject **<u>employees</u>**.

9.   **<u>Is</u>** agrees with the singular subject **<u>appeal</u>**.

10.   **<u>Are</u>** agrees with the plural subject **<u>dresses</u>**.

Key Point

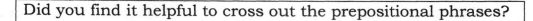

Did you find it helpful to cross out the prepositional phrases?

Indefinite Pronouns That Are Usually Singular

The pronouns that follow are usually singular and require a singular verb.

each	one	no one	someone
either	everyone	nobody	somebody
neither	everybody	anyone	

While these pronouns suggest groups of people, they actually point to individual members of the group.

EXAMPLE: See the children. <u>Each</u> wants a piece of candy.

In the above example, the pronoun <u>Each</u> refers to the children individually and requires the singular verb, wants.

EXAMPLE: Neither <u>thinks</u> that it's a good idea..

In this example, the pronoun <u>Neither</u> refers to each person in the group individually, so the subject must be singular.

Try choosing the correct verb in the following exercise.

DIRECTIONS: Underline the correct verb in the following sentences.

1.   Everybody at the game (is, are) cheering.

2.   Somebody (has, have) to so something about the situation.

3.   Neither of the clerks (want, wants) to answer the phone.

4.   Each of the television sets (need, needs) repair.

5.   One of the workmen (seem, seems) tired.

6.   No one (do, does) homework on Friday.

7.   Neither of the lawyers (was, were) present.

8.   Anyone (is, are) welcome.

9.   Someone in the guard-house (answer, answers) the phone at night.

10.   Everyone on both teams (wants, wants) to have a party.

ANSWERS

1. **Is** agrees with the singular subject **Everybody**.
2. **Has** agrees with the singular subject **Somebody**.
3. **Wants** agrees with the singular subject **Neither**.
4. **Needs** agrees with the singular subject **Each**.
5. **Seems** agrees with the singular subject **One**.
6. **Does** agrees with the singular subject **No one**.
7. **Was** agrees with the singular subject **Neither**.
8. **Is** agrees with the singular subject **Anyone**.
9. **Answers** agrees with the singular subject **Someone**.
10. **Wants** agrees with the singular subject **Everybody**.

Indefinite Pronouns That Can Be Either Singular Or Plural

The following pronouns can be either singular or plural depending upon how they are used in the sentence.

some   all   most

EXAMPLE: Some of the candy is missing.

In the above sentence the pronoun <u>some</u> is followed by the adjective phrase <u>of</u> <u>the</u> <u>candy</u>. <u>Candy</u> is singular and so the word <u>some</u> is used singularly. The verb <u>is</u> is singular.

EXAMPLE: Some of the candies are missing.

In the above sentence the pronoun <u>some</u> is followed by the adjective phrase <u>of</u> <u>the</u> <u>candies</u>. <u>Candies</u> is plural and so the word <u>some</u> is used plurally. The verb <u>are</u> is plural.

The following exercise will help you master this skill.

DIRECTIONS: Underline the correct verb in the following sentences.

1. Most of the trucks (is, are) refueled.
2. Most of the money (is, are) missing.
3. Some of the answers (was, were) incorrect.
4. All of the dancers (exercise, exercises) daily.
5. All of the programming (seem, seems) acceptable.
6. Most of the cost (is, are) covered by the tuition.

7. Some of the vegetables (seem, seems) fresh.

8. Most of the students (do, does) homework at night.

9. Some of the laundry (has, have) been folded.

10. Some of the shirts (has, have) been folded.

ANSWERS

1. **Are** agrees with the subject **Most** which is made plural by the prepositional phrase <u>of the trucks</u>.

2. **Is** agrees with the subject **Most** which is made singular by the prepositional phrase <u>of the money</u>.

3. **Were** agrees with the subject **Some** which is made plural by the prepositional phrase <u>of the answers</u>.

4. **Exercise** agrees with the subject **All** which is made plural by the prepositional phrase <u>of the dancers</u>.

5. **Seems** agrees with the subject **All** which is made singular by the prepositional phrase <u>of the programing</u>.

6. **Is** agrees with the subject **Most** which is made singular by the prepositional phrase <u>of the cost</u>.

7. **Seem** agrees with the subject **Some**, which is made plural by the prepositional phrase <u>of the vegetables</u>.

8. **Do** agrees with the subject **Most** which is made plural by the prepositional phrase <u>of the students</u>.

9. **Has** agrees with the subject **Some** which is made singular by the prepositional phrase <u>of the laundry</u>.

10. **Have** agrees with the subject **Some** which is made plural by the prepositional phrase <u>of the shirts</u>.

Indefinite Pronouns That Are Plural

The following indefinite pronouns are plural and require a plural verb.

     several   few   both   many

EXAMPLE: Several of the dancers wear ribbons in their hair.

In this sentence the pronoun <u>several</u> is the subject; the verb <u>wear</u> is the correct form.

Try these sentences. Be careful to eliminate prepositional phrases before selecting the correct verb form.

DIRECTIONS: Underline the correct verb in the following sentences.

1. Several of the glasses (is, are) chipped.

2. Few of the voters (have, has) returned.

3. Both (seem, seems) ridiculous.

4. Many (was, were) waiting on line.

5. Many of the helmets (need, needs) new straps.

6. Several of the spectators (leave, leaves) early.

7. Both of the shoes (is, are) under the stairs.

8. Few of the books (appears, appear) used.

9. Few of the jury (was, were) ready to decide.

10. Many of the injuries (has, have) been prevented.

ANSWERS

1. **Are** agrees with the plural subject **Several**.
2. **Have** agrees with the plural subject **Few**.
3. **Seem** agrees with the plural subject **Both**.
4. **Were** agrees with the plural subject **Many**.
5. **Need** agrees with the plural subject **Many**.
6. **Leave** agrees with the plural subject **Several**.
7. **Are** agrees with the plural subject **Both**.
8. **Appear** agrees with the plural subject **Few**.
9. **Were** agrees with the plural subject **Few**.
10. **Have** agrees with the plural subject **Many**.

Compound Subjects Joined By And

Most compound subjects joined by and are plural and take a plural verb.

EXAMPLE: The spoon and dish are on the table.

In this sentence the nouns spoon and dish are joined by the word and. This compound subject is followed by the plural verb are.

EXAMPLE: The cat in the basket and the dog by the fireplace make a pretty picture.

In this sentence the nouns <u>cat</u> and <u>dog</u> are joined by the word <u>and</u>. <u>In the basket</u> and <u>by the fireplace</u> are prepositional phrases modifying the nouns <u>cat</u> and <u>dog</u>. <u>Cat</u> and <u>dog</u> make up the compound subject; the plural, <u>make</u>, is the correct verb form. Again, you might find it helpful to cross out the prepositional phrases when choosing the correct verb.

Some compound subjects are considered a single item.

EXAMPLE: Spaghetti and meatballs is my favorite dinner.

In this sentence the nouns <u>spaghetti</u> and <u>meatballs</u> make up the compound subject, but because they are often served together, we consider them a single dish. The singular verb form is used.

Now, use these skills with the next group of questions.

DIRECTIONS: Underline the correct verb in the following sentences.

1. Brian and Sean (is, are) at home.

2. The books and magazines on the shelf (was, were) out of date.

3. Bacon and eggs (was, were) served for breakfast.

4. The steering wheel and column of the car (has, have) been repaired.

5. Justice and charity (is, are) virtues.

6. Sacramento and Bismarck (is, are) capital cities.

7. Macaroni and cheese (is, are) served each Wednesday.

8. The captain and the manager of the team (does, do) meet regularly.

9. Linda and her cat Thumper (has, have) been sitting by the window.

10. Clarity and color (is, are) important qualities in a diamond.

ANSWERS

1. **Are** agrees with the compound subject **Brian and Sean**.
2. **Were** agrees with the compound subject **books and magazines**.
3. **Was** agrees with the compound subject **Bacon and eggs**; because bacon and eggs make up a single dish, they are considered a singular subject.
4. **Have** agrees with the compound subject **wheel and column**.
5. **Are** agrees with the compound subject **Justice and charity**.
6. **Are** agrees with the compound subject **Sacramento and Bismarck**.

18

7. **Is** agrees with the compound subject **Macaroni and cheese**; because macaroni and cheese make up a single dish, they are considered a singular subject.

8. **Do** agrees with the compound subject **captain and manager**.

9. **Have** agrees with the compound subject **Linda and cat**.

10. **Are** agrees with the compound subject **Clarity and color**.

Compound Subjects Joined By Or, Nor, Either... Or, Neither... Nor

If the subjects joined by <u>or</u>, <u>nor</u>, <u>either...or</u>, or <u>neither...nor</u> are singular, the verb is singular.

EXAMPLE: Either the doctor or the nurse visits the patient daily.

In this sentence the nouns <u>doctor</u> and <u>nurse</u> are the subjects joined by <u>either...or</u>. Both subjects are singular and so the verb <u>visits</u> is singular. Notice that the sentence states that only one person, either the doctor or the nurse, visits the patient daily.

If one of the subjects joined by <u>or</u>, <u>nor</u>, <u>either...or</u>, or <u>neither...nor</u> is singular and the other subject is plural, the verb agrees with the subject that is closest to it.

EXAMPLE: Neither the coach nor the players are going to lunch.

In this sentence the nouns <u>coach</u> and <u>players</u> are the subjects joined by <u>Neither...nor</u>. The subject <u>coach</u> is singular and the subject <u>players</u> is plural. Because the subject <u>players</u> is closer to the verb, the verb <u>are going</u> is plural.

EXAMPLE: Neither the players nor the coach is going to lunch.
In this sentence the noun <u>players</u> and <u>coach</u> are the subjects joined by <u>Neither...nor</u>. The subject <u>players</u> is plural and the subject <u>coach</u> is singular. Because the subject <u>coach</u> is closer to the verb, the verb <u>is going</u> is singular.

DIRECTIONS: Underline the correct verb in the following sentences.

1. Neither the roses nor the magnolia tree (has, have) bloomed.

2. Bill or Joey (is, are) the attendant.

3. Neither the sedan nor the station wagon (has, have) air-conditioning.

4. Either the bride or her attendants (has, have) arrived.

5. Tara nor Donna (wear, wears) perfume.

6. Either gold or silver (make, makes) a fine gift.

7. Neither the father nor the children (was, were) excited about the shopping trip.

8. Neither the children nor the father (was, were) excited about the shopping trip.

9. Neither the frogs nor the crickets (was, were) making any noise.

10. The dog or the cat (chase, chases) the paper boy.

ANSWERS

1. The subjects <u>roses</u> (plural) and <u>tree</u> (singular) are joined by <u>Neither...nor</u>; <u>tree</u> is closer to the verb and so the verb (**has**) is singular.

2. The subject <u>Billy and Joey</u> are joined by <u>or</u> and so the verb (**is**) is singular.

3. The subjects <u>sedan</u> and <u>station wagon</u> are joined by <u>Neither...nor</u>; both are singular and so the verb (**has**) is singular.

4. The subjects <u>bride</u> (singular) and <u>attendants</u> (plural) are joined by <u>Either...or</u>; <u>attendants</u> is closer to the verb and so the verb (**have**) is plural.

5. The subjects <u>Tara</u> and <u>Donna</u> are joined by <u>nor</u> and so the verb (**wears**) is singular.

6. The subjects <u>gold</u> and <u>silver</u> are joined by <u>Either...or</u>; both are singular and so the verb (**makes**) is singular.

7. The subjects <u>father</u> (singular) and <u>children</u> (plural) are joined by <u>Neither...nor</u>; <u>children</u> is closer to the verb and so the verb (**were**) is plural.

8. The subjects <u>children</u> (plural) and <u>father</u> (singular) are joined by <u>Neither...nor</u>; <u>father</u> is closer to the verb and so the verb (**was**) is singular.

9. The subjects <u>frogs</u> and <u>crickets</u> are joined by <u>Neither...nor</u>; both are plural and so the verb (**were**) is plural.

10. The subjects <u>dog</u> and <u>cat</u> are joined by <u>or</u>; both are singular and so the verb (**chases**) is singular.

Collective Nouns

A COLLECTIVE NOUN refers to a group of persons or things. Use a singular verb if the noun is used to refer to the group as a <u>whole</u>. Use a plural verb if the members of the group are acting as <u>individuals</u>.

EXAMPLE: The <u>team</u> wins the game.

In this sentence the <u>team</u> acts as a whole in order to win the game, and so the verb <u>wins</u> is singular.

EXAMPLE: The <u>team</u> eat their sandwiches.

In this sentence the <u>team</u> acts as individuals as they each eat their own sandwiches, and so the verb <u>eat</u> is plural.

Try some examples.

DIRECTIONS: Underline the correct verb in the following sentences.

1. The class (elect, elects) a representative each year.

2. The class (wear, wears) their new tee shirts at the annual picnic.

3. The committee (fight, fights) among themselves.

4. The committee (review, reviews) proposals carefully.

5. The herd (migrate, migrates) each winter.

6. The swarm (return, returns) to its nest.

7. The troop (eat, eats) their dinners.

8. The faculty (meet, meets) at school in September.

9. The faculty (disagree, disagrees) among themselves.

10. The fleet (head, heads) for port.

ANSWERS

1. **<u>Elects</u>** agrees with <u>class</u>; <u>class</u> is singular because the group is acting as a unit.

2. **<u>Wear</u>** agrees with <u>class</u>; <u>class</u> is plural because the members are acting as individuals (each wears his own shirt).

3. **<u>Fight</u>** agrees with <u>committee</u>; <u>committee</u> is plural because the members are acting as individuals (each is fighting with the others).

4. **<u>Reviews</u>** agrees with <u>committee</u>; <u>committee</u> is singular because the group is acting as a unit.

5. **<u>Migrates</u>** agrees with <u>herd</u>; <u>herd</u> is singular because the group is acting as a unit.

6. **<u>Returns</u>** agrees with <u>swarm</u>; <u>swarm</u> is singular because the group is acting as a unit.

7. **<u>Eat</u>** agrees with <u>troop</u>; <u>troop</u> is plural because the members are acting as individuals (each is eating his own dinner).

8. **Meets** agrees with <u>faculty</u>; <u>faculty</u> is singular because the group is acting as a unit.

9. **Disagree** agrees with <u>faculty</u>; <u>faculty</u> is plural because the members are acting as individuals (they are disagreeing among themselves).

10. **Heads** agrees with <u>fleet</u>; <u>fleet</u> is singular because the group is acting as a unit.

OTHER SUBJECT - VERB AGREEMENT PROBLEMS.

The words **here** and **where** are **never** the subject of a sentence. Instead, the subject **follows** the verb, and so the subject must be found in order to use the correct verb form.

EXAMPLE: Where is the hat?

Key Point

NOTE: It is sometimes helpful to restate the sentence.

RESTATED: The hat is where?

In this sentence the subject is <u>hat</u>. <u>Hat</u> is singular and so is the verb <u>is</u>.

EXAMPLE: Here are the hats.

RESTATED: The hats are here.

In this sentence the subject is <u>hats</u>. <u>Hats</u> is plural and so is the verb <u>are</u>.

Key Point

Words stating amount are usually singular.

EXAMPLE: Fifty dollars is the correct amount.

In this sentence the noun <u>dollars</u> is the subject. It refers to <u>one</u> payment and so the verb <u>is</u> is singular.

Key Point

Some nouns ending in <u>s</u> are considered singular.

EXAMPLE: Mathematics is my favorite class.

In this sentence the noun <u>mathematics</u> ends in <u>s</u>. It is, however, one subject and so the verb <u>is</u> is singular.

Try a few questions, using the skills you have just learned.

DIRECTIONS: **Underline the correct verb in the following sentences.**

1. Here (is, are) the tickets.

2. Two thirds of the pie (has, have) been eaten.

3. Physics (has, have) not been offered this semester.

4. World economics (is, are) a critical subject.

5. There (has, have) been eleven hits this inning.

6. Four years in high school (seem, seems) like an eternity.

7. Thirty pounds (is, are) a good deal of weight to lose.

8. The mumps (is, are) an annoying disease.

9. Where (is, are) the clowns?

10. The measles (is, are) a contagious disease.

ANSWERS

1. **Are** agrees with the subject tickets.
2. **Has** agrees with the subject Two-thirds; such amounts are considered singular.
3. **Has** agrees with the subject Physics; though it ends in s, the word physics is singular in this sentence.
4. **Is** agrees with the subject economics; though it ends in s, the word economics is singular in this sentence.
5. **Have** agrees with the subject hits.
6. **Seems** agrees with the subject years; such amounts are considered singular.
7. **Is** agrees with the subject pounds; such amounts are considered singular.
8. **Is** agrees with the subject mumps; though it ends in s, the word mumps is singular in this sentence.
9. **Are** agrees with the subject clowns.
10. **Is** agrees with the subject measles; though it ends in s, the word measles is singular in this sentence.

Misplaced Modifiers

Phrases and clauses that modify other words should be placed as close as possible to the words they modify.

EXAMPLE: The sea water rose and spilled over the wall up to the top of the stone.

In this sentence the adverb <u>up</u> and the prepositional phrases <u>to the top</u> and <u>of the stone</u> are misplaced. While it is possible that the water could spill over the wall to the top of some stone on the other side of the wall, it is more likely that the wall itself is made of stone. In any event the adverb <u>up</u> is clearly misplaced; water does not spill <u>up</u>!

IMPROVED: The sea water rose <u>up to the top of the stone</u> and spilled over the wall.

Let's look at another example.

EXAMPLE: The fish was caught this morning from the dock which is being served for dinner.

In this sentence the clause <u>which is being served for dinner</u> is misplaced. The idea is ridiculous. This sentence makes it sound as if the dock is being served for dinner.

IMPROVED: The fish <u>which is being served</u> for dinner was caught this morning from the dock.

Try another example.

EXAMPLE: The boat glided from shore with its sails unfurled in the last of the early morning mist and its crew setting about their chores.

In this sentence the phrases <u>in the last</u> and <u>of the early morning mist</u> are misplaced. Since it would be awkward to place them close to the word they modify (<u>glided</u>), place them at the beginning of the sentence.

IMPROVED: In the last of the early morning mist, the boat glided from shore with its sails unfurled and its crew setting about their chores.

DIRECTIONS: Rewrite each of the following sentence so that the modifier is placed correctly.

1. Jane placed the knives, forks, and spoons on the table next to the plates and napkins before dinner.

2. The envelope is on the table which is being mailed to Ireland.

24

3. The ship headed for the port which had been damaged in the storm and needed engine repairs.

4. The championship game has resumed after twenty minutes delay of golf.

5. Jim, the singer in the band, sang several old tunes from the fifties with enthusiasm.

6. The police eliminated several suspects who may have committed the crime by checking alibis.

7. Sheila will check the pottery when it dries for flaws.

8. The magnifying glass was returned to its leather case in the drawer after it was broken.

9. The child's gloves were on both hands which were too large.

10. Steve bought a car from a salesman that needed a tune-up.

ANSWERS

1. Before dinner, Jane placed the knives, forks and spoons on the table next to the plates and napkins.
2. The envelope which is being mailed to Ireland is on the table.
3. The ship which had been damaged in the storm and needed engine repairs headed for the port.
4. The championship game of golf has resumed after twenty minutes delay.

5. Jim, the singer in the band, sang with enthusiasm several old tunes from the fifties.

6. By checking alibis the police eliminated several suspects who may have committed the crime.

7. Sheila will check the pottery for flaws when it dries.

8. After it was broken, the magnifying glass was returned to its leather case in the drawer.

9. The child's gloves, which were too large, were on both hands.

10. Steve bought a car that needed a tune-up from a salesman.

Dangling Modifiers

A dangling modifier is a phrase or clause which is acting as a modifier but has no word in the sentence that it can sensibly modify. It is a modifier <u>unattached</u> to any word in the sentence.

EXAMPLE: Running to the bus, the passing car splattered me with mud.

In this sentence the phrase <u>Running to the bus</u> is a dangling modifier. Even though the sense of the sentence suggests that this phrase refers to the speaker of the sentence, <u>me</u>, grammatically the phrase modifies the word <u>car</u>. In other words, the sentence as it is now written is equal to saying, "The passing car running to the bus splattered me with mud." This of course makes no sense.

The sentence can be corrected by changing the phrase <u>Running to the bus</u> to a clause.

IMPROVED: The passing car splattered me with mud as I was running to the bus.

OR: As I was running to the bus, the passing car splattered me with mud.

NOTE: This sentence can also be improved by altering the main clause.

EXAMPLE: Running to the bus I was splattered with mud by a passing car.

Notice in this improvement that the speaker <u>me</u> is changed to <u>I</u>.

EXAMPLE: <u>Floating in the ocean</u>, a shark attacked him.

What the underlined phrase modifies is unclear: the sentence seems to suggest that the shark was floating instead of the man indicated by the pronoun *him*. A better construction might be *He was floating in the ocean when a shark attacked him.*

DIRECTIONS: **Rewrite the following sentences so that the dangling modifiers are removed.**

1. After mowing the lawn, the grass looked beautiful.

2. When writing to the senator, my pen ran out of ink.

3. While speaking of politics, the subject of foreign aid came up.

4. Sailing down the river on a beautiful day, the sun suddenly was covered by clouds.

5. Having written the letter quickly, my message was unclear.

6. Because I am left-handed person, the scissors wouldn't work very well.

7. While traveling by train to Des Moines, my sister received the letter at home.

8. Because I found the door unlocked, the key was not necessary.

9. When choosing a new wardrobe, color and style must be considered.

10. After playing all day long, the mother tucked Alexis into bed.

ANSWERS

1. After mowing the lawn, father thought the grass looked beautiful.
2. When I was writing to the senator, my pen ran out of ink.

3. While speaking of politics, the group discussed the subject of foreign aid.

4. While we were sailing down the river on a beautiful day, the sun suddenly was covered by clouds.

5. Having written the letter quickly, I realized that my message was unclear.

6. Because I am a left-handed person, I had difficulty using the scissors.

7. While traveling by train to Des Moines, I wrote my sister a letter which she received at home.

8. Because I found the door unlocked, I did not need the key.

9. When choosing a new wardrobe, a person must consider color and style.

10. After playing all day long, Alexis was tucked into bed by her mother.

Note: **There are other possible ways to revise the sentences. Just be sure you have eliminated the dangling modifier.**

MODIFIERS THAT CAN HAVE TWO MEANINGS

Sometimes a modifier is placed in a sentence where it can have two meanings because there are two words it could be modifying.

EXAMPLE: Jimmy decided after the game was completed to call Grandma.

With the clause <u>after the game was completed</u> in its present position, the exact meaning of the sentence is unclear.

IMPROVED: After the game was completed, Jimmy decided to call Grandma.

OR: Jimmy decided to call Grandma after the game was completed.

In the first improved version Jimmy did not make his decision to call until after the game was completed. In the second version Jimmy decided either before or during the game to make the call to Grandma sometime after the conclusion of the game. Either way is correct.

Let's try a few examples.

DIRECTIONS: **Rewrite each of the following sentences so that the meaning is clear.**

1. Tim said during the television show Jerry sang beautifully.

2. The fireman asked us before we spoke for a donation.

3. The children returned to the car after the game was completed in the parking lot.

4. Remind Jane when she arrives Bill wants to meet with her.

5. The wrestler laughed that his opponent was weak before the match.

6. Dorina noted the changes during the first month Bill experienced.

7. Mrs. Thatcher told the child during the party to visit her.

8. Richie noted during his run Ed wiped his brow.

9. The train pitched suddenly tilting to the right.

10. Tell Trixie before the party at the lake begins Jim has a suggestion.

ANSWERS

1. During the television show Tim said Jerry sang beautifully.

or

Tim said Jerry sang beautifully during the television show.

2. Before we spoke, the fireman asked us for a donation.

or

The fireman asked us for a donation before we spoke.

3. After the game was completed, the children returned to the car in the parking lot.

or

The children returned to the car in the parking lot after the game was completed.

4. When she arrives, remind Jane that Bill wants to meet with her.

or

Remind Jane that Bill wants to meet with her when she arrives.

5. Before the match the wrestler laughed that his opponent was weak.

or

The wrestler laughed before the match that his opponent was weak.

6. During the first month Dorina noted the changes Bill experienced.

or

Dorina noted the changes Bill experienced during the first month.

7. During the party Mrs. Thatchet told the child to visit her.

or

Mrs. Thatchet told the child to visit her during the party.

8. During his run Richie noted Ed wiped his brow.

or

Richie noted Ed wiped his brow during his run.

9. The train pitched suddenly, tilting to the right.

or

The train pitched, suddenly tilting to the right.

(Note the use of the comma to change the meaning of the sentence.)

Suddenly the train pitched, tilting to the right.

10. Before the party at the lake begins, tell Trixie that Jim has a suggestion.

or

Tell Trixie that Jim has a suggestion before the party at the lake begins.

Verb Tense Errors

In order to show the correct time relationship of the action or statement of being in a sentence, the verb or verbs of a sentence can change form. These forms are called <u>tense</u>.

Here is an example of the six tenses using the pronoun <u>I</u> and the verb <u>talk</u>.

Present	I talk today.
Past	I talked yesterday.
Future	I shall talk tomorrow.
Present Perfect	I have talked often
Past Perfect	I had talked to her before I talked to you.
Future Perfect	I shall have talked to her by tomorrow afternoon.

The <u>present</u> <u>tense</u> is used to express an action (or state of being) going on at the present time.

The <u>past</u> <u>tense</u> is used to express an action (or state of being) that took place in the past but did not continue into the present.

The <u>future</u> <u>tense</u> is used to express an action (or state of being) going on at some time in the future.

The <u>present</u> <u>perfect</u> <u>tense</u> is used to express an action (or state being) which went on and was completed in the past before some other past action took place.

The <u>future</u> <u>perfect</u> <u>tense</u> is used to express an action (or state being) which will take place and be completed at some time in the future before some other future event.

Key Point

> If a question asks you if a sentence needs a correction, always check the sentence for verb tense errors.

EXAMPLE: I <u>finished</u> my homework when John called.

The homework was finished before John called so the correct tense and aspect would be the past perfect, in order to indicate that the action was completed before John called: *I **had** finished*... is the correct form.

Pronoun Errors

Sentences that make comparisons often use the words <u>THAN</u> and <u>AS</u>. These sentences are frequently "incomplete" to avoid repetition. Use the pronoun you would use if the sentence were "complete".

EXAMPLE: Mark is stronger than he.

In this sentence the pronoun <u>he</u> is correct. If the sentence were "completed," it would read "Mark is stronger than he is strong."

You would not say - "Mark is stronger than <u>him</u> is strong." That would be grammatically incorrect.

Look at the next two sentences.

    I like Jennie more than she.

    I like Jennie more than her.

If the first sentence is "completed," it would read, "I like Jennie more than she likes Jennie." If the second sentence is "completed," it would read. "I like Jennie more than I like her."

Key Point

> Some sentences can be completed either way while others can be completed only one way.

Use possessive personal pronouns before nouns formed by a <u>verb</u> plus <u>ing</u>.

EXAMPLE: Her ice <u>skating</u> is at championship level.

In this sentence the possessive pronoun <u>her</u> modifies the noun <u>skating</u>. Note that <u>skating</u> is the name of an activity and is made up of the verb <u>skate</u> and an <u>ing</u> ending.

Agreement Of Pronoun And Its Antecedent

Key Point

> Pronouns <u>agree</u> with their antecedents in NUMBER (SINGULAR/PLURAL) and GENDER (MASCULINE/FEMININE/ NEUTER)

EXAMPLE: The girl stated her opinion.

In this sentence the pronoun <u>her</u> refers to the noun <u>girl</u> which is <u>singular</u> and <u>feminine</u>.

The following indefinite pronouns are singular and are referred to by singular personal pronouns.

each	one	no one	anyone
either	everyone	nobody	someone
neither	everybody	anybody	somebody

32

EXAMPLE: Each of the girls stated her opinions.

In this sentence the pronoun <u>Each</u> is singular and the prepositional phrase <u>of the girls</u> indicates the feminine gender. <u>Her</u> is the correct possessive pronoun.

Key Point

Singular nouns or pronouns joined by <u>OR</u> or <u>NOR</u> are referred to by <u>SINGULAR PRONOUNS</u>.

EXAMPLE: Frank or he will bring his wrench.

In this sentence the subjects <u>Frank</u> and <u>he</u> are joined by <u>or</u>. Both are masculine and so <u>his</u> is correct.

Key Point

Nouns or pronouns joined by <u>AND</u> are referred to by <u>PLURAL PRONOUNS</u>.

EXAMPLE: The boss and the workers will eat their sandwiches.

In this sentence the subjects <u>boss</u> and <u>workers</u> are joined by <u>and</u>. <u>Their</u> is correct.

Key Point

In sentences using the relative pronouns <u>WHO</u>, <u>WHICH</u>, or <u>THAT</u>, the number of the antecedent determines the number of the verb that follows the relative pronoun.

EXAMPLE: The <u>hat</u> <u>which</u> is ripped no longer fits.

In this sentence the relative pronoun <u>which</u> refers to the noun <u>hat</u>. <u>Hat</u> is singular and so is the verb <u>is</u> that follows the relative pronoun.

DIRECTIONS: In the following sentences, select the correct word.

1.   Everyone wants (his, their) ticket back.

2.   The nurse adjusted (her, its) cap on her head.

3.   The teacher and students will hand in (her, their) tickets.

4.   The reporter that (is, are) present will turn in his story.

5.   Mary is one of the secretaries who (is, are) scheduled for a raise.

6.   Mary is the only one of the secretaries who (is, are) scheduled for a raise.

7.   Neither Jim nor his brother, who (is, are) tall, is tall enough for the job.

8. Nobody will wear (his, their) helmet.

9. The boys and girls are coloring (his, her, their) pictures.

10. The tools which (is, are) available are useless.

ANSWERS

1. **His** refers to the singular indefinite pronoun Everyone.

2. **Her** refers to the singular feminine noun nurse.

3. **Their** refers to the nouns teacher and student; they are joined by and and make up the compound subject.

4. **Is** agrees with that and is singular because that refers to the singular noun reporter.

5. **Are** agrees with who which refers to the plural noun secretaries; it is the group, secretaries, who are scheduled for the raise and Mary is one of them.

6. **Is** agrees with who which refers to the singular indefinite pronoun one; only Mary (one) is scheduled for a raise.

7. **Is** agrees with who which refers to the singular noun brother.

8. **His** refers to the singular indefinite pronoun Nobody.

9. **Their** refers to the compound plural subjects boys and girls.

10. **Are** agrees with the pronoun which which refers to the plural noun tools.

Vague Pronoun Reference

Key Point

> Sometimes the pronoun chosen could refer to more than one noun. This is very confusing. Make sure each pronoun refers back to a specific noun.

EXAMPLE: States are divided into counties and each has its own police force.

It's not clear whether *each* is referring to *states* or *counties*. A better way to write this sentence would be, "States are divided into counties and each county has its own police force."

Chapter 2: USAGE

Usage refers to making decisions about **diction**, **tone,** and **register**. An essay or lecture may be grammatically perfect, yet totally inappropriate to the situation. Elementary school lessons about science should not use specialized vocabulary, although the same vocabulary explaining the same topic would be appropriate in graduate school. A funeral eulogy would differ in tone from a newspaper obituary and one would describe the same car accident differently to friends than to an insurance company.

TONE - THE AUTHOR'S ATTITUDE

The author's attitude or feelings about what he or she has written is called the tone. Some words that describe the tone are serious, light-hearted, sarcastic, ironic, bitter and amused. You can determine the tone of the passage by the words the author uses and the manner in which he presents his ideas. Look at the following example.

HOW DOES THE SPEAKER FEEL ABOUT THE MAN HE KILLED?

A Man I Never Knew (Anonymous)

If I had only met him
 in a tavern in the town,

I know I would have let him
 share my beer and drink it down.

Instead we met on the battle-field.
 On different sides we stand.

I shot at him and saw him yield.
 His gun fell from his hand.

I killed this man I never knew.
 as he would have done to me.

Because some general dressed in blue
 said he was my enemy!

I bet he joined his army
 for the reasons I joined mine.

We had no better place to be
 no loves to leave behind.

A war does sad and strange things!
 In the field you shoot him down.

A guy who'd share your feelings
 in a tavern in the town.

You must read into the passage the feelings of the writer. However, he does use one word, the word "sad," which gives you a clue about his feelings. His quiet speech also tells you that his tone is sad rather than bitter or angry.

Look at the following three commentary examples; they give you a good idea of the different attitudes a writer can have.

WHO IS RESPONSIBLE FOR THE SUCCESS OF THE OPERA?

Congratulations must be given to the entire troupe of the Fair Meadow Company, but a few people deserve special notice. The opera, "Faust," was not only a credible musical production, but a theatrical delight as well. Usually first mention is given to the singers or the conductor, but in the case of Thursday evening's performance, it is the stage designer who deserves the roses, with a bouquet for the fashion coordinator as well. Even world-class companies with world-class budgets would have difficulty competing with the inspired and magical set designs and the stylish, spiffy modern look of the costumes.

In this commentary about opera, the writer's tone is enthusiastic. His attitude towards his subject, the opera, is very positive.

HOW DOES THE VIEWER BENEFIT FROM SUMMER T.V. PROGRAMMING?

Summertime is a great time to enjoy old favorite films on the home screen. When regular programming stops in mid-May and the network stations flood the air with re-runs, all is not lost. Local stations pick up the slack by scheduling the great oldies at an hour that doesn't require vampire stamina to enjoy them. This week the great classic thriller, "Phantom Lady," is available on channel 22 at 9 p.m. Let Bing sing you to sleep at 10 p.m. on channel 41 in "Holiday Inn." The 'good old summertime' can be a viewer's heaven if you make it a good <u>OLD</u> summertime!

The writer is very enthusiastic about old movies being shown in prime time. The tone of the commentary is enthusiastic because that is the writer's attitude toward his subject.

HOW DO HAGAR MASEFIELDS' BUILDINGS COMPARE TO OTHER BUILDINGS IN HIS TIME?

He uses materials that do not lend themselves to beauty - unpainted metal, plywood, stucco and rough concrete. Because he follows no one and no one follows him, he is easier to dislike than other American architects. At first his style was called 'California modern' but now even that term does not apply. In this age when fashionable architecture has been playful and charming, Hagar Masefield's buildings stand apart from the crowd.

The third commentary differs from the first and second. The writer is not enthusiastic about his subject - the ugly buildings of Hagar Masefield. His tone or attitude toward his subject is critical or disapproving.

HOW DOES JOHNNY DELAY GOING TO SLEEP?

Johnny's bedtime causes a battle of heroic proportions. He is a three year old military genius who can out-maneuver any senior ranking officer, otherwise known as a parent. His tactics are endless. There is the search-and-destroy "I can't find my teddy bear" tactic. When bear appears, it is evident that Johnny's room was destroyed during the search. Then there is the military funeral tactic. Whatever creature Johnny has adopted during the day always dies at night. Butterflies, crickets, even field mice, all must be buried in matchboxes complete with full military honors and a twenty-one gun salute.

The writer's style in this passage would probably not be suited to a commentary on:

1. a situation comedy
2. a children's puppet show
3. a summit conference between heads of State
4. a novel about family life
5. a baseball game

In the previous passage the writer's attitude towards his subject is one of amusement. Although he might be a bit annoyed by Johnny's behavior, the writer obviously thinks there is humor in the bedtime battle. Referring to Johnny as a three year old military genius is a great exaggeration. The writer then supports this idea with several examples of Johnny's military tactics, extending the exaggeration and the humor it causes. The writer's purpose in this passage is to amuse the reader.

In this example, the correct answer is #3. It would not be appropriate to treat a summit conference between heads of state in a light-hearted or humorous fashion. A conference between world leaders is serious business and a commentary dealing with such a topic should be written in a manner which would make that clear to the reader.

A commentary on a situation comedy could very well be written in a humorous fashion and this style would also be appropriate for a children's puppet show or a novel about family life. The last choice, a commentary on a baseball game, might not usually be treated in a humorous fashion, but it is possible to do so, especially if the event contained humorous errors on the part of the players. In that case, a humorous treatment of the subject might be very appropriate.

Chapter 3: THE STAGES OF THE WRITING PROCESS

Writing is, for the most part, a **recursive** process: a typical piece of writing is revised many times before reaching its final form. Although no two people compose in exactly the same manner, there seem to be certain stages or phases common to all writing: prewriting, drafting, and revising. The last category could be subdivided into editing and proofreading.

Prewriting, as the name implies, is the stage before actual composition. Here the writer must decide not only what to write about, but how to order and present these ideas. Other important considerations at this stage are purpose and audience. Research and formal outlines would probably be used by someone intending to write a scientific essay, whereas a poet might place more value on brainstorming or freewriting. Mathematicians are obviously fond of diagrams. A work that is historical in nature will probably start out with a *chronological* ordering, although it need not be written strictly so. A philosophical work, on the other hand, might have a *dialectical* structure where an initial idea is followed by its opposite (bravery is contrasted with cowardice, for instance) and then there is an attempt to 'reconcile' or 'synthesize' the two seemingly incompatible ideas.

Drafting is the actual composing of words into sentences and sentences into paragraphs. This is made much easier by thorough prewriting. It is not unusual for prewriting ideas to be altered during drafting. Drafting isn't simply about putting words on paper as in freewriting, but rather it is writing with an aim toward coherence and consistency.

Revising is the recursive phase of the writing process. There are two main types of revision. First, the writer may want to revise the logical structure of the work. Ideas are then changed and rearranged in relation to each other, definitions are sharpened, and there may even be some sudden revelation or inspiration. The other type of revision has to do with the mechanics of writing: correcting mistakes in spelling, punctuation and grammar, eliminating unnecessary words, adding more detail where it is called for, etc. The first type of revision is usually termed editing and the second is proofreading.

The Forms of Nonfiction Prose

The first thing one notices about prose writing is that it is organized into paragraphs. The division of writing into paragraphs reflects the writer's train of thought. Although the specific configuration and content of paragraphs will depend on the nature of the audience and the writer's purpose, all well-developed paragraphs in nonfiction prose contain three essential elements:

- **topic sentence**: expresses the main idea of that paragraph
- **support**: evidence for the main idea

- ***concluding sentence***: summarizes, emphasizes, or signals a transition to the next paragraph

These three elements serve to give coherence to writing. Ideally, no sentence in a paragraph and no paragraph in a whole work should be isolated - each has some relation to every other. The finished work should at least seem like a unified whole, not a random string of sentences.

Chapter 4: RECOGNIZING THE MAIN IDEA

No task is considered more basic to mature reading comprehension or tested more frequently than your ability to recognize the main idea of a writer's work. This is quite reasonable. For reading to be considered a meaningful act, it is imperative that you be able to identify the most important idea presented.

At its most basic level, this activity might require only that you recognize the most important thought stated in a single paragraph. This literal comprehension task is relatively easy. Signs usually abound which will point the alert reader in the correct direction. As you progress from that point, however, the task may grow more complicated. You may be asked to recognize the main idea for a passage containing several paragraphs. You may be asked to produce a statement of main idea yourself for a paragraph or passage for which the main idea is not directly stated. This inferring of a main idea is a sophisticated task but is, again, considered basic to reading comprehension.

Whether you are being asked to identify a literal or inferred main idea for a paragraph or passage, the analytical skills employed in these efforts are essentially the same. You must always be aware of the author's purpose for writing. You must be alert for materials which are irrelevant to the writer's main point. You must be alert to clues found in the structure of the materials.

The Topic Sentence

The topic sentence is a statement which identifies the subject matter of the paragraph. It is the writer's way of telling you, "This is what I will be discussing." While they may be found anywhere throughout the paragraph, topic sentences are most often the first sentence of the paragraph. The following paragraph is typical of most paragraphs. Read the paragraph and attempt to identify the topic sentence before reading further.

> Basketball is a sport which makes great physical demands on participants. The bulk of the game is given to short bursts of speed which make the lungs work hard. Along with the running are the frequent jumps for rebounds and changes of direction, both of which require great leg strength. Finally, both dribbling and shooting skills require fine coordination which is increasingly taxed by the exertion of those other aspects of the game.

You should have identified the sentence, "Basketball is a sport which makes great physical demands on participants." as the topic sentence. It is the sentence, which tells us what the paragraph will concern.

TOPIC SENTENCE	TOPIC TO BE COVERED IN THE PARAGRAPH
Basketball is a sport which makes great physical demands on participants.	The physical demands of basketball.

Sometimes the writer will place the topic sentence into the middle portion of the paragraph. The writer's purpose in doing this (besides simply varying his/her style) is to assure that you are focused on the topic at hand.

More often the writer will put the topic sentence at the end of the paragraph. The writer's purpose here is clear. By placing the topic sentence at the end of the paragraph, the writer can use the topic sentence to summarize the information which has preceded it in the paragraph. Read the paragraph which follows and attempt to identify the topic sentence before reading further.

Before jogging the prospective runner should devote at least twenty minutes to stretching exercises. While engaged in running, the jogger should try to maintain a relatively steady pace, attempting to set a pace which ensures a good cardiovascular workout without causing unnecessary strain. Following the workout, the runner should again stretch as he/she winds down. If these steps are followed, jogging will be a safe and physically rewarding activity.

You should have identified the sentence, "If these steps are followed, jogging will be a safe and physically rewarding activity." as the topic sentence of this paragraph. It is these steps that the writer is concerned with discussing.

TOPIC SENTENCE	TOPIC COVERED IN THE PARAGRAPH
If these steps are followed, jogging will be a safe and physically rewarding activity.	The steps to follow for jogging

This is a classic example of the situation in which the author uses the topic sentence as a summary statement.

If you are asking yourself why the first sentence, for example, isn't the topic sentence, the answer is clear; this paragraph is not about stretching before jogging. If it were, the entire paragraph would deal with that subject (and it simply doesn't.)

If you haven't noticed this aspect of paragraph construction, this is a crucial point. A well-written paragraph deals with only <u>one</u> topic.

Try these problems.

DIRECTIONS: Circle the correct answer.

1. There are few things in this world as beautiful as Zion National Park in Utah.   2. The rugged mountain tops of the Cougar Mountains form the bulk of the park.   3. Ponderosa pine thrive throughout, and the waters of the North Fork and East Fork Virgin Rivers flow placidly through Zion and Parunuweap Canyons respectively.   4. Checker-board Mesa rounds out this varied terrain.

1.   Select the topic sentence of the paragraph above.

        A. sentence #1   C. sentence #3

        B. sentence #2   D. sentence #4

1. The Army of the Confederacy under General Robert E. Lee arrived from the south.   2. Union forces under General George G. Meade lay waiting along the ridges.   3. When the carnage amid the wheat fields and peach orchards ended three days later, the Confederate soldiers limped home.   4. Gettysburg, a small farming town in south-central Pennsylvania, took its place among the greatest battles of all time.

2.   Select the topic sentence of the paragraph above.

        A. sentence #1   C. sentence #3

        B. sentence #2   D. sentence #4

Baseball has produced more than its share of legends in its more than one hundred year history. Connie Mack, for instance, made a place for himself in baseball's annals as both owner and manager of the great Philadelphia Athletic teams. His "million dollar infield,"featuring such stars as Joe Cronin and Jimmy Dykes was among the best ever assembled. It was Mack's longevity (he was owner for decades), however, that was his most remarkable feature.

3. Which of the following is the topic of the paragraph above?

    A. the great Philadelphia Athletic teams

    B. the "million dollar infield"

    C. baseball managers

    D. Connie Mack

1. Each fall finds the people of the Gulf states preparing for hurricane season. 2. A healthy supply of boards and nails are assembled for protecting windows and doors. 3. Supplies of canned foods are stored, radios prepared, and escape routes are planned. 4. Even so, preparations will reduce, but not eliminate, most damage.

4. Select the topic sentence of the paragraph above.

    A. sentence #1   C. sentence #3

    B. sentence #2   D. sentence #4

1. In the Forties the well-dressed woman was sporting a hemline which fell well below the knee. 2. Hemlines crept up through the Fifties, and bolted dangerously high with the miniskirts of the Sixties. 3. Fashion, that fickle phenomena, always changes, however. 4. Skirts were replaced by pants in the Seventies, and a whole new cycle began.

5.   Select the topic sentence of the paragraph above.

        A. sentence #1   C. sentence #3

        B. sentence #2   D. sentence #4

ANSWERS

1. A   The paragraph is about Zion National Park. Each sentence is directed to describing its beauty.

2. D   The paragraph is about the Battle of Gettysburg. If any of the other sentences were the topic sentence, then the entire paragraph would have been focused on the facts included in that sentence.

3. D   The paragraph is about Connie Mack. Each sentence is intended to tell the reader something more about him or his teams. Choices A and B are too general to be topic sentences, and B refers only to a single fact from the paragraph.

4. A   Sentence one states the topic of the paragraph. Each of the other choices serves as an example of what the author is trying to say about   preparations. If choice B were the topic sentence, for example, then the entire paragraph should have dealt with nails and boards. It doesn't.

5. C   The paragraph is not about any one specific trend. It is about the changes which occur in fashion. If choice D, for example, were the correct choice, then the entire paragraph would have dealt with women's pants in the '70's.

SUPPORTING DETAILS

As already stated, the writer uses the topic sentence to announce the subject matter to be covered; to identify the one topic which will be handled in the paragraph. The specific point about the subject which the author makes is the main idea. The author's move from the general topic to his/her main idea concerning that topic is handled through the use of supporting details. Let's use our original paragraph to clarify.

      Basketball is a sport which makes great physical demands on participants. The bulk of the game is given to short bursts of speed which make the lungs work hard. Along with running are the frequent jumps for

44

rebounds and changes of direction, both of which require great leg strength. Finally, both dribbling and shooting skills require fine coordination which is increasingly taxed by the exertion of those other aspects of the game.

By asking "What is the paragraph about?", you can identify the general topic of the paragraph. In this case, the answer is obviously basketball.

By asking "What is the author saying about the topic?", you can pinpoint the main idea of the paragraph. In this case the author is saying that basketball is a physically demanding sport. The "proof" of this statement is left to the supporting details. The following diagram is typical of paragraphs (such as the one we're dealing with) in which the topic sentence leads off the paragraph.

AUTHOR'S CONTENTION	AUTHOR'S PROOF/ SUPPORTING DETAILS
Basketball is physically demanding on participants.	A. Bursts of speed are hard on the lungs. B. Jumping and changes of direction require leg strength. C. Dribbling and shooting require fine coordination.

As is easily seen, the supporting details are meant to support the author's main idea. In this case the supporting details take the form of examples. Each sentence offers an example of the physical demands of basketball.

Supporting details may take forms other than simple examples. Sometimes authors will attempt to prove their contention (main idea) with an anecdote (story). At other times these supporting details may take the form of a simple description or explanation. Occasionally ideas are compared and contrasted. Read the paragraph which follows and attempt to identify the method the author is using to support the main idea.

> No one knows as well as I that human beings are creatures of habit. Born in New York City and raised there until the tender age of four, I was somewhat used to travel by bus. Unfortunately, when my parents moved us to the wilds of New Jersey, they failed to inform me of the primitive transportation system. That is how I came to be found by my worried parents, four hours after kindergarten had been released, calmly waiting for a bus which didn't exist.

In this instance the author's main idea is that people, himself included, are creatures of habit. The supporting details, the proof he offers to prove this point, take the form of a little story, or anecdote. Could the author have proven his point in some other manner? Absolutely. The only right or wrong concerning supporting details is that they must work to prove the author's main idea.

The final point concerning individual paragraphs is that all the sentences must be related. Each sentence has a specific duty. Each sentence must either be at work identifying the main idea of the paragraph or working to support that main idea. A sentence which does anything other than that is irrelevant and should not be included in the paragraph.

Read the paragraph which follows and identify the sentence which is irrelevant to the paragraph.

1. Town names often reflect the make-up of the early settlers of an area and Wyoming's towns are no different. 2. The towns Cheyenne and Shoshoni are obviously Indian gifts. 3. The towns Dubois, Teton Village, and LaBarge indicate French origins. 4. Laramie is in Wyoming. 5. Towns such as Hole-in-the-Wall, Halfway, and Lost Cabin are reminders of the occasionally eccentric nature of the early settlers.

A careful reading of the paragraph shows that every sentence is related to the origin of town names except for one. If you identified sentence number four as the irrelevant one, congratulations. The fact that Laramie is in Wyoming is not related to the point the author is trying to make.

Fortunately, you will usually not have to deal with blatantly irrelevant sentences. However, the ability to spot questionable supporting details is critical in developing more mature reading skills.

DIRECTIONS: Circle the correct answer or record it in the space provided.

Each year countless inventions are patented, and each year countless inventions and their inventors are forgotten. Only a select group of inventors have dramatically impacted upon our world. Gutenburg (and his printing press) certainly ranks among that group. James Watt, inventor of the steam engine, was an inventor of significance. The last hundred years have produced a host of significant inventors. Marconi (the radio), Birdseye (freezing techniques), and Fermi (atomic energy developments), name but a few.

1. **What method does the writer use in providing supporting details?**

      A. example   C. definition

      B. anecdote   D. comparison and contrast

In order for a species to be correctly termed a mammal, it must meet some very specific criteria. First, the animal must have hair. Second, the female must have mammary glands for feeding its young. Offspring are born live. Finally, and perhaps most technically, the red blood cells cannot contain nuclei. Any animal not meeting these criteria is not a mammal.

2. **What method does the writer use in providing supporting details?**

      A. example   C. definition

      B. anecdote   D. comparison and contrast

While not in the league of the countries Nepal and Tibet, the United States has its share of impressive mountains. Mount McKinley, for instance, stands some 20,320 feet above sea level. Also in Alaska, Mount Foraker tops 17,000 feet. Mount Lucania, Canada, stands at 17,000 feet as well. In the mainland United States, Mount Ranier and Mount Whitney both stand over 14,000 feet tall.

3. **Which sentence in the paragraph above does not support the topic covered (is irrelevant)?**

The year 1776 was a significant one in our country's history. Just two months after France and Spain agreed to give the Americans substantial monetary aid, the Declaration of Independence was approved on July 4. Things looked grim when Washington lost the Battle of Long Island on August 27th and Nathan Hale was hung as a spy on September 22, 1776. But affairs turned slightly better by year's end when Washington crossed the Delaware River and defeated the Hessions at Christmas. By 1781 the Revolutionary War ended.

4. **Select the sentence from the paragraph above which does not pertain to the topic of the paragraph.**

The expression "A fool and his money are soon parted" probably refers to all of us at one time or the other. I can still remember the time I strolled toward the boardwalk in Wildwood, a brash eleven-year-old with a spanking new five dollar bill. What I thought was the roar of the ocean was probably actually the salivating of the boardwalk hucksters as they saw me, an obvious mark, approaching. Within minutes I was broke, and not a prize had been disturbed. No cries of "We got a winner here" punctuated the night. No milk bottles scattered to the floor. No bells rang. Just a quiet, thorough, and thank God private lesson in life.

5. **Which method is the author using in providing supporting details for his/her main topic?**

      A. example   C. definition

      B. anecdote   D. comparison and contrast

ANSWERS

1. A Each supporting detail is an example of a famous inventor. B is wrong because there is no story given. C is wrong because no definition is given. D is wrong because nothing is being compared.

2. C Each detail is part of the definition of a mammal. A is wrong because no example of a mammal is given. B is wrong because no anecdote is included. D is wrong because nothing is being compared.

3. Mount Lucania, Canada, stands at 17,000 feet as well. The paragraph is about the United States mountains. Therefore, the mention of a Canadian mountain is irrelevant to the topic.

4. By 1781 the Revolutionary War ended. The topic is the events of 1776. Therefore, mention of anything having to do with 1781 is irrelevant to the topic.

5. B The main idea concerns losing money foolishly and the point is driven home by an anecdote. No example or definitions are given, so A and C are incorrect. Nothing is compared, so D is wrong.

Main Idea

The writer's whole purpose in writing is to make a point. The writer has an idea that he/she wants to express. The writer then uses the topic sentence to announce to you the subject to be covered. Then the author makes his/her point by providing you with examples in the supporting sentences. As a reader all you have to concentrate on is this fact; each paragraph should have one main idea concerning one topic.

Identifying the main idea of most paragraphs is relatively easy. Essentially, you only need to ask yourself a couple of questions. The first question to ask yourself is, "What is the topic of the paragraph?" When you've answered that simply ask, "What is the writer saying about that topic?" The answer to that second question is the main idea of the paragraph.

EXAMPLE

Few periods of American history are darker or more shameful than the last years of hostilities with the Plains Indians. November 29, 1864 marked the massacre of over three hundred Cheyenne at Sand Creek, Colorado. Only four years later, a number of survivors from Sand Creek were again set upon, attacked this time by Custer's troops on the Washita River. The final episode, the massacre of the Sioux at Wounded Knee, South Dakota, took place in 1890. Wounded Knee marked the end of significant Indian resistance of any kind.

Which statement best states the main idea of the paragraph?

1. Many Sioux were killed at Wounded Knee.

2. The final years of strife with the American Indian mark a dark period in our history.

3. Some survivors of the Sand Creek massacre were killed later at the Washita River.

4. The strife with the American Indians ended in 1890.

A review of what you already know about paragraphs will help select a correct response. First, you know that a paragraph deals with only one subject. In this paragraph the topic is the last years of hostilities with the Indians. By asking yourself, "What is the writer saying about those years?" you'll find the main idea. In this case the answer is stated for you. The writer states that they are a dark and shameful time in our history. A quick look at the possible answers would indicate that choice 2 is correct.

If you're really observant, you may have noticed that the first sentence of the paragraph is both the topic sentence and a statement of main idea. This is often true, particularly when reading paragraphs from a textbook. In terms of models, that type of paragraph structure looks something like this.

Main Idea	Supporting Details
The final years of strife with the American Indian mark a dark period in our history.	1. The Sand Creek Massacre 2. The Washita River Massacre 3. The Wounded Knee Massacre

The key here is that each supporting detail, in this case each example of our shameful handling of the Indians, builds the author's point. This is important because it offers you another way to identify the main idea. Keep this in mind: if a statement is really the main idea of a paragraph, then each sentence in the

50

paragraph should be related to that idea. For example, if you couldn't figure out the main idea of the paragraph by asking "What is the paragraph about?" and "What is the writer saying about that topic?", you can work backwards from the choices.

Look at the example and the choices again.

> Few periods of American history are darker or more shameful than the last years of hostilities with the Plains Indians. November 29, 1864 marked the massacre of over three hundred Cheyenne at Sand Creek, Colorado. Only four years later, a number of survivors from Sand Creek were again set upon, attacked this time by Custer's troops on the Washita River. The final episode, the massacre of the Sioux at Wounded Knee, South Dakota, took place in 1890. Wounded Knee marked the end of significant Indian resistance of any kind.

Which statement best states the main idea of the paragraph?

1. Many Sioux were killed at Wounded Knee.

2. The final years of strife with the American Indian mark a dark period in our history.

3. Some survivors of the Sand Creek massacre were killed later at the Washita River.

4. The strife with the American Indians ended in 1890.

If choice one were the main idea of the paragraph, then the whole paragraph should be about the Sioux being killed at Wounded Knee. A look at the paragraph shows that this is not the case. At least two separate incidents (The Washita River and Wounded Knee assaults) are also discussed. Therefore, this choice can be eliminated.

Using the same reasoning, choices three and four can also be eliminated. The paragraph is not strictly about the Washita River incident, nor does the paragraph only address the idea of the end of Indian strife.

Only statement two works as a main idea. The writer wants to point out a dark period of our history and has focused on the final years of the Indian wars. Each statement which follows lends support to that thought. Each statement serves as a neat example of the author's main idea.

In paragraphs which have no clear topic sentence, the process remains the same. You may find, however, that you will have to rely a little more on our second approach (working back toward the paragraph a choice at a time.) This is because the answer to your two questions "What is the topic of the paragraph?" and "What is the writer saying about the topic?" may not be as clear without an obvious topic sentence to attract your attention.

Read the following passage and try to figure out the main idea before reading the explanation.

> The string beans which attempted to take over the west side of the garden bring a smile to the face of Jimmy, but don't even find their way to brother Paul's plate. The beets which seemed they'd never be ready for harvest, please neither, which is just fine with father. Mom's mania for kohlrabi is understood by none, and the asparagus which father nursed from seed drives the kids from the table. "The splendor of gardening," father muses as he dines alone.

Which statement below best identifies the main idea?

1. People should agree to eat the same vegetables.

2. Jimmy and Paul disagree over the value of string beans.

3. When planting a garden, it's impossible to please everyone.

4. Most kids hate to eat vegetables.

Because this paragraph has no single sentence which neatly defines either the topic or the main idea of that topic, the reader will be making an inference in this case. By contrasting each possible main idea with the sentences of the paragraph, as was done when working with the previous sample paragraph, you can quickly eliminate choice one. Why? You can rule out choice one because the entire paragraph is not <u>about</u> why people should agree to eat the same vegetables. The author isn't saying that at all.

If choice two was the main idea, then the entire paragraph would concern only Jimmy and Paul. If option four was the main idea, why would the mother and father's choices be mentioned at all? Obviously, only choice three is diverse enough to encompass all the different sentences contained in the paragraph.

For those who are better able to understand in terms of models, what the reader is looking for is a statement which unifies the supporting details of the paragraph. In the model below, selecting a correct response means trying each statement within the main idea box. If the statement does not use each of the supporting details, you can eliminate it from consideration.

Main Idea	Supporting Details
When planting a garden, it's impossible to please everyone.	Jimmy likes string beans, Paul doesn't.
	Mother likes kohlrabi.
	Father likes beets and asparagus.

Obviously, as previously stated, only choice three works within the limits of the model. The facts contained in the sentences show you can't please everyone when planting a garden. That point, as you can now see (if you didn't before), is the writer's main idea.

DIRECTIONS: Using the previously presented information and the sample paragraphs below, answer the questions which follow. Circle the correct answer.

Though most vacationers view them as playful pups, American ranchers have a far different view of the prairie dog. Each year thousands of heads of cattle must be destroyed due to broken limbs suffered after stepping into holes left by the prairie dogs. As sheep and horses are also victims, many ranchers devote a good deal of time to the shooting and poisoning of these animals which they consider pests.

1. The paragraph tells:

    A.   How much vacationers like prairie dogs.

    B.   How cattle break their legs.

    C.   Why ranchers consider prairie dogs a nuisance.

    D.   How prairie dogs are killed.

While baseball players often make it look easy, hitting a pitched baseball is no easy task. The relatively small baseball approaches the hitter at speeds often in excess of 85 m.p.h. from just some sixty feet away. This leaves the hitter just a fraction of a second to decide whether the ball can be hit, begin his swing, and make contact with the ball. The fact that the pitcher can alter the speed at which the ball is thrown or curve the ball away from or towards the hitter, only complicates matters more.

2. The main idea of this paragraph is:

    A.   Baseballs are often thrown at over 85 m.p.h.

    B.   Hitting a pitched baseball is a difficult task.

    C.   Major league players make hitting look easy.

    D.   Baseballs are small.

In the northwest corner of the state, rolling hills, forests, and farms are the order of the day. The northeast section is an ongoing metropolis with only the imaginary city lines dividing an otherwise continuous array of apartment buildings, row houses, and condominiums. The eastern section is largely seashore-oriented, and the southern portion still depends largely on agriculture. Clearly New Jersey's a state of diverse settings.

3. **The main idea of this paragraph tells:**

A.   How diverse New Jersey's sections are.

B.   Why New Jersey is overpopulated.

C.   How important farming is in New Jersey.

D.   Where New Jersey is most crowded.

ANSWERS

1. C   The paragraph concerns ranchers and their relationship with the prairie dogs. If A were correct, the entire paragraph would be about how vacationers like prairie dogs. The same reasoning can be applied to both B and D.

2. B   If A were the choice, the entire paragraph would concern the speed of a pitched baseball. If C were correct, the entire paragraph would be about major league hitters. If D were correct, the paragraph would concern just the small size of baseballs.

3. A   Each sentence in the paragraph shows how different the sections of the state are; how diverse they are. None of the other choices work. Nothing is said about why New Jersey is overpopulated, nor how important farming is. While something is said about the crowded northeast section, it is not the main concern of the paragraph.

Expository writing is one of the most widely used forms of written discourse. Newspaper articles, book reviews, academic research papers, high school book reports, and business letters are all examples of expository writing. In this type of writing, the writer seeks to convey information as clearly and succinctly as possible, and the finished work has a factual and objective texture. There is much fact-checking and revising, especially when compared to expressive writing. This doesn't mean that expository writing is all the same. Newspaper articles use a variation of the three elements (**topic sentence**: expresses the main idea of that paragraph, **support**: evidence for the main idea, **concluding sentence**: summarizes, emphasizes, or signals a transition to the next paragraph) described above because the summary comes at the beginning rather than the end. Also, in news writing, details are given in decreasing levels of importance. Business letters are similarly efficient.

In contrast to expository writing, **persuasive writing** (sometimes called hortatory writing) seeks not only to give information but also to persuade the reader (or hearer) to do something: to change one's way of thinking or living, or to vote a certain way. The persuasive writer's topic sentence will be a statement of the desired belief, decision or proposition. ("One's actions ought to be guided by concern for humanity…"). The main body of persuasive writing is made up of reasons for doing the desired action, moving from least to most compelling ("saving the best for last"). The conclusion is usually a repetition of the main idea, using the same or almost the same words, for rhetorical effect.

Chapter 5: UNDERSTANDING LITERATURE

This section deals with three main kinds of non-literal writing: fictional narrative, drama, and poetry. Just as with nonfiction prose, fiction has a structure of thought and aims at coherence. But in fiction, certain types of imaginative experience are expressed using figurative language when needed. Ambiguity is encouraged in poetry but would be looked upon as a serious flaw in a scientific essay. Here are some of the more important devices and figures of speech used in non-literal writing:

Allegory

An allegory is a story in which the characters (people, active objects or animals) represent abstract ideas or qualities, such as goodness, evil, love, death, lust, greed, and so on.

Allegories evoke a dual interest: one is in the events, characters and setting, the other in the ideas they are intended to convey or the significance they bear. The meaning of an allegory can be religious, social, political, satirical, or of another nature, just as long as the surface story is a logical one that conveys the characters beyond into another level of meaning, that of the idea.

Two famous allegories are **The Faerie Queene** by Spenser and Bunyan's **Pilgrim's Progress**. Spenser's is a tale of imaginary creatures and their battles, but it also brings to mind how some notions of chivalry conflict. The characters represent abstract ideas. **Pilgrim's Progress** is the story of a man trying to live a godly life. However, it is also the story of Christian people in general, who must conquer their inner obstacles to faith, such as vanity and despair.

Alliteration

Alliteration is the repetition of initial consonant sounds, or any vowel sounds in successive words or syllables.

Following are some examples of alliteration. Read each one aloud, emphasizing the underlined letters or syllables.

EXAMPLE OF CONSONANT ALLITERATION:

The fair breeze blew, the white foam flew,
The furrow followed free.

EXAMPLE OF VOWEL ALLITERATION:

Apt alliteration's artful aid is often an occasional ornament in prose.

EXAMPLE OF SYLLABIC ALLITERATION:

The moan of doves in immemorial elms,
And murmuring of innumerable bees.

Allusion

Allusion is an indirect or implicit reference to something outside of the text, especially to another work of literature.

Apostrophe

Apostrophe is when the speaker addresses an absent person, an inanimate object, or an abstract idea: in *Ode on a Grecian Urn*, Keats directly addresses the urn as though it were a living person.

This device first appeared in literature as an invocation of (or prayer to) the Muses that opened Greek poetry and epics. Subsequent writers have copied that practice. There is also a good example of apostrophe in **Romeo and Juliet**, Shakespeare's tragic play. The love-smitten Juliet is alone on her balcony when she says, "O, Romeo, Romeo! wherefore art thou Romeo?" Because she addresses a person not physically present, her action is an apostrophe.

Appositive

An appositive is a phrase that renames or redescribes a subject. For example, "The Senator, *my good friend*, is wrong."

Conceit

Conceit used to mean 'concept'. It is an extended or very elaborate metaphor used often by 17th century poets like John Donne.

Denouement

The **denouement** is the final unraveling of the plot in any work that tells a story.

The denouement of **Romeo and Juliet** is the double suicide of the lovers. The denouement of **Moby Dick** by Herman Melville is the death of Captain Ahab while harpooning the great, white whale.

Didactic Writing Or Didacticism

Didacticism is literature whose primary aim is to expound some moral, political, or other teaching.

All literature exists to communicate something, so it is best not to classify a work as didactic unless the overriding concern is expressly moral or educational. The Latin writer Lucretius' book **De Rerum Natura** (On the Nature of Things) is a good example. It teaches the reader about the Epicurean philosophy of living. **Aesop's Fables**, which imply a lesson to be learned from the fabulous characters, are also examples of didactic writing. **Aesop's Fables** are allegories.

Epic

An **epic** is a long narrative poem written in lofty style, presenting characters of high social position in a series of adventures. The action is tied to one central figure of heroic proportions, and the whole poem details the history of a nation or race.

Examples of some works that are classified as epics are: ***The Iliad*** and ***The Odyssey*** (both written c. 850 B.C.) by the ancient Greek poet, Homer; ***The Aeneid*** (c. 20 B.C.) by the Latin poet, Vergil; ***Beowulf*** (c. 725A.D.), an English tale of unknown authorship (epics by unknown authors are called **folk epics**); ***Song of Roland*** (c. 1100 A.D.), a French folk epic; ***The Divine Comedy*** (1321) by the Italian, Dante; and ***Paradise Lost*** (1667) by Milton, an Englishman.

Every epic opens with a statement of theme, an invocation of a muse to inspire and instruct the writer, and action that has already begun with no exposition (the background material follows shortly; this device is known as *in media res*, Latin for "in the middle of things"). There are catalogues of ships, rosters of armies, extensive formal speeches by the main characters and complicated language in every epic. There is also the use of elaborate comparisons, called **epic similes**. A good example of epic simile comes from John Milton's ***Paradise Lost***. This is a description of a battlefield strewn with bodies:

> Angel forms, who lay entranced
> Thick as autumnal leaves that strew the brooks
> In Vallombrosa, where the Etrurian shades
> High over-arched embower; or scattered sedge
> Afloat, when with fierce winds Orion armed
> Hath vexed the Red-Sea coast, whose waves o'erthrew
> Busiris and his Memphian chivalry,
> While with perfidious hatred they pursued
> The sojourners of Goshen, who beheld
> From the safe shore their floating carcasses
> And broken chariot-wheels.

Hyperbole

A **hyperbole** is a gross exaggeration for effect, not to be taken literally.

We use hyperbole in everyday speech to color and enliven conversation, or to make a point about something.

EXAMPLE: The expressions, "It was so hot I thought I'd sweat to death," and "There were a million ants at the picnic," are hyperboles, exaggerations to make a point.

At this point try a couple questions to see how well you understand the literary terms discussed so far:

1. **In Aesop's fable "The Fox and the Grapes," the grapes allegorically represent**

   (A) fruit
   (B) goals
   (C) failure
   (D) hard work
   (E) human nature

2. **"O Romeo, Romeo! wherefore art thou Romeo?" is an example of**

   (A) alliteration
   (B) apostrophe
   (C) metonymy
   (D) epic language
   (E) hyperbole

3. **Is this the face that launched a thousand ships**
   And burnt the topless towers of Ilium?

The preceding passage is an example of

   (A) hyperbole
   (B) didacticism
   (C) allegory
   (D) epic language
   (E) alliteration

ANSWER

1. The best choice is (B). In the fable, a fox spies some juicy, luscious grapes hanging from a vine in a tree. He jumps up to pluck them several times, but falls short. Rather than find another way to reach the grapes or continue trying to jump high enough, the fox says that they are probably sour, and walks away. The grapes represent goals that individuals seek, but will not work hard enough to obtain. (A) is wrong because the grapes **are** fruit—they can not represent it. Failure to reach one's goals is represented by the actions of the fox, not by the grapes, so (C) would also be incorrect, as would (D) which is also represented by the fox's actions. (E) is the subject of the whole fable.

2. (B) is the correct choice. The person being addressed is not present; therefore, the example is, by definition, apostrophe. None of the other choices could be logically correct.

3. The passage is an example of epic language: (D) is the correct choice. It is lofty in tone, and refers to a great battle. The word "Ilium" is a strong clue to those who know that the story of the battle of Ilium is the Greek epic, **The Iliad**. (A) may have been your choice because of "thousand ships" and "topless towers", but according to Homer, a thousand Greek vessels actually did sail to Ilium. "Topless towers" is exaggeration, but it is only one small phrase from the selection, not enough to make (A) the correct answer. (C) is not a logical choice. "Topless towers" is a consonant alliteration, but again only one small part of the sample. It is not enough to warrant (E) as the correct answer.

Imagery

Imagery is use of language to represent things, actions or ideas in a descriptive manner. Images are pictures created in the mind through words.

When an author writes about a brook, babbling and bubbling around rocks and stones, he paints a picture in our minds complete with motion and sound. Imagery is detailed literary scenery that appeals to the physical senses.

Irony

Irony is contradiction between a situation in a story as it appears to the characters, and the truth as the audience knows it. The audience alone understands the ironic moment; the characters do not.

In his short story **The Gift of the Magi**, O. Henry creates a classic example of irony. A young married couple is poor, and neither has any worthwhile possessions except for the wife's long, flowing hair and the husband's antique, gold pocket watch. They love each other greatly, and when Christmas comes around they are sad because they have no money to buy expensive presents for each other. The woman sells her hair to a wig maker so that she can buy a gold watch chain for her husband; and the husband sells his watch to buy his wife a set of fine combs and brushes. Their actions, as only the audience sees, are ironic.

Another good example of irony occurs in the Greek play, **Oedipus Rex** by Sophocles. When a baby boy is born to King Laius of Thebes, the mystical Oracle of Delphi sends Laius a warning: that his son's fate is to grow up to kill his father and marry his mother. Fate, by definition, is unchangeable. The king, nevertheless, attempts to avoid the pre-determined events. He pins the baby's feet together and orders him to be abandoned on a mountain top to die.

However, the servant sent to carry out the deed feels pity for the infant and gives him to a shepherd from nearby Corinth. The shepherd takes him home, presenting him to be a son for the childless king and queen there. Oedipus grows up to be a strong, noble young man; but he is troubled by rumors that he is not the true son of the king and queen of Corinth. He visits the Oracle to ask the god Apollo for the truth of his parentage. The oracle replies only that his terrible fate is to kill his father and marry his mother.

Oedipus runs away from Corinth and his apparent family to try to prevent his fate from happening. While traveling, he is nearly run over by a chariot that is driven by his true father. The proud young man attacks and kills the man that he does not know is his true father.

Eventually, Oedipus wanders to Thebes, finding the city under siege by a sphinx, a beast that is half-woman, half-lion. The sphinx has vowed to kill all people she finds outside the city walls until they answer the riddle, "What animal walks on four legs in the morning, two legs in the afternoon and three legs in the evening?" Oedipus confronts the sphinx, answers correctly that man—in the morning as a baby crawling, in the afternoon as a full-grown creature walking, and in the evening as a bent, old being using a cane—walks so. He is correct. The sphinx kills herself, setting the city free; and the people, lacking a leader since the murder of their king (ironically by Oedipus, although no one, not even Oedipus, knows it), acclaim him as king. He marries his widowed mother, neither aware of the other's true identity. Tragedy comes to Oedipus later in the story when his identity is finally revealed by the shepherd who found him. Irony occurs when both Laius and Oedipus take actions to subvert their fates, because they actually bring their fates to pass.

Kenning

Kenning is used in Anglo-Saxon poems like *Beowulf.* It is similar to a metaphor or analogy and is usually expressed very succinctly. For example saying *bird's abode* instead of *tree.*

Litotes

Litotes is making an assertion by denying the opposite of what one wants to assert, as in *Anthony's no coward!* when one means that Anthony is brave.

Metaphor

A **metaphor** is an implied comparison between two normally unrelated things, indicating a likeness or analogy between them. The objects can be identified with each other or substituted one for the other in a sentence.

One object is actually named as the other, or the normally unrelated object is used in place of an obviously appropriate word.

SOME SENTENCES CONTAINING METAPHORS:

- His room is a garbage dump. ("room" and "garbage dump" are identified with each other)

- War is hell. ("war" and "hell" are identified with each other)

- The new teacher brought order to the zoo. ("zoo" is substituted for the logically understood word, "class")

Metonymy

Metonymy is when an adjunct stands in for the whole, as when someone says *The Vatican said yesterday...* instead of *A spokeman for the highest authority in the Roman Catholic Church said yesterday...*

Onomatopoeia

This is the use of a word whose sound suggests its meaning.

Hiss, buzz, sizzle, and slam are onomatopoetic words. Onomatopoeia also applies to whole passages of some poems and prose. An example is Edgar Allen Poe's poem *The Bells*, which in repetition of the word "bells" actually simulates the sounds of many bells ringing.

Oxymoron

Oxymoron is a phrase that contains seemingly contradictory words, such as *sinfully good*.

Now, try some more sample questions about literary terms:

1. There's a certain slant of light,
   Winter Afternoons—
   That oppresses, like the Heft
   of Cathedral Tunes—

   This passage from a poem by Emily Dickinson relies heavily on the device known as

   (A) denouement
   (B) metaphor
   (C) parody
   (D) imagery
   (E) apostrophe

2. So fierce you whirr and pound you drums—
    so shrill you bugles blow.

    "Whirr" and "pound" from this passage...

    (A) are onomatopoetic
    (B) indicate epic simile
    (C) describe metaphorically
    (D) represent didacticism
    (E) are alliterative

3. On beachy slush and sand spirits of snow fierce slanting.

    The line above illustrates Walt Whitman's use of

    (A) irony
    (B) imagery
    (C) alliteration
    (D) allegory
    (E) denouement

ANSWERS

1. (D) is the correct choice. We can eliminate (A) because there is no story told here; therefore, there could not be any kind of climax to one. (B) is not a good choice because there are no indirect comparisons; in fact, the only comparison is in lines three and four, and it is a direct comparison using the word "like". That is called a **simile**—more on that term later. (C) would not be a logical selection because there is no well-known work being made fun of in the passage. (E) would be wrong since no one except the reader is addressed.

2. (A) is the correct choice, because the words suggest their meaning with the sound they make. "Whirr" and "pound" actually mock the sound that drums make. No lofty comparisons are made in the passage, so (B) would be incorrect. In fact, no comparisons at all are made in this descriptive sample, so (C) is also incorrect. There is no overriding concern for teaching here, thus (D) is wrong. "Bugles blow" is the only alliterative phrase in the sample; "whirr" and "pound" do not involve the repetition of consonants, vowels, or syllable, therefore (E) is also logically incorrect.

3. The repetition of the consonant sound "s" runs throughout the passage in the words <u>s</u>lu<u>sh</u>, <u>s</u>and, <u>s</u>pirit<u>s</u>, <u>s</u>now, fier<u>c</u>e and <u>s</u>lanting. This is alliteration pure and simple; (C) is the correct answer. (A) is not a logical choice because no contradicting situation is presented. There is not enough of a story for anyone to say it is (D) or (E). A case might be made for (B) as a possible answer since there is description of a scene involved. However, the evidence to alliteration is greater. The best choice is (C).

Personification

Personification is a figure of speech that gives human traits (thought, action, feeling) to animals, objects or ideas. (*Anthropomorphism* is giving human shape or form to non-human things whether these things are abstract or not, such as plants, animals, etc.)

The story of Goldilocks and the three bears personifies the bears by giving them human characteristics of speech and life in a house. Whoever heard a baby bear say, "My porridge is too hot!"? George Orwell's book, **Animal Farm** is replete with personification of a farm full of animals who overthrow their cruel human master and set up a government.

HERE ARE SOME MORE PERSONIFICATIONS:

- The storm lashed the naked, helpless shore. ("Storm", given the ability to whip, and "shore", given the trait of being unclothed, personified)

- Time's cruel hand snatched her away from him. ("Time", a concept, is personified with emotion and a hand)

Satire

Satire is a form of writing that blends criticism with humor and wit, ridiculing a person or an institution with the purpose of inspiring reform.

Popular satire today is found in **MAD Magazine** and **National Lampoon**. They make fun of people, social practices, movies, commercials, politicians, television, and so on, with the motive of revealing their flaws.

Satirists have written since the Greek playwright Aristophanes (c. 400 B.C.). The Latin authors Horace (60 B.C.) and Juvenal (c. 60 A.D.) wrote satirical poems. Alexander Pope and Jonathan Swift were famous English satirists of the 18th century.

Simile

A **simile** is a direct comparison between two unlike things, using connectives such as "like" and "as."

In the sentence, "John swims like a fish," the grace and natural ability with which John swims are compared with the grace and natural ability with which a fish swims. Such a comparison is a simile. As with metaphor, two unlike things are compared in a simile (in this case, John and a fish). The key to knowing the difference between simile and metaphor is the use or absence of the words "like", "as" or other directly comparing words. A simile always has the comparing words; a metaphor does not.

SOME OTHER SIMILES:

- He eats like a horse. (A "horse" and a "man" are directly compared, introduced by the word "like".)

- That building is as tall as a mountain. (A "building" and a "mountain," again two unlike things, are directly compared. The comparison is introduced by "as.")

Symbolism

Symbolism is the use of an object to represent another object or idea. It sees the immediate, unique and personal emotional response as the proper subject of art. Symbols are used by authors to recreate in their readers the feelings or truths that are impossible to communicate verbally.

If you were to drive an unfamiliar road and to come across an octagon nailed to a post at an intersection, you would probably stop your car. That is because the octagon has become a symbol for the concept "stop." When a driver encounters an octagon along a roadside, it communicates the message to him that, for his own safety, he must stop his vehicle and check traffic. In an elementary way, that is how symbolism in literature functions.

When people see a cross atop a steeple, printed on a book cover or carved in stone over a grave, it communicates a message to them. The message is that the building, book, or grave has some Christian meaning or purpose. While the stop sign is denotative in its meaning (it spells out a precise message), the cross is connotative (it brings to mind many different messages). It can serve as a welcome to some, as a reminder of hope and goodness to others. Still others might see a cross as nothing more than the trademark of a social movement. Now we are getting close to the operation of symbolism in literature.

Authors use characters, animals, things, actions and descriptions to represent emotions or truths that can not be communicated properly by definition. In Herman Melville's novel, **Moby Dick**, a great white whale symbolizes evil. A flowing river is a popular symbol for life, or the passage of time in life, in several of the world's great literary works.

Symbols can be recognized and identified as such; but the meanings they convey, in the purest sense, can only be felt. We may attempt to describe them and analyze them, but they must be felt in order to understand their full meaning.

Synecdoche

Synecdoche is when a part stands in for the whole, such as calling an automobile *a set of wheels.*

Synesthesia

Synesthesia is speaking of one sense in terms of another, such as in the statement *The evening smelled purple.*

Theme

The theme is the central or dominating idea of a work (this includes movies, paintings and all works of art). It may be spelled out by the work or sometimes must be understood from it. Themes are always expressed in terms of all mankind and the universe.

All works of art—be they books, magazine articles, scholarly papers, statues, paintings, even buildings—have themes. The theme of much of Walt Whitman's poetry is that man is innately a good creature. The romantic English poet William Wordsworth carried the same theme further. His works tell us that in natural surroundings a man is a good being, but also one corrupted by city life.

Try a few more sample questions to test your understanding of these literary terms:

1. **The saying "as blind as a bat" is a**

    (A) metaphor
    (B) symbolism
    (C) colloquialism
    (D) simile
    (E) didacticism

2. **Two or three days and nights went by; I reckon they swum by, they slid along so quiet and smooth and lovely.**

    The passage above demonstrates a writer's use of

    (A) personification
    (B) imagery
    (C) alliteration
    (D) metaphor
    (E) epic language

3. How weary, stale, flat and unprofitable
    Seem to me all the uses of this world!
    Fie on't, ah, fie, 'tis an unweeded garden
    That grows to seed.

    The comparison of the earth and garden in this passage from Shakespeare's play, *Hamlet*, is

    (A) didactic
    (B) simile
    (C) metaphor
    (D) personification
    (E) onomatopoeia

1. (D) is the best choice. "as blind as a bat" is a direct comparison between some understood object not named (probably a person) and a bat. The words "as ...as" introduce the comparison. Metaphor requires indirect comparison by identifying or substituting a normally unrelated thing with another, thus (A) is incorrect. (C), which means a locally used expression with no meaning for people of another region, is not correct, because "blind as a bat" is used and understood in most places where English is spoken. There is no overriding concern for teaching, so (E) is wrong.

2. Personification, (A), is the best choice. Days, which are really nothing more than concepts, are given human features when the author says that "they swum by" and "they slid along." Because we could never actually see a day "swimming by," we know that (B) is incorrect; the author appeals to our humor and does not try to paint a physical picture that appeals to our physical senses through our imaginations. There is no repetition of initial consonants, vowel sounds, or syllables, thus (C) would be an illogical selection. There is no comparison in which the days are identified or substituted with another thing (such as, "the days were fish—they swum by"); therefore, (D) is wrong. Finally, the language in the passage is, while effective, uneducated, poor English. Epics are written in lofty style, so the passage could not be an example of epic language (E).

3. It is an indirect comparison in which the earth and an unweeded garden are identified with each other, without the signal words like and as. Thus, the correct answer is (C). (B) is a comparison, but a direct one used with the signal words, and it is not the answer. **Hamlet** has no overriding purpose to teach, no obvious moral, so (A) would be an illogical choice. The world is given the characteristics of an unweeded garden, a thing. Personification means attributing human characteristics to something, so (D) can not be the correct answer. There is nothing lofty about the passage; (E) would be a poor choice.

Chapter 6: FICTIONAL NARRATIVE

A few things distinguish fictional narrative from its non-fictional counterpart:

- at least some of the actions and events recounted in a piece of fiction did not actually happen

- the purpose of fiction is not merely to convey information as in a news story

- fiction relies on devices, such as "inner monologues", that would be inappropriate in a non-fictional narrative

Fiction takes many forms such as novels, novellas, short stories, and tales. Within these categories, there are numerous genres or subgenres. Narratives can be realistic, romantic, or didactic (seeking to instruct, especially in a moral sense). Some have a very objective texture, while others are very moody and subjective. Some put heavy emphasis on plot construction, while others focus more on portraying believable characters with psychological depth. Fables tend to have many fantastic elements while parables seek to make a moral point.

- **Allegory** is a story told on at least two different levels of meaning: the literal level and the 'symbolic' or 'metaphorical' level. Orwell's *Animal Farm* and Swift's *Gulliver's Travels* are about human institutions and are not works of zoology. In such a story, abstract concepts are made more 'concrete' by being embodied in characters and sensory objects.

- **Romance** is a story that emphasizes sentiment or emotion. It is not concerned with realistic scenes and characters and prefers to set its tales of love and passion in remote times and exotic places. The sense of mystery in human life is a common theme and there is usually hostility held for scientific explanations of life. Old-fashioned virtues like courage, loyalty, and honor are generally praised. Scott's *Ivanhoe* is a good example.

- **Naturalism** is a type of realistic fiction that looks at human life without any religious or mythological preconception. It places heavy emphasis on the historical and biological factors that influence human values and actions. The characters in naturalistic novels are usually working class and not very glamorous. Matters not discussed in 'polite society' are frequently depicted. Zola's *Germinal* is a good example.

- **Satire**, on the other hand, seeks not so much to accurately portray the misery of the human condition, but to ridicule social conventions and social groups. Satire frequently employs parody, mimicry, and caricature. Often the aim is didactic, as certain ways of thinking are held up as absurd or outmoded. Voltaire's *Candide* is a good example.

- **Modernist** novels, such as those written by Faulkner, Hemingway, Joyce, and Proust, comprise a mixed bag. One technique often used by modernist authors is the stream of consciousness, where a character's inner mental life is portrayed in all of its immediacy and confusion. That is, before the point at which such raw experience is given order by the logical part of the mind. There is also much juxtaposition of past and present.

Elements of Fictional Narrative

In any narrative there is a speaker. To put it another way, all narratives are written from some **point of view**. The narrator may be a character in the story, thereby limiting the narrator's knowledge of some events, especially the 'inner' events of a character's mind. In this type of narration, there may be a significant difference between the narrator's personality and that of the writer. (Fitzgerald's *The Great Gatsby* is told by Nick Carroway, and we should not assume that F. Scott Fitzgerald had exactly the same view of things as Nick.) At the other end of the spectrum, a story may be told by an **omniscient** narrator, who is not limited by time and space and who knows what is going on inside the minds of the characters. This perspective is also called the "God's-eye" view.

Besides the position of the narrator, points of view may be classified as **first-person**, **second-person**, or **third-person**. First-person narrators are aware of themselves as persons. (Melville's *Moby Dick* begins: "Call me Ishmael. Some years ago...I thought I would sail about a little and see the watery part of the world.") In contrast, the third-person approach is more objective:

She wore a pink dress...

He wiped the sweat from his brow...

It spread rapidly through the city...

Second-person narration is relatively rare:

"*You* fell asleep in the chair...."

Many fictional narratives have a main character called the **protagonist,** making the focus of the story the relationship of the protagonist to the other characters and the larger environment. The movement of the protagonist is towards some goal. The goal may be to discover truth about life or to gain knowledge about the world (or oneself) and become a mature person integrated with society or family, or to find one's way back home after years of wandering dangerously (like Odysseus in the *Odyssey*). The drama in the story comes from the obstacles that impede this progress.

The protagonist is driven to act by some conflict. One of the standard kinds of conflict identified in fiction are the protagonist's struggle against *nature* or some aspect of the natural world, be it climate, animals, or earthquakes. Also, the protagonist rebels against some institution of *society*, be it economic, political, military, or religious. Another conflict occurs when the protagonist is in competition with other individuals, himself, or herself. Of course, the same protagonist may be experiencing more than one of these conflicts.

The sequence of actions in a narrative is termed **plot**, and crucial points in the plot are points in time where the progress changes for better or worse. If the narrative is to be interesting at all, this progress should not be linear. That is, there should be turns and reversals of fortune along the way. An interesting narrative should not be entirely predictable, although through **foreshadowing** a writer will drop hints of things to come.

Another important element of narrative is **theme** (also called a motif). Theme may be defined as a recurring idea, image, or metaphor. A theme in the *Great Gatsby* is the strange combination of materialism and idealism exemplified by Jay Gatsby: He possesses material things in abundance, yet he seems to long for the simpler joys of his youth. This is also an example of conflict, and conflict often does serve as part of the theme.

Other important elements of narrative are devices such as allusion, irony, and pathos:

- **Allusion** is an indirect or implicit reference to something outside of the narrative, usually another work of literature. In Joyce's *Ulysses*, there is a sustained allusion to Homer's *Odyssey*, as the title of the former indicates. One of the purposes of calling other works to mind through allusion is contrast: the **juxtaposition** of ancient Greece and modern Dublin is meant to emphasize similarities and differences between the two things.

- **Irony** is another method of contrast and there are many varieties: in everyday life, irony involves saying one thing while meaning another, as when someone sarcastically says "Wonderful!" after hearing of a tragedy on the evening news. Socratic irony is when a very sharp-minded person pretends to be ignorant of some idea or concept. In a story or play, ***dramatic irony*** arises when one of the characters is not aware of some fact that is known to the reader or to the audience.

- **Pathos** is the quality in a narrative that arouses the reader's sympathy. One should note that sympathy is different from **empathy**. Sympathy is when we feel a sense of pity for a character, while empathy is a sense of identification with a character.

Chapter 7: THE DRAMATIC ARTS

Drama is another form of fictional writing and it has much in common with narrative and poetry. Drama, like narrative, tells a story, but differs in method of presentation. Drama also overlaps with poetry, since a play may be written in verse (although verse drama has not been much favored in modern times). There are three main genres: tragedy, comedy and melodrama:

- **Melodrama** relies on stock characters such as the brooding artist, the darkly attractive criminal, the stingy banker, etc. There is often a heavy dose of sentimentality and predictability.

- **Comedy** is a category that contains many seemingly different types of drama: Shakespeare's *The Merchant of Venice* has been put here, despite the cruel things that occur in the action. The reason why this might be considered a comedy is that it ends on a good note.

- **Tragedy** is one of the most enduring forms of drama and some of the most famous works of literature in the Western tradition are tragedies: *Oedipus Rex, Hamlet, Romeo and Juliet*, and *Faust*, just to name a few. Tragedies must end badly for the protagonist and the audience knows this, so suspense is not an important device for tragic drama. The interest in tragedy is the spectacle of a great person falling from a great height. Aristotle said that this process results in a **catharsis**, or purging, for the audience. The fact that the audience knows the fate of the protagonist allows for irony: we know that Oedipus kills his father and marries his mother, but Oedipus himself is not initially aware of this.

There is also a sense of **paradox** in the fact that a person as virtuous as the tragic hero can have such a fatal flaw. This flaw is sometimes identified as **hubris** (sometimes spelled *hybris*) which is an overwhelming pride on the part of the tragic figure. Aeschylus' Prometheus is thought to have suffered from this sort of pride, as well as Lucifer in Milton's *Paradise Lost*, Macbeth, King Lear, and Othello. Eventually, God, the gods, destiny, or fate will cut down the tragic protagonist.

The action in a tragedy is divided into episodes separated by choral odes: the chorus comments on the action and is usually taken as the "voice of the community". The structure of tragedy has five parts: exposition, complication, climax, falling action, and catastrophe. Roman dramatists, such as Seneca, and Shakespeare used this five-part division in the standard five-act structure of their plays.

Chapter 8: POETRY

Epic poetry is narrative poetry on a large scale. The most famous Western epic poems are Homer's *Iliad* and *Odyssey*, Virgil's *Aeneid*, Dante's *Divine Comedy*, and Milton's *Paradise Lost*. Epics usually involve a hero or a pilgrim on a quest or journey. A **ballad** is another kind of narrative poem, though the main character is usually less heroic than in an epic.

Lyric is a more musical type of poetry and deals with such themes as love, death, time, and nature. An **elegy** is a particularly mournful lyric. There is also much more expressiveness on the writer's part than in epic. Romantic poets of the nineteenth century such as Wordsworth, Keats, and Shelley, were fond of the lyric mode.

Dramatic poetry can be written in the form of a **monologue**, where the speaker in the poem addresses a silent listener or a character off-stage. Browning's *My Last Duchess* and Eliot's *The Love Song of J. Alfred Prufrock* are good examples of this form.

Metaphysical poetry is more of a style than a form and is identified with the seventeenth century English poets Donne, Marvell, and Herbert. Such poetry is very witty and highly intricate, requiring extremely close and careful reading. It seems very unemotional and logical when compared to Romantic poetry. To give some flavor of it, in one poem Donne compares the unity of two lovers to the legs of a compass (the mathematical instrument one uses to draw clean circles). Another famous metaphysical poem is Marvell's *To His Coy Mistress,* which is written in the general form of a logical syllogism.

Augustan poetry is eighteenth-century English poetry, so named because of its reverence to classical Greece and Rome. Its leading figure was Alexander Pope, who enjoyed writing mock-epics such as the *Dunciad*. Pope's poetry is written in heroic couplets (defined below). Other Augustan poets were Dryden and Addison.

The famous poems of the early twentieth-century are generally termed **modernist** and some of the key figures were W.B. Yeats, T.S. Eliot, Ezra Pound, Hart Crane, William Carlos Williams, and Marianne Moore. Important American poets have been Anne Bradstreet, Emily Dickinson, Walt Whitman, and Wallace Stevens.

Poetic Forms

Just as narratives are usually written in prose, poetry is usually written in verse (although there have been narratives in verse and poems in prose).

Meter And Foot

The structure of poetry is almost arithmetical when analyzed. Two elements are involved in the writing and reading of poetry: meter and foot.

Meter is the repeating pattern of stressed and unstressed syllables established in a line of poetry. The stressed syllable is also called the accented or "long" syllable, and it is marked in a line of poetry with an accent mark ('). The unstressed syllable is known as the unaccented or "short" syllable, and is marked with a cap-like symbol (∪). So, a line of verse can be characterized by the total number of syllables (syllabic verse) or by the number of stresses (accentual verse).

Foot is one unit of meter in poetry. Each unit of the repeated pattern in a line may be counted, and the length of the line is expressed by the number of feet. A foot can have two or three syllables, generally one stressed syllable and one or more unstressed syllables. A line of poetry may have one, two or as many feet as possible, but it is rare to find one with more than eight feet.

Poetic feet are named by the arrangement of stressed and unstressed syllables in the foot. The basic types are:

Name of Foot	Repeating Meter of Foot
iambic	short-long
trochaic	long-short
anapestic	short-short-long
dactylic	long-short-short
spondaic	long-long
pyrrhic	short-short

Following is an explanation of each type of metrical foot. An example from actual poetry will be given for each. It will be marked for long and short syllables to illustrate the repeating pattern for you. Read the example lines aloud; exaggerate the long and short syllables so that you can hear the pattern.

1. **IAMB**—the iambic foot is a two-syllable foot with the stress on the second syllable. This is the most common foot in English language poetry. The repeating pattern is **short syllable-long syllable**.

EXAMPLE:
$$\breve{\;}\;' \;\breve{\;}\;' \;\breve{\;}\;' \;\breve{\;}\; ' \;\;\breve{\;}\;'$$
A book of verses underneath the bough,
$$\breve{\;}\;' \;\breve{\;}\;' \;\breve{\;}\;' \;\breve{\;}\;' \;\;\breve{\;}\;\;'$$
A jug of wine, a loaf of bread—and thou.

> — Edward Fitzgerald,
>
> ### The Rubaiyat of Omar Khayyam

2. **TROCHEE**—the trochaic foot consists of a stressed syllable followed by an unstressed syllable. The repeating pattern is **long-short**, just the opposite of the iamb.

EXAMPLE:
$$'\;\breve{\;}\;'\;\breve{\;}\;'\;\breve{\;}\;'\;\breve{\;}$$
Double, double, toil and trouble,
$$'\;\breve{\;}\;'\;\;\breve{\;}\;'\;\breve{\;}\;'\;\breve{\;}$$
Fire burn and cauldron bubble.

> — William Shakespeare, **Macbeth**

3. **ANAPEST**—the anapestic foot consists of three syllables with the stress on the last syllable. The repeating pattern in the line is **short-short-long**.

EXAMPLE: With the sheep in the fold and the cows in their stalls.

4. **DACTYL**—the dactylic foot contains three syllables with the stress on the first syllable. It is the reverse of the anapest. The dactylic pattern is **long-short-short**.

EXAMPLE: Love again, song again, nest again, young again.

5. **SPONDEE**—the spondaic foot consists of two stressed syllables. Compound words are examples of spondees. Spondees are normally mixed in with other types of metrical feet in a line for variation. The repeating pattern is **long-long**.

EXAMPLE: heartbreak   childhood   football

6. **PYRRHIC**—the pyrrhic foot contains two unstressed syllables. This type of foot is rare. Like the spondee, it is interspersed in lines of poetry with other types of metrical feet for variation. It is difficult and pointless to give examples of pyrrhic feet from poetry; you will know them when you

find them if you remember that they differ from the prevailing pattern, and that they are two successive short syllables.

Lines

Now that you know the kinds of individual metrical feet and their proper names, we can concentrate on describing an entire line of poetry.

When we count the total number of feet in a line, we can give them a name that describes the length of the line. The basic kinds of lines are named by the number of feet in each:

Name of Line	Number of Feet
monometer	one-foot line
dimeter	two-foot line
trimeter	three-foot line
tetrameter	four-foot line
pentameter	five-foot line
hexameter	six-foot line
heptameter	seven-foot line
octometer	eight-foot line

Let us look at several of the examples previously used for illustrating types of metrical feet, and name the length of each line. Remember, first determine the pattern of stressed and unstressed syllables in the line of poetry; then and only then count the number of units of the pattern in each line to name its length.

EXAMPLE: Here again is the selection from **The Rubaiyat of Omar Khayyam**. It is iambic poetry. The repeating pattern is short-long:

⏑ ´ ⏑ ´ ⏑ ´ ⏑ ´ ⏑ ´

EXAMPLE: A book of verses underneath the bough,

⏑ ´ ⏑ ´ ⏑ ´ ⏑ ´ ⏑ ´

A jug of wine, a loaf of bread—and thou.

Now in your book draw a slash (/) after the last syllable in each foot (you need not draw a slash at the end of a line). The lines above should now look like this:

⏑ ´   ⏑ ´ ⏑ ´ ⏑ ´   ⏑ ´

A book / of ver / ses un / derneath / the bough,

76

<pre>
∪   ′   ∪   ′   ∪   ′   ∪   ′   ∪   ′
</pre>
A jug / of wine, / a loaf / of bread / —and thou.

Count the number of iambic feet, or units of iambic pattern, that you have made with the slashes. There are five: a five-foot line is called pentameter.

EXAMPLE: Try again with the example from Shakespeare's **Macbeth**. Remember "Double, double, toil and trouble"? Here it is properly accented. Draw slashes after each trochaic foot:

<pre>
      ′ ∪ ′ ∪   ′   ∪   ′ ∪
</pre>
EXAMPLE: Double, double, toil and trouble,

<pre>
     ′ ∪ ′   ∪   ′   ∪   ′ ∪
</pre>
Fire burn and cauldron bubble.

It should now look like this:

<pre>
      ′ ∪   ′   ∪   ′   ∪   ′   ∪
</pre>
Double, / double, / toil and / trouble,

<pre>
     ′ ∪ ′   ∪   ′   ∪   ′ ∪
</pre>
Fire / burn and / cauldron / bubble.

Count the number of feet in each line. There are four: a four-foot line is called tetrameter. It is simple, once you are familiar with the words and the process.

By combining type of feet with length of lines, we create two-word names that instantly describe the stress of syllables and the number of feet in each line. Thus, the lines from **The Rubaiyat of Omar Khayyam** are written in a form called iambic pentameter. The lines from **Macbeth** are written in trochaic tetrameter.

Just as sentences in prose are composed into paragraphs, lines of verse are composed into larger units. These larger units are called either **strophes** or **stanzas**. A stanza has a fixed number of lines: a **quatrain** has four lines, a **sestet** has six, an **octet** eight, etc. Strophes, on the other hand, have no fixed length (many narrative poems are strophic).

A **sonnet** is a stanzaic form consisting of just one stanza. The Shakespearean variety of sonnet has a total of fourteen lines which break down as follows: three quatrains followed by a couplet. In terms of meter, the sonnet is accentual: each line has (ideally) five stressed syllables out of ten total syllables. The rhyme scheme of a sonnet is *abab, cdcd, efef, gg*. Some of the most famous sonnets in English were written by Shakespeare, such as the one that begins: *Shall I compare thee to a summer's day? / Thou art more lovely and more temperate.*

Sonnets are written in a special type of meter called iambic pentameter. In this, the line may be divided into five "feet", each foot consisting of an unstressed syllable followed by a stressed one. Such a foot is called an ***iamb***. Here is a representative line of iambic pentameter from Gray's *Elegy Written in a Country Churchyard*:

"The paths of glory lead but to the grave."

The five stresses fall on *paths*, the first syllable of *glory, lead, to,* and *grave.*

A sonnet concludes with a rhyming, end-stopped couplet. Such a couplet is called a **heroic couplet**. An end-stopped line is one that ends with a punctuation mark; if the line does not end with some form of punctuation but rather spills over into the next line, it is called **enjambment**. Here is an example of enjambment from Shakespeare:

"Like to the lark at break of day arising

From sullen earth, sings hymns at heaven's gate..."

The pause in the middle of the second line above (indicated by the comma) is called a **caesura**.

At this point try some questions about the fundamentals of poetry to test your understanding of how to analyze poetry. If you do not get all of them correct, review this section again.

1. Whose woods these are I think I know.
   His house is in the village though;
   He will not see me stopping here
   To watch his woods fill up with snow.

   These lines from Frost's "*Stopping by Woods on a Snowy Evening*" are

   (A) trochaic
   (B) iambic
   (C) spondaic
   (D) plain verse
   (E) pyrrhic

2. Green pastures she views in the midst of the dale,
   Down which she so often has tripped with her pail;
   And a single small cottage, a nest like a dove's;
   The one only dwelling on earth that she loves.

   These lines by William Wordsworth are written in

   (A) iambic tetrameter
   (B) iambic pentameter
   (C) anapestic tetrameter
   (D) dactylic pentameter
   (E) dactylic tetrameter

3. Workers earn it,
   Spendthrifts burn it,
   Bankers lend it,
   Women spend it,
   Forgers fake it,
   I could use it.

   The poem quoted above is written in

   (A) trochaic dimeter
   (B iambic pentameter
   (C) trochaic tetrameter
   (D) iambic dimeter
   (E) iambic trimeter

ANSWERS

1. The repeated pattern of stressed and unstressed syllables is short-long:

   ⏑　′　　⏑　′ ⏑ ′　⏑　′
   Whose woods these are I think I know.

   Such poetry is iambic, and (B) is the correct answer. None of the others is a logical choice.

2. By going through the first two lines, marking long and short syllables, we find that the dominant metrical foot is anapestic. Note that although an iambic foot opens each line it does not change the way we name the line. Consider the iamb an incomplete anapest instead. **Always name the line by the dominant meter**. By counting the number of anapestic feet, which you should have marked by slashes:

   ⏑　′　⏑　⏑　′　　⏑ ⏑　′　　⏑ ⏑ ′
   Green pas / tures she views / in the midst / of the dale

   we find that there are four feet to a line. The length of metrical line is tetrameter. Put the two together—anapestic tetrameter—and the answer is (C). Usually, marking two lines for stress patterns and feet in a question of this type is sufficient for determining the answer. However, if you are unsure of the structure, continue marking the lines in the sample selection until the answer becomes obvious to you. Never read possible answers and try to fit one to the question; always analyze the poetic sample when you are asked to identify the structure and then look for the choice that is correct. Do not hesitate to mark your test book when you take the CLEP examination, just as you have marked your review text here. It is perfectly allowable and beneficial for you to do so.

3. After marking the first few lines for stressed and unstressed syllables:

   ′　⏑　′　⏑　′　　⏑　′　⏑
   Workers earn it, Spendthrifts burn it

   you should have found that they are trochaic. After adding slash marks between trochaic feet and counting the number in each line, you should have found them to be two-foot lines, dimeter. The correct answer is (A) trochaic dimeter. No other answer could be correct.

Rhyme

Beyond the breakdown of poetry into rhythms, as in types of feet and length of lines, there is a final consideration: rhyme. Rhyme also has technical names you should be familiar with in preparing for the Praxis examination.

Poetry means rhyme to many people, as it probably meant to ancient societies before writing was invented. Scholars theorize that ancient peoples memorized stories and passed them down from generation to generation (this is known as

oral tradition). Rhyme, it is thought, helped them remember. It is no wonder then, that the earliest words of literature were written with regular rhythm and definite rhyme. Later writers, venerating the original style of ancients such as the Greek epic poet Homer, copied their poetic style for works they deemed to be of highest significance. Even today, poetry—often rhyming, although not necessarily—has been regarded as the noblest literary expression.

Rhyme is described, generally, by three kinds of **verse forms**:

1. **RHYMED VERSE** is poetry that rhymes at the end of lines.

2. **BLANK VERSE** is poetry written in iambic pentameter without end rhyme. Shakespeare's works and all epics in English use this form.

3. **FREE VERSE** consists of lines that do not have a regular meter and do not rhyme.

Rhyme in a poem can be diagrammed by assigning consecutive letters for each new end sound.

EXAMPLE: One would diagram Shelley's **"To Wordsworth"** in this manner:

Poet of Nature, thou has wept to know		a
That things depart which never may return:		b
Childhood and youth, friendship and love's first glow,		a
Have fled like sweet dreams, leaving thee to mourn.		b
These common woes I feel. One loss is mine	5	c
Which thou too feel'st, yet I alone deplore.		d
Thou wert as a lone star, whose light did shine		c
On some frail bark in winter's midnight roar:		d
Thou hast like to a rock-built refuge stood		e
Above the blind and battling multitude:	10	e
In honoured poverty thy voice did weave		f
Songs consecrate to truth and liberty,—		g
Deserting these, thou leavest me to grieve,		f
Thus, having been, that thou shouldst cease to be.		g

The **rhyme scheme**, or diagrammed rhyme, of **"To Wordsworth"** is described as a-b-a-b-c-d-c-d-e-e-f-g-f-g. Imperfect rhymes, such as "return" and "mourn" in lines 2 and 4 and "stood" and "multitude" in lines 9 and 10, do count in the rhyme scheme and receive the same letter designation.

Once again, try some questions to measure your comprehension of these principles of poetry.

1. Now cracks a noble heart. Good night, sweet prince,
    And flights of angels sing thee to thy rest.

    The preceding lines from William Shakespeare's *Hamlet* are an example of

    (A) epic language
    (B) blank verse
    (C) heroic couplet
    (D) an alexandrine
    (E) terza rima

ANSWER: Because these lines are written in iambic pentameter without end rhyme, we know they are blank verse. Shakespeare wrote all of his plays in this style, and that is another hint that (B) is the correct answer. While the language is lofty and moving, it does not involve elaborate comparisons that signify epic language, so (A) is not the correct answer. **Heroic couplet** is rhyming iambic pentameter but these lines do not rhyme and (C) is incorrect. **Alexandrine** (D) is iambic hexameter and is an incorrect choice. **Terza rima** is a three-line stanza in iambic pentameter with interwoven rhyme scheme (a-b-a, b-c-b and so on). The example is unrhymed and consists of only two lines, so (E) is obviously incorrect.

2. Be her eternal throne
    Built in our hearts alone—
        God save the Queen!
    Let the oppressor hold
    Canopied seats of gold;
    She sits enthroned of old
        O'er our hearts Queen.

    The rhyme scheme of this verse from Shelley's **"A New National Anthem"** could be described as

    (A) a-a-b-b-c-c-d
    (B) a-b-a-b-c-d-d
    (C) a-b-a-c-d-c-d
    (D) a-a-b-c-c-c-b
    (E) a-b-c-d-a-b-d

ANSWER: The correct answer is (D).

The most familiar type of rhyme scheme is end rhyme, where the rhyming words come at the end of a line. Rhyme involves some kind of sound similarity between two words. The most familiar case is true rhyme, where the words differ only in the initial sound: *clock* and *shock* for example. **Assonance** occurs when there is only the same stressed vowel sound: *lover* and *trouble* for example. **Alliteration** is the repetition of the same initial consonant sound: *Love's Labour's Lost*.

Poetry need not have a fixed rhyme scheme: blank verse is unrhymed verse (though it is metered). A significant portion of Shakespeare's drama is written in blank verse. Free verse has neither regular rhyme nor regular meter.

Chapter 9: ASPECTS OF LINGUISTICS

Linguistics is the science of language. It studies such topics as how intrinsically meaningless units of sound are combined into larger meaningful units such as words (this property of language is sometimes called duality of patterning. It is what allows so many words to be constructed from so few sounds); the fact that words allow us to refer to things not physically present (this is called displacement); the structure and function of particular languages at particular times and places; how languages change over time; and whether there is a common underlying structure to all languages regardless of time and place.

Phonetics is the study of sounds and how these sounds are formed in the mouth cavity. The **consonants** are classified according to (1) where in the oral cavity the sound is articulated, (2) how the sound is articulated and (3) whether or not the sound is voiced. Regarding (1), consonant sounds may be *bilabial* (lips), *labiodental* (teeth touching lips), *interdental* (tongue touching teeth), *alveolar* (tongue touching the upper gum ridge), *palatal* (tongue touching hard palate), *alveolo-palatal*, *velar* (soft palate or velum), or *glottal* (upper part of larynx). (2) refers to the passage of air: *plosives* (also called stops) are made by an actual stopping of air and then an explosion of breath; *fricatives* involve air "rubbing" through a narrow opening in the mouth; *affricates* combine properties of plosives and fricatives; *nasals* result from letting air flow through the nose rather than through the oral passage; *laterals* have breath flowing around the sides of the tongue; and a *retroflex* (sometimes called *rolled*) refers to the fact that the tongue is "bent back." (Lateral and retroflex are sometimes categorized together as *liquids*.) (3) Voiced consonants involve vibration of the vocal cords:

- **P**losives: b (voiced) and p (voiceless) are bilabial; d (voiced) and t (voiceless) are alveolar; g (voiced) and k (voiceless) are velar.

- **F**ricatives: v (voiced) and f (voiceless) are labiodental; the sound of *th* in *father* (voiced) and *th* in *thin* (voiceless) are interdental; z (voiced) and s (voiceless) are alveolar; the sound of *si* in *vision* (voiced) and *sh* in *shoe* (voiceless) are alveolo-palatal; h (voiceless) is glottal.

- **A**ffricates: the sound of g in *general* (voiced) and *ch* in *chip* (voiceless) are alveolo-palatal.

- **N**asals: m is bilabial while n is alveolar; the sound of *ng* in *ring* is velar.

- **L**ateral: l is alveolar.

- **R**etroflex: the r (as in the word *retroflex*) is alveolar.

- **S**emivowels: y is palatal while w is velar.

Vowels are voiced and there is no obstruction of the airflow; they are categorized according to the position of the tongue and to whether the lips are rounded or protruding during pronunciation. The vowels in *meat, mitt, mate, met and mat* are "front vowels" because the highest part of the tongue is in front; their order reflects the position of the tongue relative to the roof of the mouth from highest to lowest. The vowels in *sue, soot, sew, saw and sot* are "back vowels" for similar reasons.

The **schwa** sound is an unstressed vowel sound, such as the *a* in comma, the *e* in cider, the *i* in family and the *o* in potassium. In making the schwa sound, the tongue is in a relatively 'middle' position compared to the other vowels. A **dipthong** is a case where there are two distinguishable vowel sounds in the same syllable as in soil, tower, and file. A vowel **digraph** is when two letters represent a single vowel sound such as the *aw* in paw.

The phonetic properties of a sound are not always a good guide to how that sound is represented by letters (**graphemes**). That is, inexperienced readers will not always be able to guess at the pronunciation of a word from its spelling (**orthography**). English has many words with unphonetic spellings: *light, phone, catalogue,* etc. **Homonyms** are words with the same pronunciation but different spellings and meanings, such as *sweet* (the taste) and *suite* (a group of rooms). **Homographs** have the same spelling but with different meanings and perhaps different pronunciations, such as *pen* (may mean the writing instrument or an enclosure for animals) or *bow* (may mean to kneel or what is used to launch an arrow, which are pronounced differently).

Phonemics, in contrast to phonetics, is not concerned with the physical nature of sounds but how different sounds which are meaningless in themselves combine to form meaningful units such as words. The fundamental units of phonemics are **phonemes**, which are sounds that when combined in different ways produce different meanings. For instance, replacing the initial /d/ phoneme in down with the /t/ phoneme produces town. On the other hand, the p in the words *plate* and *spend* seem like the same sound but they are not: the p in plate is aspirated while the p in spend is not, but this slight sound difference does not make for a difference in meaning in English.

Recognizing that a word can be broken down into a sequence of phonemes is one important approach to teaching word recognition and comprehension to beginning readers. This pedagogy goes by many names: phonemic-awareness, phonics, skills-oriented instruction, text-driven instruction, data-driven instruction, bottom-up, decoding, analysis, etc. The other main approach to reading instruction also has many designations: whole-language, holistics, meaning-oriented instruction, experience-driven instruction, top-down, hypothesis-test theory, synthesis, etc.

A **morpheme** is a meaningful sound that cannot be divided into smaller meaningful units. Thus, for a linguist, morphemes and not words are the smallest fundamental units of meaning. For example, the *s* in *boots*, the *es* in *machines*, the *en* in *oxen*, and the *ee* in feet are all morphemes which express plurality. The word *boots* consists of two morphemes meaning "an outer covering for the feet" (*boot*) and "more than one" (*-s*). The prefixes *re-* and *anti-* are morphemes which express "again" and "against." **Morphology** (the etymological root of which means 'study of form') is the study of how morphemes are put together to form words. For instance, a morphologist would notice that the morphemes *–ism*, *–tion* and *–ness* as suffixes usually designate an abstract noun in English: capitalism, reductionism, desolation, isolation, happiness, wellness, etc. The sum total of morphemes in a given language comprises that language's **lexicon** (which is embodied in its dictionary).

Semantics studies the various meanings of words and its fundamental unit is the sememe. For instance, *state* (which is called a **lexeme**) has numerous sememes: it can mean a political unit, a quality of being or existence (a state of affairs, the state of the patient), etc. **Denotation** and **connotation** are two important semantic notions: the former is the 'dictionary meaning' of a word while the latter involves the 'associations' of a word. Sometimes this difference is expressed as literal versus metaphorical meaning. For instance, the word *brother* denotes common parents but it also carries suggestions of solidarity, fraternity and sympathy for one's fellow human beings. If the connotation of a word changes over time from positive to negative it is **pejorative**, as with the word *conceit*. When the opposite change occurs, the word is **ameliorative**. When two words have roughly the same denotation, such as *cat* and *feline*, they are **synonyms**; when the denotations of two words are roughly opposite, such as *apex* and *nadir*, they are **antonyms**.

An important, though not decisive, aspect of a word's meaning is its **etymology**, which is its historical derivation. The important point is that a word's current meaning is not necessarily the same as its 'original' meaning in another language. **Cognates** are words in different languages that seem to have a similar root, perhaps somewhere in a now defunct proto-language. For example, *salt* in English would be cognate with *Salz* (German), *sale* (Italian), *sel* (French) and *sal* (Spanish and Latin). Cognate languages, like French and Italian, have similarities based on common lineage (Latin in this case).

All of the languages just mentioned are considered part of the Indo-European family of languages. The main subdivisions of the Indo-European family would include Germanic (English, German, Dutch, Danish, Swedish), Celtic (Welsh, Gaelic), Italic (Italian, Portuguese, French, Spanish, Romanian), Hellenic (Greek), Balto-Slavic (Lithuanian, Polish, Russian) and Indo-Iranian (Hindi, Bengali, Persian). Non-Indo-European language families would include Semitic (Hebrew, Arabic), Hamitic (Egyptian, Berber, Cushitic), Khoisan (Hottentot, Bushman), and Sino-Tibetan (Chinese, Burmese).

Linguists also study language as it functions in particular times, places and contexts. An **idiom** is an expression whose meaning cannot be deduced from the meaning of its parts. For instance, a non-English speaker would hardly be able to figure out the meaning of 'to bring up' based on the separate meanings of 'bring' and 'up'. Many such idioms are formed in English by attaching a preposition to a verb: to get across, to get by, to shut up, to shut down, etc. A **slang** expression is not the same as an idiomatic one: the latter is composed of 'standard' words while the former is not. A **dialect** differs from the standard language because of geographical location or social class. **Argot** is the secretive language used by closed associations, especially criminal associations, while **jargon** is the specialized language of a professional or academic group: lawyers are said to talk in *legalese*, etc. Jargon is mostly incomprehensible to the outsider, unlike **colloquial speech**, which is the familiar, common, everyday usage.

Chapter 10: RESEARCH AND RESOURCE MATERIAL

Almanac: compilation of data and statistics for a given year, including economic matters, political matters, weather, the lunar cycle, etc.

Anthology: a collection of writing by different authors of same genre (also called a compendium).

Appendix: material attached to the end of a work, explaining some aspects of the main body in greater detail.

Atlas: contains political and topographical maps and information on such matters as where to find natural resources.

Bibliography: list of recommended books; list of books by a particular author or in a particular subject; list of books consulted. An annotated bibliography includes notes on the books listed.

Dictionary: the most familiar type of dictionary gives the meaning of words, morphemes, and derivations. There are also dictionaries that give information about specialized terms, concepts and subjects, and are arranged alphabetically: dictionary of philosophy, culinary arts, etc. (encyclopedias are more general).

Glossary: explains some technical terms contained in the main text.

Handbook: similar to a dictionary or a glossary; a manual of style or usage such as those of Fowler, Strunk & White, and the University of Chicago.

Index: sometimes broken up into a subject index and a proper name index.

Manuscript: could constitute a primary source.

Thesaurus: list of synonyms and antonyms, sometimes indexed by concept.

LANGUAGE ARTS GLOSSARY

ADJECTIVE: words functioning as modifiers of nouns, typically by describing, delimiting, or specifying quantity.

ADVERB: words functioning as modifiers of verbs, adjectives, other adverbs, or clauses, typically expressing some relation of place, time, manner, degree, etc.

ALLEGORY: the representation of spiritual, moral, or other abstract meanings through the actions of fictional characters that serve as symbols.

ALLITERATION: the repetition of the same sound, as a consonant or a cluster, at the beginning of two or more stressed syllables.

ALLUSION: a passing or casual reference to something, either directly or implied.

AMELIORATIVE: improved; made better or more satisfactory.

ANTONYMS: a word opposite in meaning to another.

ARGOT: a specialized vocabulary peculiar to a particular group of people.

ASPECT: a category for which a verb is inflected, serving typically to indicate the duration, repetition, beginning, or completion of the action.

ASSONANCE: similarity of sounds in words or syllables.

AUXILIARY: supplementary; as with a verb, used to construct compound verbs.

BALLAD: a simple narrative poem, especially of folk origin, composed in short stanzas and adapted for singing.

CAESURA: a break or pause in a line of verse.

CASE: the inflection of nouns, pronouns, and adjectives indicating the syntactic relation of these words to other words on a sentence.

CATHARSIS: the purging of emotions or relieving of emotional tensions, especially through a work of art, as a tragedy or music.

CAUSATION: the act or fact of causing.

CLAUSE:	A group of words containing a subject and predicate and forming part of a sentence or constituting a whole simple sentence.
COGNATE:	descended from the same language or form.
COGNITION:	the act or process of knowing.
COLLOQUIAL SPEECH:	ordinary or familiar conversation or writing rather than formal speech or writing; informal.
CONJUNCTION:	words functioning as connectors between words, phrases, clauses, or sentences, as *and, because, but*, and *unless*.
CONNOTE:	to signify or suggest ideas, meanings, etc., in addition to the explicit or primary meaning.
CONSONANT:	a speech sound occluding, diverting, or obstructing the flow of air from the lungs.
CORRELATION:	mutual relation of two or more things, parts, etc.
CUNEIFORM:	type of writing by the ancient Akkadians, Assyrians, Babylonians, Persians, and others. Triangular marks were made in clay tablets.
DECLARATIVE:	serving to declare, state, or explain.
DENOTATION:	the explicit or direct meaning of a word or expression, as distinguished from the ideas or meanings associated with or suggested by it.
DETERMINER:	used to express quantity, etc. most important types are definite and indefinite articles.
DIALECT:	a variety of language distinguished from other varieties by features of phonology, grammar, and vocabulary and by its use by a group of speakers set off from others geographically or socially.
DICTION:	style of speaking or writing as dependent upon choice of words.
DIDACTIC:	intended for instruction.
DIGRAPH:	a pair of letters representing a single speech sound.
DIPHTHONG:	an unsegmentable, gliding speech sound varying in phonetic quality but considered to be a single sound or phoneme.
DRAFTING:	making a preliminary outline or sketch.

DRAMATIC IRONY:	irony derived from the audience's understanding of a speech or a situation not grasped by the characters in a dramatic piece.
ELEGY:	a mournful, melancholy, or plaintive poem, especially a lament for the dead.
EMPATHY:	the identification with or vicarious experiencing of the feelings, thoughts, etc., of another.
ENJAMBMENT:	the running on of the thought from one poetic line, couplet, or stanza to the next without a syntactic break.
EPIC:	a long poetic composition, usually centered upon a hero, in which a series of great achievements or events is narrated in elevated style.
ETYMOLOGY:	the history of a particular word or element of a word.
EXPOSITORY WRITING:	writing whose purpose is to explain.
FIRST PERSON:	the grammatical person used by a speaker in statements referring to himself or herself or to a group including himself or herself.
FORESHADOW:	to show or indicate beforehand.
GERUND:	a form similar to the Latin gerund in meaning and function, as in English the *–ing* form of a verb when functioning as a noun, as *writing* in *Writing is easy.*
GRAPHEME:	a unit of a writing system consisting of all the written symbols that are used to represent a single phoneme.
HEROIC COUPLET:	a set of two rhymed lines of iambic pentameter.
HOMOGRAPH:	words with the same written but of different meanings and origins, whether pronounced the same way or not.
HOMONYM:	a word the same as another in sound and spelling but different in meaning.
HUBRIS:	excessive pride or self-confidence.
IAMB:	a foot of poetry consisting of a short followed by a long.
IDIOM:	an expression whose meaning is not predictable from the usual grammatical rules of a language or from the usual meanings of its constituent elements.

INDICATIVE:	the grammatical mood used for ordinary objective statements and questions.
INFINITIVE:	the simple form of the verb, that names the action or state without specifying the subject and that functions as a noun or is used with auxiliary verbs.
INTERJECTION:	the utterance of a word or phrase expressing emotion.
INTERROGATIVE:	conveying a question.
IRONY:	the use of words to convey a meaning that is the opposite of its literal meaning.
JARGON:	the language, especially the vocabulary, peculiar to a trade, profession, or group
JUXTAPOSITION:	placing objects or ideas close together or side by side, especially for comparison or contrast.
LEXEME:	a minimal lexical unit in a language
LEXICON:	the total inventory of words or morphemes in a given language.
LYRIC:	having the form and general effect of a song.
MIMESIS:	mimicry.
MODERNIST:	the 20th century movement in the arts and taking form in any of various innovative movements and styles.
MONOLOGUE:	a dramatic or comic piece spoken entirely by a single performer.
MORPHEME:	any of the minimal grammatical units of a language, each constituting a word or meaningful part of a word that cannot be divided into smaller meaningful parts.
MORPHOLOGY:	the patterns of word formation in a language, including inflection, derivation, and compound formation.
NATURALISM:	a literary style combining a deterministic view of human nature.
NOUN:	words that can function as the subject or object in a construction and typically refer to persons, places, animals, things, states, or qualities.
OCTET:	a group of eight.

OMNISCIENT:	having complete or unlimited knowledge, awareness, or understanding.
ORTHOGRAPHY:	the art of writing words with the proper letters according to accepted usage; correct spelling.
PARADOX:	a seemingly contradictory or absurd statement that expresses a possible truth.
PARTICIPLE:	a word that can function as an adjective or be used with certain auxiliaries to make compound verb forms.
PATHOS:	the quality or power in life or art of evoking a feeling of pity or compassion.
PEJORATIVE:	having a disparaging, derogatory, or belittling effect.
PERSUASIVE WRITING:	writing that incorporates the act of advising or urging.
PHONEME:	any of the minimal units of speech sound in a language that can serve to distinguish one word from another.
PHONEMICS:	the study of phonemes.
PHONETICS:	the study of speech sounds and their production.
PHRASE:	a group of words lacking a subject and a verb, which would make it a clause.
PLOT:	the main story of a literary or dramatic work.
POINT OF VIEW:	the position of the narrator in relation to the story.
PREDICATE:	the verb and the words governed by the verb.
PREPOSITION:	words that are typically used before nouns, pronouns to form phrases.
PRONOUN:	words used as replacements or substitutes for nouns.
PROTAGONIST:	the leading character of a drama or other literary work.
QUATRAIN:	a stanza or poem of four lines.
RECURSIVE:	a rule or procedure that can be applied repeatedly.
REGISTER:	a variety of language typically used in a specific type of communicative setting.
REVISING:	altering something written or printed, in order to correct, improve, or update.

SATIRE: a literary composition in which human folly and vice are held up to scorn or ridicule.

SCHWA: the mid-central, neutral vowel sound typically occurring in unstressed syllables in English.

SECOND PERSON: the grammatical person referring to the one being addressed.

SEMANTICS: the branch of linguistics dealing with the study of meaning of language.

SENTENCE: a subject and a predicate containing a finite verb and expressing a statement, question, request, command, or exclamation.

SESTET: a group or stanza of six lines.

SLANG: very informal usage of vocabulary and idiom that is characteristically more metaphorical and playful than ordinary language.

SONNET: a poem of 14 lines, usually in iambic pentameter, with rhymes arranged in a fixed scheme, being in the Italian form divided into a major group of 8 lines followed by a minor group of six lines and in a common English form into three quatrains followed by a couplet.

STANZA: an arrangement of a certain number of lines, usually four or more, sometimes having a fixed length, meter or rhyme scheme, forming a division or a poem.

STROPHE: any separate section or extended movement in a poem, distinguished from a stanza in that it does not follow a regularly repeated pattern.

SUBJECT: something or someone represented in a literary composition or work of art, etc.

SUBJUNCTIVE: of or designating a grammatical mood typically used for grammatically subordinate statements or questions.

SYNONYM: a words having the same or nearly the same meaning.

SYNTAX: the study of the patterns of formation of sentences and phrases from words and of the rules for the formation of grammatical sentences in a language.

TENSE:	specify the time of the action or state expressed by the verb.
THEME:	the topic of the literary work.
THIRD-PERSON:	referring to anyone or anything other than the speaker or the one or ones being addressed.
TONE:	the way a literary work sounds
VERB:	words that function as the main part of a predicate, typically expressing action, state, or a relation between two things.
VOWEL:	a speech sound produced without obstructing the flow of air from the lungs.

PART II
SOCIAL STUDIES

Social Studies

The social studies section will test your knowledge of geography, world history, and United States history, and social sciences such as political science, economics, sociology, anthropology, and psychology.

Chapter 1: GEOGRAPHY

Geography may be divided into two general areas: physical and cultural. **Physical geography** is concerned with such things as topography (a topographical map shows elevations and depressions of land), climate, geomorphology (the study of land forms such as continents), and with mapping the earth. **Cultural geography** concerns itself with the man-made political boundaries and with economic and industrial issues.

Climate differs from weather in that climate refers to long-term patterns of weather. Some of the climate zones into which the earth could be divided are equatorial, tropic, temperate, and polar. An arid climate is one that receives little or no precipitation.

The earth could also be divided into different areas (called **biomes**) based on the characteristic plant and animal life found there: glacial ice, tundra, desert, grasslands, forest, jungle and wetlands. **Tundras** are plains without trees found near arctic regions such as in northern Russia. A **steppe** is similar to a tundra but is usually found further from polar regions. Savannas and pampas are types of grasslands. A **deciduous** forest is one whose trees shed their leaves annually, while a **coniferous** forest is composed of evergreen, cone-bearing trees such as pine and spruce.

A continent is a continuous mass of land above sea level. It is believed that there was once only one super-continent termed Pangaea that has since drifted into numerous different ones. The seven continents from largest to smallest are Asia, Africa, North America, South America, Antarctica, Europe, and Australia. Europe and Asia are sometimes counted as one single continent called *Eurasia*.

If an island is on the same continental shelf as the mainland, it is considered part of that continent. The largest island in the world is Greenland with an area of over 800,000 square miles. A group of islands sitting in a relatively large body of water is called an **archipelago** (an example is the Phillipines). A peninsula is a semi-island sometimes connected to the mainland by a narrow strip of land called an **isthmus** (Florida and Italy are two peninsulas).

Oceans are bodies of salt water that cover between 70 and 75% of the earth's surface. There are five oceans: the Pacific, the Atlantic, the Indian, the Antarctic, and the Arctic. Seas can be salt or fresh water and usually differentiate from oceans because they are nearly completely surrounded by land. A body of salt or fresh water completely surrounded by land is a lake. The largest sea (over 143,000 square miles in area) is the Caspian Sea in southern Russia. Other large seas (or lakes) include Lake Superior (U.S./Canada: over 31,000 square miles) and Lake Victoria in central Africa (over 24,000 square miles).

Rivers are currents of fresh water that flow from higher elevations downward until they empty into a sea. Where the river begins is called the source and where it empties into the sea is called the mouth. Some rivers have developed **deltas** at their mouths from deposits of sand and silt. Some of the important rivers of the world, starting with the longest, are the Nile in Egypt, the Amazon in Brazil, the Mississippi in the U.S., the Yangtze in China, the Volga in European Russia, and the Ganges in India.

Mountains are extreme elevations of land. Some of the more important mountain ranges are the Himalayas (Asia-Northern India), the Andes (South America's Pacific Coast), the Rockies (U.S.), the Alps (Northern Italy-Switzerland), and the Urals (Russia). Some of the highest peaks are Everest (Himalayas: 29,000 feet), Aconcagua (Andes: 22,800 ft.), Mt. McKinley (Alaska: 20,300 ft.), Kilimanjaro (Africa: 19,300 ft.), and Vinson Massif (Antarctica: 16,900 ft.).

The earth has a total surface area of approximately 200 million square miles and an equatorial circumference of about twenty-five thousand miles. The **equator** provides the reference point from which to measure north/south distances: the distance from the equator to one of the poles is divided into ninety degrees. All places on the earth that are the same distance from one of the poles are said to be on the same parallel of **latitude**. East/west distances are measured relative to the **prime meridian** (also called the Greenwich meridian because of the town in England through which it passes). The distance from the Greenwich meridian to the **International Date Line** is divided into 180 degrees. All places that are the same distance from the Greenwich meridian are said to be on the same meridian of **longitude**.

Concerning cultural geography, the most important units are countries, which are sometimes called **nation-states** (an area with its own sovereign government where the citizens share a common history and culture). Important political and/or administrative units in the United States include states, counties, cities, boroughs, townships, school districts, postal zones, and police precincts. **Demographic** maps would show the density of population in different areas. Economic maps indicate patterns of agriculture and natural resources. Historical maps show old names for cities or places of famous military battles.

Cultural geography has much overlap with the social sciences. Political scientists are interested in such things as electoral districts within a state or where the seats of authority (such as capitals) are located. Economists take an interest in such things as the location of important industries. The **Rust Belt** refers to the areas in America dominated by the steel and automobile industries and stretches from southern Michigan (Detroit), through northern

Ohio (Cleveland) and western Pennsylvania (Pittsburgh and Erie) to western New York (Buffalo). The **Wheat Belt** stretches in a north-south direction through the mid-western states of the Dakotas, Nebraska, Kansas, and Oklahoma. The **Corn Belt** stretches east-west through Ohio, Indiana, Illinois, Iowa, and Nebraska. **Silicon Valley** refers to the emergent high-tech computer industry located just south of San Francisco in cities like San Jose.

Sociologists use a number of terms to describe aspects of cultural geography. A city is defined as an area of extreme population density, usually located adjacent to a body of water. Cities, since they have no space for agriculture, are not able to provide their own food. The area upon which cities must depend for food supplies is termed the **hinterland**. The **central city** is where one finds the main government, business, and cultural activity, while the **inner city** refers to old residential areas that have grown dilapidated. **Suburbs** are residential areas on the outskirts of cities. They are politically divided from cities and are inhabited mainly by people who work in the central city. The growth of suburbs was made possible by more efficient means of transportation. The phenomenon of middle-class suburbanites moving to renovated dwellings in the inner city is known as **gentrification**.

Geography Questions

1. **Which of the following states would be considered an archipelago?**

   (A) California
   (B) Florida
   (C) Oklahoma
   (D) Hawaii

2. **Which of the following states is a peninsula?**

   (A) Illinois
   (B) Michigan
   (C) North Carolina
   (D) Georgia

3. **Which of the following countries contains tundra?**

   (A) Mexico
   (B) Brazil
   (C) Egypt
   (D) Canada

4. Which of the following is the highest mountain in North America?

(A) Mount McKinley
(B) Mount Everest
(C) Mount Rainer
(D) Mount Kilimanjaro

5. Through which of the following cities does the prime meridian pass?

(A) Washington, DC, USA
(B) Moscow, Russia
(C) Greenwich, England
(D) Paris, France

Geography Answers

1. D   Hawaii consists of a group of islands surrounded by a large body of water, the Pacific Ocean.

2. B   Michigan actually consists of two peninsulas an upper and a lower one. None of the other states listed could be considered a peninsula.

3. D   Tundra is a treeless plain in a very cold climate. Canada contains large amounts of tundra. The other countries listed are in warmer climates.

4. A   Mount McKinley (Denali) is the highest mountain in North America. When answering a question like this, remember to read carefully. Do not pick Mount Everest, which is the tallest mountain in the world.

5. C   The prime meridian passes through Greenwich, England.

Chapter 2: WORLD HISTORY

Prehistory is defined as the time before written records. The dividing line between prehistory and history is conventionally set at about 3000 BC. Humans, in the sense of *Homo sapiens sapiens*, are believed to have first appeared around 100,000 years ago. The immediate ancestors of modern humans were *Homo sapiens neanderthalensis*, *Homo habilis* and *Australopithecus*. The task of gaining knowledge about prehistorical forms of life falls to **archaeology**.

Prehistory is usually divided into periods named for the characteristic material used in making artifacts such as tools and weapons: the Stone Age, the Copper Age, the Bronze Age, the Iron Age, etc. Economically speaking, prehistory is characterized by hunting as the primary means of food acquisition, rather than agriculture. Before the end of the last ice age, hunters from Asia are believed to have crossed over a land bridge, now the Bering Strait (between present-day Russia and Alaska), into North America. This would have occurred about 30,000 BC. The receding of the ice after 10,000 BC is one of the key events of prehistory: the receding of the ice sheets caused rising sea levels and allowed more opportunities for agriculture.

History, in the sense of the history of civilization, begins in Mesopotamia around 3000 BC with the invention of the wheel and the use of writing. The type of writing used by the ancient Mesopotamians is called **cuneiform**, which uses wedges impressed into clay tablets. Around this time, the Egyptians began to use **papyrus** as writing surfaces. Much of early writing was used for commercial record keeping.

Some of the known civilizations of this time in the Middle East were Assyrians, Babylonians, Sumerians, Hittites, Chaldeans, and Hebrews. The Hebrews traced their history back to the patriarch Abraham, who lived sometime around 1500 BC. The covenant of the Hebrews with God is set forth in the **Old Testament**, the first five books of which are known collectively as the **Pentateuch** (Genesis, Exodus, Leviticus, Numbers and Deuteronomy). The remainder of the Old Testament contains the historical books (Chronicles, Kings), books of poetry (Psalms), of wisdom (Job, Ecclesiastes), and the books of the prophets (Isaiah, Ezekiel, Daniel). The Greek translation of the Old Testament is called the **Septuagint**.

The civilizations of Greece and Rome have left an enormous cultural legacy. From Greece came philosophy, mathematics, and the beginnings of science, while Rome has given us ideas on law, government, and engineering. The important political events in Greco-Roman history are the Peloponnesian War, the conquests of Alexander the Great, the Punic Wars between Rome and Carthage, the Roman Civil War which resulted in the murder of Caesar and led to the establishment of an Imperial type of government under Augustus in place of the Roman Republic, the division of the Roman Empire into western and eastern parts in about 300 AD and the collapse Rome in 476 after repeated invasions by Germanic tribes.

Figure 1 The Romans' greatest contribution to architechure was the development of the arch

By the time of its collapse, the Roman Empire had become Christianized. This was mainly because of the emperor **Constantine the Great** who in 313 legalized Christianity through the Edict of Milan. The **New Testament** is the record of God's new covenant through Jesus Christ, who came as the fulfillment of the Law of Moses. The main divisions of the New Testament are the Four Gospels, the Acts of the Apostles, the Epistles, and Revelations.

1. **The populations of the cradles of civilization were primarily:**

    (A) merchants
    (B) hunters
    (C) food gatherers
    (D) farmers

2. **The process by which one civilization shares knowledge and ideas with another civilization is called:**

   (A) cultural assimilation
   (B) cultural diffusion
   (C) imperialism
   (D) manorialism

3. **Ancient Greece was primarily a:**

   (A) great empire ruled by a monarch
   (B) great nation ruled by a democratic system
   (C) number of independent city-states
   (D) primitive civilization

4. **Socrates, Plato, and Aristotle are noted primarily for their contribution in the field of:**

   (A) science
   (B) political science
   (C) literature
   (D) philosophy

5. **The most important contribution made by the Romans to Western civilization was:**

   (A) their art, architecture, and literature
   (B) the cities and roads they built
   (C) their economic system
   (D) their political system, with its influence on law and politics

6. **Christianity might have remained a local, short-lived cult if it had not been for:**

   (A) the emperors who made it the state religion of the Roman Empire
   (B) the Germanic tribes who spread Christianity to Western Europe
   (C) the persistence of the early Christians
   (D) the rejection of Christianity by the Greeks

7. **Constantinople became the center of:**

   (A) the Greco-Roman civilization
   (B) the western region of the Roman Empire
   (C) the Byzantine culture
   (D) the Catholic Church

1. (D)   The word "cradles" indicates beginnings, and therefore farmers, not merchants allowed for great numbers of people to settle in one place. The hunting and gathering periods were before the dawn of civilizations.

2. (B)   Since the word "diffusion" means "to spread," this is the best answer. "Assimilation" means "to absorb," not "to share." Imperialism would be more concerned with conquering another culture.

3. (C)   Greece was never a nation in the modern sense, but rather a series of city-states such as Sparta and Athens. This rules out choices A and B. D can be ruled out because much of our political system, and philosophical roots can be traced back to Greece.

4. (D)   While they may have made contributions in other areas, they were primarily philosophers.

5. (D)   This question asks for the longest-lasting effect of the Romans on Western civilization. This type of question asks for the BEST answer, not just a correct one. For this reason, even though the Romans affected Western culture in all four areas, the fact that many of our laws are still based on the Roman justice system would lead you to the correct answer.

6. (A)   This type of "what if" question requires that you make an evaluation and draw a conclusion. The fact that the emperors adopted Christianity allowed it to spread throughout the empire. Chrisitianity had already been spread before Rome was conquered by the Germans or the Byzantine empire split off.

7. (C)   Rome was the center for the other answers. Remember the Byzantine empire was formed when the Roman empire was split in two. It was initially responsible for the eastern section of the Roman empire.

In western Europe, the period immediately following the collapse of the Western Roman Empire is known as the **Dark Ages**: urban life deteriorated, trade shrank and learning all but disappeared. The beginnings of the rise of Western Europe could be dated from Christmas Day in the year 800, when the Frankish king **Charlemagne** was crowned Holy Roman Emperor by the Pope. (The Holy Roman Empire in later years occupied about the same territory as modern day Germany).

Figure 2 The most impressive architectural structures during the Middle Ages was the Gothic Cathedral which represented the power and influence of the church

The Middle Ages were characterized by a form of social organization generally called **feudalism**. There were actually two distinct forms. Feudalism refers to political and military relations where a noble would receive land and privileges in return for military service. **Manorialism** (sometimes called **seignorialism**) refers to the economic relations between a lord and the serfs that worked his land. Lords had their own courts and eventually their justice would come into conflict with the king's justice. In 1215, King John of England signed the **Magna Carta**, thereby promising to respect the rights of his subjects and to follow the customary law. It is thought that the bubonic plague, usually referred to as the Black Death (about 1350), helped to weaken manorialism by creating a huge shortage of labor and thereby giving serfs more leverage in bargaining with lords.

8. **The deurbanization which took place during the decline of the Roman Empire resulted in:**

    (A) cities becoming the centers of government
    (B) industrial expansion of the empire
    (C) an agrarian society during the Middle Ages
    (D) the end of Western civilization

9. **The Middle Ages date from:**

    (A) the rise of Greece until the fall of Rome
    (B) the fall of Rome until the European discovery of America
    (C) the fall of Rome until the Crusades
    (D) the beginnings of Christianity until the Dark Ages

10. **Throughout the Middle Ages the populations of Europe tended to be fragmented and provincial mainly because:**

    (A) the lack of a common language hindered communication
    (B) transportation was primitive, therefore trade routes were not explored
    (C) the feudal system tended to isolate the people, as each estate was self-sufficient
    (D) the lack of a unifying factor, such as religion

11. **Which of the following statements best summarizes the role of the church during the Middle Ages?**

    (A) The church was the leading cause of feudalism.
    (B) The church remained the most important cultural and social influence throughout the Middle Ages.
    (C) After a long period of corruption, the church divided and its influence became fragmented.
    (D) The church was concerned only with spiritual matters, not political or economic ones.

12. **Which of the following is a contribution made by the Byzantine Empire?**

    (A) preserving the law, culture, and philosophy of the Greco-Roman civilization
    (B) development of a unique artistic style, using mosaics, gold and marble
    (C) preventing the Moslems from entering Europe from the east
    (D) All of the above were contributions of the Byzantine civilization.

ANSWERS:

8. (C) This deurbanization led to the feudal system in the Middle Ages. People moved away from the larger cities to the countryside where they became farmers

9. (B) The exact dates usually given for the Middle Ages are 476 AD to 1492 AD. With this type of question, if you know one-half of the answer, you can usually determine the correct choice. Before the fall of Rome are considered the ancient empires. The crusades are considered part of the middle ages.

10. (C) There was little need for trade or commerce under the feudal system. While it is true that there were language and transportation barriers, this was not the reason Europe was fragmented. Each lord was able to do just about whatever he wanted on his estate. There was little movement of trade between the different estates and consequently very little diffusion of ideas.

11. (B) The influence of the church overshadowed every aspect of medieval life. Not only were they one of the largest land owners during the Middle Ages, but they were often challenging the secular governments authority. This rules out choice D as an answer. The churches authority did not wane toward the end of the Middle ages. This eliminates choice C. While the church may have been used to keep the serfs in line, it was not the reason for the overall feudal structure.

12. (D) All of the choices are correct. Be sure to consider all of the answers before you make your choice.

The **Renaissance**, which began in Italy and spread to northern Europe, was a revival of classical learning and a burst of achievement in the arts. The Renaissance also overlaps with the Protestant **Reformation**: the latter begins with Martin Luther nailing his complaints against the Catholic Church on a church door in 1517 (the Ninety-Five Theses). Among Luther's problems was the sale of indulgences (pardons for sin). The response of the Catholic Church to these challenges, such as the founding of the Society of Jesus (the Jesuits), is known as the Counter-Reformation.

The 16th Century saw the beginning of European overseas expansion and colonization. Initially, Spain and Portugal were the dominant powers with Britain, Holland, and France soon following. Some of the more notable explorers were Columbus (1492: the Caribbean), Vasco de Gama (circa 1500: sailed around Cape of Good Hope and reached India), Amerigo Vespucci (circa 1500: Brazil), Balboa (1513: Pacific Ocean), Magellan (1522: first circumnavigation of the globe) and de Soto (1541: Mississippi River).

The **Enlightenment** refers to European thought and culture in the 18th century. The characteristic attitude was one of confidence that human reason could improve life on earth through science and political reform. There was a general optimism about the improvability, if not the perfectibility, of human beings and about historical progress. Religious superstitions and institutions were often criticized. Some of the key figures of this period were Voltaire, Diderot, Hume, and Kant.

Since the Reformation the most important long-term processes have been the growth of scientific thought, the evolution of nation-states and democratic institutions, and the economic and technological change known as the Industrial Revolution. The key concepts of modern science are covered in the science section of the book. Nation-states have been carved out of large multi-national empires. The two great democratic revolutions were the American Revolution (1776) and the French Revolution (1789). The Industrial Revolution saw large-scale urbanization and greater division of labor.

In terms of international relations, the early 19th century was dominated by the wars against Napoleon (1800–1815). Italy and Germany became unified states in 1860 and 1870, respectively. The twentieth century has been dominated by two world wars. The First World War (1914-18) was fought between the Central Powers (Germany, Austria-Hungary, Turkey and Bulgaria) and the Allied Powers (Britain, France, Russia, United States and Italy). The Second World War (1939-45) was fought between the Axis Powers (Hitler's Germany, Mussolini's Italy and Tojo's Japan) and the Allied Powers (Britain, Stalin's Soviet Union and the United States). The war ended with the dropping of two atomic bombs on Japan (at Hiroshima and Nagasaki) by the U.S.

From 1945-90, international relations were dominated by conflict between two "superpowers", the U.S. and the Soviet Union. This conflict is usually referred to as the **Cold War** because the two superpowers never actually fought a war directly with each other. Instead of direct war, there was war by proxy (as in Korea and Vietnam), espionage, and an arms race. The Cold War ended in 1990 with the collapse of communism in Eastern Europe and the disintegration of the Soviet Union.

17. **The philosophical movement which emphasized the human condition, rather than religious matters, and led to both the Renaissance and the Reformation, is known as:**

   (A)   enlightenment
   (B)   the Age of Reason
   (C)   humanism
   (D)   Counter Reformation

18. **The 17th and 18th centuries, because of the philosophical and intellectual movement, which stressed the importance of nationalism, individualism, and human reason, became know as:**

   (A)   the Renaissance
   (B)   the Age of Reason
   (C)   the Napoleonic Age
   (D)   Edwardism Age

19. **The most significant end-result of the English Civil War was:**

   (A)   the restoration of the monarchy
   (B)   a written constitution
   (C)   affirmation of the primacy of parliament
   (D)   election of Cromwell and the Puritans

20. The Central Powers in World War I were:

(A) Great Britain, Germany, Turkey
(B) Turkey, Russia, Germany
(C) Germany, Austria-Hungary, Turkey
(D) Germany, Great Britain, France

21. Which of the following was the most significant result of World War II?

(A) Russia was seized by the communists.
(B) The United Nations was created.
(C) Isolationism gained wide support in the United States.
(D) World leadership shifted from Europe to the United States.

22. Which of the following statements is the most accurate regarding the postwar years?

(A) For the most part, the nations of the world have become peaceful and interrelated.
(B) Western civilization has gradually declined in influence.
(C) Europe is no longer the dominant political force in the world.
(D) The third world has rejected the influences of Western civilization.

ANSWERS:

17. (C) Any word which has the suffix "ism" means belief in whatever the first part of the word is. In this case, the word "human" is used in the question, therefore "humanism" is the logical choice. Enlightenment is another term for the Age of Reason, which came after the Renaissance and the Reformation. The Counter Reformation was the Roman Catholic Church's response to the Reformation.

18. (B) Once again, a clue to the correct answer, the word "reason" is used in the question.

19. (C) The question asks for the most significant result, not the only one.

20. (C) The key to answering this question correctly is knowing whom Germany was fighting against, then eliminating the incorrect combinations. The Allies were France, Great Britain, Russia.

21. (D) Answers (A) and (C) happened after World War I. While it is correct that the United Nations was created after World War II, the question asks for the MOST significant result of the war.

22. (C) This question calls for your evaluation of trends and events during the time period in question. (A) is not the correct choice, because there have been many wars and revolutions, in addition to economic tensions. (B) is too general an answer—it may have lost in some areas (politics), but gained in others (technology). (D) is also incorrect—they may have rejected some ideas, but they may have adopted others. Therefore, (C) is the best choice.

Chapter 3: UNITED STATES HISTORY

The first successful English colonial settlements in North America were at Jamestown, Virginia, in 1607 and at Plymouth, Massachusetts, in 1620. The Spanish were dominant in the southwest while the French established colonies in Quebec Canada and Louisiana, thanks to the explorations of Champlain and LaSalle. Conflict between Britain and France came to a head in the **French and Indian War**, which ended in 1763. As a result of that conflict, Britain came to control all of the present day United States east of the Mississippi River.

Conflict between the colonists and Britain began soon after the ending of French hostilities with the Sugar Act of 1764, the Stamp Act of 1765, the Townshend Acts of 1767, and the Tea Act of 1773. The colonists' main objection to these statutes was that they imposed taxes even though the colonists had no representation in the British Parliament. ("No taxation without representation."). As punishment for the Boston Tea Party, the Intolerable Acts of 1774 closed the port of Boston and revoked the colonial charter of Massachusetts. Actual fighting broke out in 1775 at Lexington while the official break with England came on July 4, 1776 with the Declaration of Independence issued by the Second Continental Congress.

Figure 3 The second Continental Congress signing the Declaration of Independence

Penned by Thomas Jefferson, the **Declaration of Independence** spells out some principles of good and just government such as how the aim of government is to secure the natural rights of people to life, liberty, and the pursuit of happiness, and that government authority rests upon the consent of the governed. Jefferson also specifies all of the abuses and injuries of the English crown that led to the decision to revolt.

After the end of the war in 1781, the new American government was established under *Articles of the Confederation*. However, the arrangement gave little power to the federal government and inefficiency resulted. A new form of government was drawn up in Philadelphia in 1789 and the result was the **Constitution**. The Constitution gave more power to the federal government than had the Articles but because of concern over possible federal tyranny, the first ten amendments to the Constitution (the **Bill of Rights**) specifies certain limits on federal power. (These will be mentioned in the Political Science chapter).

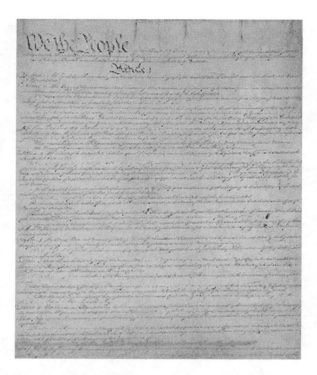

Figure 4 The United States Constitution

Among those who pushed for ratification of the Constitution with a stronger federal government were Alexander Hamilton, James Madison, and John Jay, who published a series of articles urging their views that are now referred to as the **Federalist Papers**. Those who wanted a much weaker federal government were known as Antifederalists.

The first five presidents were Washington, John Adams, Jefferson, Madison, and Monroe (this stretch of time is referred to as the "Virginia Dynasty"). In 1803, the decision in the case of *Marbury v. Madison* established the doctrine of judicial review whereby the Supreme Court would review the actions of the other two branches of the federal government to decide whether those actions were consistent with the Constitution. 1803 also saw the purchase of the Louisiana Territory from France by Jefferson. The War of 1812 with Britain ended in 1815 and, although not a clear victory for America, led to a short period of national unity and patriotism dubbed the "era of good feelings". Monroe (1817-1825) issued his famous warning (the **Monroe Doctrine**) to European powers to stay out of the Western Hemisphere, which he considered America's "sphere of influence". In the *Missouri Compromise* of 1820, Maine was admitted as a free state and Missouri was admitted as a slave state.

Andrew Jackson (president, 1829-1837) vetoed the Second Bank of the United States and became involved in the *Nullification Crisis*. The latter resulted from South Carolina's repeal of a federal tariff: did an individual state have the right to nullify a federal law in such a manner? Jackson took the view that it did not. A deal was made whereby the tariff was scaled back and South Carolina withdrew its nullification. The key political figures at this time were Henry Clay of Kentucky, Daniel Webster of Massachusetts, and John Calhoun of South Carolina.

The 1840s were dominated by the **Mexican War** whereby the U.S. gained California and New Mexico. The war ended in 1848 by the Treaty of Guadalupe-Hidalgo. The problem of whether these new areas would be slave territories or free territories was dealt with by the Compromise of 1850: California was admitted as a free state but there were no restrictions on slavery in New Mexico. In 1854, the Kansas-Nebraska Act allowed residents of those territories to decide whether to have slavery or not. In the *Dred Scott v. Sanford* decision (1857), the Supreme Court ruled that Congress did not have the authority to prohibit slavery in federal territories and that the ownership of a slave was a property right and had constitutional protection.

The U.S. in 1783

TERRITORIAL GROWTH OF THE UNITED STATES 1783-1853

The **Civil War** began in 1861 after eleven southern states seceded from the Union. The Emancipation Proclamation, freeing slaves only in rebel territories, was issued during the war in 1863. In 1865, the 13th Amendment to the Constitution officially abolished slavery in the United States. The 14th Amendment (1868) granted citizenship to former slaves and guaranteed them the equal protection of the law. The 15th Amendment (1870) protected the of former slaves' right to vote. **Reconstruction** of the South went on for about ten years from 1867-77. The government agency entrusted with helping the transition from slave to citizen was the **Freedmen's Bureau**. The Northerners who traveled south to administer and profit from reconstruction were called

carpetbaggers, while the southern whites cooperating with reconstruction were called **scalawags**.

Figure 5 Abraham Lincoln was President during the Civil War

The late 19th century was a period of industrialization for America; there was popular concern about the growth of possibly monopolistic business organizations. Congress began to regulate the railroads with the Interstate Commerce Act in 1887, and in 1890, the Sherman Antitrust Act gave government the power to take action against "trusts" that might hinder fair trade and commerce. The Sherman Act eventually was replaced by the Clayton Antitrust Act (1914), which outlawed price-fixing. Despite the concern over monopolies, the Supreme Court was very much in favor of economic rights. In its 1905 decision *Lochner v. New York*, the Court barred that state from setting a maximum-hours law in the baking industry because it interfered with free contract.

Figure 6 Children often worked long hours before laws were passed to prevent child labor abuse

With the victory in the **Spanish-American War** in 1898, America acquired interests in Cuba, Puerto Rico, Guam, and the Philippines. Theodore Roosevelt (president, 1901-09) was in favor of a greater world role for America. His foreign policy philosophy was to "speak softly and carry a big stick". At this time, America pushed for greater trade access to China (the Open Door policy), acquired the right to build a canal in Panama, and sent troops to the Dominican Republic.

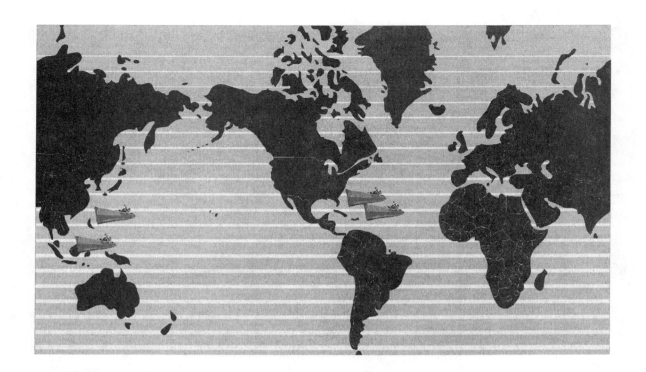

TERRITORY ACQUIRED IN THE SPANISH-AMERICAN WAR

Figure 7

The first twenty years of the 20th century is known as the **Progressive Era** (at least in domestic policy) and was characterized by demands for political reform and social action. The problems caused by industrialization were compounded by a huge wave of immigration from southern and eastern Europe. Journalists exposed horrible conditions in cities and criticized the bosses of big-city political machines, such as **Tammany Hall** in New York. These journalists were dubbed "muckrakers".

The first year of the administration of Woodrow Wilson (president, 1913-1921) was an eventful year for American government: the Federal Reserve System (a central bank) was created and two constitutional amendments were ratified. The 16th Amendment gave Congress the power to levy an income tax, while the 17th Amendment provided for the direct popular election of Senators (whereas before they were chosen by state legislatures). Wilson was president during the First World War, but his plans for a **League of Nations** (a prototype United Nations), which would have American leadership, were rejected by the Senate. The League was formed but the U.S. never joined it.

118

In response to the economic crisis of the early 1930s, referred to as the Great Depression (seriously falling output and prices, extremely high unemployment, bank failures), the administration of Franklin Roosevelt (president, 1933-1945) undertook a series of measures now commonly referred to as the **New Deal**. The "First New Deal" lasted from 1933 to 1935: the key legislation, passed within the first 100 days of the new administration, dealt with banking regulation (Glass-Steagall Act), trying to raise agricultural prices (Agricultural Adjustment Administration), and industrial recovery (National Industrial Recovery Act). The "Second New Deal" went from 1935-1938 after the Court had declared key pieces of legislation unconstitutional. The key areas were a social security system (Social Security Act) and labor relations (Wagner Act).

Figure 8 The New Deal included many large projects to put people back to work

The first important pieces of post-World War II legislation were the Employment Act (1946) and the Taft-Hartley Act (1947). The former stated that full employment would be promoted while the latter outlawed "closed shops" that would require union membership as a condition of employment. The **GI Bill** provided returning soldiers with a college education. Truman's domestic policy is called the Fair Deal. In foreign policy, Truman confronted the Soviet Union in Greece, gave massive aid to war-torn Europe (the Marshall Plan) and became enmeshed in the **Korean War** (1950-1953).

The 1950s were presided over by Dwight Eisenhower (president, 1953-1961). The economy grew, suburbs grew, the interstate highway system began, and there was peace. On the civil rights front, Eisenhower sent federal troops to Little Rock, Arkansas, to ensure compliance with desegregation of public schools. The Supreme Court's decision in *Brown v. Board of Education* (1954) declared that separate schools for blacks and whites were unconstitutional and overturned the 1896 decision of *Plessy v. Ferguson* that had enunciated the "separate but equal" doctrine. Congress further strengthened civil rights for blacks in the mid-1960s: The Civil Rights Act (1964) and the Voting Rights Act (1965) outlawed racial discrimination in employment, public accommodations, and voting.

Figure 9 There were many protests to eliminate poll taxes and literacy tests both of which kept people from voting

In foreign policy, the Cuban missile crisis (1962) resulted from a confrontation between the Kennedy Administration and the Soviet Union (under Nikita Khrushchev) over the presence of Soviet missiles in Cuba. The U.S. blockaded Cuba but a war was averted after the U.S. promised not to invade Cuba. The Kennedy years also saw the signing of a ban on above ground nuclear testing (1963).

American involvement in Vietnam began in the 1950s and gradually increased throughout the 1960s from advisors under Eisenhower, to troops under Kennedy (president 1961-63), to bombing under Lyndon Johnson (president 1963-1969). Under Nixon (president 1969-1974) bombing was expanded to the neighboring country of Cambodia. There was never a formal declaration of war. Finally, American troops pulled out in 1975.

Nixon's foreign policy was highlighted by **détente** (lessening of tension) with the Soviet Union and better relations with China. The first Strategic Arms Limitation Treaty (SALT I) was signed in 1971 by the U.S. and the Soviet Union and limited the deployment of Intercontinental Ballistic Missiles. Nixon's domestic policy was characterized by the **New Federalism**, which was a system of revenue sharing with state and local governments. Nixon resigned the presidency in August 1974 after having been impeached by the U.S. House of Representatives for obstruction of justice (but before a trial in the Senate could commence).

The 1970s was not economically a good time and was characterized by **stagflation** (an unexpected combination of high unemployment *and* high inflation). Part of the reason for this was government budget deficits to pay for the Vietnam War and the effects of oil shocks. The Organization of Petroleum Exporting Countries (OPEC) decided to cut the amount of oil that its member countries would supply on world markets, thereby forcing oil prices way up. This meant significant cost increases for industry and the laying-off of workers. By the end of the decade, both the rate of inflation and interest rates were in the double digits.

The economy did not strengthen again until after 1982. Under Reagan (president 1981-89) marginal tax rates were cut while government spending increased, especially military expenditures. An important piece of budgetary legislation passed during these years was the Gramm-Rudman Act, which set caps on government spending. Reagan's successor George H.W. Bush (president, 1989-93) put together a broad coalition of countries to oppose the invasion of Kuwait by Iraq. As a result of the Gulf War (early 1991), Iraq was expelled from Kuwait and the United Nations began to monitor Iraq's weapons facilities. Some of the notable legislation during the Clinton Administration (president, 1993-2001) included NAFTA (North American Free Trade Agreement) and welfare reform.

US History Questions

1. **Which of the following documents would have been sent to the King of England?**

   (A)   The US Constitution
   (B)   The Declaration of Independence
   (C)   The Federalist Papers
   (D)   The Bill of Rights

2. **Where was the first permanent English settlement in North America?**

    (A) Boston, Massachusetts
    (B) Plymouth, Massachusetts
    (C) Philadelphia, Pennsylvania
    (D) Jamestown, Virginia

3. **Which document was the framework for how the United States would be governed at the end of the Revolutionary War?**

    (A) The Articles of Confederation
    (B) The Declaration of Independence
    (C) The US Constitution
    (D) The Federalist Papers

4. **Which of the following wars was really an offshoot of a war between France and England.**

    (A) The War of 1812
    (B) The French and Indian War
    (C) The Revolutionary War
    (D) The American Civil War

5. **Who wrote the Declaration of Independence"**

    (A) George Washington
    (B) John Jay
    (C) John Adams
    (D) Thomas Jefferson

6. **Which of the following people did not support a strong federal government?**

    (A) James Madison
    (B) John Jay
    (C) Alexander Hamilton
    (D) Thomas Jefferson

7. **The Monroe Doctrine was concerned with what?**

    (A) ending slavery
    (B) currency exchange
    (C) health care in the united states
    (D) European colonization in the Western Hemisphere

8. **Which of the following freed all the slaves in Maryland?**

    (A) The Emancipation Proclamation
    (B) The Civil Rights Act
    (C) The 13th amendment
    (D) The Gettysburg Address

9. **What was the purpose of the Sherman Antitrust Act?**

   (A) to renew the faith in the federal government
   (B) to break up monopolies and encourage fair trade
   (C) to allow businesses to do anything they wanted
   (D) to make the North pay for the destruction done by Sherman during the Civil War

10. **Who was President when the 16th Amendment (giving congress the right to levy an income tax)?**

    (A) Franklin Roosevelt
    (B) Theodore Roosevelt
    (C) Woodrow Wilson
    (D) George Washington

11. **Which of the following was one of the major points of President Wilson's peace plan at the end of World War I?**

    (A) The United Nations
    (B) The League of Nations
    (C) Dividing Germany between France, England, Russia and the U.S.A
    (D) Outlawing submarines

12. **What major problem did Franklin Roosevelt face when he first took office?**

    (A) the outbreak of WWI
    (B) the outbreak of WWII
    (C) the great depression
    (D) the stock market crash

13. **What was President Truman's plan for rebuilding Europe?**

    (A) The Marshall Plan
    (B) The Truman Plan
    (C) The European Plan
    (D) The Cold War

14. **In which city was President Kennedy assassinated?**

    (A) New York City, NY
    (B) Washington, DC
    (C) Chicago, IL
    (D) Dallas, TX

15. **What does OPEC stand for?**

    (A) Other People's Economic Committee
    (B) Organizational Problems Enhancement Committee
    (C) Organization of Petroleum Exporting Countries
    (D) Open Package Examining Committee

US History Answers

1. B   The Declaration of Independence would have been sent to the King of England to let him know that the colonies no longer acknowledged him as their ruler. Choices A, C, and E are concerned with the governance of the United States.

2. D   Jamestown, Virginia, was the first permanent English settlement in North America. Plymouth, Massachusetts was the site of the second settlement. Boston was the site of one of the first major cities. Philadelphia was part of the Pennsylvania colony, which was started by William Penn. The Pennsylvania colony was initially settled by Quakers.

3. A   The Articles of Confederation was the initial governing document for the United States. It had many weaknesses so a new constitution was written in 1787. The new constitution had provisions for a stronger federal government.

4. B   The French and Indian War was the conflict between England and France that took place in North America. At the end of the war, in 1763, England controlled all the land east of the Mississippi except for Florida.

5. D   Thomas Jefferson wrote the Declaration of Independence.

6. D   Thomas Jefferson was a proponent of State's rights. The other three wrote the federalist papers, which supported the passage of the Constitution and a stronger federal government.

7. D   The Monroe Doctrine stated that the Western Hemisphere was closed to European colonization.

8. C   The Emancipation Proclamation only freed slaves in the rebelling territories. It wasn't until the passage of the 13th amendment that slavery was abolished throughout the country.

9. B   The Sherman Antitrust act was designed to breakup monopolies. It was used to break up large companies like standard oil.

10. C   Woodrow Wilson was President when the 16th amendment was passed.

11. B   Woodrow Wilson pushed for the formation of the League of Nations. He felt that if countries were able to get together and talk things over wars would be averted. His idea was never enacted. The United Nations was formed after World War II.

12. C   The United States was in the midst of the Great Depression when Franklin Roosevelt took office. The US did not enter WWII until his 3rd term.

13. A   President Truman's plan for rebuilding Europe after WWII was the Marshall Plan.

14. D   President Kennedy was assassinated in Dallas, TX.

15. C   OPEC stands for Organization of Petroleum Exporting Countries.

Chapter 4: POLITICAL SCIENCE

The Constitution sets up a tripartite structure of government at the federal level. These three parts are usually referred to as the three branches: the legislative branch, the executive branch, and the judicial branch. Their functions are as follows: the legislature makes the law, the executive executes or enforces the law, and the judiciary interprets or determines the meaning of the law. The highest legislative institution is the Congress, the highest executive office is the presidency, and the highest judicial body is the Supreme Court.

To prevent one branch from exceeding its authority, a system of checks and balances was worked into the relations between the three branches. For instance, the president may veto a bill passed by Congress, while this veto may be over-ridden by a two-thirds vote of members of Congress. The Supreme Court can invalidate laws passed by Congress or actions of the executive as being inconsistent with the Constitution (a process known as judicial review).

Article I of the Constitution vests legislative power in the Congress. The Congress is divided into an upper house and a lower house, resulting in what is called a bicameral legislature. The Senate is the upper house with 100 members (two from each state) whose terms last for six years. The Constitution originally stipulated that senators be chosen by state legislatures; they are now directly elected by the people as a result of the 17th Amendment, passed in 1913. The House of Representatives is the lower chamber and currently has 435 members who serve two-year terms. The number of representatives depends on population. The process of changing the number of representatives because of changes in population is called reapportionment.

Article II vests executive authority in the Presidency and specifies that the president be elected for a four-year term by the Electoral College. Each state has the same number of electors in the College as it has representatives in Congress. On Election Day, the people vote for a slate of electors to represent their state in the College and then the electors get together a few weeks later to choose a president. In practice, all of the electors from a state will cast their votes for the candidate who gets a plurality of the popular vote in their state. The number of terms that a President can serve was limited to two by the passage of the 22nd Amendment in 1951.

Article III vests judicial power in the Supreme Court. There are currently nine members but that number can be changed by Congress. Justices of the Supreme Court are appointed by the president, confirmed by the Senate, and have their positions for life. This article also gives Congress the power to establish lower courts.

The powers of the three branches are either specifically enumerated or implied: for instance, the Congress is explicitly given the power to levy taxes, declare war, coin money, borrow money, and regulate commerce. The implied powers of Congress reside in the power to make all laws "necessary and proper" to execute its enumerated powers. The president is explicitly made Commander-in-Chief by the text of the Constitution and this has been taken to imply the power to commit troops during times of military emergency, despite the fact that only Congress has the power to declare war. American troops fought in Korea and Vietnam without a formal declaration of war by Congress.

Procedures for amending the Constitution are spelled out in Article V: the usual procedure requires two-thirds of both houses of Congress and three-fourths of the state legislatures. There have been a total of twenty-six amendments, and the first ten are referred to as the Bill of Rights. Here are the more important ones, besides those already mentioned:

1st: forbids Congress from making laws that would abridge free speech or assembly or the free exercise of religion, or that would establish an official religion.

2nd: right to keep and bear arms.

4th: prevents unreasonable searches and seizures and requires probable cause for the issue of a search warrant.

5th: requires Grand Jury presentment and indictment in capital cases; cannot be tried twice for the same crime (no "double jeopardy"); protection against self-incrimination; no deprivation of life, liberty, or property without due process of law.

6th: right to a speedy and public trial by an impartial jury.

8th: prohibits excessive bail, excessive fines and cruel and unusual punishment.

10th: powers not delegated to federal government nor prohibited to the states, are reserved to the states or to the people.

12th:(1804): procedures for the electoral college.

18th:(1919): prohibition of manufacture, sale, or transport of liquor.

19th:(1920): right to vote for women.

21st:(1933): repeal of the 18th amendment.

24th:(1964): abolition of poll tax.

26th:(1971): right to vote for eighteen-year-olds.

How the words of the Constitution are to be interpreted is the job of the Supreme Court. A case gets to the Court mainly through appeals from lower courts, although the Court theoretically has original jurisdiction over such matters as disputes between states. In making decisions, the Court relies on the text of the Constitution and on previous court decisions. This respect for precedent is known as *stare decisis* (Latin for "to stay with what has been decided").

The Constitution also created a federal system. Federalism refers to the idea of balancing a strong national government with strong state governments. The fifty individual states are not mere administrative units of one national government, they are fifty separate governments with constitutions. Article I of the Constitution explicitly forbids the state governments from issuing money or entering into foreign treaties. Article VI, usually referred to as the supremacy clause, says that the Constitution along with all laws and treaties made under its authority shall be the "supreme law of the land" and that judges in every state would be bound thereby.

During the 19th century, the federal government assumed much less responsibility for the welfare of American citizens than it does today. The states make their own laws and set their own agendas but the federal government does try to nudge them in certain directions through the use of grants-in-aid, which are given to assist states with public projects (such as highways and mass transit). The federal government has threatened to hold back such money in its desire to have a uniform drinking age of twenty-one and a uniform speed limit of fifty-five. The two main types of grants-in-aid are categorical grants, which go to specifically defined areas such as highways, and block grants, which are more generally defined in order to give the state much more discretion in how the money is spent.

The federal bureaucracy is often considered the real nucleus of the national government because most civil servants retain their positions even after a change of president and cabinet. The bureaucracy is comprised of the people who actually execute and enforce the laws passed by Congress. Most civil service jobs are based on the merit system. A merit civil service was mandated by the Pendleton Act of 1883. It is divided into several functional areas, the most well known being the departments of State, Treasury, Defense, and Justice. The remaining departments are Energy, Education, Transportation, Labor, Health and Human Services, Housing and Urban Development, Agriculture, Interior, and Commerce. The most well known individual agencies are within the Justice Department: Federal Bureau of Investigation (FBI), Immigration and Naturalization Service (INS), and Drug Enforcement Administration (DEA). Independent regulatory agencies include the Federal Communications Commission (FCC), Interstate Commerce Commission (ICC) and Federal Trade Commission (FTC). There is also a mini-bureaucracy within the White House itself called the Executive Office of the President, which helps the president manage specific policy areas. The most important specific policy areas are the Office of Management and Budget (OMB), the National Security Council (NSC) and the Council of Economic Advisors (CEA).

The American system of government is often described as a form of representative democracy because the people do not directly make governmental decisions. Rather, they elect representatives to make those decisions. Voting is one way for citizens to have input in the political process. Elections in America are winner-take-all contests: if we are talking about a congressional election, the winner gets the seat and the loser gets nothing. There is no proportional representation system where a party would get a percent of the seats based on getting a percent of the votes. Also, election winners are determined by who gets a plurality of the votes without necessarily getting a majority. If the breakdown of results were Candidate X got 40%, Y got 35% and Z got 25% of the total vote, Candidate X would win, despite not getting over 50% of the votes cast.

There are other types of democracy besides the American kind, such as the types of parliamentary democracy practiced in many European countries. In Britain, the cabinet (headed by the Prime Minister) is the real organ of the executive. In contrast to our federal system, where there are strong states, France has what is called a unitary system in which there are no separate state governments but rather administrative units called departments.

Governments can be classified by different criteria: whether or not there is a constitution, for example. Some common categories include monarchy (rule by one), oligarchy (rule by the few) and polyarchy (rule by the many). Related to these are autocracy (self-rule), aristocracy (rule by the best) and democracy (rule by the people). These last three indicate not only who is ruling but also *to whose benefit* they are ruling. An aristocracy is rule by a small elite but in the interest of the whole public, whereas an oligarchy would benefit only the oligarchs. An autocrat rules for his own personal gain, while a monarch may rule in the interests of the whole nation.

What is the purpose of government? This is partly a philosophical question and different answers have been given throughout history. The American idea, based in part on the writings of English philosopher John Locke (late 17th century) and expressed by Jefferson in the Declaration of Independence, is that government exists by consent of the governed in order to protect natural rights such as life, liberty, and property. In other words, government should create the conditions under which people could pursue their ideas of happiness. People in a theoretical state of nature get together and contract to give up some liberty to a government in order to maximize their happiness. Other thinkers, such as the English philosopher Thomas Hobbes (mid 17th century), have expressed slightly dimmer views. For Hobbes, life in a state of nature without a government would be "solitary, poor, nasty, brutish, and short". Government power is a necessary evil that prevents anarchy by forcing naturally aggressive humans to obey laws. Hegel (early 19th century) thought that government was an embodiment of the increasing rationalization and liberation of the human mind. Karl Marx (mid 19th century) felt that the function of government resulted from who controlled the means of economic production.

Political Science Questions

1. **Which of the following is a check that the President has on Congress?**

   (A) Impeachment
   (B) Veto
   (C) Appropriation of funds
   (D) Declare laws unconstitutional

2. **Which of the following is a check that Congress has on the President?**

   (A) Veto
   (B) Declare laws unconstitutional
   (C) Filibustering
   (D) Overriding a veto

3. **Article one of the Constitution lists the powers of which branch of the government?**

   (A) Congress
   (B) Executive
   (C) Judicial
   (D) State

4. **Article three of the Constitution list the powers of which branch of the government?**

   (A) Congress
   (B) Executive
   (C) Judicial
   (D) State

5. **What does the first amendment protect?**

   (A) The right to bear arms
   (B) The right of free speech
   (C) The right on not needing to self-incrimination
   (D) The woman's right to vote

6. **What does the 18th amendment do?**

   (A) Grants the right to a speedy trial
   (B) Grants women the right to vote
   (C) Prohibits the sale of liquor
   (D) Prevents unreasonable searches

7. Countries ruled by just a few people are:

(A) Oligarchy
(B) Polyarchy
(C) Theocracy
(D) Monarchy

8. Countries rule by just one person are:

(A) Oligarchy
(B) Polyarchy
(C) Theocracy
(D) Monarchy

Political Science Answers

1. B   The President has veto power over all bills passed by congress.

2. D   If a President vetos a bill, Congress is able to override the veto and make the bill a law if 2/3 of the members of both houses vote for it.

3. A   Article one of the constitution lists the powers of congress.

4. C   Article three lists the powers of the judiciary

5. B   The first amendment protects the right of free speech

6. C   The 18th amendment prohibited the manufacture and sale of alcohol. It was later repealed by the 21st amendment.

7. A   Oligarchy is rule by a few.

8. D   Monarchy is rule by one.

Chapter 5: ECONOMICS

There is a distinction between descriptive (or positive) economics and normative economics. Descriptive economics try to describe the workings of an economy as it is without making any value judgements, while normative economics do not refrain from prescribing how an economy should work based on notions of efficiency, goodness, rightness, fairness, or equity. Welfare economics is normative in approach because it goes on the assumption that a desirable economy is one that promotes the welfare of its members.

Another fundamental distinction is between **macroeconomics** and **microeconomics**. Macroeconomics studies the national economy as a whole. Some of the problems that macroeconomics concerns itself with are inflation and unemployment and the desirable level of government involvement in economic matters. Microeconomics, as the term implies, studies the types of decisions made by individual households and business firms, the degrees of competition within industries, and the cost structures of business firms.

The key tools of economic analysis of markets are supply and demand. The combination of supply and demand is what determines the market price. Demand is the quantity of goods that consumers are willing to buy at various hypothetical prices. In general, *all other things being equal*, the quantity demanded will drop as the price increases. Some of the other things that influence demand are consumer income, tastes, and the prices of other substitute goods. Economists, in order to simplify analysis, focus on price as the primary influence on how much demand there will be for a particular good. The negative relation between the price of a good and the demand for it is referred to as the Law of Demand.

Price is also the primary influence on the quantity supplied to a market. However, in the case of supply there is a positive relation with price: the higher the price, the higher the quantity that businesses will be willing to supply. This is called the Law of Supply. Again, there are other factors that influence supply such as the level of technology, but price is treated as primary. So both supply and demand depend on the same variable: price.

If the market price of a good is too high, there will be too little demand. This would create an excess supply. If the seller wants to get those goods sold, the price will have to drop. The opposite situation is excess demand: this is where the price is too low in a situation where there is much more demand than supply. Here the price will rise to adjust to this fact. When, and if, the price is such that there is no excess supply or demand, the price is referred to as the equilibrium price. In other words, the equilibrium price is the price that "clears the market".

Supply and demand analysis is not only applied to markets for goods, it is also used to analyze the market for money and the market for labor. In the money market, the price of money is the interest rate and in the labor market the price of labor is the wage rate. As an example of supply/demand analysis in a labor market, if the price of labor (wage) is too low, there will be relatively few people willing to supply their labor. Then, businesses would either have to pay higher wages or reduce production.

An economic system that relies on markets and the price system as described above is called a market economy. The opposite of a market economy is a command economy, where all decisions about production and distribution are made by a central government authority (sometimes called central planning.) An economy like that of Japan falls somewhere between these two poles: the Japanese government does not own the country's important industries but it has much influence on their decisions.

A mixed economy is one that combines market forces and government regulation. (The United States is considered a mixed economy).

Key Concepts of Macroeconomics

The **gross national product** (**GNP**) is the total dollar value of all goods and services produced in a country in a given year. It is a measure of output and includes such things as cars, shaves at the barber shop, and legal services. To make sure that a rise in GNP didn't simply result from a rise in prices, the GNP number is usually adjusted for a rise in prices. This is called Real GNP. Real GNP is further adjusted for population: Real GNP per capita is real GNP divided by the number of people in the country.

A **recession** is a temporary and natural decline in output; it is officially defined as two consecutive quarters of GNP decline. During a recession workers are laid off and the unemployment rate rises. A **depression** is a sustained period of falling output, falling prices, and very high unemployment (during the Great Depression the unemployment rate reached 25%.) The unemployment rate is the number of people out of work as a percentage of the whole labor force. This would include people who are between jobs. Because there will always be people in such a situation, the lowest unemployment rate thought attainable is 4-6 %. This is referred to as the natural rate of unemployment and such a situation would be called full employment. Stabilization policy refers to government payments such as unemployment insurance that go up during periods of recession.

Inflation is defined as a rise in the general level of prices. Another often used definition is that inflation is "too much money chasing too few goods". If output were to stay the same yet people had more money to spend on this output, one could expect prices to rise (all other possible factors being equal). Because of inflation, a dollar buys less than what it could buy before the price rise. The most widely used measure of inflation is the **Consumer Price Index** (CPI) which tracks the price of a typical basket of goods of a typical household.

Fiscal policy is the taxing and spending policy of the government. When the federal government spends more money than it takes in from taxes, the result is a budget deficit. The government may want to run a deficit in order to stimulate the economy either by cutting taxes or spending more or both. A deficit is usually financed by the issuance of treasury bonds.

The government derives its tax revenue from many different sources: income tax, capital gains tax, estate tax, etc. A tax can be categorized by whether it is progressive or regressive. Under a progressive tax system, the tax paid represents a higher percentage of the person's income (the higher the income, the higher the percentage). The income tax is an example of a progressive tax where income above a certain amount is taxed at a higher marginal rate. A regressive tax is one that falls more heavily on lower incomes. The sales tax is such a tax since lower income people spend a greater percentage of income on life's necessities.

Monetary policy refers to the government's efforts to regulate the money supply. This task is entrusted to the Federal Reserve Bank. The money supply is defined variously but it is essentially the sum total of cash and any instrument that can be easily converted to cash in order to make purchases (such as checking and savings accounts). The Federal Reserve is a bank for banks and it regulates the money supply by making it more or less expensive for member banks to borrow from it.

To give an example: if the Federal Reserve Bank judges that the economy is getting too "hot" and inflation might become a problem, the Federal Reserve Bank may decide to tighten the money supply by raising rates for member banks. The result would be that, because of the new higher cost of borrowing, member banks would borrow less from the Federal Reserve Bank, and in turn would raise rates on their business customers. Businesses would borrow less for investment and may lay off workers.

Money is defined by economists as having three main functions. It is a store of value, it is a medium of exchange, and it is a unit of account. In the past, money was made of something that had intrinsic value like gold or silver. The paper money of today is a type known as fiat money, which has value because the government has decreed it legal tender.

Key Microeconomics Concepts

Microeconomists study how markets work in various types of industries. A perfectly competitive market would be one in which there are many firms supplying essentially the same product. The firms take the market price as a given over which they have no control. The opposite of a perfectly competitive market is a monopolistic one. In this situation, there is only one supplier of the product and there are no close substitutes. There is a downside though: since the monopolistic firm is the sole supplier there are no other firms to bear the pain of any drop in demand. If the monopoly tries to raise its price, demand will fall and so will revenues. In practice, firms are neither extreme: **oligopoly**, a situation where there are only a few suppliers, is more common. The American auto industry might be an example of this. Oligopolies have been known to attempt price-fixing, which is illegal.

Antitrust policy is the government's attempt to prevent monopolies from existing. The first antitrust statute dates back to 1890 (the Sherman Act) and was written to prohibit "any combination in restraint of trade". Because of the vagueness of this language, the Sherman Act was replaced by the Clayton Act in 1914. Some of the more notable break-ups (or attempted break-ups) have been John D. Rockefeller's Standard Oil in 1911, AT&T in the 1980s, and Microsoft in 2000.

Concerning the international economy, governments typically impose tariffs on imported goods. When a government raises tariffs (taxes on imports) so high that a significant portion of imports is discouraged, it is called **protectionism**. The opposite of protection is free-trade. Exchange rates between countries are either fixed or floating. A floating exchange rate is one that is allowed to fluctuate according to supply and demand. When we want to buy more foreign goods, they must be paid for in the foreign country's currency. This will increase the demand for that foreign currency and the value of that foreign currency will appreciate relative to the U.S. dollar. Some of the international institutions that resulted from the Second World War were the World Bank, the International Monetary Fund (IMF), and the General Agreement on Tariffs and Trade (GATT). The latter has since become the World Trade Organization (WTO).

1. **Microeconomics includes which of the following features?**

   I. fiscal policy
   II. business decisions
   III. consumer theory
   IV. family decisions
   V. money and banking

   (A) II and III
   (B) III and IV
   (C) III, IV and V
   (D) I and III

2. **Which is an example of barter?**

   (A) depositing a paycheck in your account
   (B) exchanging a personal check for a desired item
   (C) using cash to purchase a desired item
   (D) exchanging three eggs for two heads of lettuce

3. **When a government determines a financial plan for spending revenues, it is setting**

   (A)   monetary policy
   (B)   the business cycle
   (C)   fiscal policy
   (D)   financial opportunities

4. **The value of goods and services is set by**

   (A)   the quantity of other goods and services that can be exchanged for it
   (B)   the amount of money needed to buy one unit of the goods and services
   (C)   the amount of land, labor and capital needed to produce the goods and services
   (D)   the amount of profit the business man desires

5. **During the 1930's in the United States, which phase of the business cycle predominated?**

   (A)   business prosperity
   (B)   recession
   (C)   recovery
   (D)   depression

6. **An example of an autonomous, self-sufficient economic order would be**

   (A)   a man residing alone in a seashore villa
   (B)   a man residing alone on a deserted island
   (C)   a man residing alone on a tenant farm
   (D)   a man residing alone in a city apartment

7. **All of the following are examples of a command economy EXCEPT**

   (A)   government controls during wartime
   (B)   the feudal system
   (C)   a communist government
   (D)   a son learning his father's trade

8. **Price for a product in a free market is determined by which of the following?**

   (A)   supply and demand
   (B)   supply only
   (C)   demand only
   (D)   production costs alone

9. **The Law of Diminishing Returns states that**

(A) the amount of output will first decrease, and then increase, as the variable factor increases

(B) the amount of output will first decrease slightly and then decrease rapidly, as the variable factor increases

(C) the amount of output will first increase slightly, and then increase rapidly, as the variable factor increases

(D) the amount of output will first increase, and then decrease, as the variable factor increases

ANSWERS:

1. (B)   The other items listed are factors of macroeconomics.

2. (D)   Barter is direct exchange and does not involve cash or payment by check.

3. (C)   Monetary policy determines currency; the business cycle is short-run fluctuations in general prices; businessmen use financial opportunities to maximize profits.

4. (A)   (B) is the price of goods and services; (C) and (D) determine the cost, but if consumers do not want a particular good or service, the value of it will go down.

5. (D)   This period in American history is known as the Great Depression.

6. (B)   In (A), (C) and (D) it can be assumed that the man is buying goods (food, clothing, etc.) and services (a maid to clean the villa). Only in (B) is he totally self-sufficient.

7. (D)   While the father is an authority figure, this type of father-to-son economy is based on tradition. A common economy has an authority directing the activities of many.

8. (A)   Supply and demand go hand in hand in determining price. If people desire an item and it is in short supply, the price will surely go up. Production costs do contribute to price, but if few people want the item, the price will go down.

9. (D)   For example, as more farmers work on an acre of land, output will increase to that point where the marginal product meets the average product (and the farmers start to get in one another's way).

Chapter 6: SOCIOLOGY

Sociology is the study of how the individual relates to the larger society by virtue of belonging to various groups: family, clan, community, church, profession, occupation, etc. Some of the main areas include kinship relations, the influence of ethnicity, the class structure of society, urbanization and how cities relate to suburbs and rural areas, how social institutions come to have power and authority, and deviant and criminal behavior.

One of the most important types of groups that an individual belongs to is called a primary group. The family and one's ethnic group are important examples. The bonds between the individual and members of the primary group are ones of affection and nurturing. It is this group that is responsible for socialization, which is the process of learning the mores, customs, and values

This process is responsible for giving children a sense of identity and belonging. A secondary group, on the other hand, is one that an individual chooses to join, such as a profession or political party.

Two of the most important concepts employed by sociologists originate from German sociology: Gemeinschaft and Gesellschaft. The former is roughly translated as "community" while the latter means "society". The connotations of these terms are just as important as their literal meaning. Gemeinschaft is the kind of social existence one finds in primary groups, where there are bonds of affection and loyalty. Gesellschaft suggests a more fleeting association with others based on calculations of self-interest such as in commerce and business.

Sociology studies the division of society into classes. Stratification refers to the hierarchical ordering of social groups according to rank or status, as with the caste system in India. Society may be stratified according to wealth, political power, or educational attainment. Mobility refers to the ease with which an individual can move from one stratum into another. Division of labor is a concept used to describe the changes in economic relations since the Industrial Revolution. Dividing work into smaller and more easily manageable specialized tasks allows for much greater economic productivity.

Power is the ability to coerce someone while authority is the right to use power. Sociology is interested in how power becomes authority and how social institutions such as governments acquire legitimacy. There is also an interest in how institutions *lose* legitimacy and how reform, or even outright revolution, comes about.

Sociology Questions

1. With which of the following would a sociologist not be concerned?

(A) how a person relates to himself
(B) how a person relates to his family
(C) how a person relates to his community
(D) how a person relates to people on his job

2. Which of the following is not a secondary group?

(A) Office coworkers
(B) Church groups
(C) Families
(D) Chess clubs

3. Which of the following would a sociologist not study?

(A) Class mobility
(B) Individual emotional well-being
(C) Authority
(D) Power

Sociology Answers

1. A Sociologists study how people relate to each other, so a sociologist would not study how a person relates to himself.

2. C Families are a primary group. Secondary groups are ones that people choose to belong.

3. B Sociologist are very interested in class mobility, authority, and power. Psychologist are concerned with individual emotional well-being.

Chapter 7: ANTHROPOLOGY

Physical anthropology refers to archaeology, while cultural anthropology has much overlap with sociology. Anthropology tends to study either remains of prehistoric cultures or primitive cultures that still exist. Since aspects of physical anthropology were included in the World History section, this section will cover cultural anthropology.

When studying different cultures, the anthropologist is careful to avoid ethnocentrism, which is the evaluation of a foreign culture by the standards of one's own culture. As a matter of fact, some anthropologists refrain from making *any* evaluations of the culture under study in the belief that science ought to be value-free. The belief that certain behaviors, such as cannibalism, ought not to be morally judged but seen in their cultural context, is known as cultural relativism.

Two processes studied by anthropology are **acculturation** and **assimilation**, which are related but distinct. Acculturation refers to a situation of contact between two cultures where one of them is changed through being absorbed by the other. Assimilation, on the other hand, is a process whereby *both* cultures are changed by being fused into one new culture.

Anthropologists also study kinship groups. Kinship ties may be the result of blood or marriage or could include legally defined relations, such as adoptive parents or religiously sanctioned roles like godparents. Primitive societies are dominated by such primary groups and individuals in such a society do not have very much freedom in choosing the paths their lives will take.

Lineage may be traced matrilineally or patrilineally. In matrilineal descent, ancestry is traced through the mother, while patrilineal descent is traced through the father. If both are used it is called bilateral descent, while if either can be used it is called ambilineal descent.

Anthropologists try to get a handle on culture by studying the literature, myths, symbols, and rituals of a group. Some important terms in this area are **animism**, which is a belief that supernatural beings can inhabit things such as animals and plants; **totemism**, where an animal or a plant comes to symbolize the bonds of unity within a kinship group and where it would be taboo to kill this special animal or plant; and **shamanism**, where the shaman is someone with a special connection to the unseen spirits that inhabit the world.

Shamans are sometimes referred to as "witch doctors".

Anthropology Questions

1. **Which of the following is a problem for anthropologists?**

   (A) Cultural relativity
   (B) Assimilation
   (C) Acculturization
   (D) Ethnocentrism

2. **Which of the following is the term used for one culture being absorbed by another?**

   (A) Cultural relativity
   (B) Assimilation
   (C) Acculturation
   (D) Ethnocentrism

3. **When parental lineage is traced through the mother, the lineage is said to be:**

   (A) Matrilineal
   (B) Patrilineal
   (C) Bilateral descent
   (D) Ambilineal

Anthropology Answers

1. D   When studying other cultures, anthropologist must ignore belief of their own culture and only base their views on the culture they are studying. It is often difficult to get rid of all biases.

2. C   Acculturation is where another culture absorbs one culture. Assimilation is where the two cultures combine to form a new culture.

3. A   Lineage traced through the mother is matrilineal. Lineage traced through the father would be patrilineal. Lineage traced through both parents is bilateral descent.

Chapter 8: PSYCHOLOGY

Psychology studies the mind and its relation to behavior. **Behavioral psychology** would tend to favor the word "brain" instead of "mind" and would qualify "behavior" with "observable" in its attempt to be more scientific. The main areas of psychological study are conditioning and learning, personality formation, social behavior, abnormal conditions such as psychosis, and the biological basis for behavior. Whereas sociology places more emphasis on the group, psychology gives greater attention to the individual.

Cognition is the faculty of the mind that engages in rational thinking, such as processing information received by the senses, forming ideas and concepts, devising theories and hypotheses, and weighing choices in order to make decisions. Psychologists define intelligence as the level of cognitive functioning of an individual. It is frequently measured by an IQ test. IQ stands for Intelligence Quotient and is defined as a person's mental age, divided by the person's chronological age, times 100. A ten-year-old with the mental age of a twelve-year-old would have an IQ of (12/10) × 100 or 120.

There are two main types of **conditioning** studied by psychologists: classical (or Pavlovian) conditioning and operant (or instrumental) conditioning. A classical case is the result of Pavlov's famous study of dogs, where the sound of a bell would cause the dogs to salivate because the sound had become associated with food. A case of operant conditioning would involve an animal learning to operate a device in order to obtain a desired result.

An influential theorist in the field of learning and development has been **Jean Piaget,** who saw the process of learning as one of assimilation and accommodation, both of which involve some sort of adaptation. The child assimilates new objects into its pre-existing patterns of thinking and behavior. However, when the objects are not easily assimilated, the child accommodates by modifying its patterns of thinking and behavior. Piaget identified various stages of cognitive development:

- *sensory-motor stage*: sucking or throwing any object within reach

- *pre-operational stage*: capacity for memory, make-believe and symbolism but not yet able to see the world from any point of view but their own

- *concrete operational stage*: able to perform concrete operations such as counting discrete objects

- *abstract operational stage*: able to reason abstractly about objects, numbers, etc.

As far as personality development through childhood, the theories of **Sigmund Freud** have also been very influential. Freud divided the mind into three parts:

- the *id:* the aggressive part

- the *ego*: the rational or calculating part which tries to balance the desires of the id with the standards of society

- the *superego*: the moral part of the mind.

Freud further divided the mind into the conscious and the unconscious. Freud's pupil Jung broke with his teacher and developed his own ideas about archetypes, which are universal symbols embedded in the human psyche. Some common terms from psychoanalysis are ***repression*** (burying a painful experience in the subconscious), ***projection*** (attributing one's problems to external people or things) and ***sublimation*** (channeling a potentially destructive impulse into socially useful or sanctioned activities such as sports or art).

Freud and Jung were interested in the causes of **neurosis**, which is a relatively mild problem. The person experiencing neurosis can function and has little or no difficulty distinguishing reality from illusion or delusion. Some common symptoms of a neurosis are nightmares and the milder forms of depression. On the other hand, **psychosis** is a much more severe disorder. A psychotic person is generally not a functioning member of society and is unable to distinguish between reality and his or her own fantasies. Some specific psychoses are schizophrenia and paranoia. The terms **psychopathic** and **sociopathic** are generally used to describe people who tend to express their sickness in socially unacceptable or criminal ways. Other aspects of social behavior studied by psychology are conformity (adapting one's behavior to societal or group expectations), deviant behavior (deviating from the behavioral norms of one's society), and mass behavior (why do individuals do things in crowds, like rioting at a football game, that they wouldn't do otherwise?).

Psychology Questions

1. **Which of the following is not an example of classical conditioning?**

   (A) A rat running to the lighted side of a maze.
   (B) A monkey pushing a lever to get a banana.
   (C) A dog barking when a doorbell rings.
   (D) A cat coming when it hears a can opener.

2. **After having a stroke Bob has lost the ability to talk and reason. He likes to pick objects and smell them. At which stage of cognitive development is he operating?**

   (A) Sensory-motor stage
   (B) Pre-operational stage
   (C) Concrete operational stage
   (D) Abstract operational stage

3. **Blaming one's coworkers for getting fired at work is an example of:**

   (A) Repression
   (B) Projection
   (C) Sublimation
   (D) Neurosis

Psychology Answers

1. B   Classical conditioning is when there is a direct response to a stimulus. Operant conditioning is when a subject initiates an action to get the desired result. In case B the monkey is initiating the action. In the other cases the animal are responding to a stimulus.

2. A   Bob's stroke was severe. He has regressed to the initial stage where senses; feel, touch and taste, are most important. Essentially he has regressed all the way back to exploring his environment.

3. B   Projection is when people blame others for their problems. Repression is when problems are caused because painful events from the past are buried in the subconscious. A neurosis is a mild psychological disorder and sublimation is channeling potentially destructive behavior into a positive activity.

SOCIAL STUDIES GLOSSARY

ACCULTURATION: the process of adopting the cultural traits or social patterns of another group.

ANIMISM: the belief that natural objects, natural phenomena, and the universe itself possess souls.

ARCHAEOLOGY: the scientific study of historic or prehistoric peoples and their cultures by analysis of their artifacts, inscriptions, monuments, and other remains.

ARCHIPELAGO: a large group or chain of islands.

ASSIMILATION: the merging of cultural traits from distinct cultural groups.

BEHAVIORAL PSYCHOLOGY: the branch of psychology that derives its concepts from observation of the behavior of living organisms.

BILL OF RIGHTS: the first ten amendments of the Constitution.

BIOME: a major geographic region that contains a distinctive community of plants, animals, fungi, etc.

CARPETBAGGER: a Northerner who went to the South after the Civil War to profit from the unsettled conditions.

CENTRAL CITY: a densely populated city that is the core or center of a metropolitan area.

CHARLEMAGNE: ("Charles the Great") AD 742-814, king of the Franks; as Charles I, first emperor of the Holy Roman Empire 800-814.

CIVIL WAR: the war in the United States between the North and the South.

CLIMATE: the composite or generally prevailing weather conditions of a region, including temperature, air pressure, humidity, precipitation, cloudiness, and winds, throughout the year, averaged over a series of years.

COLD WAR: intense political, military, and ideological rivalry between nations, short of armed conflict; such rivalry after World War II between the U.S.S.R. and the U.S. and their respective allies.

CONDITIONING: a process of changing behavior by rewarding or punishing a subject each time an action is performed.

CONIFEROUS:	evergreen trees and shrubs, as those of the pine and cypress families, that bear both seeds and pollen on dry scales arranged as a cone.
CONSTANTINE THE GREAT:	AD 288?-337, Roman emperor 324-337; legally sanctioned Christian worship.
CONSTITUTION:	the fundamental law of the U.S., framed in 1787 and put into effect in 1789.
CONSUMER PRICE INDEX:	the change in the cost of common goods and services paid by a typical consumer, expressed as the percentage change in total cost of these same items over a base period.
CORN BELT:	a region in the midwestern U.S., especially Iowa, Illinois, and Indiana, known for raising corn and cornfed livestock.
CULTURAL GEOGRAPHY:	the branch of geography that is concerned with man-made political boundaries and with economic and industrial issues.
CUNEIFORM:	composed of slim triangular or wedge-shaped elements, as the characters used in writing by the ancient Akkadians, Assyrians, Babylonians, Persians, and others.
DARK AGES:	the period in European history from about AD 476 to about 1000 marked by repressiveness and a lack of advanced knowledge, etc.
DECIDUOUS:	shedding the leaves annually, as certain trees or shrubs.
DECLARATION OF INDEPENDENCE:	the formal statement, written by Thomas Jefferson and adopted on July 4, 1776 by the Second Continental Congress, declaring the thirteen American colonies free and independent of Great Britain: there were fifty-six signers.
DELTA:	a nearly flat plain of alluvial, often triangular, deposit between diverging branches of the mouth of a river.
DEMOGRAPHICS:	the statistical data of a population, especially those showing average age, income, education etc.
DEPRESSION:	a low state of functional activity or an economic downturn
DÉTENTE:	a relaxing of tension, especially between nations.

ENLIGHTENMENT: a European philosophical movement of the 17th and 18th centuries, characterized by belief in the power of reason and by innovations in political, religious, and educational doctrine.

EQUATOR: the great circle of the earth that is equidistant from the North Pole and the South Pole.

FEDERALIST PAPERS: a set of eighty-five articles written by Alexander Hamilton, James Madison, and John Jay published in 1787 and 1788, analyzing the Constitution of the United States and urging its adoption.

FEUDALISM: the political, military, and social systems in the Middle Ages, based on the holding of lands in fief or fee and in the resulting relations between lord and vassal.

FREEDMAN'S BUREAU: the government agency which helped former slaves in their transition to freedom and citizenship.

FRENCH AND INDIAN WAR: that part of the Seven Years' War (between England and France) which was fought in America from 1754 to 1763

FREUD: Sigmund, 1856-1939, Austrian neurologist: founder of psychoanalysis.

GENTRIFICATION: the upgrading of run-down urban neighborhoods by affluent people who buy and renovate the properties, thereby displacing the resident poor

GI BILL: the bill which gave funds for college education as an incentive to enlist in the armed forces.

GROSS NATIONAL PRODUCT: the total monetary value of all goods and services produced in a country during one year.

HINTERLAND: the remote or less developed parts of a county; an inland area supplying goods to a port.

INFLATION: a steady rise in the level of prices.

INNER CITY: a central and usually older part of the city, densely populated, often deteriorating, and inhabited mainly by the poor.

INTERNATIONAL DATE LINE:	an imaginary line drawn north and south through the Pacific Ocean, largely along the 180th meridian: it is the line at which, by international agreement, each calendar day begins at midnight, so that when it is Sunday just west of the line, it is Saturday just east of it.
INTERSTATE COMMERCE ACT:	established a United States federal commission in 1887 to regulate the commerce between the States
ISTHMUS:	a narrow strip of land, bordered on both sides by water, connecting two larger bodies of land.
KOREAN WAR:	the war (1950-53) between North Korea, aided by Communist China, and South Korea, aided by the U.S. and other United Nations.
LATITUDE:	the angular distance, measured north or south from the equator, of a point in the earth's surface, expressed in degrees.
LEAGUE OF NATIONS:	an association of nations, established January 10, 1920 by the Versailles treaty, to promote international cooperation and peace: it was dissolved in April 1946, and was succeeded by the United Nations after World War II.
LONGITUDE:	angular distance east or west in the earth's surface, as measured in degrees, from the prime meridian at Greenwich, England.
MACROECONOMICS:	the study of large economic systems (as a nation) comprised of different sectors.
MAGNA CARTA:	the charter of liberties forced from King John by the English barons at Runnymede, June 15, 1215.
MANORIAL:	a lord's house and adjoining lands over which he exercised control.
MEXICAN WAR:	the war between the U.S. and Mexico, 1846-48.
MICROECONOMICS:	the branch of economics dealing with particular aspects of an economy, as the price-cost relationship of a firm.
MONETARY POLICY:	the government's efforts to regulate the money supply in a country.

MONROE DOCTRINE: stated by President Monroe in 1823 that the U.S. opposed further European colonization of or intervention in the Western Hemisphere.

NATION-STATE: a sovereign state inhabited by a fairly homogeneous group of people who share a feeling of common nationality.

NEUROSIS: a functional disorder in which feelings of anxiety, obsessional thoughts, compulsive acts, and physical complaints without objective evidence of disease.

NEW DEAL: the economic and social policies and programs introduced by President Franklin D. Roosevelt and his administration.

NEW FEDERALISM: a system of revenue sharing with state and local governments.

NEW TESTAMENT: the collection of the books of the Christian Bible, comprising the Gospels, Acts of the Apostles, the Epistles, and the Revelation of St. John the Divine.

OLD TESTAMENT: the complete Bible of the Jews, comprising the Law, the Prophets, and the Hagiographa. The first of the two main divisions of the Christian Bible.

OLIGOPOLY: the market situation in which prices and other factors are controlled by a few sellers.

PAPYRUS: a material on which to write prepared from thin strips of the pith of the papyrus plant laid and pressed together, used by the ancient Egyptians, Greeks, and Romans.

PENTATEUCH: the first five books of the Old Testament: Genesis, Exodus, Leviticus, Numbers, and Deuteronomy.

PHYSICAL GEOGRAPHY: the branch of geography concerned with natural features and phenomena of the earth's surface.

PIAGET: Jean, 1896 - 1980, Swiss cognitive psychologist.

PREHISTORY: human history in the period before recorded events, know mainly through archaeological discoveries, study, research, etc.

PRIME MERIDIAN:	the meridian running through Greenwich, England, from which longitude east and west is reckoned.
PROGRESSIVE ERA:	the first twenty years of the twenty-first century, characterized by demands for political reform and social action.
PROJECTION:	to give another person or object the feelings, thoughts, or attitudes present in oneself.
PROTECTIONISM:	the practice of protecting domestic industries from foreign competition by imposing import duties or quotas.
PSYCHOPATHIC:	pertaining to psychopathy; engaging in amoral or antisocial acts without feeling remorse.
PSYCHOSIS:	a mental disorder characterized by symptoms, as delusions or hallucinations, that indicate impaired contact with reality.
RECESSION:	a period of economic decline when production, employment, and earnings fall below normal levels.
RECONSTRUCTION:	the process by which the states that had seceded were reorganized as part of the Union after the Civil War.
REFORMATION:	the 16th-century movement for reforming the Roman Catholic Church, which resulted in the establishment of the Protestant churches.
RENAISSANCE:	the activity, spirit, or time of the great revival of art, literature, and learning in Europe beginning in the 14th century and extending to the 17th century, marking the transition from the medieval to the modern world.
REPRESSION:	the suppression from consciousness of distressing or disagreeable ideas, memories, feelings, or impulses.
RUST BELT:	the Great Lakes states and adjacent areas of the eastern U.S. in which much of the work force has traditionally been employed in manufacturing and metals production.
SCALAWAGS:	a white Southerner who supported Republican policy during Reconstruction, often for personal gain.

SEPTUAGINT: the oldest Greek version of the Old Testament, traditionally said to have been translated by 70 or 72 Jewish scholars at the request of Ptolemy II.

SHAMANISM: the animistic religion of North Asia, expressing a belief in powerful spirits that can be influenced only by shamans.

SILICON VALLEY: area in North California, in the Santa Clara valley region, where many high-technology companies are located.

SOCIOPATHIC: a person whose behavior is antisocial and who lacks a sense of moral responsibility or social conscience.

SPANISH-AMERICAN WAR: the war between the U.S. and Spain in 1898.

STAGFLATION: an inflationary period accompanied by rising unemployment and lack of increase in business activity.

STEPPE: an extensive plain without trees.

SUBLIMATION: the diversion of energy of (a sexual or other biological impulse) from its immediate goal to one of a more acceptable social, moral, or aesthetic nature.

SUBURB: lying immediately outside a city or town, especially a smaller residential community.

TAMMANY HALL: a Democratic political organization in New York City, founded in 1789 as a fraternal society and associated with corruption and abuse of power.

TOTEMISM: the practice of having a natural object or an animate being, as the emblem of a clan, family, or group.

TUNDRA: treeless plains of the arctic regions of Europe, Asia, and North America.

WHEAT BELT: the expanse of land stretching in a north-south direction through the mid-western states of the Dakotas, Nebraska, Kansas, and Oklahoma.

PART III
MATHEMATICS

The Praxis Elementary Education Content Knowledge test covers the following topics

- Integers
- Fractions
- Decimals
- Percents
- Geometry
- Algebra
- Coordinate Geometry
- Statistics

Check the Praxis web site for your specific test information and to see if you will be able to use a calculator.

Chapter 1: Number Properties

Section 1: Numbers and Number Systems

We count discrete objects using the natural, or counting, numbers:
$$\{1, 2, 3, 4, 5,...\}$$

If we include zero in the above set, we get the set of whole numbers:
$$\{0, 1, 2, 3, 4, 5,...\}$$

If we include the negative whole numbers in the above set, we get the set of **integers**:

$$\{...-3, -2, -1, 0, 1, 2, 3,...\}$$

As you may have noticed, the set of positive integers is the same as the set of counting numbers.

For example:

2 is an integer, a whole number and a counting number

0 is an integer and a whole number

-2 is only an integer

Rational numbers can be expressed as a ratio of two integers.

Finally, if you include all fractions in the set of integers, you get the set of **real numbers**. 0, $\sqrt{2}$, $-\frac{1}{3}$ and π are all real numbers. Any number that can be represented using the above sets of numbers is a real number.

The last type of number is the complex numbers. Complex numbers are those with an imaginary component, and imaginary numbers result from trying to take the square root of a negative number.

Section 2: Integers

Integers are a well-defined set of numbers having certain properties. Integers have the property of closure with respect to certain operations. If you add two integers, the sum will **_always_** be an integer; thus the set of integers is said to be closed with respect to addition. The set of integers is also closed with respect to multiplication and subtraction, but it is **not** closed with respect to division. Both 2 and 3 are integers but 2/3 is not an integer.

Integers are either odd or even. An even integer is divisible by two, while an odd integer is not. Addition, subtraction, and multiplication of odds and evens display some patterns. These patterns could be summed up as follows:

(even) ± (even) = (even)

(even) ± (odd) = (odd)

$$(\text{odd}) \pm (\text{odd}) = (\text{even})$$
$$(\text{even}) \times (\text{even}) = (\text{even})$$
$$(\text{even}) \times (\text{odd}) = (\text{even})$$
$$(\text{odd}) \times (\text{odd}) = (\text{odd})$$

Saying that one integer is divisible by another integer means after division there is no remainder. There are a few tricks to determine whether a given integer is divisible by another integer. For instance:

If the given integer is even (its units digit is 0, 2, 4, 6 or 8) then it is divisible by 2.

If the sum of the digits is divisible by 3, then the integer is divisible by 3.

If the number represented by the final two digits is divisible by 4, then the integer is divisible by 4.

If the units digit is 0 or 5, then the integer is divisible by 5.

If the integer is divisible by 2 and by 3, then it is divisible by 6.

If the number represented by the final three digits is divisible by 8, then the integer is divisible by 8.

If the sum of the digits is divisible by 9, then the integer is divisible by 9.

Where permitted, use your calculator to easily determine divisibility.

EXAMPLE: Is 5216 divisible by 8?

SOLUTION: On your calculator punch in 5216, then the division sign (÷), then 8 and finally the equals sign (=). The display should show 652, which is a whole number. Since the quotient is a whole number, 5216 is in fact divisible by 8.

EXAMPLE: Is 144 is divisible by 7?

SOLUTION: You would punch in as in the previous example, and the display would show 20.571428571428 (or thereabouts, depending on how many digits your calculator can display) which is definitely not a whole number. Therefore, 144 is not divisible by 7.

If an integer a is divisible by an integer b, then b is called a **factor** of a (and a is called a **multiple** of b). By way of definition, every integer except for 0 is a factor of itself and 1 is a factor of every integer. As an example, here are the *positive* factors of 24:

{1, 2, 3, 4, 6, 8, 12, 24}

Here are *all* of the factors of 24:

{-24, -12, -8, -6, -4, -3, -2, -1, 1, 2, 3, 4, 6, 8, 12, 24}

In order to determine the *prime* factors of an integer, we need to first define **prime**. An integer is prime if its only two factors are 1 and itself. (An alternative way to say this is that a prime is divisible only by 1 and itself.) The first prime integer (and the only even prime) is 2. Besides 2, all primes are odd. Here are the first ten primes:

{2, 3, 5, 7, 11, 13, 17, 19, 23, 29...}

Incidentally, if an integer other than 0 or 1 is not prime, it is called **composite**. (4 is thus the first composite integer.)

Considering the example above, we can now enumerate the prime factors of 24:

{2, 3}

24 could be written as the product of its prime factors: (2)(2)(2)(3) or 2^3 (3). The fact that an integer can be written uniquely as the product of primes is the Fundamental Theorem of Arithmetic:

4 = (2)(2)

6 = (2)(3)

8 = (2)(2)(2)

9 = (3)(3)

10 = (2)(5)

12 = (2)(2)(3)

14 = (2)(7), etc.

The factors of a number always constitute a finite set. On the other hand, the multiples of a number always constitute an infinite set. The multiples of 7:

{7, 14, 21, 28, 35, 42, 49,...}

Notice that 7 is a multiple of itself. Every integer is a multiple of itself.

Given two different integers, we may sometimes need to find the greatest factor that the two integers have in common. This number is called the **greatest common factor** (or **greatest common divisor**) of the two integers. The GCF of two integers is the greatest integer that divides both of them evenly. As an example, it is not too difficult to see that the GCF of 6 and 9 is 3 or that the GCF of 12 and 24 is 12.

EXAMPLE: What is the GCF of 105 and 378?

SOLUTION: The systematic method for finding the GCF of two integers is called the **Euclidean Algorithm**, after its originator (Euclid). The first step is to recognize that the GCF of 105 and 378 cannot be greater than 105. Quick inspection also shows that 105 does not divide into 378 evenly but rather leaves a remainder of 63. So the GCF of 105 and 378 is the same as the GCF of 63 and 105. 63 does not divide into 105 evenly, but leaves a remainder of 42. The initial problem has now been reduced to finding the GCF of 42 and 63, which is easily found to be 21.

The **least common multiple** of two integers is the least integer that both divide into evenly. The LCM is useful when trying to find a common denominator for two fractions that are being added. For example, the LCM of 4 and 10 is 20. Simply multiplying the two integers will give a common multiple, but it will not necessarily be the *least* common multiple. 4 and 10 both go into 40 evenly, but 40 is not the least common multiple.

Integer Practice Problems

1. **If a is an integer, which of the following is (are) also?**

   A. $\dfrac{2a + 2}{2}$

   B. $\dfrac{a + 2}{2}$

   C. $\dfrac{2a + 1}{2}$

2. **If b is odd, what are the 3 odd numbers after b?**

3. **If a is even, is xyab even or odd where x, y, and b are integers?**

4. **What happens to c when d is doubled if $c = 3d^2$?**

5. **What is the 7th prime number?**

6. **A perfect number is any number equal to the SUM of its factors, including 1 but excluding the number itself, what is the first perfect number?**

7. **If x is odd and y is even, is (xy) + (x + y) odd or even?**

8. **If P is a negative fraction, which is larger P^2 or P^3?**

9. **If a is odd and b is even, is $a^3 \times b^3$ odd or even?**

10. **Is the square of an even number divided by another even number always odd, always even or may it be either?**

157

ANSWERS:

1. A. $\dfrac{2a + 2}{2} = \dfrac{2(a + 1)}{2} = a + 1$ Therefore, A is an integer.

   B. $\dfrac{a + 2}{2} = \dfrac{a}{2} + \dfrac{2}{2} = \dfrac{a}{2} + 1$ Therefore, B is an integer only when a is even.

   C. $\dfrac{2a + 1}{2} = \dfrac{2a}{2} + \dfrac{1}{2} = a + \dfrac{1}{2}$ Therefore, C is not an integer.

2. b + 2, b + 4, b + 6

3. a is even; therefore, any number of factors will produce an even integer (assuming x, y and b are integers).

4. $c = 3d^2$ $c = 3(2d)^2$
   $$c = 3 \times 4d^2$$
   $$c = 12d^2$$

   Therefore, c is 4 times (or 2^2) larger.

5. The 7th prime number is 17. The first 6 prime numbers are 2, 3, 5, 7, 11, and 13.

6. The first perfect number is 6, since 6 = 3 + 2 + 1. The next perfect number would be 28 because 28 = 14 + 7 + 4 + 2 + 1.

7. Odd, because xy is even, xy + y is even. x + an even = even + odd = odd.

8. P is negative. Therefore, P^3 is negative. P^2 is positive, so $P^2 > P^3$.

9. Even, because a^3 is odd, b^3 is even, and odd × even = even.

10. It is impossible to determine the quotient of two even numbers.

    EXAMPLE: $\dfrac{6^2}{4} = \dfrac{36}{4} = 9(\text{odd})$, $\dfrac{8^2}{4} = \dfrac{64}{4} = 16(\text{even})$

    It might not be an integer.

    EXAMPLE: $\dfrac{2^2}{16} = \dfrac{4}{16} = \dfrac{1}{4}$

Key Point

Fractions represent parts of wholes. We need them because not everything in the world is measurable with integers. The top of a fraction is called the numerator and the bottom is called the denominator. The denominator gives the "name" or "family" of the fraction, for instance $\frac{1}{5}, \frac{2}{5}, \frac{3}{5}$, etc. all belong to the family of fifths. The numerator tells how many we have of a particular family.

$$\frac{3}{8} = \frac{numerator}{denominator}$$

The figure below is divided into eight equal pieces. The fraction of the figure that is shaded is $\frac{3}{8}$. Eight represent the total number of pieces that the figure is divided into. Eight represents the whole figure. Three represents the part of the figure that is shaded. By placing the number that represents the part (3) over the number that represents the whole (8), we represent the part of the figure that is shaded as a fraction ($\frac{3}{8}$).

$$\text{Fraction Shaded} = \frac{\text{Pieces Shaded}}{\text{Total Pieces}} = \frac{3}{8}$$

As you work with fractions, you'll find that two fractions may very well be equal even though they are expressed in different forms. Therefore, it will be helpful for you to be able to change from one form into another.

Section 1: Reducing A Fraction To Lowest Terms

The figure below is divided into 12 equal parts. Four of the parts are shaded.

One way to express the fraction that is shaded is to places the number of shaded parts (4) over the total number of parts (12). This fraction is $\frac{4}{12}$.

If we consider the figure as a collection of six columns, 2 of which are shaded, we could express the fraction as the number of shaded columns (2) over the total number of columns (6). This fraction is $\frac{2}{6}$.

Now suppose we kept the same number of blocks and the same number of shaded blocks, but rearranged them to look like the figure below.

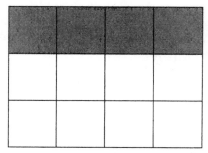

If we consider the figure as a collection of 3 rows, 1 of which are shaded, we could express the fraction as the number of shaded rows (1) over the total number of rows (3). This fraction is $\frac{1}{3}$.

All three fractions, $\frac{4}{12}$, $\frac{2}{6}$, and $\frac{1}{3}$ express the relationship between the 4 shaded boxes to the total number of boxes. These fractions have the same value, and we say that they are **equivalent**.

The relationship that is expressed in lowest terms is the fraction $\frac{1}{3}$. A fraction can be reduced if there is a whole number that can be divided evenly into both the numerator (top) and denominator (bottom). A fraction has been reduced to **lowest terms** if there is no longer any whole number, other than one, that can be divided evenly into both the numerator and denominator.

In our example, the fraction $\frac{4}{12}$ can be reduced to the fraction $\frac{2}{6}$ by dividing both the numerator and denominator by the whole number 2.

$$\frac{4 \div 2}{12 \div 2} = \frac{2}{6}$$

However, this fraction is not reduced to lowest terms because there is still a whole number that will divide evenly into 2 and 6. The number 2 will divide evenly into both the numerator and denominator.

$$\frac{2 \div 2}{6 \div 2} = \frac{1}{3}$$

We could have gotten the same result by dividing the numerator of the original fraction (4) and the denominator of the original fraction (12) each by the number 4.

$$\frac{4 \div 4}{12 \div 4} = \frac{1}{3}$$

Working with a fraction in its lowest terms will give you a better sense of its relative size. It will also help you add and subtract fractions, which we will cover in a later section.

Example: Reduce $\frac{36}{90}$ to lowest terms.

Solution: The largest number that can be divided evenly into 36 and 90 is 18, but chances are it will not be the first one you see. It is more likely that you would see that 9 divides evenly into both numbers. There is not just <u>one</u> correct way to start the problem. However, there is only <u>one</u> correct answer.

$$\frac{36 \div 9}{90 \div 9} = \frac{4}{10}$$

At this stage, you have reduced the fraction, but not to its lowest terms. Both 4 and 10 can be divided evenly by the number 2.

$$\frac{4 \div 2}{10 \div 2} = \frac{2}{5}$$

The answer is $\frac{2}{5}$. There is no whole number, other than one, that can be divided evenly into both 2 and 5.

Example: Reduce $\frac{20}{35}$ to lowest terms.

Solution: The largest number that can be divided evenly into 20 and 35 is 5.

$$\frac{20 \div 5}{35 \div 5} = \frac{4}{7}$$

Example: Reduce $\frac{175}{250}$ to lowest terms.

Solution: It might be helpful to think of these numbers in terms of dollars and cents. Ask yourself how many quarters are in $1.75? How many quarters are there in $2.50? There are 7 quarters in $1.75 and 10 quarters in $2.50.

$$\frac{175 \div 25}{250 \div 25} = \frac{7}{10}$$

Example: Reduce $\frac{72}{108}$

Solution: $\frac{72 \div 36}{108 \div 36} = \frac{2}{3}$

The largest number that divides evenly into 72 and 108 is 36. Don't feel badly if you didn't initially identify 36. Maybe you saw 2, or maybe 9. Dividing both numerator and denominator by 2 would result in the fraction $\frac{36}{54}$. If you divided 72 and 108 by 9, you would end up with the fraction $\frac{8}{12}$. In both cases these fractions can still be reduced. As long as you continue to find a number that can be divided evenly into both the numerator and denominator of the fraction, you can continue to reduce the fraction. Ultimately, you will end up at the same result, $\frac{2}{3}$.

Reducing to Lowest Terms Problems

Reduce the following fractions to lowest terms.

1. $\frac{14}{21}$

2. $\frac{66}{99}$

3. $\frac{20}{50}$

4. $\frac{49}{84}$

5. $\frac{375}{525}$

6. $\frac{24}{27}$

7. $\frac{42}{63}$

8. $\frac{105}{165}$

9. $\frac{180}{260}$

10. $\frac{68}{76}$

11. $\frac{18}{42}$

12. $\frac{125}{600}$

13. **List the following three fractions from highest to lowest.**

$$\frac{5}{24}, \frac{12}{48}, \frac{9}{72}$$

14. **Five relatives are to share in a $100,000 inheritance. According to the will, Rudi is to get $\frac{2}{16}$, Colleen is entitled to $\frac{7}{28}$, Bob gets $\frac{3}{9}$, Irene's share is $\frac{3}{36}$, and finally Brady gets $\frac{5}{24}$. Put the five relatives in order of highest share to lowest share.**

Reducing to Lowest Terms Solutions

1. $\quad \dfrac{14}{21} = \dfrac{14 \div 7}{21 \div 7} = \dfrac{2}{3}$

2. $\quad \dfrac{66}{99} = \dfrac{66 \div 11}{99 \div 11} = \dfrac{6}{9} = \dfrac{6 \div 3}{9 \div 3} = \dfrac{2}{3}$

3. $\quad \dfrac{20}{50} = \dfrac{20 \div 10}{50 \div 10} = \dfrac{2}{5}$

(Note: You can cancel zeros in the numerator and denominator as long as you cancel an equal number in both.)

$$\frac{2\cancel{0}}{5\cancel{0}} = \frac{2}{5}$$

4. $\quad \dfrac{49}{84} = \dfrac{49 \div 7}{84 \div 7} = \dfrac{7}{12}$

5. $\quad \dfrac{375}{525} = \dfrac{375 \div 25}{525 \div 25} = \dfrac{15}{21} = \dfrac{15 \div 3}{21 \div 3} = \dfrac{5}{7}$

Remember: How many quarters in $3.75? How many quarters in $5.25?

6. $\quad \dfrac{24}{27} = \dfrac{24 \div 3}{27 \div 3} = \dfrac{8}{9}$

7. $\quad \dfrac{42}{63} = \dfrac{42 \div 7}{63 \div 7} = \dfrac{6}{9} = \dfrac{6 \div 3}{9 \div 3} = \dfrac{2}{3}$

8. $\quad \dfrac{105}{165} = \dfrac{105 \div 5}{165 \div 5} = \dfrac{21}{33} = \dfrac{21 \div 3}{33 \div 3} = \dfrac{7}{11}$

9. $\quad \dfrac{180}{260} = \dfrac{18\cancel{0}}{26\cancel{0}} = \dfrac{18 \div 2}{26 \div 2} = \dfrac{9}{13}$

10. $\dfrac{68}{76} = \dfrac{68 \div 4}{76 \div 4} = \dfrac{17}{19}$

11. $\dfrac{18}{42} = \dfrac{18 \div 6}{42 \div 6} = \dfrac{3}{7}$

12. $\dfrac{125}{600} = \dfrac{125 \div 25}{600 \div 25} = \dfrac{5}{24}$

13. In a later section, we will discuss an easier solution path to this problem, but for now we must use the one skill we have developed, and that is, reducing each fraction to lowest terms.

There is no number that will divide evenly into both 5 and 24, so $\dfrac{5}{24}$ is already reduced to lowest terms. The largest number that will divide evenly into 12 and 48 is 12. $\dfrac{12}{48}$ reduces to $\dfrac{1}{4}$. Finally, the largest number that divides evenly into 9 and 72 is 9. $\dfrac{9}{72}$ reduces to $\dfrac{1}{8}$. So the three fractions are $\dfrac{5}{24}$, $\dfrac{1}{4}$, and $\dfrac{1}{8}$. It is easy to see that $\dfrac{1}{4}$ is larger than $\dfrac{1}{8}$, but where does $\dfrac{5}{24}$ fit into the picture? Well, $\dfrac{5}{24}$ is larger than $\dfrac{4}{24}$ but smaller than $\dfrac{6}{24}$. $\dfrac{4}{24}$ reduces to $\dfrac{1}{6}$ and $\dfrac{6}{24}$ reduces to $\dfrac{1}{4}$. So, $\dfrac{5}{24}$ is larger than $\dfrac{1}{6}$, but smaller than $\dfrac{1}{4}$. If it is larger than $\dfrac{1}{6}$, it is certainly larger than $\dfrac{1}{8}$.

$\dfrac{12}{48}$, $\left(\dfrac{1}{4}\right)$ is larger than $\dfrac{5}{24}$, and $\dfrac{5}{24}$ is larger than $\dfrac{9}{72}$ $\left(\dfrac{1}{8}\right)$. The correct sequence is $\dfrac{12}{48}$, $\dfrac{5}{24}$, and $\dfrac{9}{72}$.

The relationship would have been easier for us to see had we only reduced each fraction so that each denominator was 24. Dividing both 12 and 48 by 2, we would get $\dfrac{6}{24}$. Dividing both 9 and 72 by 3, we would get $\dfrac{3}{24}$. Now, it is easy to see that $\dfrac{6}{24}$ is larger than $\dfrac{5}{24}$ which, in turn, is larger than $\dfrac{3}{24}$. The number 24 is called the common denominator and is the key to that easier solution. As promised, we will study common denominators in a future section.

14. If you reduce each fraction to lowest terms the result would be:

$$\frac{2}{16} = \frac{1}{8}$$

$$\frac{3}{9} = \frac{1}{3}$$

$$\frac{7}{28} = \frac{1}{4}$$

$$\frac{3}{36} = \frac{1}{12}$$

$$\frac{5}{24} = \frac{5}{24}$$

The first four fractions are easy to sequence. If you keep the value of the numerator the same (in this case, 1) you decrease the value of the fraction as you increase the denominator. $\frac{1}{3}$ is larger than $\frac{1}{4}$, which is larger than $\frac{1}{8}$, which is larger than $\frac{1}{12}$. From the previous problem, we know that $\frac{5}{24}$ is smaller than $\frac{1}{4}$ but larger than $\frac{1}{8}$. Therefore, the proper sequence of fractions is:

$$\frac{3}{9} \left(\frac{1}{3}\right), \ \frac{7}{28} \left(\frac{1}{4}\right), \ \frac{5}{24}, \ \frac{2}{16} \left(\frac{1}{8}\right), \text{ and } \frac{3}{36} \left(\frac{1}{12}\right)$$

The proper sequence of relatives is: Bob, Colleen, Brady, Rudi, and Irene.

Section 2: Improper Fractions and Mixed Numbers

Key Point

Fractional numbers that are greater than 1 can be written in two different forms. One form is much better to work with when you are multiplying or dividing fractions. The other is better when you have to judge relative size. So, it is important that you are able to work with both and change from one form to the other.

$\frac{19}{5}$ is an Improper Fraction.

An Improper Faction is a fraction with a numerator that is larger than the denominator.

As we will see later in this book, this is the form we will use when we are multiplying or dividing fractions. However, in this form, it is difficult to evaluate its relative size.

Is $\frac{19}{5}$ larger than 5?

Is $\frac{19}{5}$ smaller than 3?

Would you rather earn 4 times more than you do now or $\frac{19}{5}$ more than you do now?

In order to judge relative size, we actually perform the division that this fraction defines. We divide 19 by 5. 5 goes into 19, 3 times with 4 remainder. The remainder is written over the original denominator, in this example, 5, forming the fraction $\frac{4}{5}$. Then we write this fraction next to the whole number 3.

$$\frac{19}{5} = 3\frac{4}{5}$$

The final result is $3\frac{4}{5}$. This is called a **Mixed Number**. A mixed number is made up of 2 parts, a whole number and a fraction that is greater than zero but less than 1.

Key Point

To review, in order to change an improper fraction to a mixed number, divide the denominator of the improper fraction into the numerator. Write the remainder over the original denominator. This fractional remainder is written next to the whole number. Remember, if we start with a fraction of 5, we end with a fraction of 5.

$3\frac{4}{5}$ is a number that is greater than 3, but less than 4. So:

Is $\frac{19}{5}$ larger than 5? **NO**

Is $\frac{19}{5}$ smaller than 3? **NO**

Would you rather earn 4 times more than you do now or $\frac{19}{5}$ more than you do now? **4 times more.**

Let's try some more problems.

Example: Change $\frac{51}{8}$ to a mixed number.

Solution: $\frac{51}{8}$ $51 \div 8 = 6$ with a remainder of 3

$$\frac{51}{8} = 6\frac{3}{8}$$

Example: Change $\frac{13}{5}$ to a mixed number.

Solution: $\frac{13}{5}$ $13 \div 5 = 2$ with a remainder of 3

$$\frac{13}{5} = 2\frac{3}{5}$$

Changing From a Mixed Number to an Improper Fraction

A visual representation of $3\frac{4}{5}$ would be 3 rows, each with 5 blocks and a fourth row with only 4 blocks.

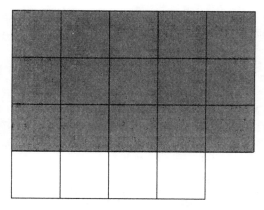

If we consider 5 blocks as a full row, then the last row is only $\frac{4}{5}$ of a row. The fastest way to count how many blocks there are is to consider that there are 3 full rows with 5 blocks each. To find the total number of blocks in these 3 rows, we would multiply 3 by 5, which is 15. To find the total number of blocks in the figure, we would have to add the 4 blocks from the partial row.

$$3 * 5 = 15$$
$$15 + 4 = 19$$

Key Point

> To change a mixed number to an improper fraction, multiply the whole number by the denominator of the fraction and add this product to the numerator of the fraction. The sum is placed over the original denominator.

Changing $3\frac{4}{5}$ back to an improper fraction, we would multiply 3 by 5 (15) and add 4 = 19. 19 is placed over the original denominator (5). $3\frac{4}{5} = \frac{19}{5}$.

Regardless of which direction we move in, we start with a fraction of 5 and we end with a fraction of 5.

Example: Change $7\frac{4}{5}$ to an improper fraction.

Solution:

Step 1: Multiply the whole number (7) by the denominator (5).

$5 \times 7 = 35$

Step 2: Add the product (35) to the numerator (4).

$35 + 4 = 39$

Step 3: Put the result (39) over the original denominator (5).

Mixed Number $\rightarrow 7\frac{4}{5} = \frac{39}{5} \leftarrow$ **Improper Fraction**

Example: Change $5\frac{3}{7}$ to an improper fraction.

Solution: $7 \times 5 = 35$ $35 + 3 = 38$

$5\frac{3}{7} = \frac{38}{7}$

Improper Fractions and Mixed Numbers Sample Problems

Directions: **Change the following improper fractions to mixed numbers and reduce to lowest terms.**

1. $\frac{15}{8}$ 2. $\frac{29}{12}$

3. $\frac{62}{11}$ 4. $\frac{110}{25}$

5. $\frac{42}{24}$ 6. $\frac{82}{9}$

Directions: Change the following mixed numbers to improper fractions.

7. $3\frac{4}{9}$ 8. $1\frac{1}{4}$

9. $11\frac{2}{3}$ 10. $7\frac{3}{4}$

11. $8\frac{6}{7}$ 12. $9\frac{2}{5}$

13. Of the following fractions, which is the largest?

$$\frac{7}{4}, \frac{3}{2}, 3\frac{1}{8}, \frac{10}{3}, \frac{15}{5}$$

14. Arrange the following fractions in descending order.

$$\frac{19}{6}, \frac{17}{3}, 4\frac{2}{5}, \frac{27}{10}, \frac{23}{4}$$

Improper Fractions and Mixed Numbers Sample Problem Solutions

1. 8 goes into 15, once with 7 remainder

$$\frac{15}{8} = 1\frac{7}{8}$$

2. 12 goes into 29, twice with 5 remainder

$$\frac{29}{12} = 2\frac{5}{12}$$

3. 11 goes into 62, 5 times with 7 remainder

$$\frac{62}{11} = 5\frac{7}{11}$$

4. 25 goes into 110, 4 times with 10 remainder

$$\frac{110}{25} = 4\frac{10}{25} = 4\frac{2}{5}$$

5. 24 goes into 42, once with 18 remainder

$$\frac{42}{24} = 1\frac{18}{24} = 1\frac{3}{4}$$

6. 9 goes into 82, 9 times with 1 remainder

$$\frac{82}{9} = 9\frac{1}{9}$$

7. 9 x 3 + 4 = 31

$$3\frac{4}{9} = \frac{31}{9}$$

8. 4 x 1 + 1 =

$$1\frac{1}{4} = \frac{5}{4}$$

9. 3 x 11 + 2 = 35

$$11\frac{2}{3} = \frac{35}{3}$$

10. 4 x 7 + 3 = 31

$$7\frac{3}{4} = \frac{31}{4}$$

11. 7 x 8 + 6 = 62

$$8\frac{6}{7} = \frac{62}{7}$$

12. 5 x 9 + 2 = 47

$$9\frac{2}{5} = \frac{47}{5}$$

13.

$$\frac{7}{4} = 1\frac{3}{4}$$

$$\frac{3}{2} = 1\frac{1}{2}$$

$$3\frac{1}{8} = 3\frac{1}{8}$$

$$\frac{10}{3} = 3\frac{1}{3}$$

$$\frac{15}{5} = 3$$

After all of the improper fractions have been converted to mixed numbers, it is easy to see that $\frac{10}{3}$ or $3\frac{1}{3}$ is the largest quantity.

14.

$$\frac{19}{6} = 3\frac{1}{6}$$

$$\frac{17}{3} = 5\frac{2}{3}$$

$$4\frac{2}{5} = 4\frac{2}{5}$$

$$\frac{27}{10} = 2\frac{7}{10}$$

$$\frac{23}{4} = 5\frac{3}{4}$$

The largest number is either $5\frac{2}{3}$ or $5\frac{3}{4}$. To be precise in our determination we would have to express both fractions in some common fashion. This is called a common denominator and is a topic for later discussion. For now, it is only necessary to know that each time you add 1 to both the numerator and denominator of a fraction, the resulting fraction is larger in size than the original fraction. Therefore, $\frac{2}{3}$ is less than $\frac{(2+1)}{(3+1)}$ or $\frac{3}{4}$. So, $5\frac{3}{4}$ is larger than $5\frac{2}{3}$. The remainder of the sequence follows without difficulty, as it is easy to see that $4\frac{2}{5}$ is larger than $3\frac{1}{6}$, which, in turn, is larger than $2\frac{7}{10}$. In their original form the sequence in descending order is:

$$\frac{23}{4}, \frac{17}{3}, 4\frac{2}{5}, \frac{19}{6}, \frac{27}{10}$$

Section 3: Adding Fractions with Common Denominators

Key Point

The denominator of a fraction **names** the fraction. You can only add or subtract fractions with the same name, or denominator. For example, you can add $\dfrac{5}{7} + \dfrac{6}{7} = \dfrac{11}{7} = 1\dfrac{4}{7}$ together because they are **all fractions of 7**. They have a **Common Denominator of 7**. When this is the case, you need only add the numerators together. **Do Not add the denominators** together. If you add fractions of 7 together, you end up with a fraction of 7. The name does not change.

Example: Find the sum of $\dfrac{4}{9}$ and $\dfrac{8}{9}$.

Solution: In this case the **common denominator is 9** – both numbers are fractions of 9. We add the numerators and the denominator remains the same.

$$\frac{4}{9} + \frac{8}{9} = \frac{12}{9}$$

We can **divide** numerator and denominator **by 3** and reduce the fraction to $\dfrac{4}{3}$.

Additionally, we can write the result as a mixed fraction $1\dfrac{1}{3}$.

Example: Add $\dfrac{5}{8} + \dfrac{5}{8}$ and reduce to lowest terms.

Solution: $\dfrac{5}{8} + \dfrac{5}{8} = \dfrac{5+5}{8} = \dfrac{10}{8}$

$$\frac{10}{8} = \frac{10 \div 2}{8 \div 2} = \frac{5}{4}$$

$$\frac{5}{4} = 5 \div 4 = 1\frac{1}{4}$$

Adding Fractions With a Common Denominator Problems

Directions: Convert to improper fractions if possible. Always reduce to lowest terms.

1. $\dfrac{6}{17} + \dfrac{3}{17} =$

2. $\dfrac{4}{9} + \dfrac{2}{9} + \dfrac{7}{9} =$

3. $\dfrac{9}{25} + \dfrac{11}{25} =$

4. $\dfrac{11}{40} + \dfrac{3}{40} + \dfrac{19}{40} =$

5. $\dfrac{3}{8} + \dfrac{5}{8} + \dfrac{7}{8} =$

6. $\dfrac{5}{12} + \dfrac{11}{12} =$

7. Each of the objects below has been divided so that all of its parts are of equal size. Express each shaded region as a fraction and find the sum of all the shaded areas.

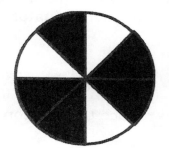  

Adding Fractions With a Common Denominator Solutions

1. $\dfrac{6}{17} + \dfrac{3}{17} = \dfrac{6+3}{17} = \dfrac{9}{17}$

2. $\dfrac{4}{9} + \dfrac{2}{9} + \dfrac{7}{9} = \dfrac{4+2+7}{9} = \dfrac{13}{9} = 1\dfrac{4}{9}$

3. $\dfrac{9}{25} + \dfrac{11}{25} = \dfrac{9+11}{25} = \dfrac{20}{25} = \dfrac{4}{5}$

4. $\dfrac{11}{40} + \dfrac{3}{40} + \dfrac{19}{40} = \dfrac{11+3+19}{40} = \dfrac{33}{40}$

5. $\dfrac{3}{8} + \dfrac{5}{8} + \dfrac{7}{8} = \dfrac{3+5+7}{8} = \dfrac{15}{8} = 1\dfrac{7}{8}$

6. $\dfrac{5}{12} + \dfrac{11}{12} = \dfrac{5+11}{12} = \dfrac{16}{12} = \dfrac{4}{3} = 1\dfrac{1}{3}$

7. In the first figure, which is a circle, five of the eight sections are shaded. The first fraction is therefore equal to $\frac{5}{8}$.

In the second figure, which is a rectangle, three of the eight sections are shaded. The third fraction is therefore equal to $\frac{3}{8}$.

Finally, in the third figure, which is a square, four of the eight sections are shaded. The third fraction is therefore equal to $\frac{4}{8}$.

$$\textbf{Sum of the shaded areas } = \frac{5}{8} + \frac{3}{8} + \frac{4}{8} =$$

$$\textbf{Sum of the shaded areas } = \frac{5+3+4}{8} = \frac{12}{8} = 1\frac{1}{2}$$

Key Point

Section 4: Subtracting Fractions with Common Denominators

As in addition, you can only subtract fractions that have the same denominator (name). If they do, then solving this problem is just a matter of subtracting the numerators and writing the difference over the common denominator.

Example: Subtract $\dfrac{13}{30}$ from $\dfrac{19}{30}$.

Solution: Subtract 13 from 19, and place the difference, 6, over the common denominator of 30.

The number 6 divides evenly into both the numerator and denominator. So, $\dfrac{6}{30}$ can be reduced to $\dfrac{1}{5}$.

Example: Of a class of 25 students, $\dfrac{2}{5}$ are out with the flu. Express, as a fraction, the number of students left in class.

Solution: 25 Total Students

Flu	Flu			

$\dfrac{2}{5}$ Have the Flu.

To answer the question, it is not important to know the total number of students. $\dfrac{2}{5}$ represents the fraction of students who have the flu. All of the students would be represented by the number 1. To find the fraction that represents the students still in

176

the classroom, we subtract $\frac{2}{5}$ from 1. How many fifths is the number 1? It's all 5 of the fifths. We can write the number 1 as $\frac{5}{5}$, and the subtraction as:

$$\frac{5}{5} - \frac{2}{5} = \frac{3}{5}$$

Subtracting Fractions With a Common Denominator Problems

1. $\dfrac{5}{9} - \dfrac{2}{9} =$
2. $\dfrac{7}{12} - \dfrac{1}{12} =$

3. $\dfrac{23}{24} - \dfrac{8}{24} =$
4. $\dfrac{9}{40} - \dfrac{5}{40} =$

5. $\dfrac{8}{11} - \dfrac{3}{11} =$
6. $\dfrac{19}{30} - \dfrac{13}{30} =$

7. **Of a class of 24 students, half are out with the flu and 6 more are at band practice. Express as a fraction the number of students left in the class.**

Subtracting Fractions With a Common Denominator Solution

1. $\dfrac{5}{9} - \dfrac{2}{9} = \dfrac{5-2}{9} = \dfrac{3}{9} = \dfrac{1}{3}$

2. $\dfrac{7}{12} - \dfrac{1}{12} = \dfrac{7-1}{12} = \dfrac{6}{12} = \dfrac{1}{2}$

3. $\dfrac{23}{24} - \dfrac{8}{24} = \dfrac{23-8}{24} = \dfrac{15}{24} = \dfrac{5}{8}$

4. $\dfrac{9}{40} - \dfrac{5}{40} = \dfrac{9-5}{40} = \dfrac{4}{40} = \dfrac{1}{10}$

5. $\dfrac{8}{11} - \dfrac{3}{11} = \dfrac{8-3}{11} = \dfrac{5}{11}$

6. $\dfrac{19}{30} - \dfrac{13}{30} = \dfrac{19-13}{30} = \dfrac{6}{30} = \dfrac{1}{5}$

7. Half of the class is out with the flu. That equals 12 of the 24 students or $\dfrac{12}{24}$.

Six students are at band practice or $\frac{6}{24}$.

The fraction of the students remaining is the difference between a full class $\frac{24}{24}$ and those absent $\frac{18}{24}$.

Fraction present $= \frac{24}{24} - \frac{18}{24} = \frac{(24-18)}{24} = \frac{6}{24}$ or $\frac{1}{4}$

Section 5: Finding and Using a Common Denominator

Key Point

If the fractions you wish to add or subtract do not have a common name (common denominator), such as $\frac{3}{7}$ and $\frac{2}{5}$, then you have to rename each one so that they do both have the same denominator.

We know that $\frac{3}{7} = \frac{6}{14} = \frac{9}{21} = \frac{12}{28} = \frac{15}{35}$

We know that $\frac{2}{5} = \frac{4}{10} = \frac{6}{15} = \frac{8}{20} = \frac{10}{25} = \frac{12}{30} = \frac{14}{35}$

We can write both fractions, $\frac{3}{7}$ and $\frac{2}{5}$, as fractions of 35. 35 is the **Common Denominator.**

Key Point

For the two fractions that we are working with, the common denominator is a number that both 7 and 5 can divide evenly into. If you cannot immediately think of such a number, the product of the 2 denominators will always work. This may not get you the smallest common denominator, but it will give you a common denominator.

In our example, the product of the two denominators is 35.

$$\frac{3}{7} \rightarrow \frac{?}{35}$$ 7 goes into 35, 5 times
5 times 3 is 15.

$$\frac{3}{7} = \frac{15}{35}$$

$$\frac{2}{5} \rightarrow \frac{?}{35}$$ 5 goes into 35, 7 times
7 times 2 is 14.

$$\frac{2}{5} = \frac{14}{35}$$

Now we can add the fractions together.

$$\frac{3}{7} + \frac{2}{5} = \frac{15}{35} + \frac{14}{35} = \frac{29}{35}$$

Example: What is the sum of $\frac{2}{3}$ and $\frac{4}{5}$?

Solution: 3 and 5 are the denominators and they have a LCM of 15:

$$\frac{2}{3} + \frac{4}{5} = \frac{10}{15} + \frac{12}{15} = \frac{22}{15} = 1\frac{7}{15}$$

$\frac{2}{3}$ was written as $\frac{10}{15}$ and $\frac{4}{5}$ was rewritten as $\frac{12}{15}$. Example:

Example: Subtract $\frac{2}{9}$ from $\frac{5}{6}$.

Solution: First we must find a common denominator – a number that both 6 and 9 divide evenly into. If we have trouble finding one, we can always use their product, 54. But this is not the smallest common denominator. The smallest number that both 6 and 9 divide evenly into is 18.

6 goes into 18, 3 times

9 goes into 18, 2 times

$\frac{5}{6} \rightarrow \frac{?}{18}$ 6 goes into 18, 3 times

3 times 5 is 15.

$\frac{5}{6} = \frac{15}{18}$

$\frac{2}{9} \rightarrow \frac{?}{18}$ 9 goes into 18, 2 times

2 times 2 is 4.

$\frac{2}{9} = \frac{4}{18}$

$\frac{5}{6} - \frac{2}{9} = \frac{15}{18} - \frac{4}{18} = \frac{11}{18}$

Finding a Common Denominator Problems

1. Change $\frac{4}{5}$ to a fraction of 20.

2. Change $\frac{7}{10}$ to a fraction of 20.

3. Change $\frac{3}{4}$ to a fraction of 12.

Finding a Common Denominator Solutions

1. $\dfrac{4}{5} = \dfrac{16}{20}$ 5 goes into 20, 4 times; 4 times 4 is 16.

$\dfrac{4}{5} \searrow\!\!\!\nearrow \dfrac{16}{20}$

2. $\dfrac{7}{10} = \dfrac{14}{20}$ 10 goes into 20, 2 times; 2 times 7 is 14.

$\dfrac{7}{10} \searrow\!\!\!\nearrow \dfrac{14}{20}$

3. $\dfrac{3}{4} = \dfrac{9}{12}$ 4 goes into 12, 3 times; 3 times 3 is 9.

$\dfrac{2}{4} \searrow\!\!\!\nearrow \dfrac{9}{12}$

Adding and Subtracting Fractions With Unlike Denominators Problems

DIRECTIONS: Solve the following problems. Answers should be in simplified form.

1. Add $\dfrac{2}{3}$ and $\dfrac{1}{4}$.

2. $\dfrac{2}{9} + \dfrac{1}{6} =$

3. $\dfrac{5}{12} + \dfrac{2}{3} + \dfrac{7}{24} =$

4. Add $\dfrac{6}{7}$ and $\dfrac{4}{21}$.

5. Add $\dfrac{4}{5}$ and $\dfrac{7}{10}$.

6. $\dfrac{5}{6} + \dfrac{3}{4} =$

7. $\dfrac{3}{4} - \dfrac{2}{3} =$

8. $\dfrac{1}{2} - \dfrac{5}{24} =$

9. $\dfrac{11}{12} - \dfrac{5}{18} =$

10. Subtract $\dfrac{2}{5}$ from $\dfrac{21}{25}$.

11. **Before the football game started, Richard and 23 of his closest friends decided to order pizza. When asked their preference, half said anything's okay, $\dfrac{1}{6}$ said anything but anchovies, and another quarter requested sausage and peppers. The remainder wanted nothing extra. What fraction of Richard's friends like plain pizza?**

12. **Colleen spends $\dfrac{1}{4}$ of her monthly take home pay on rent, $\dfrac{1}{8}$ on food and clothes, $\dfrac{3}{40}$ on heat and electricity, $\dfrac{1}{5}$ on insurance and repayment of loans, $\dfrac{1}{10}$ on transportation, and $\dfrac{1}{16}$ on phone, water, and other bills and miscellaneous household items. What fraction of her take home pay is left for entertainment and savings?**

Adding and Subtracting Fractions With Unlike Denominators Solutions

1. The common denominator is 12.

$$\dfrac{2}{3} \to \dfrac{8}{12} \qquad \dfrac{1}{4} \to \dfrac{3}{12}$$

$$\dfrac{2}{3} + \dfrac{1}{4} = \dfrac{8}{12} + \dfrac{3}{12} = \dfrac{11}{12}$$

2. The common denominator is 18.

$$\dfrac{2}{9} \to \dfrac{4}{18} \qquad \dfrac{1}{6} \to \dfrac{3}{18}$$

$$\dfrac{2}{9} + \dfrac{1}{6} = \dfrac{4}{18} + \dfrac{3}{18} = \dfrac{7}{18}$$

3. The common denominator is 24.

$$\dfrac{5}{12} \to \dfrac{10}{24} \qquad \dfrac{2}{3} \to \dfrac{16}{24}$$

$$\dfrac{5}{12} + \dfrac{2}{3} + \dfrac{7}{24} = \dfrac{10}{24} + \dfrac{16}{24} + \dfrac{7}{24} = \dfrac{33}{24} = 1\dfrac{9}{24} = 1\dfrac{3}{8}$$

4. The common denominator is 21.

$$\dfrac{6}{7} \to \dfrac{18}{21}$$

$$\dfrac{6}{7} + \dfrac{4}{21} = \dfrac{18}{21} + \dfrac{4}{21} = \dfrac{22}{21} = 1\dfrac{1}{21}$$

5.   The common denominator is 10.

$$\frac{4}{5} \rightarrow \frac{8}{10}$$

$$\frac{4}{5} + \frac{7}{10} = \frac{8}{10} + \frac{7}{10} = \frac{15}{10} = 1\frac{5}{10} = 1\frac{1}{2}$$

6.   The common denominator is 12.

$$\frac{3}{4} \rightarrow \frac{9}{12} \qquad \frac{5}{6} \rightarrow \frac{10}{12}$$

$$\frac{3}{4} + \frac{5}{6} = \frac{9}{12} + \frac{10}{12} = \frac{19}{12} = 1\frac{7}{12}$$

7.   The common denominator is 12.

$$\frac{3}{4} \rightarrow \frac{9}{12} \qquad \frac{2}{3} \rightarrow \frac{8}{12}$$

$$\frac{3}{4} - \frac{2}{3} = \frac{9}{12} - \frac{8}{12} = \frac{1}{12}$$

8.   The common denominator is 24.

$$\frac{1}{2} \rightarrow \frac{12}{24}$$

$$\frac{1}{2} - \frac{5}{24} = \frac{12}{24} - \frac{5}{24} = \frac{7}{24}$$

9.   The common denominator is 36.

$$\frac{11}{12} \rightarrow \frac{33}{36} \qquad \frac{5}{18} \rightarrow \frac{10}{36}$$

$$\frac{11}{12} - \frac{5}{18} = \frac{33}{36} - \frac{10}{36} = \frac{23}{36}$$

10.   The common denominator is 25.

$$\frac{2}{5} \rightarrow \frac{10}{25}$$

$$\frac{21}{25} - \frac{2}{5} = \frac{21}{25} - \frac{10}{25} = \frac{11}{25}$$

11.   First, we want to add the fractions $\frac{1}{2}$, $\frac{1}{6}$, and $\frac{1}{4}$ together. We could get a common denominator by multiplying 2, 4, and 6 together, but this is not the smallest common denominator. Although you could use 24 to solve the problem, 12 is the smallest common denominator.

2 goes into 12, 6 times so $\frac{1}{2} = \frac{6}{12}$

6 goes into 12, 2 times so $\dfrac{1}{6} = \dfrac{2}{12}$

4 goes into 12, 3 times so $\dfrac{1}{4} = \dfrac{3}{12}$

The sum of these three fractions is $\dfrac{11}{12}$. The fraction of friends who prefer their pizza plain is equal to:

$$\dfrac{12}{12} - \dfrac{11}{12} = \dfrac{1}{12}$$

12. First, we have to find the common denominator of 4, 5, 8, 10, 16, 40. 4, 5, 8 and 10 all divide evenly into 40. 16, however, does not. The next higher multiple of 40 is 80. We know that 4, 5, 8, and 10 will divide evenly into 80 because they divided evenly into 40. 80 is also divisible by 16, so 80 is our common denominator.

4 goes into 80, 20 times; so $\dfrac{1}{4} = \dfrac{20}{80}$

8 goes into 80, 10 times; so $\dfrac{1}{8} = \dfrac{10}{80}$

40 goes into 80, 2 times; so $\dfrac{3}{40} = \dfrac{6}{80}$

5 goes into 80, 16 times; so $\dfrac{1}{5} = \dfrac{16}{80}$

10 goes into 80, 8 times; so $\dfrac{1}{10} = \dfrac{8}{80}$

16 goes into 80, 5 times; so $\dfrac{1}{16} = \dfrac{5}{80}$

Now add the fractions together to get a total.

$$\dfrac{20}{80} + \dfrac{10}{80} + \dfrac{6}{80} + \dfrac{16}{80} + \dfrac{8}{80} + \dfrac{5}{80} =$$

The sum of these six fractions is $\dfrac{65}{80}$. The amount of income remaining for entertainment and savings is:

$$\dfrac{80}{80} - \dfrac{65}{80} = \dfrac{15}{80} \text{ or } \dfrac{3}{16}$$

Colleen has $\dfrac{3}{16}$ of her take home pay left for entertainment and savings.

Section 6: Adding and Subtracting Mixed Numbers

Key Point

When adding or subtracting mixed numbers you will perform the appropriate operation on the whole numbers separately from the fractions. Actually, it is as if you were seeking the solution to **two** problems instead of **one**. The fraction in your final answer, of course, will be simplified (reduced to lowest terms), if possible.

Let's try some examples.

Example: Add $3 \dfrac{5}{18}$ and $7 \dfrac{1}{18}$

Solution:

$3 \dfrac{5}{18}$ $3 + 7 = 10$ addition of the whole numbers

$+ 7 \dfrac{1}{18}$ $\dfrac{5}{18} + \dfrac{1}{18} = \dfrac{6}{18}$ addition of the fractions

$+ 10 \dfrac{6}{18} = 10 \dfrac{1}{3}$ combine the two and reduce the fraction to

lowest terms

Example: The difference between $9 \dfrac{3}{8}$ and $2 \dfrac{1}{4}$ is:

1) $11 \dfrac{1}{4}$

2) $5 \dfrac{1}{4}$

3) $7 \dfrac{5}{8}$

4) $7 \dfrac{1}{8}$

5) $11 \dfrac{4}{12}$

Solution: The word **difference** is your clue that this is a subtraction problem.

$$9 \frac{3}{8}$$
$$-2 \frac{1}{4}$$
$$\overline{\quad 7 \frac{1}{8}}$$

$$\frac{3}{8} - \frac{1}{4} = \frac{3}{8} - \frac{2}{8} = \frac{1}{8}$$

$$9 - 2 = 7$$

$$7 \frac{1}{8}$$

Choice "4" is the correct response.

HINT: It is helpful in a problem of this type to first determine the approximate size of the answer. You are asked to find the difference between a number larger than 9 and a number slightly larger than 2. You will get an answer slightly larger than 9 minus 2, or 7. This eliminates responses 1, 2, and 5. Careful inspection would even eliminate response 3. This can save you a great deal of time.

Key Point

> If the problem involves subtracting a larger fraction from a smaller one, you will have to "borrow" from the whole number.

Example: Subtract $5 \frac{7}{8}$ from $11 \frac{3}{8}$.

Solution: $\frac{7}{8}$ is larger than $\frac{3}{8}$. How can you solve this problem?

You will "borrow" 1 from the whole number 11, decreasing the 11 in size by 1 and leaving 10. The one you "borrowed" is added to the $\frac{3}{8}$ in the form of $\frac{8}{8}$.

$$\frac{3}{8} + \frac{8}{8} = \frac{11}{8}$$

So, you have transformed $11\frac{3}{8}$ into its equivalent form $10\frac{11}{8}$. Now you can perform the subtraction. Remember to leave your answer in simplified form.

$$11\frac{3}{8} = 10\frac{11}{8}$$
$$-5\frac{7}{8} = 5\frac{7}{8}$$

$$5\frac{4}{8} = 5\frac{1}{2}$$

Step 1: Convert the fractions so that they have a common denominator and that the number being subtracted is smaller than the number it is subtracted from. Then subtract.

$\frac{3}{8}$ is changed to $\frac{11}{8}$, $\frac{11}{8} - \frac{7}{8} = \frac{4}{8} = \frac{1}{2}$

Step 2: Subtract the whole number portion of the problem.

$$10 - 5 = 5$$

Step 3: Put the parts together.

$$5\frac{1}{2}$$

Key Point

IN REVIEW:
To perform the operation of "borrowing", remember the following rules:
I.   Decrease the whole number by one.
II.   Add the denominator to the numerator.
III. Put new numerator over the original denominator.

Example: $11\frac{3}{8} = 10\frac{3+8}{8} = 10\frac{11}{8}$

Working With Mixed Numbers Problems

Directions: Perform the appropriate operation.

1. $3\dfrac{5}{12} + 6\dfrac{2}{12}$ 2. $5\dfrac{4}{9} + 12\dfrac{2}{9}$

3. $1\dfrac{1}{7} + 4\dfrac{3}{7} + 2\dfrac{5}{7}$ 4. $20\dfrac{1}{2} - 10\dfrac{5}{16}$

5. $9\dfrac{4}{15} - 7\dfrac{7}{15}$

6.   The length of the wall in Bob's bedroom is $12\dfrac{1}{2}$ feet. Along this wall he plans to put a dresser measuring 3 feet 11 inches and a desk to hold his computer and printer. The desk measures 6 feet 5 inches. What is the maximum distance these two pieces of furniture can be apart?

Working With Mixed Numbers Solutions

1.
$$\begin{array}{r} 3\dfrac{5}{12} \\[2mm] +6\dfrac{2}{12} \\[2mm] \hline 9\dfrac{7}{12} \end{array}$$
    $3 + 6 = 9$

    $\dfrac{5}{12} + \dfrac{2}{12} = \dfrac{7}{12}$

    This fraction cannot be reduced any lower.

2.
$$\begin{array}{r} 5\dfrac{4}{9} \\[2mm] +12\dfrac{2}{9} \\[2mm] \hline 17\dfrac{6}{9} = 17\dfrac{2}{3} \end{array}$$
    $5 + 12 = 17$

    $\dfrac{4}{9} + \dfrac{2}{9} = \dfrac{6}{9}$

    This fraction can be reduced by dividing by 3.

3.
$$\begin{array}{r} 1\dfrac{1}{7} \\[2mm] 4\dfrac{3}{7} \\[2mm] +2\dfrac{5}{7} \\[2mm] \hline 7\dfrac{9}{7} = 8\dfrac{2}{7} \end{array}$$
    $1 + 4 + 2 = 7$

    $\dfrac{1}{7} + \dfrac{3}{7} + \dfrac{5}{7} = \dfrac{9}{7}$

    The improper fraction in the answer must be reduced to a mixed number.

4.

$$20 \frac{1}{2} = \quad 20 \frac{8}{16} \qquad 20 - 10 = 10$$

$$-10 \frac{5}{16} = \quad 10 \frac{5}{16} \qquad \frac{8}{16} - \frac{5}{16} = \frac{3}{16}$$

$$10 \frac{3}{16} \qquad \text{This fraction cannot be reduced.}$$

NOTE: In this problem, it was necessary to first find a common denominator (16) before you could solve the problem. Each skill you learn is used to help you perform other operations. It is important that you master each one before you go on to the next.

5.

$$9 \frac{4}{15} = \quad 8 \frac{19}{15} \qquad 8 - 7 = 1$$

$$-7 \frac{7}{15} = \quad 7 \frac{7}{15} \qquad \frac{19}{15} - \frac{7}{15} = \frac{12}{15}$$

$$1 \frac{12}{15} = 1 \frac{4}{5} \qquad \text{It is necessary to reduce this fraction to lowest terms by dividing by 3.}$$

6. This problem involves several steps.

First, we have to determine how much space the furniture will take up.

There are 12 inches in a foot, so the dresser is $3 \frac{11}{12}$ and the desk is $6 \frac{5}{12}$ feet. Adding these two figures together we get:

$$3 \frac{11}{12} \qquad\qquad 3 + 6 = 9$$

$$+ 6 \frac{5}{12} \qquad\qquad \frac{11}{12} + \frac{5}{12} = \frac{16}{12}$$

$$9 \frac{16}{12} = 10 \frac{4}{12} \qquad \text{Don't reduce this fraction yet because you will want your final answer to be in inches or feet.}$$

Now that we know the amount of space the two pieces take up, we can find the amount of space that would be left.

The maximum space between these two pieces of furniture would be the difference between $12 \frac{6}{12}$ (the length of the wall) and $10 \frac{4}{12}$ (the amount of space the two pieces would need).

$$12\ \frac{6}{12}$$

$$+\ 10\ \frac{4}{12}$$

$$2\ \frac{2}{12}$$

$12 - 10 = 2$

$$\frac{6}{12} + \frac{4}{12} = \frac{2}{12}$$

$\frac{2}{12}$ feet equals 2 inches so the final answer is 2 feet 2 inches.

Section 7: Multiplying Fractions

1	2	3	4			
5	6	7	8			
9	10	11	12			

The figure above is divided into 24 equal parts.

24   Total Squares

16   Shaded Squares

12   Numbered Squares

$\dfrac{16}{24} = \dfrac{2}{3}$ of the squares are shaded

$\dfrac{12}{16} = \dfrac{3}{4}$ of the shaded squares are numbered

$\dfrac{12}{24} = \dfrac{1}{2}$ of the squares are numbered

Two-thirds of the parts are shaded. Three-quarters of the shaded parts are numbered. Put another way, $\dfrac{3}{4}$ of the $\dfrac{2}{3}$ are numbered. In an arithmetic problem, the word "of" translates into multiplication. Three-quarters of two-thirds equals $\dfrac{3}{4}$ times $\dfrac{2}{3}$.

We can see from the figure that 12 of the 24 squares are numbered, so we know that the result of the multiplication is $\dfrac{12}{24}$ or $\dfrac{1}{2}$. But what are the rules for multiplying two or more fractions together?

Key Point

Rule 1:	You do not need a common denominator in order to multiply fractions.
Rule 2:	When multiplying two or more fractions together, first rewrite any mixed numbers as improper fractions.
Rule 3:	Multiply the numerators together and place this product over the product of the denominators.

191

So, in our example:

$$\frac{3}{4} \times \frac{2}{3} = \frac{6}{12} = \frac{1}{2}$$

Example: Multiply $\frac{3}{5}$ by $\frac{2}{7}$.

Solution: $\frac{3}{5} \times \frac{2}{7} =$

$$\frac{3 \times 2}{5 \times 7} = \frac{6}{35}$$

Example: Solve $1\frac{1}{3}$ times $\frac{4}{5}$.

Solution: $1\frac{1}{3} \times \frac{4}{5} =$

Remember to convert $1\frac{1}{3}$ to an improper fraction.

$$1\frac{1}{3} = \frac{4}{3}$$

THEREFORE: $\frac{4}{3} \times \frac{4}{5} =$

$$\frac{4 \times 4}{3 \times 5} = \frac{16}{15} = 1\frac{1}{16}$$

Key Point

A procedure called **canceling** might make the operation of multiplication easier for you. This aid is similar to simplifying fractions, except that in canceling you are looking for a number that will divide evenly into any one of the numerators and any one of the denominators. For instance, in our example where we were multiplying $\frac{3}{4}$ and $\frac{2}{3}$, we could divide the numerator of the first fraction and the denominator of the second fraction by 3. Also, the denominator of the first fraction and the numerator of the second fraction are both divisible by 2.

$$\frac{{}^{1}\cancel{3}}{2\cancel{4}} \times \frac{{}^{1}\cancel{2}}{1\cancel{3}} = \frac{1 \times 1}{2 \times 1} = \frac{1}{2}$$

Key Point

Cancelling makes the problem easier to solve. However, if you do not cancel, you will still get the correct answer.

Example: Multiply $\frac{4}{13}$ by $\frac{7}{8}$.

Solution: The number 4 divides evenly into 4 and into 8.

$$\frac{{}^{1}\cancel{4}}{13} \times \frac{7}{\cancel{8}_{2}}$$

4 goes into 4, 1 time

4 goes into 8, 2 times

The problem simplifies to:

$$\frac{1}{13} \times \frac{7}{2} = \frac{1 \times 7}{13 \times 2} = \frac{7}{26}$$

You could also solve this problem by first multiplying and then reducing the answer. However, the multiplications are larger and more time consuming. Also simplification is not as easy to see as the canceling was.

$$\frac{4}{13} \times \frac{7}{8} = \frac{4 \times 7}{13 \times 8} = \frac{28}{104} = \frac{28 \div 4}{104 \div 4} = \frac{7}{26}$$

Example: Solve $3\frac{1}{3} \times \frac{3}{20} \times \frac{2}{7}$

Solution: $3\frac{1}{3} \times \frac{3}{20} \times \frac{2}{7}$ **FIRST**, rewrite $3\frac{1}{3}$ as $\frac{10}{3}$.

$\frac{10}{3} \times \frac{3}{20} \times \frac{2}{7}$ **NEXT**, cancel where possible

10 goes into 10 and 20

3 goes into 3 and 3

2 goes into 2 and 2

$$\frac{{}^{1}\cancel{10}}{{}_{1}\cancel{3}} \times \frac{{}^{1}\cancel{3}}{{}_{1}{}_{2}\cancel{20}} \times \frac{{}^{1}\cancel{2}}{7} = \frac{1}{7}$$

Now, try some practice problems.

Multiplication of Fractions Problems

DIRECTIONS: Perform the following multiplications and leave your answer in simplified form. (Watch for the different signs that indicate multiplication.)

1. $\dfrac{6}{11} \times \dfrac{2}{3}$

2. $4\dfrac{1}{2} \times \dfrac{4}{15}$

3. $\dfrac{2}{5} \cdot \dfrac{25}{8}$

4. $\dfrac{(7)}{(9)} \dfrac{(3)}{(28)}$

5. $2\dfrac{1}{4} \times \dfrac{16}{27}$

6. $\dfrac{12}{21} \times 2\dfrac{1}{9}$

7. Before the football game started, Richard and 23 of his friends decided to order pizza. When asked their preference, half said anything is okay, $\dfrac{1}{8}$ said anything but anchovies, and another quarter requested sausage and peppers. The remainder wanted nothing extra. What fraction of Richard's friends like plain pizza? You solved this problem in an earlier section and obtained the answer of $\dfrac{1}{12}$ of Richard's friends like plain pizza. Now determine, how many people comprise $\dfrac{1}{12}$ of the group.

8. One-tenth of Cherie's monthly budget goes for miscellaneous bills other than rent, heat and electric. Her phone bill represents one-quarter of the miscellaneous bills. What fraction of her total monthly budget is her phone allowance? If her total budget is $2,000, how much is her phone allowance?

Questions 9 and 10 refer to the following information.

Anneliese has picked out the perfect color of pink to paint her bedroom. The manager of the paint store says that to make that shade he needs to mix a $1\frac{1}{2}$ gallons of white paint with 3 quarts of red paint. Anneliese only needs half this amount.

9. What fraction of a gallon of white paint should the manager use?

10. What fraction of a gallon of red paint should the manager use?

Multiplication of Fraction Solutions

1. $\dfrac{6}{11} \times \dfrac{2}{3} = \dfrac{6 \times 2}{11 \times 3} = \dfrac{12}{33} = \dfrac{4}{11}$ or $\dfrac{^2\cancel{6}}{11} \times \dfrac{2}{\cancel{3}_1} = \dfrac{4}{11}$

2. $4\dfrac{1}{2} \times \dfrac{4}{15} = \dfrac{9}{2} \times \dfrac{4}{15} = \dfrac{^3\cancel{9}}{_1\cancel{2}} \times \dfrac{^2\cancel{4}}{_5\cancel{15}} = \dfrac{3 \times 2}{1 \times 5} = \dfrac{6}{5} = 1\dfrac{1}{5}$

3. $\dfrac{2}{5} \cdot \dfrac{25}{8} = \dfrac{^1\cancel{2}}{_1\cancel{5}} \cdot \dfrac{^5\cancel{25}}{_4\cancel{8}} = \dfrac{1 \times 5}{1 \times 4} = \dfrac{5}{4} = 1\dfrac{1}{4}$

4. $\dfrac{(7)}{(9)} \dfrac{(3)}{(28)} = \dfrac{^1\cancel{7}}{_3\cancel{9}} \times \dfrac{^1\cancel{3}}{_4\cancel{28}} = \dfrac{1 \times 1}{3 \times 4} = \dfrac{1}{12}$

5. $2\dfrac{1}{4} \times \dfrac{16}{27} = \dfrac{9}{4} \times \dfrac{16}{27} = \dfrac{^1\cancel{9}}{_1\cancel{4}} \times \dfrac{^4\cancel{16}}{_3\cancel{27}} = \dfrac{1 \times 4}{1 \times 3} = \dfrac{4}{3} = 1\dfrac{1}{3}$

6. $\dfrac{12}{21} \times 2\dfrac{1}{9} = \dfrac{^4\cancel{12}}{21} \times \dfrac{19}{_3\cancel{9}} = \dfrac{76}{63} = 1\dfrac{13}{63}$

7. You have already worked the problem to the point where you know that $\dfrac{1}{12}$ of the 24 people like plain pizza.

$$\dfrac{1}{12} \text{ of } 24 = \dfrac{1}{_1\cancel{12}} \times \dfrac{^2\cancel{24}}{1} = 2$$

8. Cherie's phone allowance is $\dfrac{1}{4}$ of $\dfrac{1}{10}$.

$$\frac{1}{4} \times \frac{1}{10} = \frac{1}{40}$$

$$\frac{1}{1\cancel{40}} \times \frac{\overset{50}{\cancel{2000}}}{1} = \$50$$

9. To get the correct shade, but half the amount, they have to use half of each color. To find the amount of white paint to use, they have to take half of $1\frac{1}{2}$.

$$\frac{1}{2} \times 1\frac{1}{2} = \frac{1}{2} \times \frac{3}{2} = \frac{3}{4}$$

They will use $\frac{3}{4}$ of a gallon of white paint.

10. Since the original formula called for 3 quarts of red paint, they will use half of 3.

$$\frac{1}{2} \times 3 = \frac{3}{2} \text{ quarts}$$

There are 4 quarts in a gallon

They will use $\frac{3}{2}$ quarts x $\frac{1\,\text{gallon}}{4\,\text{quarts}} = \frac{3}{8}$ gallons of red paint.

Section 8: Division of Fractions

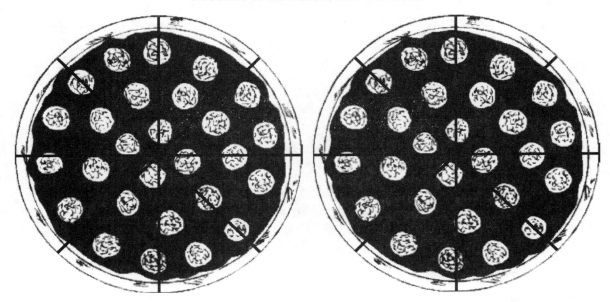

If the rule for dividing fractions is difficult for you to remember, it may be because ever since you were small, when a quantity had to be divided, it became smaller. However, if you divide a quantity by a fraction that is less than one, the result is greater than the original quantity. Think of two pizzas. Each is divided into pieces that are one-eighth the size of the original pie. You start out with two pieces (2 pizzas), and you end up with 16 individual pieces. Put another way, 2 divided by $\frac{1}{8}$ equals 16.

The rule for dividing by a fraction is to invert the fraction you are dividing by and proceed with the problem as if it were a multiplication problem.

In our example, $2 \div \frac{1}{8} = 2 \times 8 = 16$

Let's try another example.

Example: Divide $\frac{4}{7}$ by $\frac{3}{5}$.

Solution: $\frac{4}{7} \div \frac{3}{5} =$ The divisor must be inverted. $\frac{3}{5}$ is changed to $\frac{5}{3}$.

$\frac{4}{7} \cdot \frac{5}{3} =$ Then you proceed with the multiplication problem.

$\frac{(4)(5)}{(7)(3)} = \frac{20}{21}$

Notice how this problem used two different forms for multiplication, the dot and parentheses. On the test you will be expected to know the different symbols for multiplication, make sure you know them.

Try another example.

Example: Solve $\dfrac{4}{11} \div \dfrac{6}{22}$

Solution: $\dfrac{4}{11} \div \dfrac{6}{22} =$ Invert the divisor.

$\dfrac{4}{11} \cdot \dfrac{22}{6} =$ Cancel where possible. 11 divides into 11 and 22.

2 divides into 4 and 6.

$\dfrac{^2 4}{_1 11} \cdot \dfrac{^2 22}{_3 6} = \dfrac{2 \times 2}{1 \times 3} = \dfrac{4}{3} = 1\dfrac{1}{3}$

Here is a different type of division problem.

Example: Reduce $\dfrac{^7/_{12}}{^{21}/_8}$

Solution: Remember, the line that separates the numerator and denominator of a fraction stands for division. Therefore, the problem you are faced with is dividing $\dfrac{7}{12}$ by $\dfrac{21}{8}$.

$\dfrac{7}{12} \div \dfrac{21}{8} =$

$\dfrac{7}{12} \cdot \dfrac{8}{21} =$

$\dfrac{^1 7}{_3 12} \cdot \dfrac{^2 8}{_3 21} = \dfrac{1 \times 2}{3 \times 3} = \dfrac{2}{9}$

Division of Fraction Problems

1. $\dfrac{11}{12} \div \dfrac{3}{4}$

2. $\dfrac{6}{7} \div \dfrac{4}{9}$

3. $\dfrac{2}{13} \div \dfrac{8}{11}$

4. $\dfrac{15}{16} \div 4\dfrac{1}{2}$

5. The length of the wall in Bob's bedroom is $12\frac{1}{2}$ feet. Along this wall he plans to put a dresser measuring 3 feet 11 inches and a desk to hold his computer and printer. The desk measures 6 feet 5 inches. What is the maximum distance these two pieces of furniture can be apart?

6. Using the information from problem #5, how far apart (in inches) will the two pieces of furniture be if Bob wants an equal distance from the wall to the dresser, between the dresser and the desk, and between the desk and the wall?

Division of Fraction Solutions

1. $\quad \dfrac{11}{12} \div \dfrac{3}{4} = \dfrac{11}{12} \times \dfrac{4}{3} = \dfrac{11}{{}_3\cancel{12}} \times \dfrac{\overset{1}{\cancel{4}}}{3} = \dfrac{11}{9} = 1\dfrac{2}{9}$

2. $\quad \dfrac{6}{7} \div \dfrac{4}{9} = \dfrac{6}{7} \times \dfrac{9}{4} = \dfrac{\overset{3}{\cancel{6}}}{7} \times \dfrac{9}{{}_2\cancel{4}} = \dfrac{27}{14} = 1\dfrac{13}{14}$

3. $\quad \dfrac{2}{13} \div \dfrac{8}{11} = \dfrac{2}{13} \times \dfrac{11}{8} = \dfrac{\overset{1}{\cancel{2}}}{13} \times \dfrac{11}{{}_4\cancel{8}} = \dfrac{11}{52}$

4. $\quad \dfrac{15}{16} \div 4\dfrac{1}{2} = \dfrac{15}{16} \div \dfrac{9}{2} = \dfrac{15}{16} \times \dfrac{2}{9} = \dfrac{\overset{5}{\cancel{15}}}{{}_8\cancel{16}} \times \dfrac{\overset{1}{\cancel{2}}}{{}_3\cancel{9}} = \dfrac{5}{24}$

5. The dresser is 3'11" and the computer desk is 6'5". This is a total length of 9'16" or, more correctly stated, 10'4". If we subtract 10'4" from the total length of the wall (12' 6") the difference (2' 2") is the maximum distance that the two pieces of furniture can be apart.

Note: This problem was solved in the working with mixed numbers section (pg. 31) refer back if you need a more complete explanation.

6. In problem 5 we discovered that the total unused space was 2 feet 2 inches. The problem is now to divide the space into 3 equal pieces.

2 feet 2 inches = 26 inches

$26 \div 3 = 26 \times \dfrac{1}{3} = \dfrac{26}{3} = 8\dfrac{2}{3}$ inches

Section 9: Ratios

Rational numbers are those that can be exactly expressed as fractions: for instance, 0.5, 3.2 and – 0.2 are all rational since they can be expressed exactly as $\frac{1}{2}$, $\frac{32}{10}$ and $-\frac{1}{5}$. π and $\sqrt{2}$ are examples of irrational numbers. When written as decimals, the digits of irrational numbers go on forever without any pattern. One way to think about the difference between rational and irrational numbers is this: the marks on a ruler represent rational numbers, ¼, ½, ¾, etc. If you tried to measure a length that was irrational, say the diagonal of a square with a side equal to 1 unit, the length would always fall between two marks of the ruler, even if you divided the ruler into billionths, trillionths, and so on. A rational number written as a fraction is called a **ratio**.

A ratio is a comparison of two quantities and is an expression of their relative size. You can encounter ratios at a school board meeting: "There are 24 students for every one teacher"; In currency exchange: "You will get 9 German Marks for every 4 U.S. Dollars"; The breakdown of the job force: "There are 2 women for every 3 men".

A ratio can be expressed as a fraction $\frac{2}{3}$, or using a colon – 2:3. Order is important. Obviously, $\frac{2}{3}$ and $\frac{3}{2}$ are not equal. Nor is 2:3 and 3:2.

Example: 24 : 9 is equivalent to which of the following:

  1) 3:2   2) $\frac{15}{3}$ 3) $\frac{8}{3}$ 4) 12:3   5) $\frac{2}{3}$

Solution: Both 24 and 9 can be divided by 3, so the ratio can be reduced to 8:3, or $\frac{8}{3}$. "3)" is the correct answer.

Example: Nancy is 18 years older than her 8 year old daughter. What will the ratio of Nancy's age to her daughter's age be in 6 years?

Solution: Nancy is currently 26 years old. She will be 32 in 6 years. Her daughter will be 14. The ratio will be 32 : 14 or 16 : 7.

Section 10: Proportions

A proportion is a relationship that expresses two equal ratios. From our previous example, we know that:

$$\frac{24}{9} = \frac{8}{3}$$

24 and 9 are in the same ratio as 8 and 3.

In the proportion above, 24 is the first term of the proportion, 9 is the second, 8 is the third, and 3 is the fourth. The second and third terms (9 and 8) are called the means and the first and fourth terms (24 and 3) are called the extremes.

In a proportion, the product of the means is equal to the product of the extremes. An easier way to remember this is the expression "cross-multiplying".

$$\frac{24}{9} \diagdown\!\!\!\!\diagup \frac{8}{3}$$ The product of the means, 9 * 8, is equal to the product of the extremes, 24 * 3. They're both equal to 72.

Example: Find the third term of the proportion $\frac{3}{5} = \frac{?}{25}$.

Solution: 3 * 25 = 5 * ?

75 = 5 * ?

75 = 5 * **15**

$$\frac{3}{5} = \frac{15}{25}$$

Example: Find the fourth term of the proportion $\frac{5}{6} = \frac{15}{?}$

Solution: 5 * ? = 6 * 15

5 * ? = 90

5 * **18** = 90

$$\frac{5}{6} = \frac{15}{18}$$

Ratio and Proportion Problems

1. **Simplify the ratio 28 : 6**

2. **The ratio 18 : 12 is equivalent to which of the following?**

1) $\frac{6}{4}$ 2) 3 : 2 3) 2 : 1 4) $\frac{3}{4}$ e) 2 : 3

3. **Find the third term of the proportion** $\frac{3}{8} = \frac{?}{24}$.

4. **Find the fourth term of the proportion** $\frac{7}{9} = \frac{35}{?}$

5. **Find the first term of the proportion** $\frac{?}{4} = \frac{18}{24}$.

6. **Find the second term of the proportion** $\frac{11}{?} = \frac{55}{15}$.

7. **Edmund, at age 54, is 48 years older than his daughter, Katie. What is the ratio of Edmund's age to his daughter's age? What will the ratio be in 6 years?**

8. **Gail spends** $\frac{1}{4}$ **of her monthly take home pay on rent,** $\frac{1}{8}$ **on food and clothes,** $\frac{3}{40}$ **on heat and electric,** $\frac{1}{5}$ **on insurance and repayment of loans,** $\frac{1}{10}$ **on transportation, and** $\frac{1}{16}$ **on phone, water, other bills, and miscellaneous household items. What is the ratio of rent expense to heat and electric? If Gail spends $1,200 on rent, how much does she allow for heat and electric?**

9. **Daniel is allowed to watch 2 hours of television for every 3 hours he puts in studying. On the average, Daniel studies 10 hours each week. On the average, how much TV time is he allowed?**

Ratios and Proportions Solutions

1. The numbers 28 and 6 are divisible by 2.

   28 : 6 = 14 : 3.

2. Eliminate "4" and "5" because the larger number is not first. The numbers 18 and 12 are divisibly by 6.

   18 : 12 = 3 : 2. The answer is "2."

3. $\frac{3}{8} \diagup\!\!\!\!\diagdown \frac{?}{24}$ 3 x 24 = 8 x ?   72 = 8 x ?   72 = 8 x 9   ? = 9

4. $\dfrac{7}{9} = \dfrac{35}{?}$ $7 \times ? = 9 \times 35$ $7 \times ? = 315$ $7 \times 45 = 315$ $? = 45$

5. $\dfrac{?}{4} \diagup\!\!\!\!\diagdown \dfrac{18}{24}$ $? \times 24 = 4 \times 18$ $24 \times ? = 72$ $24 \times 3 = 72$ $? = 3$

6. $\dfrac{11}{?} \diagup\!\!\!\!\diagdown \dfrac{55}{15}$ $11 \times 15 = ? \times 55$ $165 = ? \times 55$ $165 = 3 \times 55$ $? = 3$

7.   **Part One:**   If Edmund is 48 years older than his daughter, his daughter is 6 years old. The correct ratio is 54:6 or 9:1.

      Part Two: In six years, Edmund will be 60 years old and his daughter will be 12. The correct ratio is 60:12 or 5:1.

8.   **Part One:**   The two fractions we are comparing are $\dfrac{1}{4}$ and $\dfrac{3}{40}$. One approach would be to write both fractions in terms of the common denominator, 40. The result is $\dfrac{10}{40}$ and $\dfrac{3}{40}$. Out of every 40 dollars spent, 10 dollars is spent on rent and 3 dollars is spent on heat and electric. The ratio is 10:3.

      Another approach is to remember that a ratio is a division. We are dividing $\dfrac{1}{4}$ by $\dfrac{3}{40}$. This is the same as multiplying $\dfrac{1}{4}$ by $\dfrac{40}{3}$.

$$\dfrac{1}{\underset{1}{\cancel{4}}} \times \dfrac{\overset{10}{\cancel{40}}}{3} = \dfrac{10}{3}$$

      Part Two: The proportion is: 10 is to 3 as 1200 is to what number? We have to solve for the fourth member of the proportion.

$$\dfrac{10}{3} \diagup\!\!\!\!\diagdown \dfrac{1200}{?}$$

      10 goes into 1200, 120 times

      120 times 3 = 360

      ? = 360

9.   The ratio of study time to TV time is 3 : 2.

      3 is to 2 as 10 is to what number?

      $\dfrac{3}{2} = \dfrac{10}{?}$ $3 \times ? = 2 \times 10$ $3 \times ? = 20$ $? = \dfrac{20}{3}$ or $6\dfrac{2}{3}$ hours.

The decimal form of a number is something that you are familiar with because you work with money on a daily basis and dollars and cents use a decimal format. We'll see that decimals are easier to work with than fractions, but it is important that you can work with both and be able to change from one format to the other.

First, let's look at some basic equivalents between decimal form and fractional form of numbers.

Decimal	Definition	Fraction
.1	1 tenth	$\dfrac{1}{10}$
.01	1 one hundredth	$\dfrac{1}{100}$
.001	1 one thousandth	$\dfrac{1}{1000}$

and so on.

Section 1: Changing From Decimal Form to Fraction Form

Changing from decimal form to fraction form is easy. Use the following steps:

Step 1: The numerator of the fraction will be the decimal number.

Step 2: The denominator will be the number one followed by a number of zeros equal to the number of decimal places in the original decimal number.

Example: Change .63 to a fraction.

Solution: Step 1: The numerator will be 63.

Step 2: There are two decimal places in the fraction .63. The denominator will be the number one with 2 zeros (100).

Therefore, $.63 = \dfrac{63}{100}$.

Example: 0.295 can be written as:

$$\frac{2}{10} + \frac{9}{100} + \frac{5}{1000}$$

Note that adding zeros to the right of both the numerator and denominator does not change the value: $.8 = \dfrac{8}{10} = \dfrac{80}{100} = \dfrac{800}{1000}$, etc.

If you are changing a decimal to a fraction, and there is a whole number to the left of the decimal, the result will be a mixed number.

Example: Write 7.91 as a fraction.

Solution: 7.91 has a whole number part (7) and a decimal part (.91). Your answer will have a whole number part and a fraction part. The decimal is written as $\frac{91}{100}$ and written to the right of the whole number.

Therefore, $7.91 = 7\frac{91}{100}$

Example: Write 38.35 as a mixed number.

Solution: $38.35 = 38\frac{35}{100}$

Example: Change .231 to a fraction.

Solution: The numerator will be 231. Since there are three places or digits to the right of the decimal, the denominator of the fraction will be the number one followed by 3 zeros.

Therefore, $.231 = \frac{231}{1000}$

Example: Change 3.926 to a fraction.

Solution: The whole number, 3, is written to the left of the fraction whose numerator is 926 and whose denominator is equal to 1, followed by 3 zeros.

Therefore, $3.926 = 3\frac{926}{1000}$

This fraction can be reduced by dividing both the numerator and denominator by 2.

$3.926 = 3\frac{926}{1000} = 3\frac{463}{500}$

Section 2: Changing From Fraction Form to Decimal Form

Key Point

> Changing from a fraction to a decimal is a matter of dividing the denominator into the numerator

Example: Change $\frac{3}{4}$ to a decimal.

Solution: $\frac{3}{4} = 3 \div 4 = .75$

Example: Which of the following is equivalent to $\frac{3}{8}$?

    1) .25   2) .5   3) .625   4) .375   5) .1667

Solution:

$$\frac{3}{8} = 8\overline{)3.000} = .375$$

$$\begin{array}{r} .375 \\ 8\overline{)3.000} \\ \underline{2\,4} \\ 60 \\ \underline{56} \\ 40 \\ \underline{40} \\ 0 \end{array}$$

The decimal equivalent of $\frac{3}{8}$ is .375. The correct answer is 4).

Converting Decimals and Fractions Problems

Directions: Change the following decimals to fractions.

    1. .369   2. 7.25

    3. .024   4. 13.8

    5. 4.76   6. .005

Directions: Change the following fractions to decimals.

    7. $\frac{7}{8}$ 8. $\frac{1}{4}$

    9. $\frac{4}{5}$ 10. $\frac{9}{2}$

    11. $\frac{19}{25}$ 12. $4\frac{7}{10}$

    13. $\frac{18}{20}$ 14. $12\frac{3}{8}$

Converting Decimals and Fractions Solutions

1. $.369 = \dfrac{369}{1000}$

2. $7.25 = \dfrac{725}{100}$ or $7\dfrac{25}{100} = 7\dfrac{1}{4}$

3. $.024 = \dfrac{24}{1000} = \dfrac{3}{125}$

4. $13.8 = \dfrac{138}{10}$ or $13\dfrac{8}{10} = 13\dfrac{4}{5}$

5. $4.76 = \dfrac{476}{100}$ or $4\dfrac{76}{100} = 4\dfrac{19}{25}$

6. $0.005 = \dfrac{5}{1000} = \dfrac{1}{200}$

7. $\dfrac{7}{8} = 8\overline{)7.000} = .875$ ($.875$)

8. $\dfrac{1}{4} = 4\overline{)1.00} = .25$ ($.25$)

9. $\dfrac{4}{5} = 5\overline{)4.0} = .8$ ($.8$)

10. $\dfrac{9}{2} = 2\overline{)9.0} = 4.5$ (4.5)

11. $\dfrac{19}{25} = 25\overline{)19.00} = .76$ ($.76$)

    A quick way to do this problem is to multiply the numerator and the denominator by 4.

    $\dfrac{19}{25} = \dfrac{19 \times 4}{25 \times 4} = \dfrac{76}{100} = .76$

    If your denominator is equal to 10, 100, 1000 etc., you only need to shift the decimal point in the numerator. Shift the decimal to the left the number of places equal to the number of zeros in the denominator.

12. $\dfrac{7}{10} = .7$; $4\dfrac{7}{10} = 4.7$

13. Reduce $\dfrac{18}{20}$ to $\dfrac{9}{10}$. Then, just move the decimal point one place to the left.

$$\dfrac{18}{20} = .9$$

14. $\dfrac{3}{8} = 8\overline{)3.000} = .375$; $12\dfrac{3}{8} = 12.375$

Section 3: Rounding Decimals

As we've already discussed, the first position to the right of the decimal is called the tenths position, the second position to the right of the decimal is called the hundredths position, and the third position to the right of the decimal is called the thousandth position. It continues from there, ten thousandth, hundred thousandth, etc.

Key Point

If we want to round a decimal number, say .375 to the nearest hundredth, we are basically asking is .375 closer to .38 or .37. In order to do this we must examine the digit to the right of the hundredth position. This would be the thousandth position. If this digit is 5 or greater, we will add 1 to the hundredth digit and drop the thousandth digit. If this digit is 4 or less, we leave the hundredth position as is and drop the thousandth digit. In our example, .375, the thousandth digit is 5 or greater, so we increase the hundredth digit by 1 to 8, and drop the 5.

.375 rounded to the nearest hundredth is **.38**

.375 rounded to the nearest tenth is **.4**

Example: Round 17.29 to the nearest whole number.

Solution: In this problem you are asked if 17.29 is closer to 17 or 18. You are rounding to the "ones" position, so we look at the digit immediately to the right. That digit is 2. Since it is 4 or less, we leave the ones digit as is and drop all the digits to the right. 17.29 rounded to the nearest whole number is 17.

Section 4: Addition and Subtraction of Decimals

Key Point

The one thing to keep in mind when adding decimal numbers is that you form a column of the decimals that you wish to add. The decimal points must line up one under the other.

Example: Add .19 + 2.6 + .384

Solution:
```
     .190
    2.600
  +  .384
    3.174
```

Example: 3.5 + 28 + .02 + 5.348

Solution:
```
    3.500
   28.000
     .020
  + 5.348
   36.868
```

Key Point

Subtraction must be handled in the same way as addition. Line up the decimal points.

Example: Subtract 4.974 from 8.26.

Solution:
```
    8.260
  - 4.974
    3.286
```

Example: 17.29 - 3.694, rounded to the nearest hundredth

1) 13.596   2) 13.71   3) 13.50   4) 13.59   5) 13.60

Solution:
```
   17.290
  - 3.694
   13.596
```

210

The correct answer is 5).

Example: $58.236 - 17.04 = 58.236$

Solution 58.236

                     $\underline{-\ 17.040}$

                        41.196

Example: If John did $\frac{1}{4}$ of a job in one day and .3 the next, how much did he complete in both days?

Solution: Either: $\frac{1}{4} + \frac{3}{10} = \frac{5}{20} + \frac{6}{20} = \frac{11}{20}$ or $.25 + .3 = .55$

Look at the answers to see which form to change to.

Example: Add $\frac{1}{3}$, .2 and .75.

Solution: Change: .2 to $\frac{2}{10}$ or $\frac{1}{5}$ and   .75 to $\frac{75}{100}$ or $\frac{3}{4}$

Add: $\frac{1}{3} + \frac{1}{5} + \frac{3}{4} = \frac{20}{60} + \frac{12}{60} + \frac{45}{60} = \frac{77}{60} = 1\frac{17}{60}$

Example: $\frac{2}{5} - .068 = .400 - .068 = .332$

Can you do this problem by changing .068 to a fraction and proving the answer is the same? You will find this is a little more difficult, but it will allow you to use either form if required.

Key Point

| NOTE: | In dealing with fractions such as $\frac{2}{3}, \frac{1}{3}, \frac{1}{9}$ etc., remember they are repeating decimal forms and it is usually best to use the fraction form in calculations and then convert the answer to decimal form if required. |

Adding and Subtracting Decimals Problems

Directions: **Combine the following decimals.**

1. $3.8 + .297 + .55 =$

2. $9.21 + 6.592 =$

3. $12.16 + 9.5 =$

4. $629.86 + 318.6 =$

5. $6.2 + 18.4 + .39 =$

6. $5.61 - 3.4 =$

7. $18.18 - 9.9 =$

8. $462.49 - 289.64 =$

9. $.751 - .026 =$

10. $9.078 - 8.64 =$

11. On May 9th, her birthday, Holly deposited $1,446.94 in her checking account. She made another deposit of the same amount at the end of the month. On the 7th of May, she wrote a check for $91.20 to cover her phone bill and another for $72.77 to cover her electric. On the 26th of the month, she wrote checks to cover her charge account (269.20), her monthly bill for car insurance ($123.50), and her next month's rent ($1,125.00). If her beginning balance on May 1st was $319.57, how much money did she have in her account on May 20th? On May 31st? Does Holly have enough money in her account to pay $668.70 for an oil delivery on May 26th?

Adding and Subtracting Decimal Solutions

1.
```
  3.800
   .297
+  .550
  4.647
```

2.
```
  9.210
+ 6.592
 15.802
```

3.
```
 12.16
+ 9.50
 21.66
```

4.
```
 629.86
+ 318.60
 948.46
```

5.
```
  6.20
 18.40
+  .39
 24.99
```

6.
```
  5.61
- 3.40
  2.21
```

7.
```
 18.18
- 9.90
  8.28
```

8.
```
 462.49
- 289.64
 172.85
```

9.
```
 .751
- .026
 .725
```

10.
```
 9.078
- 8.640
  .438
```

11. Because this is a complicated problem, you may find it helpful to first set up a schedule listing dates bills and deposits are made and include the questions you need to answer. Also, this is an excellent problem to practice using your calculator.

May 1 - $319.57 balance

May 7 - $ 91.20 paid phone

$ 72.77 paid electric

May 9 - $1,446.94 deposited in account

May 20 - How much is in the account?

May 26 - $269.20 paid charge account

$123.50 paid insurance

$1,125.00 paid rent

Does Holly have enough in his account to pay the $668.70 oil bill?

May 31 - $1,446.94 deposited in account

How much is in the account on this date?

Before Holly made the deposit, she wrote two checks:

$91.20   (Phone)

+ 72.77   (Electric)

$163.97

That reduced her account balance by $163.97. Her beginning balance was $319.57. Subtracting $163.97 from $319.57, that left her with $155.60 in her account.

$319.57

− 163.97

$155.60

Later that week she deposited $1,446.94, increasing her balance to $1,602.54.

$155.60

+1446.94

$1602.54   (May 20th balance)

After depositing her paycheck, she wrote checks totaling $1,517.70.

$269.20   (Charges)

123.50   (Insurance)

+1125.00   (Rent)

$1517.70

This reduced her account balance to $84.84.

$1602.54
-1517.70
$84.84

Therefore, she cannot pay her oil bill until the end of the month when she deposits an additional $1,446.94. Then her balance will be $1,531.78.

$84.84
$+1446.94$
$1531.78 \qquad$ (May 31st balance)

Section 5: Multiplication and Division of Decimals

Multiplication

Key Point

In multiplication, the important point to remember is the number of decimal places in your answer must be equal to the sum of the decimal places in your problem

Example: Find the product of 3.6 and 5.4

Solution: There is 1 decimal place in the first number and 1 in the second. Therefore, the product will have 2 decimal places.

$$\begin{array}{r} 3.6 \\ \times\, 5.4 \\ \hline 144 \\ \underline{1800} \\ 19.44 \end{array}$$

Example: The product of 9.1 and 7.9 is:
1) 112.69
2) 71.89
3) 73.169
4) 42.89
5) 73.64

Solution:

$$\begin{array}{r} 9.1 \\ \underline{\times\, 7.9} \\ 819 \\ \underline{6370} \\ 71.89 \end{array}$$

Key Point

Apply relative size of the numbers to the problem. This will give you the relative size of the answer. You are multiplying a number that is a little larger than 9 by a number that is a little less than 8. The answer should be about 72. That would allow you to eliminate answer choices "1" and "4". Choice "3" can also be eliminated because there will be only 2 decimal places in the answer, and choice "5" can be eliminated because the answer must end with the number 9 (9 x 1 = 9). Therefore choice "2" can be shown to be the correct answer without even multiplying the problem out. Being able to notice relative size and looking at the decimal answers can save you a large amount of time on the test.

Division

Key Point

> When dividing by a decimal, shift the decimal point as many places to the right as is necessary to make the divisor (the number you are dividing by) a whole number. You must then shift the decimal point of the dividend (the number you are dividing into) an equal number of places. The decimal point in the quotient (the answer) is placed immediately above the decimal in the dividend.
>
> NOTE: You may need to add zero after the decimal point is placed in the dividend.

Example: Divide .00105 by 3.5

Solution: $3.5\overline{)\ .00105}$

$$
\begin{array}{r}
.0003 \\
35\overline{)\ .0105} \\
\underline{105} \\
0
\end{array}
$$

Example: Divide 25 by 3.21 and round your answer to one decimal place

Solution: $3.21\overline{)\ 25}$

$$
\begin{array}{r}
7.78 \\
321\overline{)\ 2500.00} \\
\underline{2247} \\
2530 \\
\underline{2247} \\
2830 \\
2568
\end{array}
$$

To round your answer to the nearest tenth, examine the digit to it's right which is 8. It is 5 or greater, so increase 7 by 1 and drop the remaining decimals. The rounded answer is 7.8

Multiplying and Dividing Decimal Problems

Directions: **Multiply the following decimals.**

1. (3.29) (1.8)

2. 16.2 x .23

3. (12.29) (7.42)

4. .091 x 3.28

5. (110.4) (8.1)

Directions: **Divide the following decimals**

6. .0105 by 3.5

7. 17.08 by 2.8

8. 62.985 by 16.15

9. 77.361 by 21.4

10. 117 by 8.3 rounded to 2 decimal places

Multiplying and Dividing Decimal Solutions

1.
```
    3.29
  x 1.8
   2632
   3290
  5.922
```

2.
```
   16.2
  x .23
    486
   3240
  3.726
```

3.
```
   12.29
  x 7.42
    2458
   49160
  860300
 91.1918
```

4.
```
    3.28
  x .091
     328
    2952
 .29848
```

5.
```
   110.4
  x 8.1
    1104
   88320
  894.24
```

6. $3.5\overline{)}.0105$ = $35\overline{)}.105$
```
      .003
  35).105
      105
        0
```

7. $2.8\overline{)}17.08$ = $28\overline{)}170.8$
```
      6.1
  28)170.8
      186
       28
       28
        0
```

8. $16.15\overline{)}62.985$ = $1615\overline{)}6298.5$
```
          3.9
  1615)6298.5
        4545
        1453 5
        1453 5
             0
```

9. $21.4\overline{)}77.361$ = $214\overline{)}773.610$
```
          3.615
  214)773.610
       642
       1316
       128 4
         3 21
         2 14
         1070
         1070
            0
```

218

10. $8.3\overline{)117}$ = $83\overline{)1170.000}$ = 14.10 rounded to 2 decimal places.

$$
\begin{array}{r}
14.096 \\
83\overline{)1170.000} \\
\underline{83} \\
340 \\
\underline{332} \\
800 \\
747 \\
530 \\
498
\end{array}
$$

Section 1: Changing Between Decimal and Percent Form

Changing from a Decimal to a Percent

Key Point

Percent is another way that you can refer to a part of 100. 1 percent is 1 part of 100. 100 percent is 100 parts of 100, or the entire quantity. The symbol for percent is "%"

Changing from decimal form to percent form is just a matter of shifting the decimal point two places to the right and adding the percent symbol.

For example:

.25 = 25%   .325 = 32.5%

Changing from a Percent to a Decimal

Key Point

In problems where you want to find a percent of a number, you will perform a multiplication. But in order to do that, you will have to convert the percent into a decimal. You can probably see that changing from a percent to a decimal is just as easy as changing from a decimal to a percent – just reverse the procedure. In other words, shift the decimal point two places to the left and drop the percent symbol.

For example:

62% = .62   35.4% = .354   45½% = 45.5% = .455

Changing Decimals and Percents Problems

Change the following decimals to percents.

1. .67   2. .0031   3. 5.97   4. .801

5. .093

Change the following percents to decimals.

6. 50%   7. 32 1/4%   8. 6.4%   9. .098%

10. 320%

Changing Decimals and Percents Solutions

1. .67 = .67.% = 67%

2. .0031 = .00.31 = .31%

3. 5.97 = 5.97.% = 597%

4. .801 = .80.1% = 80.1%

5. .093 = .09.3% = 9.3%

6. 50% = .50. = .5

7. 32 1/4% = 32.25% = .32.25 = .3225

8. 6.4% = .06.4 = .064

9. .098% = .00.098 = .00098

10. 320% = 3.20. = 3.2

Section 2: Changing Between Fraction and Percent Form

Changing from a Fraction to a Percent

Key Point

In order to change a fraction to a percent, you must first change the fraction to decimal form. Once you've done that, you have, as mathematicians like to point out, reduced it to a previously solved problem. That being, changing a decimal to a percent.

Example: Change $\frac{5}{8}$ to a percent

Solution: $\frac{5}{8} = 8\overline{)5.000}^{.625} = 62.5\%$

Changing from a Percent to a Fraction

Key Point

The % symbol expresses a division by 100. You can drop it as long as you express that division some other way. One way to show that 100 divides a number is to write the number as the numerator of a fraction with 100 as the denominator.

Example: Write 72% as a fraction.

Solution: $72\% = \frac{72}{100} = \frac{18}{25}$

Example: Write 12.5% as a fraction.

Solution: $12.5\% = \frac{12.5}{100} = \frac{125}{1000} = \frac{1}{8}$

Example: Change $4\frac{1}{6}$% to a fraction.

Solution: $4\frac{1}{6} = \frac{25}{6}\% = \frac{25}{600} = \frac{1}{24}$

Changing Fraction and Percent Problems

Change the following fractions to percents.

1. $\frac{2}{5}$ 2. $\frac{3}{8}$ 3. $3\frac{1}{4}$ 4. $\frac{17}{20}$

5. $\frac{9}{25}$

Change the following percents to fractions.

6. 27%   7. 9.4%   8. 37 1/2%   9. 7 1/4%

10. 120%

Changing Fraction and Percent Solutions

1. $\dfrac{2}{5} = 5\overline{)2.0}^{.4}$

   .4 = .40.% = 40%

2. $\dfrac{3}{8} = 8\overline{)3.000}^{.375}$

   .375 = .37.5% = 37.5%

3. $3\dfrac{1}{4}$ = 3.25 = 3.25.% = 325%

4. $\dfrac{17}{20} = 20\overline{)17.00}^{.85}$

   .85 = .85.% = 85%

5. $\dfrac{9}{25} = \dfrac{9 \times 4}{25 \times 4} = \dfrac{36}{100}$ = .36 = .36.% = 36%

6. 27% = $\dfrac{27}{1 \times 100} = \dfrac{27}{100}$

7. 9.4% = $\dfrac{94}{10 \times 100} = \dfrac{94}{1000} = \dfrac{47}{500}$

8. $37\dfrac{1}{2}$% = $\dfrac{75}{2 \times 100} = \dfrac{75}{200} = \dfrac{3}{8}$

9. $7\dfrac{1}{4}$% = $\dfrac{29}{4 \times 100} = \dfrac{29}{400}$

10. 120% = $\dfrac{120}{1 \times 100} = \dfrac{120}{100} = \dfrac{6}{5} = 1\dfrac{1}{5}$

Section 3: Word Problems Dealing With Percent

Taking A Percent of a Number

There are basically three types of percent word problems. The first type we will discuss is taking the percent of a number. You may find it the easiest of the three types because it is one you work with the most often in everyday life.

Key Point

> The word **of** in English is translated into the arithmetic operation multiplication. The phrase "20% of 165" is translated into 20% times 165.

In order to perform the multiplication, you must first rewrite 20% as a decimal.

20% = .20

$$\begin{array}{r} 165 \\ \times\ .20 \\ \hline 33.00 \end{array}$$

First change the percent to the decimal equivalent form.

20% = .2   20% of 165 = 33

Example: Find 15% of 70

Solution: 15% = .15

$$\begin{array}{r} 70 \\ \times\ .15 \\ \hline 350 \\ 700 \\ \hline 10.5 \end{array}$$

15% of 70 = 10.5

Now, look at a very common type of situation in which you will have to use this skill – when you need to calculate sales tax on an expensive item.

Example: Bill is thinking of buying a riding mower that costs $2,250. Bill lives in New Jersey where the sales tax is 6%. What is the total cost of the mower?

Solution: The sales tax is 6% of $2,250. In arithmetic, the word "of" translates to multiplication.

$2250 * 6% = $2250 * .06 = $135.00 The sales tax is $135.00.

The total cost is $2,250 + $135.00 = $2,385.

Example: Calculate a 20% tip on a $55.00 dinner.

Solution: Again, our answer is the product of the original number, 55, and the percentage, 20%. The easiest way to do this is first to find 10% of the number and double that answer, since 20% is twice 10%. We use 10% because it is easy to calculate. Multiplying by 10% simply shifts the decimal point one place to the left of the number.

$55 \times 10\% = 5.5$

When we double this result, we get 11. 20% of $55.00 is $11.00.

Key Point

Section 4: Expressing a Number as a Percent of Another

The second type of percent word problem is one in which you need to express one number as a percent of another. For example, finding what percentage 24 is of 96. As a fraction, this would be written as $\frac{24}{96}$. The **part** is always placed in the **numerator**, and the **whole** is always in the **denominator**. To get a decimal, you would divide 96 into 24 and get .25. This result is more easily obtained if you first reduce $\frac{24}{96}$ to $\frac{1}{4}$.

Shifting the decimal point two places to the right gives the desired result of 25%.

Example: If you earn \$165 on a \$3000 savings account what percentage interest does this represent?

Solution: Restating the question yields, "What percent of 3000 is 165?"

$$\frac{\text{Part} \rightarrow \quad 165}{\text{Whole} \rightarrow 3000} = \frac{165 \div 5}{3000 \div 5} = \frac{33}{600} = \frac{11}{200}$$

$$200 \overline{)11.000} = 5.5\%$$
$$\quad\quad .055$$
$$\quad\quad \underline{10\ 00}$$
$$\quad\quad\quad 1\ 000$$
$$\quad\quad\quad \underline{1\ 000}$$
$$\quad\quad\quad\quad\quad 0$$

Example: During the 2000 – 2001 season, the nationally ranked Rutgers University women's basketball team won 23 games and lost 8. What was their winning percentage rounded to the nearest tenth of a percent?

Solution: The number of games won was 23. The total number of games played was 23 plus 8, or 31. Using your calculator to help with the division, the percentage won was:

23/31 = .7419 = 74.19%

Rounded to the nearest tenth = 74.2%

Section 5: One Number Represents a Percentage of an Unknown Number

Key Point

The third type of percentage word problem is perhaps the most confusing for people. It is the type in which you are told that one number represents a percentage of an unknown number and you are asked to find the original number.

Example: 15 is 20% of what number.

Solution: First translate the English into math.

15 = 20% times some number.

To find the unknown number we must reverse the process. You must divide the answer 15 by 20%.

$15 \div 20\% = 15 \div .20$

```
        75.
  .2.)15.0.
      14
      10
      10
       0
```

15 is 20% of 75

Example: A store is running a 35% sale on all jewelry. A pair of earrings is on sale for $55.25. What was the original price of the earrings? How much money would you save buying the item on sale?

Solution: When you know the percentage and know the "answer", you find the original number by dividing the answer by the percentage. Since there was a 35% sale, we know that $55.25 represents 65% of the original number. Use your calculator to help you with the following division:

$55.25 \div .65 = 85.$

The original price was $85.00. You would save the difference between $85.00 and $55.25, or $29.75.

Percentage Word Problems (Remember you may use your calculator)

1. Find 17% of 64.

2. Find 160% of 49.

3. Find 5% of $820.

4. Find the interest on a $480 loan if the interest charge is 10%.

5. Calculate a 20% tip on a $15.00 dinner.

6. What percent of 65 is 13?

7. What percent of 90 is 16.2?

8. If a $25.00 late penalty is charged on a $500.00 washer/dryer, what percent is the penalty?

9. A high school basketball team wins 15 games and loses 5. What is their winning percentage?

10. Six is 75% of what number?

11. Twenty-six is 40% of what number?

12. A football team that lost 4 times, lost 25% of their games. How many games did they play?

13. Bob had a 60% success rate with his indoor plants. If 24 survived, how many plants did he start with?

14. A local ski shop announces a 50% sale on all ski jackets in stock. The ad goes on to say that selected items will be marked down an additional 50% at the cash register. If you were to take advantage of the double reduction, what would the final marked down price by on an item that originally sold for $180.00? What was the total dollar discount? What was the total percent discount? What would the total cost to you be if you had to pay 5% sales tax?

15. Mary Lou opens up an IRA account so that she can save money for her retirement. Each year she puts away $2\frac{3}{4}$% of her annual income and each year her investment grows at $7\frac{1}{2}$% interest on amounts that were on deposit for a-full year. She earns $20,000 the first year and gets a 10% raise the next year. If she always make her IRA contribution at the end of the year, how much money will be in her account at the end of the second year?

Percent Word Problem Answers

1.
$$\begin{array}{r} 64 \\ \times\ .17 \\ \hline 448 \\ 650 \\ \hline 10.88 \end{array}$$

2.
$$\begin{array}{r} 49 \\ \times\ 1.60 \\ \hline 2940 \\ 4900 \\ \hline 78.40 \end{array}$$

3.
$$\begin{array}{r} 820 \\ \times\ .05 \\ \hline 41.00 \end{array}$$
or 10% of 820 = 82.0   5% = $\frac{1}{2}$ 10% = 82 ÷ 2 = 41

4.
$$\begin{array}{r} 480 \\ \times\ .10 \\ \hline 48.00 \end{array}$$
or 10% of 480 = 48.0

5.
$$\begin{array}{r} 15.00 \\ \times\ .20 \\ \hline 3.0000 \end{array}$$
or 10% of 15 = 1.5   20% = (2)10% = (1.5)(2) = 3

6. $\dfrac{13}{65} = 65\overline{)13.00} = 20\%$

$$\begin{array}{r} .20 \\ 65\overline{)13.00} \\ 13\ 0 \\ \hline 00 \end{array}$$

7. $\dfrac{16.2}{90} = 90\overline{)16.20} = 18\%$

$$\begin{array}{r} .18 \\ 90\overline{)16.20} \\ 9\ 0 \\ \hline 7\ 20 \\ 7\ 20 \\ \hline 0 \end{array}$$

8. $\dfrac{25}{500} = 500\overline{)25.00} = 5\%$

$$\begin{array}{r} .05 \\ 500\overline{)25.00} \\ 25\ 00 \\ \hline 00 \end{array}$$

9. $\dfrac{15}{15+5} = \dfrac{15}{20} = 20\overline{)15.00} = 75\%$

$$\begin{array}{r} .75 \\ 20\overline{)15.00} \\ 14\ 0 \\ \hline 1\ 00 \\ 1\ 00 \\ \hline 0 \end{array}$$

10. $\dfrac{6}{75\%} = \dfrac{6}{.75} = .75\overline{)6.00} = 75.\overline{)600}$

$$\begin{array}{r} 8 \\ 75.\overline{)600} \\ \underline{600} \\ 0 \end{array}$$

6 is 75% of 8

11. $\dfrac{26}{40\%} = \dfrac{26}{.4} = .4\overline{)26.0} = 4.\overline{)260}$

$$\begin{array}{r} 65 \\ 4.\overline{)260} \\ \underline{24} \\ 20 \\ \underline{20} \\ 0 \end{array}$$

26 is 40% of 65

12. $\dfrac{4}{25\%} = \dfrac{4}{.25} = .25\overline{)4.00} = 25.\overline{)400}$

$$\begin{array}{r} 16 \\ 25.\overline{)400} \\ \underline{25} \\ 150 \\ \underline{150} \\ 0 \end{array}$$

They played 16 games.

13. $\dfrac{24}{60\%} = \dfrac{24}{.6} = .6\overline{)24.0} = 6.\overline{)240}$

$$\begin{array}{r} 40 \\ 6.\overline{)240} \\ \underline{24} \\ 00 \end{array}$$

He started with 40 plants.

14. An item selling for $180.00 would initially be marked down to $90.00 (half or 50% of $180.00). At the register, the $90.00 would be reduced again by 50% of $45.00. The final sales price of $45.00 represents a total savings of $135.00 ($180.00 - $45.00).

The total discount was 75% $\dfrac{135}{180} = \dfrac{3}{4}$

10% of $45.00 is $4.50. 5% would be $2.25

$45.00 + $2.25 = $47.25

The total cost of the jacket with tax equals $47.25.

15. The problem as a whole may seem very involved and complicated, but if we break it into its parts, we can see that it simply involves a series of decimal multiplications and additions.

At the end of the first year, Mary Lou deposits $2\frac{3}{4}\%$ of $20,000.

$2\frac{3}{4}\% = 2.75\% = .0275$

$$\begin{array}{r} .0275 \\ \times\ 20000 \\ \hline 550.0000 \end{array}$$

With some practice, you could do this in your head. To multiply .0275 by 10,000 you would simply move the decimal 4 places to the right. The result is 275. Multiplying by 20,000 would produce a value twice as large, or 550.

So at the end of the first year the account stands at $550.00

Mary Lou's raise in the second year equals 10% of $20,000 = $2,000. Her salary, therefore, is $22,000. Her contribution at the end of the year equals $605.00.

```
      .0275
   x  22000
     550000
    5500000
    605.0000
```

Key Point

> Now do not forget that her first contribution earns interest for a full year.

Her total balance at the end of the second year is:

$550 + 7 $\frac{1}{2}$% interest on $550 + $605

The interest is:

```
    .075
   x 550
    3750
   37500
   41.250
```

The total account is:

$550.00	amount deposited 1st year
41.25	interest earned on 1st year's amount
+ 605.00	amount deposited 2nd year
$1196.25	

Section 6: Using Formulas

You will need to understand when it is appropriate to apply a specific formula, and to know how the data in a particular problem relates to the components of the formula.

The following three examples demonstrate this requirement. You may use your calculator on all problems.

Example: It's time for Bob to buy a minivan, and he has already qualified for a $15,000 loan. He finds a car he likes, but the sticker price is $23,750. However, the car company is offering a $1,500 cash rebate, and the dealer is offering a $750 customer loyalty discount. Since Bob is a loyal customer, the dealer also sent him a vehicle allowance voucher in the mail for $955 if he buys a car during their Leadership Celebration next weekend. If Bob wants to put aside $1,000 for sales tax, how much of a trade-in must the dealer offer him in order to make a deal?

- (1) $5,545
- (2) $6,545
- (3) $7,295
- (4) $7,500
- (5) $8,250

Solution: **The correct answer is (2).**

Bob qualified for a $15,000 loan, but wants keep $1000 in reserve, so he only has $14,000 to spend. Subtracting his discounts and rebates from the sticker price of the car, brings the cost down to $20,545.

$23,750.00
  $1,500.00 (rebate)
     $750.00 (loyalty discount)
-    $955.00 (voucher)
  $20,545.00

If Bob only has $14,000 to spend, the trade-in has to cover the difference between these two numbers.

$20,545.00
- $14,000.00
     $6,545.00 = trade-in value.

Example: Colleen loans $10,000 for 4 years to Michelle. Michelle agrees to pay back the loan and simple interest at an annual rate of $8\frac{3}{4}\%$. How much, in total, will she pay back at the end of the four years?

    (1) $875
    (2) $3,500
    (3) $10,875
    (4) $13,500
    (5) $15,000

Solution: **The correct answer is (4).**

Interest = Principal × Rate × Time

Interest = 10,000 × .0875 × 4

Interest = 3,500

Total payback = Principal + Interest

Total Payback = $10,000 + $3,500 = $13,500

Example: Marissa averages 50 mph on her way to work and makes the trip in 45 minutes. How many miles does she travel to work?

    (1) 12.5
    (2) 25
    (3) 37.5
    (4) 50
    (5) $66\frac{2}{3}$

Solution: **The correct answer is (3).**

Distance = Rate × Time

$45 \text{ minutes} = \frac{45}{60} = \frac{3}{4} \text{ hour}$

$\text{Distance} = 50 \times \frac{3}{4}$ or $50 \times .75$

Distance = 37.5

This is an easy solution to estimate. Half of 50 is 25 and 100% of 50 is 50.

75%, or $\frac{3}{4}$, is half way between these two numbers. You know that the answer is greater than 25, so (1) and (2) must be incorrect. You also know that the answer is less than 50, so (4) and (5) must also be incorrect. The only possible correct answer is (3).

Chapter 5: NUMBER RELATIONSHIPS AND FORMULAS

Section 1: Word Problems With Decimals and Fractions

Many of the problems do not require a formula, but you will need to know what arithmetic operation to perform (addition, subtraction, multiplication, or division) and be able to work with the fraction, decimal, and percent forms that we've already covered. On the following pages, we'll cover some examples of decimals and fractions.

 $1.09

 $.69

Example: A quart of soda normally sells for $.69. A half gallon sells for $1.09. If there are four quarts to a gallon, what is the savings if you buy a gallon of seltzer by the half gallon container instead of individual quarts?

Solution: Two half gallons would cost 2 times $1.09 or $2.18.

If you were to buy individual quarts, you would have to buy 4 to make up a gallon. 4 times $.69 = $2.76.

The savings is $2.76 - $2.18 = $.58.

$1.09 $.53

Example: Using the information from the previous problem, if the quarts are on sale this week for 53¢, what is the best buy for a gallon of seltzer?

Solution: Four quarts at 53¢ each would cost a total of $2.12.

You have already determined that two half gallons would cost $2.18.

So, this week, the quarts are the better buy. The savings would be 6 cents ($2.18 – $2.12). Sometimes the savings are not always in the larger container.

Example: It's time for Bob to buy a minivan, and he has already qualified for a $15,000 loan. He finds a car he likes, but the sticker price is $23,750. He has saved $5,000 and the sales tax will be 6%. If he can save $350 per week how long until he can buy the car.
(1) 10 weeks
(2) 11 weeks
(3) 14 weeks
(4) 15 weeks
(5) over a year

Solution: **The correct answer is (4).**

Bob qualified for a $15,000 loan and he currently has $5,000 in savings, so this means he currently had $20,000 to pay for the car. The total cost of the car is equal to the price of the car plus the tax.

$23,750 + (.06)($23,750) = $25,175

The amount Bob still needs to save is equal to the total price minus the amount he has currently saved.

$25,175 - $20,000 = $5,175

The number of weeks is equal to the amount needed to be saved divided by the amount that is saved each week. This number must then be rounded up to the nearest whole week.

$5,175 ÷ $350 = 14.78... It will take him 15 weeks.

3.7 pounds

53 oz.

$3 \frac{3}{4}$ pounds

Example: If there are 16 ounces to a pound, which is heaviest, a bag weighing 3.7 pounds, one weighing 53 ounces, or one weighing $3 \frac{3}{4}$ pounds?

Solution: Dividing 16 into 53, we convert 53 ounces into $3 \frac{5}{16}$ pounds.

Next, convert the fraction into decimal form:

53 ounces = $3 \frac{5}{16}$ pounds = 3.3125 pounds

$3 \frac{3}{4}$ pounds, written in decimal form, is 3.75

Our third weight, 3.7, is already in decimal form. Obviously, 3.75 is the largest decimal, so $3 \frac{3}{4}$ pounds is the heaviest weight.

Section 2: The Concept of "Average"

Key Point

> Most often when we use the term "average" we are referring to the **Arithmetic Mean**.
>
> To find the **Mean** of a group of numbers, you simply sum all the number values and divide by the number of items you're adding together.

Example: A 10 question quiz resulted in the following scores:

$$3, 4, 5, 5, 6, 7, 7, 7, 10$$

What is the mean test score?

Solution: There are 9 test scores, so the number of items is 9. The sum of those 9 items is 54. The mean is equal to $54 \div 9 = 6$.

Key Point

> The **Median** defines a middle point. It is the number value of one of the items we are examining. It is uniquely positioned such that there are an equal number of items whose value is less than the median as those whose value is greater than the median.

Example: Using the example above of our test scores:

$$3, 4, 5, 5, 6, 7, 7, 7, 10$$

Solution: 6 would also be the median score. There are 4 quiz scores below 6 and 4 above.

Key Point

> The **Mode** of a series of numbers is number value that occurs most frequently within the series.

Example: Using our example one more time, we see that the most common quiz score is 7. It occurs 3 times. The next most frequent value is 5. The remaining test values occur one time each. So, the most frequent value, 7, is the mode of the test scores.

Key Point

> The **range** of a set of numbers is the values between the highest and the lowest value in the set. In the above set, the range is 3 – 10.

Example: What is the median of the following 9 numbers:

2, 8, 10,10,14,15,18,19, 21

1) 10
2) 13
3) 14
4) 18
5) 21

Solution: **The correct answer is 3).**

There are 4 values less than number 14 and four numbers greater than 14, so 14 is the median.

13 is the mean. It's equal to the sum of all the numbers (117) divided by the number of items, which is 9.

10 is the mode. It is the only value that occurs twice.

Example: The difference between the mean and the mode of the numbers:

6, 10, 11, 16, 11, 19, and 11 is:

1) 0
2) 1
3) 11
4) 12
5) 16

Solution: **The correct answer is (2).**

The mean of these numbers is 12, which is equal to the sum (84) divided by the number of items (7).

The mode is the most common value which is also 11, it occurs three times. The difference between these two numbers is 1.

Zero is the difference between the median and the mode. The median is also 11. There are two items that have value less than 11 (6 and 10) and two items that have value greater than 11 (16 and 19).

Chapter 6: GEOMETRIC SHAPES AND RELATIONSHIPS

Our study of Geometry will be covered in two chapters. This chapter will concentrate on a discussion of basic shapes, relationships of sides and angles, and the formulas for perimeter and area. Chapter eight will cover coordinate geometry.

Section 1: Information About Geometric Figures

The three basic elements in geometric reasoning are points, lines, and angles. Lines are formed from numerous points and angles are formed from the intersection, or tangency, of lines. Before you begin your review of geometric formulas, it is important for you to become familiar with the various types of angles and their relationships to each other. Angles are classified according to the number of degrees they contain. Also, there are certain truths that are constant for different types of geometric figures.

Key Point

| The total number of degrees in a circle is 360°. |

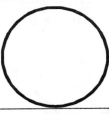

Key Point

| Angles are measured in degrees and can be classified according to the number of degrees in them. |

An angle whose measure is between 0° and 90° is an **ACUTE** angle.

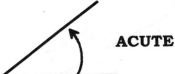

ACUTE

An angle whose measure is 90° is called a **RIGHT** angle. The symbol to indicate a right angle is ⌐,

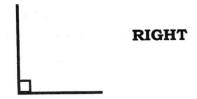

RIGHT

Angle whose measure is between 90° and 180° is an **OBTUSE** angle.

OBTUSE

Angle whose measure is 180° is a **STRAIGHT** angle.

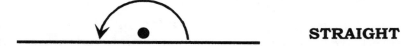

STRAIGHT

Key Point

Two angles whose sum is 180° are **supplementary**.

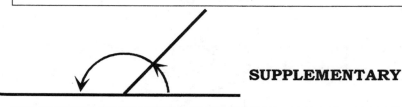

SUPPLEMENTARY

Key Point

Two angles whose sum is 90° are **complementary**.

COMPLEMENTARY

If two straight lines intersect, then four angles are formed.

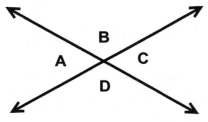

The angles A and C are equal, as are the angles B and D. These pairs of equal angles are called **vertical angles**. There are also four pairs of supplementary angles (angles that add up to 180°): A and B, B and C, C and D, and D and A.

If two parallel lines are intersected by a third line (a *transversal*), then the diagram will look something like this:

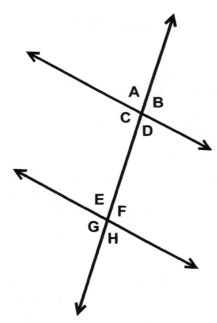

Because of the parallel lines, angles A, E, and H are all equal to each other and angles B, F, and G are all equal to each other. Angle A is supplementary with angle F and with angle G; angle B is supplementary with angle E and with angle H, etc. Some terminology: angles A and H are called **alternate exterior angles**, angles C and F are called **alternate interior angles**, angles A and E are called **corresponding angles** and angles C and E are called **consecutive angles**.

Let's try some questions. You will be able to answer these questions from the information you have just learned.

Item 1 is based on the following diagram.

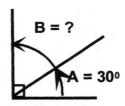

1.   **If angle A is 30°, what is the size of angle B?**

        (1)   40°
        (2)   75°
        (3)   60°
        (4)   150°

Solution: Because you can see from the diagram that the 2 angles form a right angle and you know that the number of degrees in a right angle is 90°, you can easily pick the correct answer, 60° or number (3). Also, the two angles are complementary, equal 90°. 30 + 60 = 90

Item 2 is based on the following diagram.

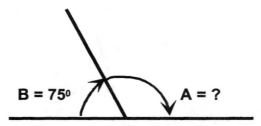

B = 75⁰   A = ?

2.   **If angle B is 75°, what is the size of angle A?**

    (1)   50°
    (2)   130°
    (3)   75°
    (4)   105°

Solution: Because you know from the diagram that the 2 angles form a straight angle or are supplementary angles, you would easily pick answer number (4). There are 180° in a straight angle,

75 + 105 = 180.

Let's continue our review.

Key Point

The total number of degrees in the angles of a triangle is 180°.

How might this help you answer a question? Let's take a look.

3.   **In a given triangle, $\angle A = 90°$, $\angle B = 45°$. What is the measure of $\angle C$?**

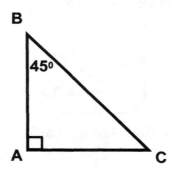

    (1)   90°
    (2)   45°
    (3)   180°
    (4)   75°

Solution: Because you know that the sum of the angles in a triangle is 180°, you know immediately that the correct answer is 45° or number (2).

242

Key Point

The total number of degrees in a four-sided figure (square, parallelogram, trapezoid rectangle) is 360°

Item 4 is based on the following diagram.

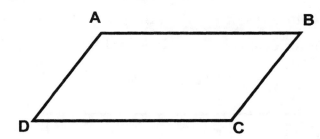

4.   If ∠A = 120°, ∠B = 60°, and ∠C = 120°, how many degrees are in ∠D?

       (1)   60°
       (2)   45°
       (3)   120°
       (4)   75°
       (5)   80°

Solution: The correct answer is number (1). The total number of degrees in the angles of a parallelogram is 360°. 120 + 60 + 120 = 300.

360 - 300 = 60.

Section 2: The Rectangle

WORDS TO KNOW IN THIS SECTION

PERIMETER: the sum of the length of the sides of a figure

AREA: size measurement enclosed by a 2 dimensional figure

The rectangle is a four-sided figure, all angles are right angles and opposite sides are equal.

The first formula we will use is one for finding the **PERIMETER** of a rectangle.

Key Point

> Perimeter of a rectangle is equal to twice the length, plus twice the width.
>
> P = 2L + 2W

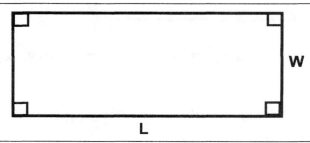

W

L

Key Point

> Length and width could also be referred to as base and height.
>
> P = 2b + 2h

Example: Find the perimeter of a rectangle whose length is 10 inches and width is 4 inches.

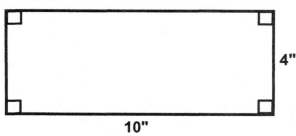

4"

10"

Solution: P = 2l + 2w

P = 2(10") + 2(4")

P = 20" + 8"

P = 28 inches

244

Example: Find the perimeter of a rectangle whose length is 3 inches and width is 8 inches.

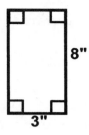

8"

3"

Solution: P = 21 + 2w

P = 2(3") + 2(8")

P = 6" + 16"

P = 22 inches

Example: Find the perimeter of a rectangle whose length is 9" and whose width is 3".

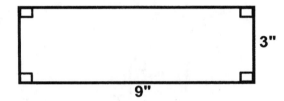

3"

9"

1) 12"
2) 27"
3) 6"
4) 2'

Solution: P = 2(1) + 2(w)

P = 2(9") + 2(3")

P = 18" + 6"

P = 24"

There are 12" in a foot, so 24 inches equals 2 feet. The correct answer is (4), 2'.

Key Point

The second formula we need to discuss is one for finding the **AREA** of a rectangle. The area of a rectangle is equal to length times width. It is written as:

A = 1 x w

This could also be written as A = b x w. b represents base and w represents width.

Key Point

The unit of measure for area is **square** units.

Example: Find the area of rectangles used in the previous examples.

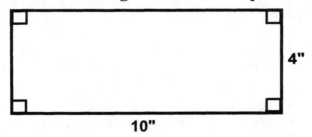

Solution: A = l x w
A = 10" x 4"
A = 40 sq. in.

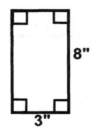

Solution: A = l x w
A = 3" x 8"
A = 24 sq. in.

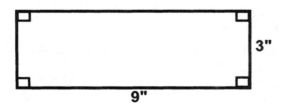

Solution: A = l x w
A = 9" x 3"
A = 27 sq. in.

Section 3: The Square

The square is a rectangle with four equal sides.

Key Point

The **PERIMETER** of a square is equal to 4 times the side.

P = 4s

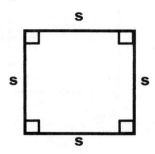

Let us look at the following examples.

Example: Find the perimeter of a square whose side is 6'

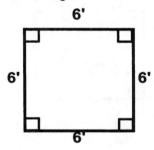

Solution: P = 4s
             P = 4(6')
             P = 24 ft.

Example: Find the perimeter of a square whose side is 1 foot.

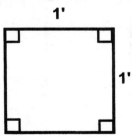

Solution: P = 4s
             P = 4(1")
             P = 4 ft.

Key Point

The **AREA** of a square is equal to side times side, or side squared. The formula is written as:

A = s x s or A = s²

Applying the formula for the area of a square on the squares in previous examples, we get the following:

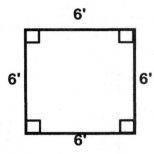

A = s x s
A = 6' x 6'
A = 36 sq. ft.

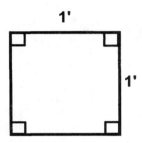

A = s x s
A = 1' x 1'
A = 1 sq. ft.

Here is another example.

Example: Find the number of square inches in a square foot.

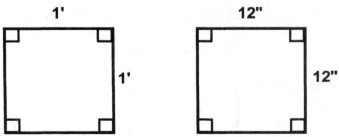

Solution: A = s x s
A = (12")(12")
A = 144 sq. in.

There are 144 square inches in one square foot.

Section 4: The Triangle

A triangle is a three-sided figure.

A triangle also has three angles. The two most important properties of all triangles regardless of type are:

Key Point

> The three angles *must* add up to 180^0.
>
> Each side must be greater that the difference in length of the other two sides and less than the sum of the length of the other two sides. (For instance, if two sides of a triangle are of lengths 3 and 5, the third side must be between 2 and 8.)

To begin the review, let's look at the different types of triangles.

Triangles can be placed into categories according to the type of angles they have.

ACUTE - has three acute angles

RIGHT - has one right angle

OBTUSE - has one obtuse angle

EQUIANGULAR - has three angles of equal measure

Triangles may also be categorized by length of their sides

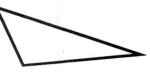

SCALENE - has no sides the same length

ISOCELES - has 2-sides the same length

EQUILATERAL - all sides are the same length

The diagram below refers to question 1.

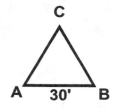

1. **If Triangle ABC is an equilateral triangle and side AB is 30 feet, what is the length of side AC?**

    (1) 45 ft.
    (2) 60 ft.
    (3) 30 ft.
    (4) 50 ft.

Solution: Because you know that all sides in an equilateral triangle are equal, you can quickly see the correct answer is, number (3), 30 ft.

Let's continue our review of the formulas used to find area and perimeter.

Key Point

The **PERIMETER** of a triangle is equal to the sum of the sides. $P = a + b + c$

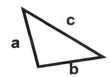

250

Example: Find the perimeter of a triangle whose sides are 3', 4' and 5'.

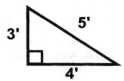

Solution: P = a + b + c
            P = 4' + 3' + 5'
            P = 12'

Example: Find the perimeter of this triangle.

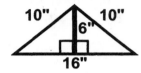

Solution: P = a + b + c
            P = 16" + 10" + 10"
            P = 36"

Key Point

> The AREA of a triangle is equal to $\frac{1}{2}$ the base times the height. It is written as:
>
> $A = \frac{1}{2} b \times h$

The height of the triangle will be the side of the figure only if the side forms a right angle (90°) with the base. A right angle is indicated as ⌐ in a drawing.

Example: Find the area of this triangle.

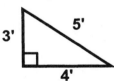

Solution: $A = \frac{1}{2} b \times h$

            $A = (\frac{1}{2})(4')(3')$

            $A = (2')(3')$
            $A = 6$ sq. ft.

Example: Find the area of this triangle.

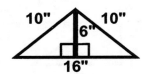

Solution: A = $\frac{1}{2}$ b x h

A = ($\frac{1}{2}$)(16")(6")

A = (8")(6")

A = 48 sq. in.

Section 5: The Pythagorean Theorem

Key Point

One of the formulas you'll be given is the Pythagorean Theorem, but before we discuss this formula, we must first introduce the arithmetic operation of taking a square root. The square root of a number is a number that when multiplied by itself will give us the original number.

Square Root is denoted by the symbol $\sqrt{}$.

$$\sqrt{9} = 3 \qquad\qquad \sqrt{81} = 9$$

Key Point

The Pythagorean Theorem states that if we square the length of both sides of a right triangle, and then take the square root of their sum, the result will be the length of the hypotenuse

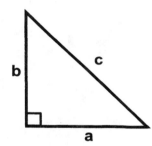

In the figure at the left, **a** and **b** are the sides of a right triangle. **c** is the hypotenuse. The relationship expressed in the Pythagorean Theorem can be expressed by the formula:

$c^2 = a^2 + b^2$, or

$$c = \sqrt{a^2 + b^2}$$

Example: Find the length of the hypotenuse of a right triangle whose sides are 3 feet and 4 feet.

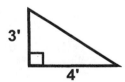

Solution: a = 3 and b = 4

$C^2 = a^2 + b^2 = 3^2 + 4^2$

$C = \sqrt{3^2 + 4^2} = \sqrt{9 + 16} = \sqrt{25} = 5$ feet

Example: Find the length of the second leg of a right triangle whose side is 5 inches and hypotenuse is 13 inches.

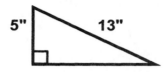

Solution: $a = 5$ and $c = 13$
$13^2 = 5^2 + b^2$
$169 = 25 + b^2$
$144 = b^2$
$\sqrt{144} = \sqrt{b^2} = b$
$12 = b$

Key Point

Sometimes the lengths of all three sides of a right triangle are integers, such as in the above examples. If we multiply all the sides of a 3-4-5 right triangle by 2, we get a 6-8-10 right triangle. 3-4-5 and 6-8-10 right triangles are similar to each other. Not all right triangles have integer sides.

Example: Find the length of the hypotenuse of a right triangle whose sides are 5 inches and 9 inches.

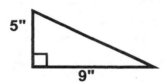

Solution: $a = 5$ and $b = 9$
$c^2 = 5^2 + 9^2$
$c = \sqrt{5^2 + 9^2} = \sqrt{25 + 81} = \sqrt{106} \cong 10.2956$ inches

Section 6: Similar Triangles

Two Triangles are similar if their corresponding angles are equal and their corresponding sides are proportional.

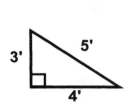

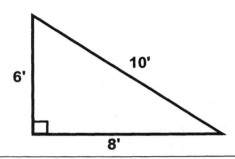

If we can show that the corresponding angles (angles that are in the same position in each triangle) of one triangle are equal to the corresponding angles of a second triangle, the triangles are similar and the corresponding sides (sides that are in the same position in each triangle) will be proportional. In the example below, we have 2 right angles. The 2 angles formed by intersecting lines are equal. That means the third angles of the triangles are equal. The corresponding sides are the ones opposite the equal angles.

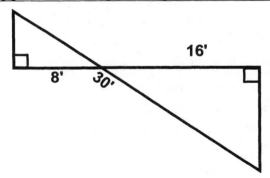

Example: If the horizontal line is cut into 8 foot and 16 foot segments by the 30 foot diagonal, what is the length of the hypotenuse of the smaller triangle?

Solution:

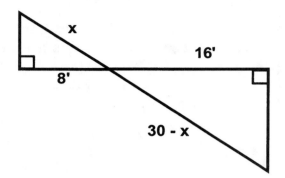

$$\frac{8}{x} = \frac{16}{30 - x}$$

16x = 240 − 8x
24x = 240
x = 10

Example: If ∠a = 70°, and ∠c is a right angle, what is the measurement of ∠e?

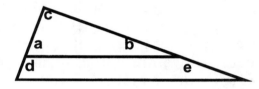

Solution: The triangle with angles c, a, and b, is similar to the triangle with angles c, d, and e.

∠a = ∠d and ∠b = ∠e .

Since we know that there are 180° in a triangle, and the sum of ∠a and ∠c = 160°, then ∠b = 20°.

Since ∠b = ∠e, then ∠e also = 20°.

Section 7: The Parallelogram

Key Point

A parallelogram is a four-sided figure with opposite sides parallel (the sides, if extended, would never intersect) and equal. The **PERIMETER** of a parallelogram is equal to 2 times the base, plus 2 times the side. It is written as:

P = 2b + 2c

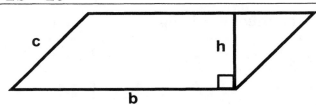

Let us apply this formula to the following examples.

Example: Find the perimeter of a parallelogram whose parallel sides are 10' and 5'.

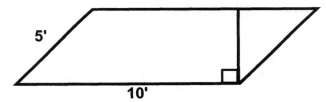

Solution: P = 2b + 2c
P = 2(10') + 2(5')
P = 20' + 10'
P = 30'

Example: Find the perimeter of the parallelogram in the figure below.

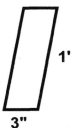

Solution: P = 2b + 2c
P = 2(3") + 2(1')
P = 2(3") + 2(12")
P = 6" + 24"
P = 30"

You must work in a common unit, which is why we change from 1' to 12" in the third step.

Key Point

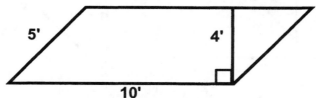

The **AREA** of a parallelogram is equal to base times height. The formula differs from that of the rectangle only in that the height of the parallelogram is not necessarily the side of the figure.

A = b x h

Example: Find the area of this figure if the height is equal to 4'.

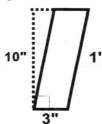

Solution: A = b x h
A =(10')(4')
A = 40 sq. ft.

Example: Find the area of the figure below if the height is 10 inches.

Solution: A = b x h
A = (3")(10")
A = 30 sq. in.

Perimeter and Area of Squares, Rectangles, Triangle, and Parallelogram Problems

The following 3 examples refer to the four figures below. Figure (A) is a rectangle, figure (B) is a square, figure (C) is a parallelogram, and figure (D) is a right triangle. The solutions and explanations follow on the next page.

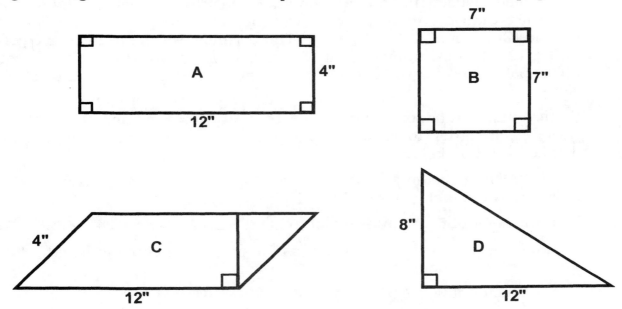

1. **In which two figures are the perimeters equal?**

   (1) (A) and (C)
   (2) (A) and (D)
   (3) (B) and (C)
   (4) There are no 2 perimeters that are equal

2. **In which two figures are the areas equal?**

   (1) (A) and (C)
   (2) (A) and (D)
   (3) (B) and (C)
   (4) There are no 2 areas that are equal

3. **Which figure has both the largest perimeter and largest area?**

   (1) (A)
   (2) (B)
   (3) (C)
   (4) No figure has both the largest perimeter and largest area..

Perimeter and Area of Squares, Rectangles, Triangle, and Parallelogram Solutions

1.   1)   By simple inspection, this is obvious. Perimeter is equal to the sum of the sides, and (A) and (C) are both 4-sided figures with sides of equal length.

With some inspection, you can conclude that the perimeter of figure (D) is greater than the rectangle or parallelogram. The perimeter of figures (A) and (C) is equal to 8 + 12 + 12. The perimeter of the triangle is equal to 8 + 12 + a third number that we know to be greater than 12 because the hypotenuse of a right triangle is greater in length than either of its sides.

From a time standpoint this is the best way to approach to problem. However, in order to reinforce the use of formulas, we'll work out a detailed solution below.

Figure (A) is a rectangle. The opposite sides are equal in length. So, there are two 4 inch sides and two 12 inch sides.

The perimeter of figure (A) is equal to 2(4″) + 2(12″) = 8″ + 24″ = 32″

Figure (B) is a square. All four sides of a square are equal in length. So, there are four 7 inch sides.

The perimeter of figure (B) is equal to 4(7″) = 28″

Figure (C) is a parallelogram. The opposite sides are equal in length. So, there are two 4 inch sides and two 12 inch sides.

The perimeter of figure (C) is equal to 2(4″) + 2(12″) = 8″ + 24″ = 32″

Figure (D) is a right triangle. To find the length of the hypotenuse, use the Pythagorean Theorem.

The length of the third side equals

$$\sqrt{(8)^2 + (12)^2} = \sqrt{64 + 144} = \sqrt{208} = 14.42$$

The perimeter of figure (D) is approximately equal to

8″ + 12″ + 14.42″ = 34.42″

The correct answer is (1).

2.   2)   By inspection, we see we have a rectangle that has a height of 4″ and a base of 12″. We also have a triangle with a twice the height (8″) and the same base measurement (12″). Since the area of a rectangle is **l x h** and the area of a triangle is $\frac{1}{2}$**l x h**, we see that the rectangle (figure A) and the triangle (figure D) have the same area.

As with the previous problem, this time-saving method is the best way to approach to problem. However, we will again provide a detailed solution to reinforce the use of formulas.

Figure (A) is a rectangle. Its vertical side (4″) is its height and its horizontal side (12″) is its length.

The area of figure (A) = **l x h,** or, 4″ x 12″ = 48 sq. in.

Figure (B) is a square. All four sides of a square are equal in length. So, the height and the length are both 7″.

The area figure (B) is equal to 7″ x 7″ = 49 sq. in.

Figure (C) is a parallelogram. We don't know the height of the figure, but the perpendicular distance between the two 12″ sides must be less than slanted side (4″). So, we know that the area of figure (C) must be less than the area of figure (A).

Figure (D) is a right triangle, so its height is equal to the length of its perpendicular side (8″). The length of the triangle is 12″.

The area of figure (D) = $\frac{1}{2}$**l x h** or, $\frac{1}{2}$ x 8″ x 12″ = 48 sq. in.

The correct answer is (2).

3.   4)   We know from the previous two solutions that the square is larger in area (49 sq. ″) than either the rectangle or triangle (48 sq. ″), but it's smaller in perimeter (28″) than the rectangle (32″). Therefore none of the figures has both the largest area and perimeter.

The correct answer is (4).

Key Point

The last four-sided figure we will look at is the trapezoid. A trapezoid is a four-sided figure having only two sides parallel. The parallel sides are called the **bases**. They are labeled **b** and **b'**. The **PERIMETER** of the trapezoid is equal to the sum of the four sides.

P = a + b + c + b'

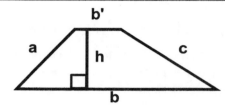

Let us apply this formula to the following problems.

Example: Find the perimeter of a trapezoid whose bases are 9" and 3" and whose sides are 4" and 5".

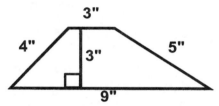

Solution: P = a + b + c + b'
P = 4" + 3" + 5" + 9"
P = 21"

Example: Find the perimeter of the trapezoid below.

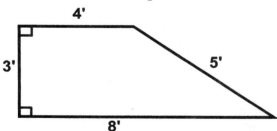

Solution: P = a + b + c + b'
P = 3' + 4' + 5' + 8'
P = 20'

Key Point

The **AREA** of a trapezoid is equal to the **average** of the bases times the height.

$$A = \frac{b + b'}{2} \cdot h$$

Example: Find the area of the trapezoid in figure below.

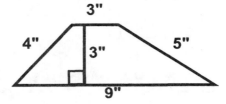

Solution:
$$A = \frac{b + b'}{2} \cdot h$$
$$A = \frac{3" + 9"}{2} \cdot 3"$$
$$A = \frac{12"}{2} \cdot 3"$$
$$A = 6" \cdot 3"$$
$$A = 18 \text{ sq. in.}$$

Example: Find the area of the trapezoid in the figure below.

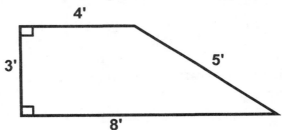

Solution:
$$A = \frac{b + b'}{2} \cdot h$$
$$A = \frac{4' + 8'}{2} \cdot 3$$
$$A = \frac{12'}{2} \cdot 3'$$
$$A = 6' \cdot 3'$$
$$A = 18 \text{ sq. ft.}$$

Section 9: Perimeter and Area Review

Let us review the figures we have studied so far by placing them next to each other. The appropriate formulas are under each diagram.

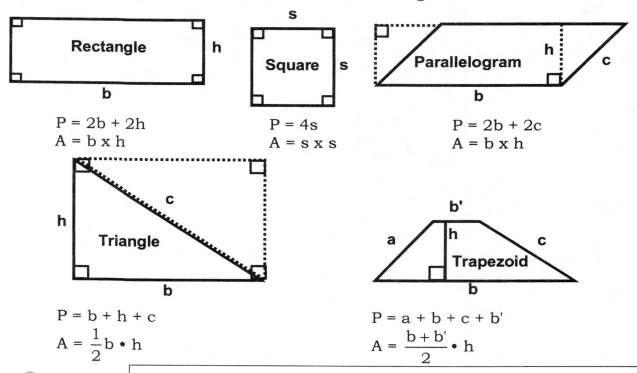

Rectangle

P = 2b + 2h
A = b x h

Square

P = 4s
A = s x s

Parallelogram

P = 2b + 2c
A = b x h

Triangle

P = b + h + c
$A = \frac{1}{2}b \cdot h$

Trapezoid

P = a + b + c + b'
$A = \frac{b + b'}{2} \cdot h$

Key Point

The dotted lines are used to show you that it is logical that the area of a parallelogram is the same as a rectangle and that the area of a triangle is half that of a rectangle. Notice that all area formulas involve a product of base times height, with the trapezoid using an average of its two bases.

Section 10: The Circle

A circle is a collection of points equidistant from a given point called the center. Because of its shape, the terms and formulas used are different from the figures we have already covered. It is important that you know what the terms mean before you try to work any problems dealing with circles.

Let's take a look at them.

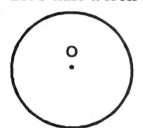

In this figure, the point O is the center of the circle. A circle is named by the point in the center. In this case we would say circle O.

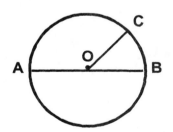

A **chord** of the circle is a line segment joining two points on the circle. A chord that passes through the center of the circle is called a **diameter**. Chord AB is a diameter.

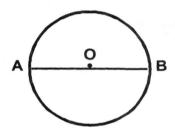

A line segment that joins the center with any point of the circle is called a **radius**. OA, OB and OC are all radii of the circle.

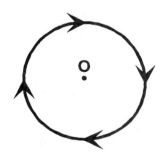

The **circumference** of a circle is equivalent to the perimeter of a rectangle. It is the distance around a circle.

A constant used in the formula for finding the circumference of a circle is written like this Π. It is equal to 3.14 or $\frac{22}{7}$. You can use either form, decimal or fraction. Use the one that matches the other numbers you are using in the problem.

The formula for finding the **circumference** of a circle is:

C = 2Πr

The formula for finding the **area** of a circle is Π times the radius squared (r x r).

A= Πr²

Example: Find the circumference and area of the circle below.

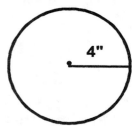

4"

Solution:

C =	2Πr	A =	Πr²
C =	2Π(4")	A =	Π(4")(4")
C =	2 (4") Π	A =	(4")(4")(Π)
C =	8Π" *** See Note**	A =	16Π sq. in. *** See Note**

$$C = 8(\frac{22}{7})"$$ A = 16(3.14) sq. in.

$$C = \frac{176}{7} \text{ inches}$$ A = 50.24 sq. in.

$$C = 25 \frac{1}{7} \text{ inches}$$

*NOTE: On the examination, check the form of the multiple-choice answers. You may not have to take your answer beyond this point.

Example: Find the area of the shaded region below.

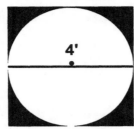

Solution:

NOTE: If the diameter is 4', then the radius is half as large or 2'.
Area of the square = s x s

$$A = 4' \times 4'$$

$$A = 16 \text{ sq. ft.}$$

Area of the circle = Πr^2

$$A = \Pi(2')(2')$$

$$A = 4\Pi \text{ sq. ft.}$$

Area of shaded region = Area of square - area of circle

Area of shaded region = $(16 - 4\Pi)$ sq. ft.

Numerical Relationships and Geometric Formulas Problems

1.   If 6" square tile costs 45 cents each, how much is this by the square foot?

2.   If Jennifer drinks 6 eight-ounce glasses of water each day, how many gallons of water would she drink in a week?

3.   Twice a year, Neil donates a pint of blood at his company's blood drive. He will get a certificate from the blood bank when he donates a total of one gallon. How long will this take?

Find the perimeter and area of the following figures:

4.

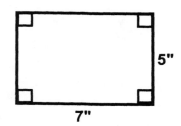

RECTANGLE

5.

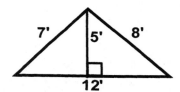

SQUARE

6.

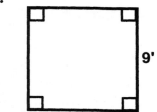

TRIANGLE

7.

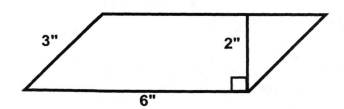

PARALLELOGRAM

8.

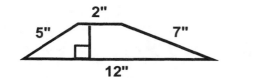

Find the perimeter   Find the area

TRAPEZOID

9.

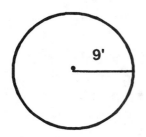

CIRCLE

10. If there are 43,560 square feet in an acre, which lot is larger, one that is a quarter acre or one that measures 100 feet along the front and is 120 feet deep?

Numerical Relationships and Geometric Formulas Solutions

1. If the tile is 6 inches on a side, it would take 4 tiles to cover an area 12 inches by 12 inches. Therefore, 1 square foot would cost 4 times .45 or $1.80.

2. There are 16 oz. in a pint, so six 8 oz. glasses would equal 3 pints a day. Over a week, this would equal 7 times 3 or 21 pints. If there are 2 pints to a quart and 4 quarts to a gallon, then there are 8 pints in a gallon. By dividing 8 into 21, we see that 21 pints is $2 \frac{5}{8}$ gallons.

3. As we saw in the previous problem, there are 8 pints in a gallon. Neil starts by donating one pint, so has 7 more to donate. If he donates twice a year, it will take him $3 \frac{1}{2}$ more years to donate a total of one gallon.

4. P = 2(7") + 2(5") = 14" + 10" = 24"

   A = (7")(5") = 35 sq. in.

5. P = 4(9') = 36'

   A = (9')(9') = 81 sq. ft.

6. P = 12' + 8' + 7' = 27'

$$A = \frac{1}{2}(12')(5') = (6')(5') = 30 \text{ sq. ft.}$$

7. $P = 2(6'') + 2(3'') = 12'' + 6'' = 18''$

   $A = (6'')(2'') = 12 \text{ sq. in.}$

8. $P = 5'' + 2'' + 7'' + 12'' = 26''$

   $A = \dfrac{2'' + 12''}{2} \cdot 3'' = 7'' \cdot 3'' = 21 \text{ sq. in.}$

9. $C = 2\Pi r = 2\Pi (9') = 18\Pi'$

   $A = \Pi r^2 = \Pi(9')(9') = 81\Pi \text{ sq. ft.}$

10. First, we have to find the size of the second lot. The area is 100' times 120' or 12,000 square feet. The easiest way to compare the two lots, is to multiply both by 4. In the first case, we will get one acre. In the second, we will get 48,000 square feet, which is more than an acre. The second lot, therefore, is the larger one.

Key Point

> **VOLUME** is the size enclosed by a 3-dimensional figure.

We will now take a look at the formulas used to find the volume of a few geometric figures. The first is the rectangular solid.

RECTANGULAR SOLID

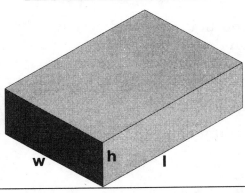

Key Point

> The volume of a rectangular solid is equal to length times width, times height. The formula is written as:
>
> V = 1 x w x h
>
> The unit of measure for volume is cubic units.

Example: Find the volume of the figure below.

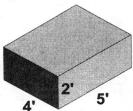

Solution: V = 1 x w x h

V = 5' x 4' x 2'

V = 40 cubic feet

Cube

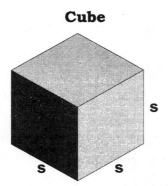

Key Point

The second figure we will consider is the cube. It is the three dimensional counterpart to the square. The volume of a cube is equal to side times side times side or side-cubed. The formula is written as:

$$V = s \times s \times s \text{ OR } V = s^3$$

Example: What is the volume of the cube below?

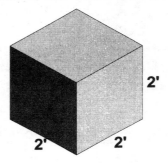

Solution: $V = s \times s \times s$ or s^3

$V = 2' \times 2' \times 2'$

$V = 8$ cu. Ft.

CYLINDER

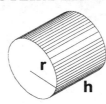

Key Point

The last geometric solid we will discuss is the cylinder. The volume of a cylinder is equal to Π times radius-squared times height. An easy way to remember this is that the volume is equal to the area of the circular top times the height. The formula is written as:

$$V = \Pi r^2 h$$

Example: Find the volume of the figure below.

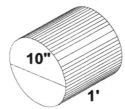

10"

1'

Solution: In order to find the volume of the cylinder, you must first find the radius. Second, change the height to inches. If the diameter is 10", then the radius is 5". The height is 1' or 12", so:

V = Πr²h

V = Π(5")(5")(12")

V = 300Π cubic inches.

Volume Problems

DIRECTIONS: Find the volume of the following figures.

1.   **A cube with a side equal to 9 inches.**

2.   **A cylinder whose radius is one foot and whose height is 6 inches.**

3.   **A rectangular solid whose length is 7 ft., width is 8 ft. and height is 6 ft.**

4.   **A cube with a side of $\frac{1}{2}$ a foot.**

5.   **A cylinder, given the area of its top as 16 Π sq. inches and its height is 9 inches.**

Volume Solutions

1.   V = 9" x 9" x 9"

V = 729 cu. in

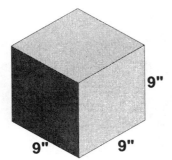

9"

9"   9"

2 . $V = \Pi (12") (12") (6")$ 864Π cu. in.

or $V = \Pi(1')(1')(\frac{1'}{2}) = \frac{1}{2}\Pi$ cu. ft.

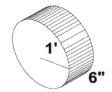

3. $V = 7' \times 8' \times 6'$

$V = 336$ cu. ft.

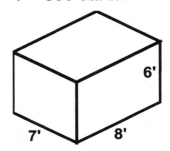

4. $V = \frac{1'}{2} \times \frac{1'}{2} \times \frac{1'}{2} = \frac{1}{8}$ cu. ft.

or $V = 6" \times 6" \times 6" = 216$ cu. in.

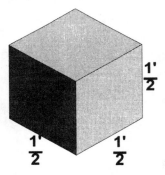

5. $V = \Pi r^2 h$

$V = $ Area $\times$ h

$V = 16\Pi" \times 9"$

$V = 144\Pi$ cu. in.

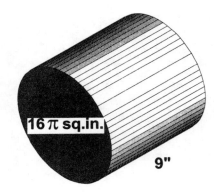

16 π sq.in.

9"

274

Chapter 7: ALGEBRA

Section 1: Algebraic Expressions

The expression (5)(4) or 5 * 4 represents the product of 5 and 4 which we know equals 20.

Key Point

> The expression (5)(X) or 5 * X represents the product of 5 and some number. X is a **Variable**. When something is variable, it is unknown. In this case, it's the value of X that can unknown.

If X = 3, then 5 * X = 5 * 3 = 15

If X = 7, then 5 * X = 5 * 7 = 35

Key Point

> The product of 5 * X can also be written in its most common form 5X. 5X is called an **Algebraic Term**. With our introduction of algebraic terms, we will no longer use "x" as a symbol of multiplication. X will be a variable.

3X + 7 is an **Algebraic Expression**. It's made up of one, or more, algebraic terms. Its value is a function of X. The number 3 is called the **Coefficient** of X. 7 is a **Constant**.

In the expression Y = 3X + 7, Y is a **Function** of X; its value is dependent on the value of X.

As we substitute different values for X, we generate new values for Y.

If X = 1, then Y = 3(1) + 7 = 10

If X = 7, then Y = 3(7) + 7 = 28

Example: If Y = X + 12, what is the value of Y, when X = 3?

    1) 3
    2) 12
    3) 13
    4) 15
    5) 36

Solution: Substituting 3 in for X, we get Y = 3 + 12 = 15

4) is the correct answer.

Example: If $Y = \dfrac{2X + 7}{3X}$ what does Y equal when X = 3?

Solution: $Y = \dfrac{2(3) + 7}{3(3)} = \dfrac{6 + 7}{9} = \dfrac{13}{9} = 1\dfrac{4}{9}$

The basic unit in algebra is called a **term**. An algebraic term consists of four parts, some of which are not always written explicitly but rather are 'understood': (1) the variable, (2) the coefficient, (3) the sign and (4) the exponent.

Here are three terms:

$5n^2$

$- \frac{1}{4} y^3$

x

In the first term, the sign is understood to be positive, the coefficient is 5, the variable is n and the exponent is 2. In the second term, the sign is negative, the coefficient is $\frac{1}{4}$, the variable is y and the exponent is 3. In the third term, only the variable is shown; the other three understood parts are a positive sign, a coefficient of 1, and an exponent of 1.

The four operations on algebraic terms have certain limits because of the variable. As far as addition goes, only like algebraic terms can be added. Like terms are ones with the same variable part (where the variable has the same exponent):

$x + y$ (different variable parts so they can't be added)

$x^2 + x^3$ (different exponents so they can't be added)

$2x - 5x$ (like terms; the sum is $-3x$)

Multiplication and division can't be done on different variables. If the variables are the same but the exponents are different, three key rules must be observed:

Product rule: when multiplying exponentials, add the exponents.

$$x^2 x^5 = x^7$$

Quotient rule: when dividing exponentials, subtract the exponents.

$$\frac{x^2}{x^5} = x^{-3}$$

Power of a power: multiply the exponents.

$$\left(x^2\right)^{-5} = x^{-10}$$

There are also two key rules to be aware of when dealing with radicals:

Product rule: the square root of the product equals the product of the square roots.

$$\sqrt{50} = \sqrt{25}\sqrt{2} = 5\sqrt{2}$$

Quotient rule: the square root of the quotient equals the quotient of the square roots.

$$\frac{\sqrt{75}}{\sqrt{3}} = \sqrt{\frac{75}{3}} = \sqrt{25} = 5$$

Distributing and Factoring

Suppose that you had an expression like this:

$$2x\,(x - y)$$

Inside the parentheses cannot be added, so the only operation possible is multiplying the $2x$ by $(x - y)$. This is done following the distributive property: the $2x$ must be multiplied by every individual term inside the parentheses:

$$2x\,(x - y) = 2xx - 2xy$$
$$= 2x^2 - 2xy$$

Key Point

> Another commonly used form of distribution is required when multiplying a binomial times a binomial, such as $(x + 2)(x - 5)$. In this case, each of the two terms within one set of parentheses must be multiplied by each of the terms in the other set of parentheses, giving a total of four separate multiplications. The mnemonic device frequently employed here is FOIL, which stands for **F**irst, **O**utside, **I**nside, **L**ast. The *first* terms are x times x, the *outside* terms are x times -5, the *inside* terms are 2 times x, and the *last* terms are 2 times -5.
>
> $$(x + 2)(x - 5) = x^2 - 5x + 2x - 10 = x^2 - 3x - 10$$

The inverse process of distributing is called **factoring** and there are three methods of factoring with which you should be familiar: the greatest common factor method, the difference of two squares method, and trinomial factoring.

EXAMPLE: Rewrite $2x^2y - 6yx^3$ in factored form.

SOLUTION: Factor out the greatest common factor. The GCF of 2 and -6 is 2, the GCF of x^2 and x^3 is x^2, and the GCF of y and y is, of course, y. So the GCF of the two terms is $2x^2y$. So the original expression in factored form is $2x^2y\,(1 - 3x)$.

The difference of two squares method requires that the expression to be factored be of the form $x^2 - y^2$, such as $m^2 - 9$ or $t^2 - 25$. Here are some examples:

$$x^2 - 49 = (x)^2 - (7)^2 = (x+7)(x-7)$$
$$t^2 - 25 = (t)^2 - (5)^2 = (t+5)(t-5)$$
$$m^2 - 9 = (m)^2 - (3)^2 = (m+3)(m-3)$$
$$x^2 - y^2 = (x)^2 - (y)^2 = (x+y)(x-y)$$

To factor a trinomial such as $x^2 + 4x - 21$, you should inspect the coefficient of x, in this case 4, and the non-variable term, in this case –21. Now find the two numbers that when multiplied give –21 and when added give you 4. The two numbers are 7 and –3. Now you could rewrite the trinomial as $(x + 7)(x - 3)$. To check this, multiply by the FOIL method mentioned above and you will wind up with the original trinomial.

Section 2: Equations

$14 + 3 = 17$ is an equation. It has terms on both sides of an equal sign and, in fact, the terms must be equal in value. If we were to add something to one side of the equation, we would have to add an equal amount to the other side.

$$14 + 3 + 4 = 17 + 4$$

If we were to take something away from one side of the equation, we would have to take an equal amount away from the other side.

$$14 + 3 - 2 = 17 + 4 - 2$$

Key Point

An equation that has an algebraic term on at least one side of the equal sign is an Algebraic Equation.

For Example: $X + 5 = 50$

X is an unknown. However, we're looking for the value of X that will make both sides of the equation equal. What number plus 5 equals 50? In this case, you might be able to figure this out in your head. The number is 45. In general, though, how would we solve an algebraic equation?

Key Point

Remember that your algebraic equation is a balanced scale. If you add something to one side, you must add the same value to the other side. If you multiply one side by a number, you must multiply the other side by the same number. The same goes for subtraction and division.

So, starting with:

$$\begin{array}{r} X + 5 = 50 \\ -5 = -5 \\ \hline X = 45 \end{array}$$

Example: Solve for X, if $2X + 9 = 15$

Solution:

$$\begin{array}{r} 2X + 9 = 15 \\ -9 = -9 \\ \hline 2X = 6 \end{array}$$ First, subtract 9 from both sides of the equation

$$\frac{2X}{2} = \frac{6}{2}$$ Next, divide both sides by 2

$$X = 3$$

Example: If 3X − 12 = 48, what is X equal to?

                1) 12
                2) 16
                3) 20
                4) 36
                5) 60

Solution:

$$
\begin{array}{rl}
3X - 12 = & 48 \\
+12 = & +12 \\
\hline
3X = & 60
\end{array}
$$
First, add 12 to both sides of the equation

$$\frac{3X}{3} = \frac{60}{3}$$
Next, divide both sides by 3

X = 20

The correct answer is 3).

Example: For what value of X is $\frac{2}{3}X - 5 = 13$ a true statement?

                1) $5\frac{1}{3}$
                2) 8
                3) 12
                4) 18
                5) 27

Solution: $\frac{2}{3}X - 5 = 13$ First, add 5 to both sides of the equation

$\frac{2}{3}X - 5 + 5 = 13 + 5$

$\frac{2}{3}X = 18$ Next, multiply both sides by 3/2

$\frac{3}{2} \cdot \frac{2}{3}X = 18 \cdot \frac{3}{2}$

X = 27

Key Point

You could also do this in two steps by first multiplying both sides by 3 and then dividing both sides by 2.

The correct answer is 5).

Equation Problems

1. **If 15 = X – 9, what does X equal?**

    1) 6
    2) 15
    3) 24
    4) 9
    5) 10

2. **If 3X + 4 = 16, what does X equal?**

    1) 12
    2) 20
    3) 3
    4) 4
    5) $\dfrac{20}{3}$

3. **If 5X – 30 = 2X, what does X equal?**

    1) 10
    2) 3
    3) 6
    4) $\dfrac{30}{7}$
    5) 15

4. **If 9X – 8 = 2X + 6, what does X equal?**

    1) 3
    2) $\dfrac{8}{9}$
    3) $\dfrac{14}{9}$
    4) 2
    5) $\dfrac{6}{7}$

5. **If X + 12 = 5X – 12, what does X equal?**

    1) 6
    2) 0
    3) 4
    4) 3
    5) 2

6. If $\frac{3}{4}X + 8 = 20$, what does X equal?

    1) 12
    2) 9
    3) 28
    4) 21
    5) 16

7. If $\frac{5x + 3}{4} = 7$, what does X equal?

    1) 2
    2) $\frac{4}{5}$
    3) 25
    4) 5
    5) $\frac{12}{5}$

8. If $\frac{2}{3}X + 1 = \frac{1}{3}X + 5$, what does X equal?

    1) 12
    2) 9
    3) 28
    4) 21
    5) 16

9. After a busy night at the restaurant, the waiters and waitresses count up their tips. Tom earned twice as Don, and Jennie earned as much as the two of them combined. If the total tips for the three of them came to $270.00, how much did Tom earn?

    1) $30
    2) $45
    3) $90
    4) $115
    5) $135

10. Mike and Karen live 55 miles apart. They hop in their cars and drive towards each other, but Mike travels faster than Karen, and when the two meet, he ends up traveling 5 miles farther than Karen. How far did Mike travel before the two met?

   1) 20
   2) 25
   3) 30
   4) 35
   5) 40

Algebra Solutions

1.
$$15 = X - 9$$
$$+9 = +9$$
$$24 = X$$

The correct answer is 3).

2.
$$3X + 4 = 16$$
$$-4 = -4$$
$$3X = 12$$

$$\frac{3X}{3} = \frac{12}{3}$$

$$X = 4$$

The correct answer is 4).

3.
$$5X - 30 = 2X$$
$$+30 = +30$$
$$5X = 2X + 30$$

$$5X = 2X - 30$$
$$-2X = -2X$$
$$3X = +30$$

$$\frac{3X}{3} = \frac{30}{3} \,, \ X = 10$$

The correct answer is 1).

4.

$$9X - 8 = 2X + 6$$
$$ +8 = +8$$
$$9X = 2X + 14$$

$$9X = 2X + 14$$
$$-2X = -2X$$
$$7X = +14$$

$$\frac{7X}{7} = \frac{14}{7}, \quad X = 2$$

The correct answer is 4).

5.

$$X + 12 = 5X - 12$$
$$ +12 = +12$$
$$X + 24 = 5X$$

$$X + 24 = 5X$$
$$-X = -X$$
$$24 = 4X$$

$$\frac{24}{4} = \frac{4X}{4}, \quad X = 6$$

The correct answer is 1).

6.

$$\frac{3}{4}X + 8 = 20$$
$$\phantom{\frac{3}{4}X} -8 = -8$$
$$\frac{3}{4}X = 12$$

$$\frac{4}{3} \cdot \frac{3}{4}X = 12 \cdot \frac{4}{3}$$
$$X = 16$$

The correct answer is 5).

7.

$$\frac{5X + 3}{4} = 7$$

$$4 \cdot \frac{5X + 3}{4} = 7 \cdot 4$$

$$5X + 3 = 28$$

$$5X + 3 = 28$$
$$\underline{\quad -3 = -3}$$
$$5X = 25$$

$$\frac{5X}{5} = \frac{25}{5} = 5$$

The correct answer is 4).

8.

$$\frac{2}{3}X + 1 = \frac{1}{3}X + 5$$
$$\underline{\quad -1 = -1}$$
$$\frac{2}{3}X = \frac{1}{3}X + 4$$

$$\frac{2}{3}X = \frac{1}{3}X + 4$$

$$-\frac{1}{3}X = -\frac{1}{3}X$$

$$\frac{1}{3}X = 4$$

$$3 \cdot \frac{1}{3}X = 3 \cdot 4 = 12$$

The correct answer is 1).

9.   Let X represent amount of tips that Don earned. Since Tom earned twice as much as Don, we will let 2X represent Tom's tips. Jennie earned as much as Tom and Don combined, so that would be represented as X + 2X, or 3X. We also know that the sum of the tips equals $270. So,

X + 2X + 3X = 270

6X = 270

$$\frac{6x}{6} = \frac{270}{6}$$

X = 45

Remember, though, that X represents Don's tips. The question wants us to find the amount Tom earned. That is equal to 2X, or $90.

The correct answer is 3).

10.   Let X represent the distance that Karen traveled. Since Mike traveled 5 miles farther, his distance will be represented by X + 5. We also know that the total distance traveled by the both of them is the 55 miles that originally separated them. So,

X + X + 5 = 55

2X + 5 = 55

  - 5 = - 5

2X = 50

$$\frac{2x}{2} = \frac{50}{2}$$

X = 25

Remember, though, that X represents Karen's distance. The question asked how far Mike traveled. That is equal to X + 5, or 30 miles

The correct answer is 3).

Section 3: Inequalities

A relationship can be stated between two quantities that is not an equality, in which case we are dealing with an inequality. Like the relation of equivalence, the relations "greater than" and "less than" have certain properties. For instance, the transitive property expresses the **axiom** if $a > b$ and $b > c$, then $a > c$.

Key Point

One of the most important properties of inequalities is that multiplying or dividing both sides by a negative *reverses* the direction of the inequality symbol. (Multiplying or dividing both sides by a positive, or adding or subtracting from both sides, does *not* change the direction.)

EXAMPLE: If $-2x + 5 > 11$, what are the possible values of x?

SOLUTION: Just solve for x as you would in an equation, remembering that multiplying or dividing both sides by a negative reverses the inequality.

$-2x + 5 > 11$ (given)

$-2x > 6$ (subtracted 5 from both sides)

$x < -3$ (divided both sides by -2, thereby reversing inequality sign)

So x has to be a number less than -3 (in other words, to the left of -3 on the number line). This result could be graphed on the real number line like this:

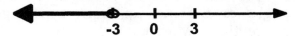

The hollow circle at -3 indicates that x is less than but *not* equal to -3. If x were less than *or* equal to -3 (in symbols, $x \le -3$), then the hollow circle would be filled in.

Chapter 8: Coordinate Geometry

Section 1: Points in Space

Coordinate or Analytical Geometry deals with location and relationship of points found on a two-dimensional surface. This surface is divided into 4 parts by two intersecting perpendicular lines called axes. The horizontal line is the x-axis and the vertical line is the y-axis. They're like horizontal and vertical number lines. An ordered pair of numbers, where the first number is always the distance traveled along the x-axis and the second number is the distance traveled along the y-axis, defines every point in this space.

Key Point

> The point where the x-axis and y-axis meet is called the origin. It is the point where measurement originates. You move "0" in an x direction and "0" in a y direction to get there. We represent the origin by the notation (0,0), where the first number is the value you move in an x direction and the second number is the value you move in a y direction. Moving to the right or moving up from the origin is considered a positive direction. Moving to the left or moving down from the origin is considered moving in a negative direction.

Example: Locate the point (5,2)

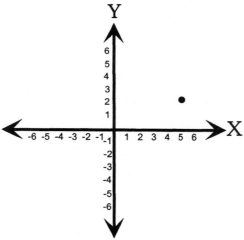

Solution: You would locate the point (5,2) by moving from the origin 5 spaces to the right and 2 spaces up.

288

Example: Locate the point (-1,-1)

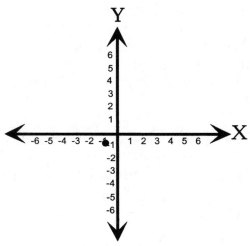

Solution: You would locate the point (-1,-1) by moving from the origin 1 space to the left and 1 space down.

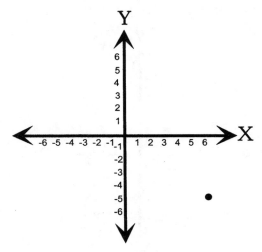

Example: What are the coordinates of the above point?

    1) (6 , 5)
    2) (6 , -5)
    3) (-6 , 5)
    4) (-6 , -5)

Solution: In order to locate the point, from the origin, you move 6 units to right (+6) and 5 units down (-5). The point is (6, -5).

The correct answer is 2).

Section 2: Finding the Midpoint

Key Point

When you are given two points and want to find the midpoint, the steps to follow are straightforward. Simply add the two X coordinates together and divide by two to find the X coordinate of the midpoint. Then add the two Y coordinates together and divide by two to find the Y coordinate of the midpoint.

$$\frac{X_1 + X_2}{2} = X_m \qquad\qquad \frac{Y_1 + Y_2}{2} = Y_m$$

Example: Find the midpoint of the points (2,3) and (4,5).

Solution: $\dfrac{X_1 + X_2}{2} = X_m \qquad\qquad \dfrac{Y_1 + Y_2}{2} = Y_m$

$$\frac{2+4}{2} = \frac{6}{2} = 3 = X_m \qquad\qquad \frac{3+5}{2} = \frac{8}{2} = 4 = Y_m$$

The midpoint equals (3,4)

Example: Grid in the midpoint of the points (-2,1) and (6,-1).

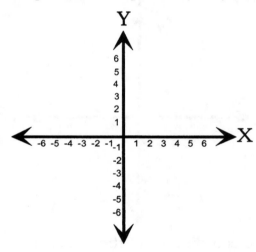

Solution: $$\frac{X_1 + X_2}{2} = X_m \qquad\qquad \frac{Y_1 + Y_2}{2} = Y_m$$

$$\frac{-2 + 6}{2} = \frac{4}{2} = 2 = X_m \qquad\qquad \frac{1 + (-1)}{2} = \frac{0}{2} = 0 = Y_m$$

The midpoint equals (2,0)

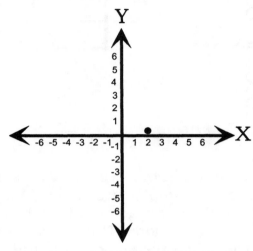

Example: Find the midpoint of the points (12,3) and (3,-5).

    1) (-9,-2)

    2) (7.5,1)

    3) (7.5,-1)

    4) (7.5,4)

    5) (7.5,-4)

Solution: $$\frac{X_1 + X_2}{2} = X_m \qquad\qquad \frac{Y_1 + Y_2}{2} = Y_m$$

$$\frac{12 + 3}{2} = \frac{15}{2} = 7.5 = X_m \qquad\qquad \frac{3 + (-5)}{2} = \frac{-2}{2} = -1 = Y_m$$

The midpoint equals (7.5,-1)

The correct answer is 3).

Section 3: Graphing a Straight Line

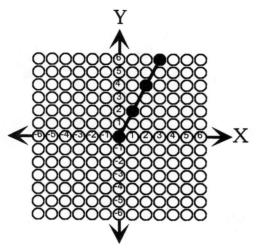

X	Y
0	0
1	2
2	4
3	6

When we connect any two points in our grid, and we extend our line, we notice that there is a constant relationship between the x and y coordinates of any point located on the line. In the example above, each time we move "1" in an X direction, we move "2" in a Y direction. This relationship between the change in Y over the change in X is called the slope of the line. The larger the positive slope, the steeper the angle of the line as you move from left to right. Lines with positive slopes rise from left to right. Lines with negative slopes fall from left to right.

Key Point

> In general, straight lines are represented by the equation:
>
> y = mx + b

The coefficient of x, m, is the slope of the line and the constant, b, is the y-intercept, which is the point at which the line crosses the y-axis. The y intercept has an x coordinate of zero. In our example above, the y-intercept is 0. The point (0,0) is called the origin.

If in the equation y = mx + b, we substitute 0 for x, we see that y = b. This shows us that, in fact, b is the value of y where the line crosses the y-axis.

If we wanted to find the equation of the line that passed through the points on our graph, we would first find the slope of the line. Remember that the slope is the ratio of the change in Y over the change in X.

The change in Y as you move from (0,0) to (1,2) is 2. The change in X is 1. The slope, m, is $\frac{2}{1}$ or 2.

So, we know that the equation is in the form y = 2x + b. Substituting any pair of values for x and y, we can solve for b.

$$y = mx + b$$
$$0 = 2(0) + b$$
$$0 = b$$

The equation is $y = 2x$

Example: What are the coordinates of the y-intercept for the line represented by $Y = \dfrac{2}{3}X - 7$

     1) (0,7)
     2) (2,3)
     3) (-7,0)
     4) (0,-7)
     5) (0,0)

Solution: In this example, the value of "b" is –7, so the y-coordinate of the y-intercept is –7. The x-coordinate of the y-intercept is always zero. So the y-intercept is (0,-7).

The correct answer is 4).

Example: What is the slope of a line that goes through the points (1,5) and (3,9).

Solution: The measurement in the change in y from (1,5) to (3,9) is the difference between the two y values. The difference between 9 and 5 is 4. The change in the x values is the difference between 3 and 1, or 2. The change in y (4) over the change in x (2) defines the slope of the line. The slope, "m" is equal to $\dfrac{4}{2}$, or 2.

Example: What is the equation of a line that goes through the points (1,5) and (3,9).

Solution: So, now we know that the equation that defines the line passing through (1,5) and (3,9) is of the form:

$$y = 2x + b$$

We also know that when x = 1, y = 5. So, we can substitute these values into the equation, and solve for b.

$$y = 2x + b$$

$$5 = 2(1) + b$$

$$5 = 2 + b$$

$$3 = b$$

The equation of the line that crosses through both (1,5) and (3,9) is:

$$y = 2x + 3$$

Example: What is the equation of a line that goes through the points (6,0) and (12,4).

Solution: The measurement in the change in y from (6,0) to (12,4) is the difference between the two y values. The difference between 4 and 0 is 4. The change in the x values is the difference between 12 and 6, or 6. The change in y (4) over the change in x (6) defines the slope of the line. The slope, "m" is equal to $\frac{4}{6}$, or $\frac{2}{3}$.

So, now we know that the equation that defines the line passing through (6,0) and (12,4) is of the form:

$$y = \frac{2}{3}x + b$$

We also know that when x = 6, y = 0. So, we can substitute these values into the equation, and solve for b.

$$y = \frac{2}{3}x + b$$

$$0 = \frac{2}{3}(6) + b$$

$$0 = 4 + b$$

You have to subtract 4 from 4 in order to get zero, so b must be -4

The equation of the line that crosses through both (6,0) and (12,4) is:

$$y = \frac{2}{3}x - 4$$

Example: Below are values of x and y along a straight line. Find the missing value in the table.

x	y
4	19
2	13
0	?

1) 7
2) -7
3) 5
4) -5
5) 0

Solution: The slope of the line (m) is equal to the change in y over the change in x. This is equal to:

$$\frac{(19-13)}{(4-2)} = \frac{6}{2} = 3$$

So, the equation of our line is equal to $y = 3x + b$. We know that $y = 13$ when $x = 2$ so we can substitute these values in our equation.

$y = 3x + b$

$13 = 3(2) + b$

$13 = 6 + b$

$7 = b$

Our equation is $y = 3x + 7$. When $x = 0$, $y = 7$.

The correct answer is 1).

Section 4: Distance Between Two Points

Key Point

The distance between two points is represented by the formula $\sqrt{(X_2 - X_1)^2 + (Y_2 - Y_1)^2}$, where the coordinates of the starting point are (X_1, Y_1) and the coordinates of the end point are (X_2, Y_2). By subtracting one X coordinate from the other, we are calculating the change in the X value, or the distance traveled in an X direction. By subtracting one Y coordinate from the other, we are calculating the change in the Y value, or the distance traveled in an Y direction.

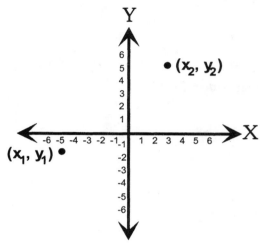

If you think of the distance traveled in the X direction as the base of a right triangle, and the distance traveled in the Y direction as the side of a right triangle, then the distance between the two points is the hypotenuse of the right triangle.

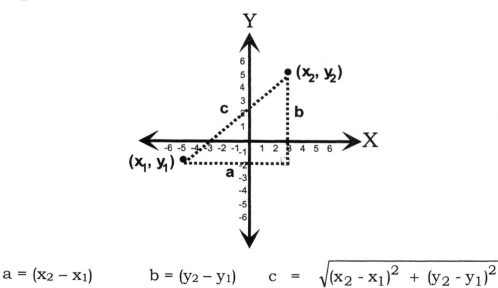

$$a = (x_2 - x_1) \qquad b = (y_2 - y_1) \qquad c = \sqrt{(x_2 - x_1)^2 + (y_2 - y_1)^2}$$

So, the formula:

$$\sqrt{(x_2 - x_1)^2 + (y_2 - y_1)^2}$$

is simply an application of the Pythagorean Theorem.

Example: Find the distance between the two points below.

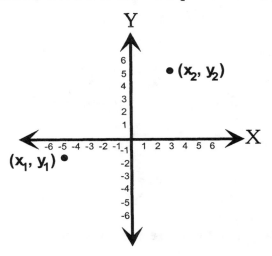

Solution: The coordinates of the first point are (-5,-2). The coordinates of the second point are (3,5)

$X_2 = 3$ and $X_1 = -5$; $X_2 - X_1 = 8$

$Y_2 = 5$ and $Y_1 = -2$; $Y_2 - Y_1 = 3$

$$\sqrt{(x_2 - x_1)^2 + (y_2 - y_1)^2} = \sqrt{8^2 + 7^2} = \sqrt{64 + 49} = \sqrt{113}$$

The distance between the two points is about 10.63 units.

Example: Find the distance between the two points (1,6) and (5,12)

Solution: $X_2 = 5$ and $X_1 = 1$; $X_2 - X_1 = 4$

$Y_2 = 12$ and $Y_1 = 6$; $Y_2 - Y_1 = 6$

$$\sqrt{(x_2 - x_1)^2 + (y_2 - y_1)^2} = \sqrt{4^2 + 6^2} = \sqrt{16 + 36} = \sqrt{52} = 7.21$$

Coordinate Geometry Problems

1. **Locate the point (6,-3) on the grid below.**

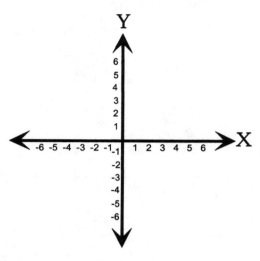

2. **Locate the point (-4,-5) on the grid below.**

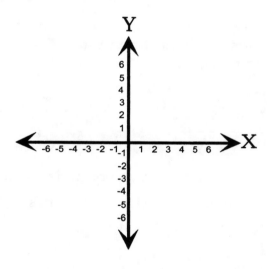

3. **Locate the point (4,5) on the grid below.**

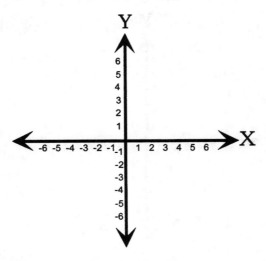

4. **Locate the point (-6,2) on the grid below.**

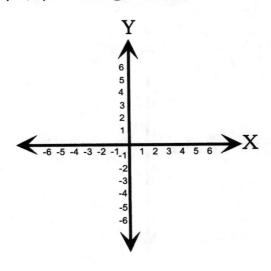

5. Locate the point (0,-3) on the grid below.

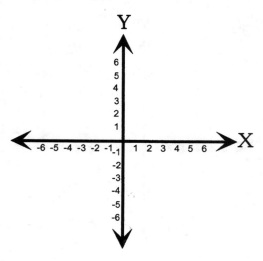

6. Locate the point (-2,0) on the grid below.

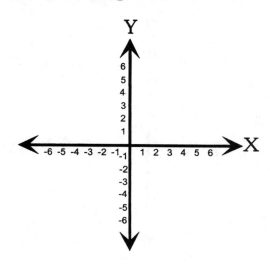

7. Grid in the midpoint of the points (-3,4) and (-1,2).

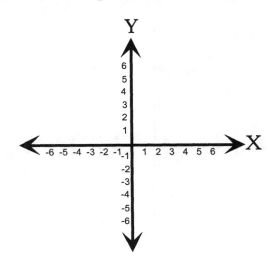

8. What is the midpoint of the points (8,2) and (12,-8)?

    1) (8,0)
    2) (-4,10)
    3) (-4,-6)
    4) (20,-6)
    5) (10,-3)

9. What is the y-intercept of the line with and equation of y = 3x + 4?

    1) (4,0)
    2) (0,3)
    3) (0,-3)
    4) (0,-4)
    5) (0,4)

10. What is the y-intercept of the line with the equation of $y = \frac{1}{4}$?

    1) (4,0)
    2) (0,4)
    3) (0,0)
    4) $(0,\frac{1}{4})$
    5) $(\frac{1}{4},0)$

11. Grid in the y-intercept of the equation y = -2x – 3.

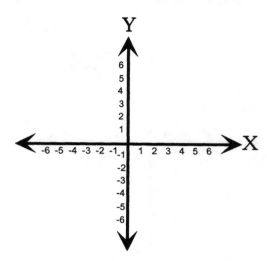

12. What is the slope of the line with the equation y = 2x – 3?

    1) 2
    2) 3
    3) –3
    4) –2
    5) $-\dfrac{2}{3}$

13. What is slope of the line with and equation of y = 3x + 4?

    1) 4
    2) -4
    3) -3
    4) $\dfrac{3}{4}$
    5) 3

14. What is the slope of the line with the equation of y = $\dfrac{1}{4}$?

    1) 4
    2) 0
    3) -4
    4) $\dfrac{1}{4}$
    5) $-\dfrac{1}{4}$

15. **What is the equation of a line that passes through the points (3,5) and (5,8)?**

        1) $y = 1.5x + .5$

        2) $y = 15x$

        3) $y = \dfrac{2}{3}x + \dfrac{1}{2}$

        4) $y = \dfrac{2}{3}x - \dfrac{1}{2}$

        5) $y = x - \dfrac{1}{2}$

16. **What is the length of a line that connects the points (3,5) and (5,8)?**

        1) 5

        2) 4

        3) 3.6

        4) 13

        5) 17.72

17. **What is the length of a line that connects the points (-2,2) and (4,10)?**

        1) 3

        2) 4

        3) 5

        4) 6

        5) 10

Coordinate Geometry Solutions

1. The point (6,-3) is located by moving in the X direction 6 spaces to the right and in the Y direction 3 spaces down.

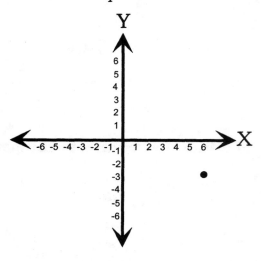

2. The point (-4,-5) is located by moving in the X direction 4 spaces to the left and in the Y direction 5 spaces down.

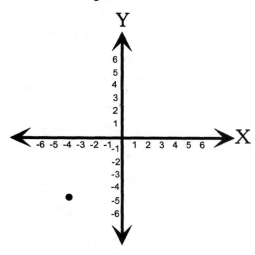

3. The point (4,5) is located by moving in the X direction 4 spaces to the right and in the Y direction 5 spaces up.

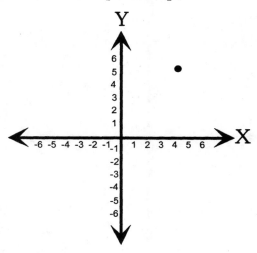

4. The point (-6,2) is located by moving in the X direction 6 spaces to the left and in the Y direction 2 spaces up.

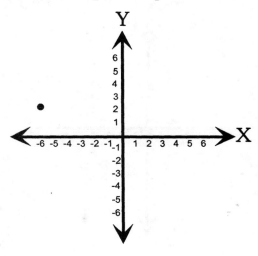

5. The point (0,-3) is located by moving in the X direction 0 spaces and in the Y direction 3 spaces down.

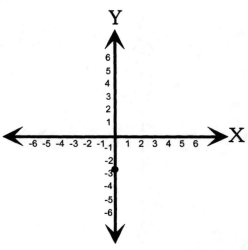

6. The point (-2,0) is located by moving in the X direction 2 spaces to the left and in the Y direction 0 spaces.

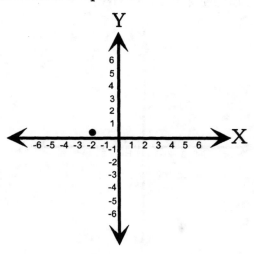

7.
$$\frac{X_1 + X_2}{2} = X_m \qquad\qquad \frac{Y_1 + Y_2}{2} = Y_m$$

$$\frac{(-3) + (-1)}{2} = \frac{-4}{2} = -2 = X_m \qquad\qquad \frac{4 + 2}{2} = \frac{6}{2} = 3 = Y_m$$

The midpoint equals (-2,3)

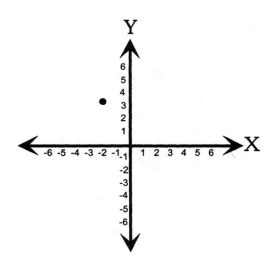

8.
$$\frac{X_1 + X_2}{2} = X_m \qquad\qquad \frac{Y_1 + Y_2}{2} = Y_m$$

$$\frac{8 + 12}{2} = \frac{20}{2} = 10 = X_m \qquad\qquad \frac{2 + (-8)}{2} = \frac{-6}{2} = -3 = Y_m$$

The midpoint equals (10,-3)

The correct response is 5).

9. To find the y-intercept you plug 0 into the equation for x.

y = 3(0) + 4 = 4

The y-intercept equals (0,4)

The correct response is 5).

10. A line with the equation $y = \frac{1}{4}$ has no slope. For any x, y equals $\frac{1}{4}$.

Therefore, when x = 0, y will equal $\frac{1}{4}$.

The correct response is 4).

11. The equation y = -2x – 3 has a y intercept of (0,-3).

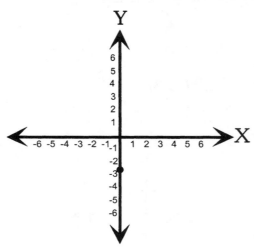

12. The slope of a line is equal to the coefficient of x in its equation.

y = 2x – 3   The slope equals 2.

The correct response is 1).

13. The slope of a line is equal to the coefficient of x in its equation.

y = 3x + 4   The slope equals 3.

The correct response is 5).

14. The slope of a line is equal to the coefficient of x in its equation.

$y = 0x + \dfrac{1}{4}$ The slope equals 0.

The correct response is 2).

15. The slope of the line (m) is equal to the change in y over the change in x. This is equal to:

$$\frac{(8-5)}{(5-3)} = \frac{3}{2} = 1.5$$

So, the equation of our line is equal to y = 1.5x + b. We know that y = 8 when x = 5 so we can substitute these values in our equation.

y = 1.5x + b

8 = 1.5(5) + b

8 = 7.5 + b

.5 = b

Our equation is y = 1.5x + .5

The correct answer is 1).

16. $X_2 = 5$ and $X_1 = 3$; $X_2 - X_1 = 2$

$Y_2 = 8$ and $Y_1 = 5$; $Y_2 - Y_1 = 3$

$$\sqrt{(x_2 - x_1)^2 + (y_2 - y_1)^2} = \sqrt{2^2 + 3^2} = \sqrt{4+9} = \sqrt{13} = 3.605$$

When evaluating the square root of 13, you can use your calculator and the square root function key to approximate your answer.

The correct answer is 3).

17. $X_2 = 4$ and $X_1 = -2$; $X_2 - X_1 = 6$

$Y_2 = 10$ and $Y_1 = 2$; $Y_2 - Y_1 = 8$

$$\sqrt{(x_2 - x_1)^2 + (y_2 - y_1)^2} = \sqrt{6^2 + 8^2} = \sqrt{64+36} = \sqrt{100} = 10$$

When evaluating the square root of 13, you can use your calculator and the square root function key to approximate your answer.

The correct answer is 5).

Combinatorial math involves the principles of counting. One example would be computing the number of different outfits possible given 3 different blouses and 3 different skirts. The total number of different outfits is 3 × 3 or 9, and this illustrates the general principle which is that if you have x different choices for one thing and y different choices for another, then there are $x × y$ total possible choices.

EXAMPLE: How many different possible ways can the objects A, B, and C be arranged without repetition and where order is important?

SOLUTION: There are 6 possible ways:

A, B, C

A, C, B

B, A, C

B, C, A

C, A, B

C, B, A

Thus there are 6 **permutations** of the 3 objects A, B and C. Permutations are like sets, but there is a difference: if two sets have the same members, they are equal but not so with permutations. All of the 6 permutations above have the same members but in different orders. That's the essential thing about permutations: the order matters.

Key Point

If there is a large number of objects, the number of permutations will be too large to actually enumerate all of them as we did in the above example, so a quick formula would be useful: if there are n objects, then there are $n!$ permutations, assuming no repetition ($n!$ is read 'n factorial'.) In the above example, there are 3! ways to arrange the three objects, and 3! is translated as 3 × 2 × 1. Why? Because for the first slot in our three-member set we had 3 choices (A, B, or C). Once we made a choice for the first slot, we had only 2 choices left for the second slot (since we assumed no repetition); and after the first two slots were filled, there was only 1 choice left for the third and final slot.

EXAMPLE: How many different ways can I arrange a set of 6 different colored flags?

SOLUTION: I have six different ways that I can fill the first position. Once I've filled the first position, there are 5 flags left, so I have 5 choices for the second position, 4 for the third, and so on.

6* 5 * 4 * 3 * 2 * 1

Each way I can fill the first position is paired with each way I can fill the second position, etc. This pairing implies multiplication, and, in fact, the total number of permutations is

6 * 5 * 4 * 3 * 2 * 1 or 720 permutations.

This product can also be written as **6!** (called 6 factorial).

EXAMPLE: From the same set of 6 different colored flags, how many different arrangements of three flags can I make?

SOLUTION: 6 * 5 * 4 = 120

This could also be written as $\dfrac{6 \cdot 5 \cdot 4 \cdot 3 \cdot 2 \cdot 1}{3 \cdot 2 \cdot 1} = \dfrac{6!}{3!}$

In general, the formula for the permutations of n things taken r at a time, or $_nP_r$, is $\dfrac{n!}{(n-r)!}$, where n equals the total number of objects and r equals the number chosen.

EXAMPLE: Marisa bought 5 new blouses, 3 new skirts, and 2 new pairs of shoes for her new job. If she works Monday through Friday, how many weeks can she go without wearing the same outfit twice?

(A)   1   (B)   3   (C)   6   (D)   2

SOLUTION: First, we have to find how many different outfits can she make. She has 5 choices for the blouse, which can be paired with any one of 3 choices for the skirt, which, in turn, can be paired with either of the 2 choices for the shoes.

5 * 3 * 2 = 30

So, she can make 30 different outfits. But how many weeks can she go without repeating an outfit? That would be $\dfrac{30}{5}$ or 6 weeks.

The correct answer is (C).

Combinations

What if the order did not matter (but still assuming there is no repetition)? Then we would simply find the number of combinations of the objects.

EXAMPLE: How many 3-person committees could be formed from a pool of 5 people?

SOLUTION: Call these 5 people A, B, C, D, and E. The number of permutations of these five people would be 5×4×3 or 60. Included in these 60 permutations would be sets with the same members but in different orders. For combinations order does not matter so these extra permutations should be eliminated. Do this by dividing 60 by the number of permutations of 3 objects or 3×2×1. So the number of combinations of 5 things taken 3 at a time is 60/6 or 10.

Key Point

The formula for the number of combinations of n things taken r at a time (no repetition) is

$$\frac{n!}{r!\,(n-r)!}$$

EXAMPLE: The Senior Class Council is made up of one representative from each of the 12 Senior Homerooms. They are going to pick 3 members to serve as a subcommittee to plan the Senior Prom. How many different subcommittees are possible?

(A) $\dfrac{12!}{9!3!}$ (B) $\dfrac{12!}{9!}$ (C) $\dfrac{12!}{3!}$ (D) $\dfrac{12!}{9!(9-3)!}$

SOLUTION: If order were important in the selection we would have 12 * 11 * 10. But that would be counting every three-member panel 3! times. The committee of Fred, Sally, and George and the committee of Sally, Fred, and George would be considered two different committees if order were important. However, we know that this is the same committee, regardless of the order in which we picked the 3 names. So, we must divide 12 * 11 * 10 by 3! to eliminate the repetition.

The number of subcommittees = $\dfrac{12 \cdot 11 \cdot 10}{3!} = \dfrac{12 \cdot 11 \cdot 10 \cdot 9!}{3!9!} = \dfrac{12!}{3!9!}$.

The correct answer is (A). When multiplied out, it is 220.

EXAMPLE: How many different hands of 5 cards can you deal from a 52-card deck?

SOLUTION: The order that you receive the cards is unimportant. The only thing you care about what 5 cards you have at the end of the deal.

We already know that if order were important, we have $_{52}P_5 = \dfrac{52!}{47!}$.

What's the impact of considering order? I'm counting each hand of 5 cards 5! times. If I divide the number of permutations by 5!, I'll have the number of combinations.

$$_{52}C_5 = \frac{52!}{47!*5!} = \frac{52*51*50*49*48*47!}{47!*5!} = \frac{52*51*50*49*48}{5*4*3*2*1}$$
$$= 13*17*10*49*24 = 2{,}598{,}960$$

Probability

To find the probability of flipping "heads" with a coin, we form a fraction: the bottom of the fraction will be the total number of possible outcomes (in this case 2); the top of the fraction will be the total number of favorable outcomes (in this case 1). So the probability of flipping a head is 1 out of 2 or ½ or 50%. The probability of an event must be 0 or 1 or some fraction between 0 and 1. If the probability of an event is 0, then the event cannot happen (for instance, flipping a head *and* a tail on one flip); if the probability is 1, then the event is certain to happen (for instance, flipping a head *or* a tail on one flip).

EXAMPLE: If you roll a die, what is the probability that you will roll an even number?

SOLUTION: The set of favorable outcomes = {2, 4, 6}

The set of total outcomes = {1, 2, 3, 4, 5, 6}

$P(\text{even}) = \dfrac{3}{6} = \dfrac{1}{2}$

EXAMPLE: What is the probability that you draw an Ace from a 52-card deck?

SOLUTION: There are four favorable outcomes = the Ace of spades, hearts, diamonds, & clubs. There are 52 total outcomes.

$P(\text{Ace}) = \dfrac{4}{52} = \dfrac{1}{13}$

The probability of not getting an ace is $\dfrac{48}{52}$ or $\dfrac{12}{13}$. The probability that an event doesn't occur is equal to 1 - P(Event).

EXAMPLE: What is the probability that a single draw from a standard 52-card deck will yield a number divisible by 3?

(A) $\frac{3}{52}$ (B) $\frac{1}{13}$ (C) $\frac{3}{13}$ (D) $\frac{2}{13}$

SOLUTION: There are 3 numbers divisible by 3 (3, 6, and 9) and there are 4 of each in the deck, so there are 12 favorable outcomes. There are 52 total outcomes. The probability is $\frac{12}{52}$ or $\frac{3}{13}$. The correct answer is (C).

EXAMPLE: Bob has 7 shirts, each a different color. He randomly selects 3 shirts to pack for a business trip. What is the probability that he packs the blue, yellow, and white shirts?

(A) 210   (B) $\frac{1}{840}$ (C) $\frac{1}{35}$ (D) $\frac{1}{210}$

SOLUTION: $_7C_3 = \frac{7!}{3!4!} = \frac{7*6*5}{3*2*1} = 7*5 = 35$

There are 35 possible combinations of shirts, only 1 of which is blue, yellow, and white. There is only one favorable outcome out of 35 total outcomes. The probability is $\frac{1}{35}$.

(C) is the correct answer.

Combination Of Events

What if you were asked the probability of flipping two consecutive heads or the probability if two coins were flipped at the same time that they would both come out heads? These are two examples of so-called **independent events**: the outcome of one flip does not affect the probability of heads coming up on the *other* flip. To calculate the probability, simply multiply the probabilities of the individual flips: the probability of heads on the 1ˢᵗ flip is ½ and it is also ½ on the 2ⁿᵈ. So the overall probability of heads coming out both times is ½ × ½ or ¼. **Mutually exclusive events** are events that cannot happen at the same time (for instance the probability of flipping a head *and* a tail on one flip).

EXAMPLE: What is the probability of drawing a diamond *or* a jack from a deck of cards?

SOLUTION: The probability of drawing a diamond is 13/52 (or 25%) and the probability of drawing a jack is 4/52 (a little less than 8%). But there is 1 card that is both a diamond *and* a jack, and this outcome must be deducted otherwise we would be counting this card twice in the calculations: 13/52 + 4/52 − 1/52 = 16/52 (about 31%). So the probability of drawing a diamond *or* a jack is about 31%.

EXAMPLE: If you deal 2 cards from a 52 card deck, what is the probability that both are Aces?

SOLUTION: This is equal to the probability that you draw an ace on the first card times the plus the probability that you draw an ace on the second card (given that you already drew an Ace on the first card).

P(2 Aces) = P(Ace on first card) * P(Ace on second card) =

$$\frac{4}{52} * \frac{3}{51} = \frac{12}{2652}$$

The key here is that the first card is not replaced in the deck, so there are only 3 aces remaining for the second card and only 51 cards remaining in the deck.

PRACTICE PROBLEMS

1. What is the probability of drawing a picture card from a 52-card deck?

    (A) $\frac{1}{13}$ (B) $\frac{4}{13}$ (C) $\frac{1}{52}$ (D) $\frac{3}{13}$

2. What is the probability that you can flip a coin three times and get heads each time?

    (A) $\frac{1}{8}$ (B) $\frac{1}{2}$ (C) $\frac{1}{4}$ (D) $\frac{3}{8}$

3. In a game of 21 (blackjack) you have a 10 and a 3. What is the probability that your next card will give you a total of 19, 20, or 21 (assume the 10 and 3 are the only cards drawn from the deck so far)?

    (A) $\frac{3}{13}$ (B) $\frac{6}{25}$ (C) $\frac{3}{52}$ (D) $\frac{3}{50}$

4. What is the probability that it will not rain on a given day if the probability that it will rain is 1/3?

    (A) $\frac{1}{3}$ (B) $\frac{1}{6}$ (C) $\frac{2}{3}$ (D) $\frac{1}{2}$

5. If you draw one of 24 slips of paper numbered consecutively from 1 - 24, what is the probability of drawing a number exactly divisible by 3?

    (A) $\frac{2}{3}$ (B) $\frac{1}{24}$ (C) $\frac{5}{8}$ (D) $\frac{1}{3}$

6. What is the probability that a random draw of a card from a deck is a 9 or 8?

    (A) $\frac{8}{13}$ (B) $\frac{2}{13}$ (C) $\frac{1}{13}$ (D) $\frac{4}{13}$

7. If you are to choose a committee of 4 people from a group of 8, how many different committees are possible?

    (A) 100   (B) 32   (C) 64   (D) 70

8. How many different telephone area codes can be formed using the digits 0 - 9, if 0 isn't used for the first digit?

    (A) 500   (B) 1000   (C) 900   (D) 729

9. How many triangles can be formed from a set of 8 different points, no three of which lie in a straight line?

    (A) 336   (B) 60   (C) 70   (D) 56

10. How many even three-digit numbers are there?

    (A) 500   (B) 400   (C) 4450   (D) 100

ANSWERS PRACTICE PROBLEMS

1. D   There are 12 picture cards in a deck. Therefore, there are $\frac{12}{52}$ or $\frac{3}{13}$ chances of getting a picture card.

2. A   The probability of getting heads 3 times would be $\frac{1}{2} \times \frac{1}{2} \times \frac{1}{2}$ or $\frac{1}{8}$.

3. B   If the next card drawn were a 6, 7, or 8, you would have a total of 19, 20, or 21. Since there are 4 of each, there are a total of 12 favorable cards. Since there are 50 cards left, the probability would be $\frac{12}{50}$ or $\frac{6}{25}$.

4.   C.   The probability that an event will happen, plus the probability it will not, must give a sum of 1. Therefore, the probability it will not happen is $1 - \frac{1}{3}$ or $\frac{2}{3}$.

5.   D   There are 8 numbers from 1-24 which are divisible by 3. The probability is, therefore, $\frac{8}{24}$ or $\frac{1}{3}$.

6.   B   The probability of getting a 9 or 8 is $\frac{8}{52}$, or $\frac{2}{13}$.

7.   D   The number of committees would be $_8C_4 = \frac{8 \times 7 \times 6 \times 5}{4 \times 3 \times 2 \times 1}$ or 70.

8.   C   For the first digit, you have a choice of 9 digits (1-9). For the second and third digits you have a choice of 10 digits each. Therefore, there are $9 \times 10 \times 10$ or 900.

9.   D   Each triangle requires 3 points. From 8 points there are 8 C 3 possible triangles. $8\ C\ 3 = \frac{8 \times 7 \times 6}{3 \times 2 \times 1} = 56$.

10.   C   The first digit can be 1-9; the second, 0-9; the third can only be 0, 2, 4, 6, 8 or 5 digits. Then there are $9 \times 10 \times 5$ or 450 even 3-digit numbers.

Chapter 10: SET THEORY

A set is a group of objects where membership in the group is clearly defined. In other words, given an object we should be able to say either that it is a member of a hypothetical set or that it is not. If two sets consist of the same members, then they are equal sets. If a number a is a member of a set X the notation would be $a \in X$.

Sets can be broken down into smaller sets. The smaller sets are called **subsets** of the original set. By way of definition, a set is considered a subset of itself; also, there is a set with special properties called the empty or **null set**, which is defined as the set with no members; the null set is denoted $\{\}$ or $\varnothing$.

EXAMPLE: How many subsets are there of set A if A={2, 4, 6, 8}?

SOLUTION: Set A has 16 total subsets:
$$\{\{2\},\{4\},\{6\},\{8\},\{2,4\},\{2,6\},\{2,8\},\{4,6\},\{4,8\},\{6,8\},\{2,4,6\},\{2,4,8\},$$
$$\{2,6,8\},\{4,6,8\}, \{2,4,6,8\} \text{ and } \{ \}\}.$$

In general, a set with n members has 2^n total subsets (which includes the set itself and the empty set.) If set C is a subset of set A and C has less members than A, then C is considered a proper subset of A. Consider the following three sets:

$$A=\{1, 3, 5, 7\}$$
$$B=\{1, 3, 5, 7\}$$
$$C=\{1, 3, 5\}$$

Both sets B and C are subsets of set A, but set C is also a *proper* subset of set A because it has fewer members. The notation would be $B \subseteq A, C \subset A$.

Operations can be done on two or more sets, the most important being union, intersection, and difference. The union of two sets denotes the members that are in one set *or* the other. If A={1,2,3} and B={3,4,5} then the union of A and B, denoted $A \cup B$, is {1,2,3,4,5}. The intersection of A and B is defined as the members that are in both A *and* B; in other words, intersection refers to the members that two sets have in common. Using the previous sets as examples, the intersection of A and B, denoted $A \cap B$, is {3}. If two sets have no members in common, that is, if their set of intersection is an empty set, then the two sets are said to be **disjoint** in relation to each other. The difference between two sets A and B, denoted A – B, is all of the members that are in A but not in B. (Similarly, B – A denotes all members in B that are not in A).

The above type relationships could be represented with Venn diagrams where instead of putting members within braces they are put within circles to indicate membership.

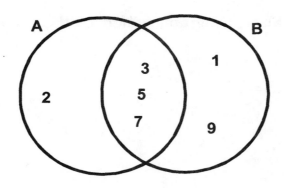

Here's a list of some of the relations we can deduce from the diagram:

$A = \{2, 3, 5, 7\}$ or $A = \{$all primes less than 8$\}$

$B = \{1, 3, 5, 7, 9\}$ or $B = \{$all odds greater than 0 but less than 10$\}$

$$A \cup B = \{1, 2, 3, 5, 7, 9\}$$
$$A \cap B = \{3, 5, 7\}$$
$$A - B = \{2\}$$
$$B - A = \{1, 9\}$$

EXAMPLE: In the Venn Diagram below, the shaded region represents which relationship?

(A) $A \cup B$

(B) $A \cup (B \cup C)$

(C) $A \cup C$

(D) $A \cup (B \cap C)$

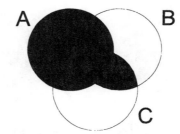

By inspection, we see that we've shaded all of circle A plus the area where circles B and C meet, or intersect. So, we are joining A with the intersection of B and C. The correct answer is (D).

EXAMPLE: Given the Venn Diagram, which of the following statements are true?

I. A ∪ B = {4, 6, 8}

II. A ∩ C = {5, 6, 7}

III. B ∩ C = {16, 24}

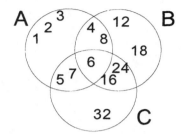

(A) I and II　　(B) II only　　(C) All　　(D) None

SOLUTION: A is obviously false because it doesn't even include all the elements of A.

{4, 6, 8} is the intersection of the two sets. Therefore, we can eliminate a) and c). B is true which eliminates D as a response. The correct answer is B.

Practice Problems — Set Theory

Questions 1 - 5 refer to the following:

A = {1, 2, 3, 4, 5}

B = {2, 3, 5, 8, 9}

C = {2, 4, 6, 7, 8}

1.　What is A ∪ B?

(A) {2,3}　　(B) {2,3,5}　　(C) {1,4,8,9}　　(D) {1,2,3,4,5,8,9}

2.　What is A ∩ B?

(A) {1,2,3,4,5,8,9}　(B)　　{∅} (C)　　{2,4}　　(D) {2,3,5}

3.　What is A ∪ (B ∩ C)?

(A) {2,3,5}　　(B) {1,2,3,4,5,8} (C) {2,3,4,5}　　(D) {2,3,4,5,6,7,8,9}

4.　How many subsets of C are there?

(A) 5　　(B) 7　　(C) 32　　(D) 16

5.　What is (A ∩ B) ∩ C?

(A) {2}　　(B) {2,3,5}　　(C) {∅}　　(D) {2,3,4,5,6,8}

320

6. If A = {x: -1 < x ≤ 3} and B = {X: x ≥ 3}, then A ∪ B =?

    (A) x < -1   (B) x > -1   (C) x ≥ 3   (D) x ≥ -1

7. In the Venn diagram below, the shaded region represents which of the following?

    (A) A ∪ B ∪ C
    (B) A ∩ B ∩ C
    (C) (B ∪ C) ∩ A
    (D) (A ∩ C) ∪ C

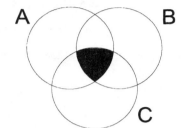

8. Based on the Venn diagram below, which of the following statements is true?

    (A) A ∪ B = {2,4}
    (B) A = {1,2,3,4,6,8}
    (C) A ∩ B = {2,4}
    (D) B = {1,2,3,4,6,8}

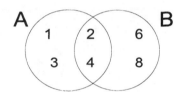

ANSWERS

1. D   A ∪ B contains all of the elements included in either A or B.

2. D   A ∩ B contains only those elements common to both sets.

3. B   The intersection of B and C is {2,8}. The union of {2,8} with A = {1,2,3,4,5} is {1,2,3,4,5,8}.

4. C   There are 5 elements so there are 2^5 or 32 subsets including the null set and the set itself.

5. A   A ∩ B is {2,3,5}; {2,3,5} ∩ {2,4,6,7,8} is {2}.

6. B   A is the set of numbers greater than -1 and less than or equal to 3. B is the set of numbers greater than or equal to 3. A ∪ B is the set of numbers greater than -1.

7. B   The shaded part represents the elements common to A and B and C or   A ∩ B ∩ C. Using the elements defined in problems 1 - 7, the intersection of the 3 sets would be {2}.

8. C   The intersection of A and B includes those elements common to both sets, or in the Venn diagram those elements included in the area where the 2 circles intersect. A ∩ B = {2,4}.

MATHEMATICS GLOSSARY

ABSOLUTE VALUE: the magnitude of a quantity, irrespective of sign; the distance of a quantity from zero.

ACUTE: an angle less than 90°.

ADDITIVE: the function of the union or sum of two quantities.

ALGORITHM: a set of rules for solving a problem in a finite number of steps.

ALTERNATE ANGLE: one of a pair of nonadjacent angles made by the crossing of two lines by a third line.

AMELIORATIVE: to make or become better or more satisfactory.

ASSOCIATIVE PROPERTY: The grouping of items does not change the quantity.

$(a + b) + c = a + (b + c)$

AXIOM: a proposition in logic or mathematics that is assumed without proof for the sake of studying the consequences that follow from it.

BINARY: involving two.

COMMUTATIVE PROPERTY: having the property that one term operating on a second is equal to the second operating on the first, as $a \times b = b \times a$.

COMPOSITE: made up of separate parts or elements.

COMPOUND: composed of two or more parts.

CONGRUENCE: a relation between two numbers in which the numbers give the same remainder when divided by a given number.

COORDINATE: any of the magnitudes that serve to define the position of a point or line.

CORRESPONDING ANGLE: two nonadjacent angles made by the crossing of two lines by a third line, one angle being interior, the other exterior, and both being on the same side of the third line.

DISTANCE: the amount of time or space between two points.

DISTRIBUTIVE PROPERTY: having the property that terms in an expression may be expanded in a particular way to form an equivalent expression. $a(b + c) = ab + bc$

DOMAIN:	the set of values assigned to the independent variables of a function.
EQUILATERAL:	a figure having all its sides equal.
FACTOR:	one of two or more numbers, algebraic expressions, or the like, that when multiplied together produce a given product.
GREATEST COMMON DIVISOR:	the largest number that is a common divisor of a given set of numbers.
GREATEST COMMON FACTOR:	another name for greatest common divisor.
HYPOTENUSE:	the side of a right triangle opposite the right angle.
IMPROPER FRACTION:	a fraction having the numerator greater than the denominator.
INTEGER:	one of the positive or negative numbers 1,2,3, etc., or zero.
INVERSE FUNCTION:	the function that replaces another function when the dependent and independent variables of the first function are interchanged for an appropriate set of values of the dependent variable.
ISOSCELES:	having two sides equal.
LEAST COMMON MULTIPLE:	also called lowest common multiple; the smallest number that is a common multiple of a given set of numbers.
LEG:	one of the sides of a triangle other than a base or hypotenuse.
LINEAR EQUATION:	a first-order equation involving two variables: its graph is a straight line in the Cartesian coordinate system.
LONG DIVISION:	division, usually by a number of two or more digits, in which each step of the process is written down.
MEAN:	something midway between two extremes; one way to express average.
MEDIAN:	the middle number in a given sequence of numbers, or the average of the middle two numbers when the sequence has an even number of numbers.
MIDPOINT:	a point at the middle.

MIXED NUMBER:	a number consisting of a whole number and a fraction or decimal, as 4 1/2 or 4.5.
MODE:	the most common value in a sample.
MODULUS:	a quantity by which two given quantities can be divided to yield the same remainders.
MULTIPLE:	a number that can be evenly divided by another number.
MULTIPLICATIVE:	having the power of multiplying.
MUTUALLY EXCLUSIVE EVENTS:	events in which the occurrence of one precludes the occurrence of the other.
NULL SET	an empty set.
OBTUSE:	an angle greater than 90° but less than 180°.
PERMUTATIONS:	changing the order of set elements arranged in a particular way.
POLYGON:	a figure having three or more sides.
PRIME NUMBER:	a positive integer that is not divisible without remainder by any integer except itself and 1.
PROPER FRACTION:	a fraction having the numerator less than the denominator.
PROPORTION:	comparative relation between things as to size, quantity, number, etc.
PYTHAGOREAN THEOREM:	the theorem that the square of the hypotenuse of a right triangle is equal to the sum of the squares of the other two sides.
QUADRILATERAL:	A four-sided figure
RADIUS:	a straight line extending from the center of a circle or sphere to the circumference or surface.
RANGE:	the set of all values attained by a given function throughout its domain.
RATIO:	the relation between two similar magnitudes with respect to the number of times the first contains the second.
RATIONAL NUMBER:	a number that can be expressed exactly by a ratio of two integers.
REAL NUMBER:	a rational number.

RECIPROCAL: Two numbers which when multiplied yield 1.

Ex. 1/3 * 3 =1

RIGHT ANGLE: the angle formed by two intersecting perpendicular lines; an angle of 90°.

RIGHT TRIANGLE: a triangle having a right angle (90^0).

SLOPE: The change y divided by the change in x for a given line.

SUBSET: all elements in the set can be found in another set.

TERM: each of the members of which a mathematical expression separated by signs (+, -, *, ÷)

TRANSITIVE PROPERTY: the property stating if a=b and b=c, then a=c.

VERTICAL ANGLE: one of two opposite and equal angles formed by the intersection of two lines.

PART IV
SCIENCE

This section covers

- History of Science
- The Scientific Method
- Chemistry
- Biology
- Earth Science
- Physics

Science

The science section of the test covers life science (biology), earth science (geology), astronomy, physical science (physics), and chemistry. There may also be a few questions on scientific methodology and the history of science.

Chapter 1: SCIENTIFIC METHOD

Science, in the modern sense, is a well-defined way of understanding the world and discovering truths about the world. It is defined not only by *what* it studies but also by *how* it studies. To put it another way, method is just as important as content. The characteristics of this method could be summed up as follows: science aims to be empirical, objective, and systematic.

To say that science is **empirical** is to say that it is based on observation. There is more to scientific method than this, but observation seems to be necessary. To appreciate the role of observation in science, one could contrast science with other general approaches to the world: history cannot directly observe the objects of its study, while philosophy places equal or greater importance on thought relative to observation.

That science is *systematic* is to say that it is not haphazard or random. Scientific thought has a structure, scientific investigations must proceed within certain parameters, and scientific questions must be formulated in a certain way. (It is not enough for a scientist to ask "why?" without any further definition.) A new theory or discovery must be related to the existing structure of knowledge and that structure will be changed because of this addition. This structure is sometimes referred to as a **paradigm**, or model. One such paradigm would be the heliocentric model of planetary motion where the earth and other planets revolve in elliptical orbits around the sun. The planets are kept in their orbits by the gravitational attraction between them and the sun.

The scientific method essentially consists of observation, reasoning, and testing. The exact sequence of steps will not be the same in every case, but the process is typical. First, an observation of some event in the world is made. From this, a reasonable guess (**hypothesis**) to explain the event is formulated. Then, testing of the hypothesis through the gathering of data occurs. After this, the scientist will reason whether the hypothesis has been confirmed or not. At this point, if the hypothesis is not confirmed, it is either discarded or modified. If the hypothesis is modified, the updated version is again tested by experimentation. On the other hand, if the hypothesis is repeatedly confirmed, it will take on the status of a **theory**. Some theories seem so fundamental that they are called laws. For example, Newton's laws concerning motion, the laws of thermodynamics, etc.

Scientific reasoning falls under two broad categories: inductive and deductive. Inductive reasoning involves moving from particular to general. A particular event, such as the sun rising in the east, is observed to happen so many times that the observer is led to formulate a general rule such as "the sun always rises in the east" or "the probability is that the sun will rise in the east." The problem with induction is that it can only formulate probabilities, not necessities. There is no guarantee that the sun will always behave in a certain way or that it will even exist at a certain point in the future.

Deductive reasoning moves in the opposite direction: general to particular. This type of reasoning starts with a general premise or *postulate* that all reasonable people would accept, such as "all living things change over time" and deduces theorems from this general principle such as "human beings change over time." If one accepts the premise as true, one *must* accept the theorem that follows logically from it. The theorem is then tested experimentally to establish its scientific validity. The problem with deduction is that there may not be agreement as to the meanings of the words used in the premises. For instance, in the premise "all living things change over time" there may be debate over what counts as a "living thing," the meaning of "change," and what kind of time scale ought to be used.

Causation is a key concept in scientific explanations and it ought to be distinguished from **correlation**. Two events or phenomena may be correlated without causation. For instance, there seems to be a correlation between speed limits and the number of automobile accidents: as the speed limit increases so does the number of accidents, but this should not be taken to mean that speed limits "cause" accidents.

Scientific explanations tend to take certain forms, the most notable of which are teleological, functional, structural, and reductional types of explanation. *Telos* means "goal" or "purpose" in Greek and so a **teleological** explanation refers to some purpose. An example would be explaining the fact that humans have feet by saying that humans have feet for the purpose of mobility. A **functional** explanation would examine how feet actually function in specific circumstances without making reference to any one purpose that they are supposed to have. **Structural** explanations break down the objects of study into their constituent parts and how these parts combine to form a whole that is more than the sum of its parts. **Reductional** explanations reduce a phenomenon to something that is more scientifically treatable, such as when someone says that the mind is nothing more than the chemical workings of the brain.

When conducting experiments, a **control group** is often used for comparison. The primary group under study and the control group have the same characteristics except for the variable being studied. This allows the scientist to 'isolate' the effects of the variable. **Dependent variables** change when the other variables change. **Independent variables** are not changed by changing other variables.

Chapter 2: SCIENTIFIC MEASUREMENT

Since science often has to deal with quantities that are either very large or very small, it has developed a shorthand notation to express these quantities. For instance, the distance to the edge of the universe is about 100 trillion trillion meters, which is a 1 followed by 26 zeros. A much more economical way of expressing this huge number would be 10^{26}. The system of scientific notation is thus based on powers of 10, where the exponent indicates the number of zeros to the right of the units place. Thus one million is 1×10^6, 2,405 is 2.405×10^3, and a trillion is 1×10^{12}. Very small quantities involve division: 1 millionth is 1 divided by a million, (0.000001) which can be expressed as 1×10^{-6}.

Science uses standard prefixes to indicate factors:

deka	Ten	10^1	deci	One-tenth	10^{-1}
hecto	Hundred	10^2	centi	One-hundredth	10^{-2}
kilo	Thousand	10^3	milli	One-thousandth	10^{-3}
mega	Million	10^6	micro	One-millionth	10^{-6}
giga	Billion	10^9	nano	One-billionth	10^{-9}
tera	Trillion	10^{12}	pico	One-trillionth	10^{-12}

Thus a nanosecond (1×10^{-9}) is a billionth of a second and a kilometer (1×10^3) is a thousand meters.

Unfortunately, there isn't one universal system of units, so conversion of units from one system to another is often necessary. The two systems between which conversion usually takes place are the metric system and the English system. The English system is the one used by most people in the United States, however the scientific community usually uses the metric system. Examples of English units of distance would be inches, feet, yards, miles, etc. The pound is the English unit of weight. In both systems, the standard unit of time is the second.

To convert units of length between systems, simply multiply by fractions equal to one until you have the correct units to which you are looking to convert. For instance if you want to convert inches to centimeters:

1 inch = 2.54 centimeters

$$Y \text{ inches} \times \frac{2.54 \text{ centimeters}}{1 \text{ inch}} = 2.54Y \text{ centimeters}$$

If you needed to convert a certain number of feet to its equivalent number of meters, the sequence would go something like this: feet to inches, inches to centimeters, centimeters to meters. (A meter is equivalent to 100 centimeters.)

As an example, convert 6 feet to meters using only the fact that 1 in.=2.54 cm.

$$6 \, \text{ft} \left(\frac{12 \, \text{in}}{1 \, \text{ft}} \right) \left(\frac{2.54 \, \text{cm}}{1 \, \text{in}} \right) \left(\frac{1 \, \text{m}}{100 \, \text{cm}} \right) = \frac{(6)(12)(2.54) \, \text{m}}{100} = 1.8288 \, \text{m}$$

So 6 feet equals approximately 1.83 meters. The key strategy in the above conversion is arranging the fractions so that the unwanted units would cancel out, leaving only the desired unit of meters. Inside each of the three parentheses to the left is a fraction equal to 1; these fractions do not change the value of the quantity, only its units.

Chapter 3: THE HISTORY & DEVELOPMENT OF SCIENCE

Modern science is the result of over two millennia of labor: wondering, questioning, experimenting, etc. The two key historical periods are ancient Greece and Europe since about the 16th century. Here are some of the key figures:

- Pythagoras (circa 500 BC): related the three sides of a right triangle in the famous theorem that bears his name. $a^2 + b^2 = c^2$

- Democritus (circa 400 BC): theorized that matter was composed of indivisible pieces called *atoma*.

- Hippocrates (circa 400 BC): the "father of medicine".

- Euclid (circa 300 BC): laid out the principles of plane geometry that are still taught in schools.

- Archimedes (circa 250 BC): principle that a body in fluid loses weight equal to the weight of the fluid that it displaces; discovered lever and pulley.

- Ptolemy (circa 150 AD): geocentric theory that the heavenly bodies revolve around the earth in circular orbits.

- Copernicus (circa 1540): superceded Ptolemaic system with the heliocentric theory that the earth revolves around the sun and the earth spins on its axis.

- Kepler (circa 1600): the planets revolve around the sun in elliptical, not circular, orbits.

- Galileo (circa 1600): invented refracting telescope; discovered free-fall acceleration.

- Newton (circa 1687): (described below in Physics section.)

- Linnaeus (circa 1735): outlined the classification scheme for living things used in biology.

- Bernoulli, Daniel (circa 1740): speed of a fluid and pressure of the fluid are inversely proportional.

- Lavoisier (died 1794): named oxygen and hydrogen; invented nomenclature for chemical systems.

- Avogadro (circa 1810): two equal volumes of gas, at same temperature and pressure, contain an equal number of molecules.

- Dalton (circa 1810): matter composed of atoms of differing weights that combine in predictable ratios.

- Faraday (circa 1830): electromagnetic induction.

- Darwin (1859): theory of evolution by natural selection.

- Mendel (1866): particulate theory of inheritance in which genes are passed on independently of each other.

- Maxwell (1873): related electricity and magnetism.

- Pasteur (d 1895): theorized that disease was caused by germs outside of the body.

- Curie, Marie and Pierre (1898): discovered radium.

- Rutherford (1911): discovered the atomic nucleus.

- Bohr (1913): postulated orbits for electrons.

- Einstein (circa 1920): curvature of space-time; related mass and energy.

- Planck (circa 1920): energy emitted in discrete packets called 'quanta'.

- Heisenberg (1925): formulated the 'uncertainty principle' which says that if one knows the velocity of a high-speed particle like an electron, then one can't be absolutely certain of its position, and converse.

- Fermi (1942): first uranium chain-reaction; named the neutrino.

Section 1: Structure And Composition Of The Atom

Chemistry involves the study of matter and it transformations. Matter has 3 physical states: solids, liquids and gases. The basic building block of all matter is the atom.

Question 1:

What is the basic building block of matter?

      a. atoms
      b. gases
      c. liquids
      d. solids

Atoms

Atoms are made of three subatomic particles, protons, neutrons and electrons. Protons are positively charged and have a mass of 1 amu (atomic mass unit). Electrons are negatively charged and have a mass of $\frac{1}{1800}$ amu or nearly zero. Neutrons have no charge and have a mass of 1 amu.

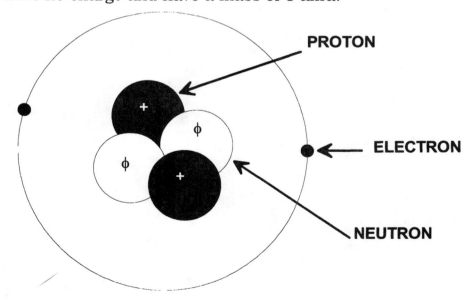

Atomic Weight

Protons and **neutrons** are located in the **nucleus** (the center) of the atom. Since each of these particles weighs one atomic mass unit, together, they make up the **atomic weight** (how much the atom weighs) of the atom.

Atomic weight may accompany the chemical element symbol in certain problems. It is the number written as a superscript to the upper left of the chemical symbol.

EXAMPLE: ^{195}Pt

^{70}Ga

Question 2:

What makes up the nucleus?

a. protons
b. neutrons
c. electrons
d. a and b

Isotopes

The identity of an atom is determined by the number of protons. For example, hydrogen always has one proton. Although the <u>atoms of the same element contain the same number of protons</u>, the number of neutrons may vary, producing isotopes. For example, an atom of uranium may be expressed as ^{238}U, ^{235}U or ^{234}U, depending upon the specific atomic weight. These U atoms are referred to as **isotopes**. Isotopes are atoms with the same number of protons (thus are the same element), but different atomic weights because they have a different number of neutrons. In normal chemical reactions isotopes react the same way.

Question 3:

Which of the following is the best definition for an isotope?

a. atoms with the same number of protons
b. atoms with the same number of neutrons
c. atoms with the same number of electrons
d. atoms with the same number of protons but with a different number of neutrons

Many atoms have isotopic forms.

ISOTOPES OF HYDROGEN

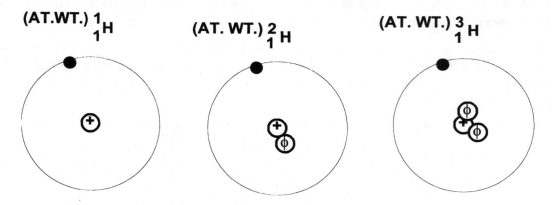

(AT.WT.) ^1_1H (AT. WT.) ^2_1H (AT. WT.) ^3_1H

All of these are hydrogen atoms because they have one proton and one electron. But, they all are isotopes of hydrogen because they have different atomic weights.

ATOMIC WEIGHTS OF CARBON

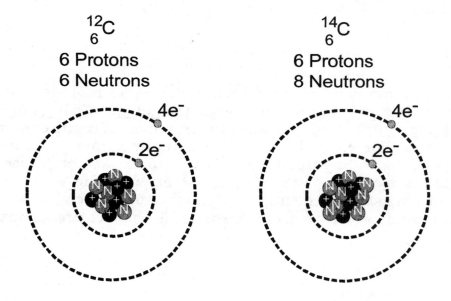

$^{12}_6C$

6 Protons
6 Neutrons

$^{14}_6C$

6 Protons
8 Neutrons

4e⁻ → $4e^-$

2e⁻ → $2e^-$

Both of the above are carbon atoms because they have 6 p⁺ and 6 e⁻. They are isotopes of carbon because they have different atomic weights of the same element.

Question 4:

Which of the following is true of isotopes?

      a. they all react differently
      b. they have a different number of protons
      c. they have a different number of electrons
      d. they have a different number of neutrons

Atomic Number Protons

The number of protons in the nucleus determines the atomic number of the atom. Each element (group of similar atoms) has its own atomic number. When this number accompanies the chemical symbol, it is placed to the lower left of the symbol. Often the atomic number is not written down because the element symbol also tells the atomic number.

Atomic Weight 1 H Atomic Weight 7 Li Atomic Weight 238 U
Atomic Number 1   Atomic Number 3   Atomic Number 92

Question 5:

What is the best definition for atomic number?

      a. the number of electrons in the atom
      b. the number of protons in the atom
      c. the number of neutrons in the atom
      d. the number of protons and neutrons in the atom

Electrical Charges Of The Atom

The number of protons in the nucleus determines the number of electrons present in an **atom**. Atoms are electrically **neutral**. For every proton there is an electron. The positive electrical charge of the proton is cancelled by the negative electrical charge of the electron. (In an atom, (p^+) charges = (e^-) charges, leaving the atom in a neutral state electrically).

Question 6:

How many electrons would oxygen have if it has eight protons?

      a. four
      b. eight
      c. sixteen
      d. twenty-four

Electrons

Electrons are located outside the nucleus at sites called orbits/shells/levels (take your choice, they all mean the same site).

Levels

An atom may contain up to seven levels.

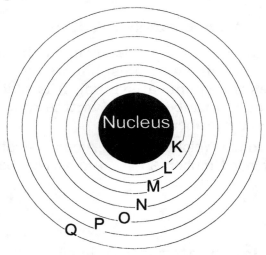

EXAMPLES:

$_1^1 H$ $_{17}^{35} Cl$ $_{92}^{238} U$

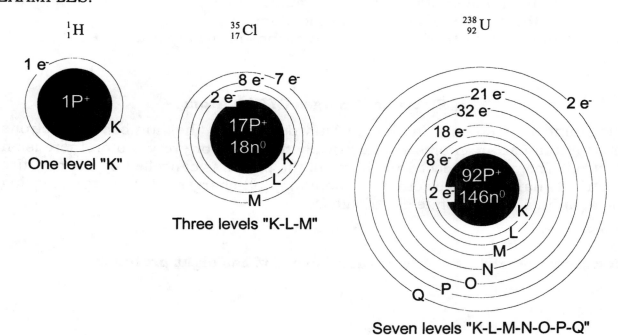

One level "K"   Three levels "K-L-M"

Seven levels "K-L-M-N-O-P-Q"

Question 7:

Electrons are located in

    a. orbits.
    b. shells.
    c. levels.
    d. all of the above.

Section 2: Number of Elements

There are ninety-two elements naturally occurring in nature. There are also a number of man-made atoms, but these disintegrate quickly back to the natural ninety-two.

Chemical Symbols

Each element has its own chemical symbol. This symbol may be one capital letter or a capital letter followed by a lower case letter.

EXAMPLES: H   hydrogen   C   carbon

                  He helium   Ca calcium

Here is a list of common chemical symbols you might be expected to know for the examination:

CHEMICAL SYMBOL	ELEMENT	CHEMICAL SYMBOL	ELEMENT
1. Al	Aluminum	11. Na	Sodium
2. Ca	Calcium	12. S	Sulfur
3. C	Carbon	13. U	Uranium
4. Cu	Copper	14. Zn	Zinc
5. Fe	Iron	15. Hg	Mercury
6. Pb	Lead	16. Br	Bromine
7. Mg	Magnesium	17. N	Nitrogen
8. P	Phosphorus	18. O	Oxygen
9. K	Potassium	19. H	Hydrogen
10. Si	Silicon	20. Cl	Chlorine

Elements 1-14 exist naturally as solids; 15 and 16 exist as liquids. Numbers 17-20 exist as diatomic gases.

Elements are grouped in a periodic table according to common properties. The **alkali metals** are soft and react very easily with other elements. Examples are Lithium (Li), Sodium (Na), Potassium (K), and Cesium (Cs). The **halogens** are nonmetals that occur as diatomic molecules and have a tendency to gain electrons, thereby forming negative ions (such as when chlorine reacts with sodium to form salt). Fluorine (F), Chlorine (Cl), Bromine (Br) and Iodine (I) are examples of halogens. The **noble gases** (sometimes called *inert* or *rare* gases) are generally unreactive with other elements except under extremely controlled laboratory conditions. Some examples of the noble gases are Helium (H), Neon (Ne), Argon (Ar), Krypton (Kr), Xenon (Xe), and Radon (Rn).

Question 8:

Which of the following are solids at room temperature?

> I   OXYGEN
>
> II POTASSIUM
>
> III CARBON

a. I only
b. I and III only
c. II and III only
d. all of the above

Section 3: Diatomic Molecules And Compounds

The diatomic gases have a **subscript** written to the lower right of the chemical symbol (O_2, H_2, N_2, and Cl_2) indicating the number of atoms in the molecule.. These gases exist in their free state as a pair of atoms and referred to as a **diatomic molecule** (two atoms forming one molecule).

Compounds

Given the right circumstances, atoms, elements, molecules and compounds may react with each other to form new products. The products formed may be new compounds or released.

Atoms are single atoms not chemically bonded together.

Elements are single type of atom either alone or chemically bonded together.

Molecules are two or atoms chemically bonded together. The atoms can be the same, or different.

Question 9:

When two like atoms form a chemical bond, what are they called?

      a. a joint
      b. a joining
      c. a bicompound molecule
      d. a diatomic molecule

Section 4: Chemical Reactions

When two **elements** combine, the properties of the **product** will be different from the elements. Look at the example of what happens when hydrogen and oxygen combine to form the **compound**, water.

TWO ELEMENTS	hydrogen + oxygen $\Rightarrow$ water		
SYMBOLS	$H_2 +$ (unbalanced)	$O_2 \Rightarrow$	H_2O
PHYSICAL PROPERTIES	gases, odorless, tasteless, colorless		liquid, odorless, tasteless, colorless
CHEMICAL PROPERTIES	very explosive	supports combustion	<u>NOT</u> explosive and does <u>NOT</u> support combustion

Question 10:

Which of the following is true?

    a.   The products of a reaction always have the same properties as the reactants.
    b.   The products of a reaction always have a blend of the properties of the reactants.
    c.   There are always more products than reactants.
    d.   The products will have properties independent from those of the reactants.

Now, look at what happens when two compounds are combined. This reaction is called a **double replacement reaction**:

Two Compounds

sodium hydroxide + hydrochloric acid $\Rightarrow$ sodium chloride + water

When this is written as an equation using the symbols that represent the compounds it would look like this:

SYMBOLS $\qquad$ NaOH + HCl $\Rightarrow$ NaCl + H_2O

IMPORTANT POINTS FOR YOU TO KNOW WHEN WORKING WITH ELEMENTS, COMPOUNDS, AND REACTIONS:

- (OH) with or without brackets, usually denotes a **base**.
- H beginning a chemical formula usually denotes an **acid**.
- an acid + a base combine to form a salt and water

Using this information with the previous equation, we see that Na (OH) is a base, HCl is an acid and that they combined to form NaCl, which is a salt, and H_2O, which is water.

$\qquad$ BASE + ACID $\Rightarrow$ SALT + WATER

$\qquad$ Na (OH) + HCl $\Rightarrow$ NaCl + H_2O

When a compound and an element are combined to form a new product the process is called a **single replacement reaction**.

Look at the following example of a single replacement reaction.

$\qquad$ Sodium Chloride + Fluorine $\Rightarrow$ Sodium Fluoride + Chlorine

Using the symbols that represent these chemicals, the equation would look like this:

SYMBOLS $\quad$ NaCl + F_2 $\Rightarrow$ NaF + Cl_2

$\qquad$ (unbalanced)

Question 11:

Which of the following is a double replacement reaction?

    I. $LiOH + HCl \Rightarrow LiCl + H_2O$

    II. $H_2 + O_2 \Rightarrow 2H_2O$

    III. $C + O_2 \Rightarrow CO_2$

  a. I only
  b. II only
  c. III only
  d. II and III only

The Law Of Conservation Of Matter

At this point, it would be wise to study the **Law of Conservation of Matter**. Simply stated: <u>matter can neither be created nor destroyed</u>.

Look at the following reaction formula, $H_2 + O_2 \Rightarrow H_2O$.

It is true that hydrogen and oxygen combine to form water. However, the <u>correct amount</u> of H_2 must combine with the <u>correct amount</u> of O_2 in order to produce H_2O.

The "CORRECT" amount of reactants in a reaction (the ingredients are called reactants) is the <u>least</u> amount that allows the reaction to proceed. H_2O is the proper formula for water. H_2 and O_2 is the proper way to represent the reactants. Unfortunately, in the overall formula there is <u>NO</u> equality.

    H_2 two atoms of hydrogen (one molecule)

    O_2 two atoms of oxygen (one molecule)

    H_2O two atoms hydrogen, one atom oxygen (one molecule)

      $H_2 + O_2 \Rightarrow H_2O$

      2 : 2   2:1

In the reaction as written, one oxygen has been "lost". The Law of Conservation of Matter states this cannot happen. In order to remedy the situation and comply with the Law, a balance must be struck on each side of the arrow.

Suppose we use two molecules of H_2 (four atoms) on the left side of the arrow and two molecules of water on the right side of the arrow.

    <u>2</u>H_2 $+ O_2$ $\Rightarrow$ <u>2</u> H_2O

    4 H ATOMS + 2 O ATOMS $\Rightarrow$ 4 H ATOMS + 2 O ATOMS

This balances our equation - the amount of matter on the right side of the arrow (the products) equals the amount of matter on the left side of the arrow (the reactants):

	H_2	O_2 $\Rightarrow$	H_2O
UNBALANCED	1 molecule 2 atoms	1 molecule 2 atoms	1 molecule water = 2 atoms hydrogen and 1 atom of oxygen
BALANCED	$2H_2$ 2 molecules of <u>2 atoms each</u>	+ O_2 $\Rightarrow$ 1 molecule <u>of 2 atoms</u>	$2 H_2O$ 2 molecules <u>of water</u>
	4 atoms (2x2) of hydrogen	2 atoms (1x2) of oxygen	2x2 hydrogen 4 atoms hydrogen
			2x1 oxygen <u>2 atoms of oxygen</u>

Question 12:

Why is it necessary to balance equations?

a. so that you are not creating matter
b. to make everything easier
c. to make everything harder
d. to produce more oxygen

Section 5: Covalent Bonding

When atoms form bonds they can either give up, take away, or share electrons. The sharing of electrons is called **covalent bonding**.

EXAMPLE: $2 H_2 + O_2 \Rightarrow 2 H_2O$

4 H + 2 O will produce 2 molecules of H_2O

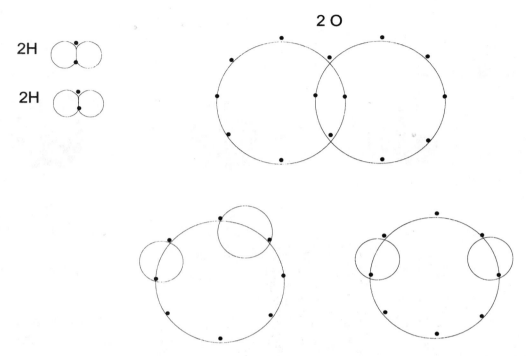

The two diatomic molecules of hydrogen combine with the one diatomic molecule of oxygen. During the reaction, the diatomic molecules of hydrogen and oxygen are broken apart and reassembled.

Question 13:

When hydrogen and oxygen form a molecule, which of the following is true?

> a. They share the electrons.
> b. The oxygen takes electrons from the hydrogen.
> c. The hydrogen takes electrons from the oxygen.
> d. Nothing happens to the electrons.

Section 6: Ionic Bonding

Another kind of chemical bonding is the **ionic bond**. In this type of bond the electrons are moved from one atom to another. Positively charged ions (cations) combine with negatively charged ions (anions) to form neutral salts.

EXAMPLE:

$$2\ Na\ +\ Cl_2 \rightarrow 2\ NaCl$$

(to simplify, we'll work with only one atom of Na, Cl, and one molecule of NaCl)

EXAMPLE:

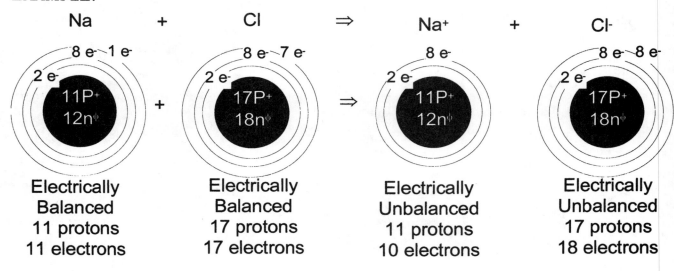

Na⁺ and Cl⁻ can be written with + and - indicating they are charged (electrically **UN**balanced). They are now called **IONS** because they no longer fit the definition of an atom.

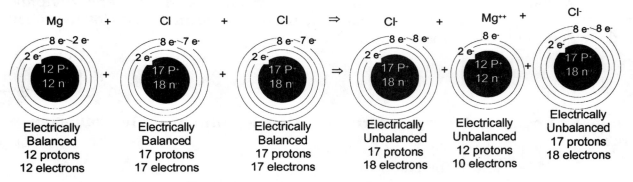

Question 14:

What is the product of an ionic reaction?

    a. a covalent molecule
    b. a salt
    c. free ions
    d. a gas

Section 7: Types Of Molecules

Two important kinds of solutions in chemistry and everyday life are **acids** and **bases**. An acid is an aqueous solution with a relatively high concentration of positive hydrogen ions (H^+). A base has a relatively high concentration of hydroxide ions (OH^-). pH measures the concentration of H^+. A low pH means a higher hydrogen ion concentration and more acidity, while a high pH means that the solution is basic. Some common acids include lemon juice and vinegar, while some common bases are household bleach and ammonia. Milk would be neutral on the pH scale.

Organic molecules (generally speaking, those containing carbon) are important for basic biological processes. The four most common are:

- Carbohydrates: from the standpoint of molecular structure, carbohydrates are also known as polysaccharides (complex sugars). In human biology, they provide energy.

- Lipids: from the standpoint of molecular structure, lipids are also called triglycerides. They are fats that function in energy storage and provide the structural components of cells.

- Proteins: molecularly known as polypeptides, proteins carry out control functions in the body.

- Nucleic acids: are composed of nucleotides and function in the storage of genetic information.

Elements other than carbon that are important for living things are nitrogen, oxygen, hydrogen, phosphorus, and sulfur.

You have now completed your review of chemistry. Before you take the chapter test, check your answers to the chemistry questions that appeared in the chapter.

ANSWERS - CHAPTER QUESTIONS

1. a. The paragraph states the basic building block is the atom and that it makes up all matter.

2. d. The paragraphs state both protons and neutrons are found in the nucleus, and that together they make up the atomic weight of an atom.

3. d. The last paragraph gives the best definition of an isotope. It says isotopes have the same number of protons, but different atomic weights because they have different numbers of neutrons.

4. d. The examples reinforce what we saw in the previous paragraphs, that isotopes have a different number of neutrons.

5. b. The passage states the atomic number is the number of protons in the nucleus.

6. b. The paragraph states atoms have as many electrons as protons. If oxygen has eight protons, it would also have eight electrons.

7. d. The first paragraph states electrons are found in levels, shells, and orbits, and that they all mean the same thing.

8. c. Looking at the chart provided we can see that oxygen is a diatomic gas, potassium is a solid, and carbon is a solid. That makes c your best answer.

9. d. The first paragraph tells about diatomic molecules. It says that they are two like atoms that are joined together. When unlike atoms are joined, the product is called a compound.

10. d. Looking at the reaction in the given example, the only answer that fits is the products will have properties independent from the reactants. In the example you go from having two gases to having a liquid. That is definitely not a blending of properties. We ended up with fewer products than reactants, and it is not stated that all reactants must explode.

11. a. A double replacement reaction is when two ions swap places. The only reaction that does that is the first reaction.

12. a. The paragraphs state the reason it is necessary to balance equations is that you cannot create matter.

13. a. The paragraphs state hydrogen and oxygen form a covalent compound. This means that they share electrons.

14. b. In an ionic reaction, the reactants would combine to make an ionic compound, often a salt.

Review the areas which you answered incorrectly and then take the chapter test.

As you take this short quiz, remember that the material you just studied is used as the reading comprehension material for these questions. If you need to do so, refer back to the part of the text that will help you choose the correct answer.

CHAPTER TEST - CHEMISTRY

1. Mg^{++} is the symbol for
   a. magnesium
   b. magnesium with two protons
   c. magnesium ion
   d. magnesium compound
   e. magnesium with balanced charges

2. Covalent means
   a. loss of electrons
   b. gain of electrons
   c. decay of electrons
   d. sharing of electrons
   e. addition of neutrons to the nucleus

3. The chemical formula for an acid begins with the element
   a. O
   b. Cl
   c. F
   d. OH
   e. H

4. Of the following elements, only __?__ exists naturally as a liquid.
   a. Br
   b. F
   c. Cl
   d. Zn
   e. O

5. In the element carbon, only the number of ____?____ may vary.
   a. protons
   b. neutrons
   c. protons and neutrons
   d. electrons
   e. electrons and protons

6. Atoms of the same element having different atomic weights are

    a. isobars.
    b. isotherms.
    c. isohyets.
    d. isotopes.
    e. isotonic.

7. The atomic weight of an element equals the number of

    a. protons.
    b. protons plus electrons.
    c. protons plus neutrons.
    d. neutrons plus electrons.
    e. neutrons.

8. When an acid and a base react, the products are

    a. two acids.
    b. two bases.
    c. an acid and a base.
    d. a very complex compound, neither acid nor base.
    e. salt and water.

9. What is transferred when an ionic bond forms?

    a. protons
    b. electrons
    c. neutrons
    d. protons plus electrons
    e. neutrons plus protons

10. The reason equations must be balanced is

    a. It looks better that way.
    b. All electrons must be accounted for.
    c. Molecules are different than elements.
    d. Metals are different than non-metals.
    e. The Law of Conservation of Matter.

ANSWERS - CHAPTER TEST CHEMISTRY

1. c)
2. d)
3. e)
4. a)
5. b)
6. d)
7. c)
8. e)
9. b)
10. e)

Section 1: The Cell

In order for us to understand how living things function, we must first understand the basic unit of life. Every living thing we see, both plants and animals, is made up of the same basic building block, the cell. There are differences between cells, but it is surprising how similar most cells are to each other.

Let's take a look at what a typical animal cell looks like so you can get an idea of what some of the basic parts do, and what they look like.

ANIMAL CELL

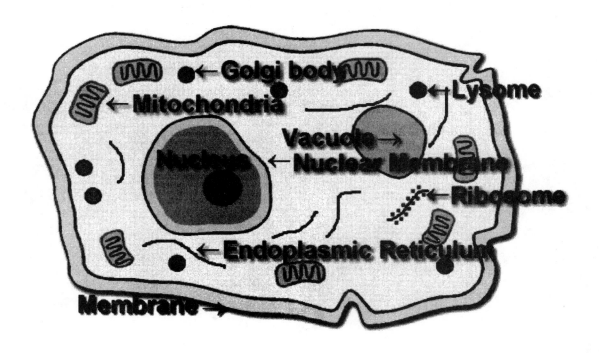

1. **Centrioles** -   Aid in spindle formation during cell division. It makes sure that the chromosomes (the genetic material) go to the right place.

2. **Endoplasmic Reticulum** - A structure used to separate areas of the cell. It looks much like the cell membrane.

3. **Cell Membrane** - Holds the cell together. It also has the job of letting things in and out of the cell. It is very thin, and goes all around the outside of the cell.

4. **Nuclear Membrane** - Separates nucleus from rest of cell body.

5. **Chromatin** - the "genetic" material of the cell. It is responsible for determining what the cell does.

6. **Golgi Body** - stores proteins.

7. **Ribosome** - site where protein synthesis occurs.

8. **Nucleolus** - supplies m-RNA chemicals for protein synthesis.

9. **Mitochondria** - site where energy for cell functions is released.

10. **Cytoplasm** - a gel-like substance containing the following: water, minerals, vitamins, proteins (enzymes), carbohydrates, fats (lipids), and nucleic acids. This is the fluid in a cell.

11. **Vacuole** - a space within the cell that stores food, water, or waste material.

12. **Lysome** - aids in the breakdown of proteins.

Now, let's try some questions. The answers are found in the material you have just read.

Question 1:

Which of the following if missing would cause the cell to die for lack of energy?

      a.   the ribosome
      b.   the cell membrane
      c.   the nucleus
      d.   the mitochondria

Question 2:

The main function of the cell membrane is

      a.   protein synthesis.
      b.   regulation of things entering and leaving the cell.
      c.   energy production.
      d.   cell reproduction.

SOME THINGS TO REMEMBER:

1.   Chromatin forms chromosomes during reproduction.

2.   The cell membrane and nuclear membrane allow substances to pass through - water, gases, food, waste, etc.

3.   The nucleus controls metabolism, growth, and reproduction.

The following illustration points out the major differences between the plant and the animal cell. Most of the parts remain the same, but plants have several extra parts because they do different jobs than animal cells.

PLANT CELL

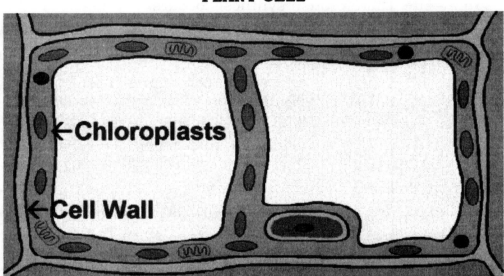

Plant cells usually do not have the mobility of animal cells. Thus, they have a need for protection from their surrounding environment. This protection comes in the form of a non-living cell wall made of cellulose. This is a hard material. A common form we know is wood.

The **chloroplasts** in plant cells manufacture their own food. They are green in color and contain chlorophyll, which is used to collect energy from the sun. This energy is used to help make food for the plant cell.

Question 3:

The cell wall in a plant is

        a.   living and made of cellulose.
        b.   living and made of chlorophyll.
        c.   dead and made of cellulose.
        d.   dead and made of chlorophyll.

Question 4:

The main function of the cell wall is

    a.   protection.
    b.   movement.
    c.   energy production.
    d.   photosynthesis.

Section 2: How Plants Get Their Food

The food making process in green plant cells is called **photosynthesis.**

The following equation explains what occurs during the photosynthesis reaction.

$$\text{light energy} + 6CO_2 + 6H_2O \xrightarrow[\text{+ enzymes}]{\text{Chlorophyll}} C_6H_{12}O_6 + 6O_2$$

The light energy changes to chemical energy in the chloroplasts. The chemical energy is used to unite carbon dioxide (CO_2) with water (H_2O) to produce sugar ($C_6H_{12}O_6$) and oxygen (O_2), which is released as a gas.

From this process of photosynthesis, all the food for all the plants and animals is produced. Plants make food and grow; animals then eat these plants, which gives them food.

Question 5:

During photosynthesis, what two molecules are combined?

    a. water and sugar
    b. sugar and oxygen
    c. water and carbon dioxide
    d. water and oxygen

Question 6:

If it were not for photosynthesis,

   a. all the plants would die.
   b. all the animals would die.
   c. animals would take over the earth.
   d. both plants and animals would die.

- A plant cell that does not make its own food may be **parasitic** (living off other plants or animals) or **saprophytic** (Living off dead plants or animals).

OTHER POINTS TO REMEMBER:

- Animals are **heterotrophic**, capture their food. They do not make it. They must eat and then break down their food to get energy.

- Most plants are **autotrophic**, make their own food.

- Any form of energy may be converted to any other form. In fact, this must regularly be done if the organism is going to survive.

- **Herbivores** eat plants

- **Carnivores** eat animals

- **Omnivores** eat both plants and animals

- **Primary consumers** eat plants

- **Secondary consumers** eat primary consumers

- **Decomposers** eat dead plants and animals

- In addition to the food chain there is also a **nitrogen cycle**. Nitrogen gas (N_2) exists abundantly in the atmosphere. It must be converted to different forms such as ammonium (NH_4^+) or nitrate (NO_3^-) ions in a process called **fixation** before it can be used by living things.

Different species are organized into communities, communities interact in an **ecosystem**, and the sum total of all living things is the **biosphere**. The biosphere would include the lithosphere (soil and rocks), the hydrosphere (oceans), and atmosphere (air). Species interact with one another and over time develop characteristic relations: these types of reciprocal relations are called **symbiosis**. The three main types are:

- **Commensalism**: one benefits, the other is neither harmed nor benefited.

- **Mutualism**: both organisms benefit.

- **Parasitism**: one benefits, other is harmed.

Question 7:

Which of the following is true?

      a. Animals can make their own food.
      b. Fish can make their own food.
      c. All plants make their own food.
      d. Some plants can not make their own food.

Section 3: DNA, RNA And Protein Synthesis

DNA (deoxyribonucleic acid) makes up the genes that form the chromosomes. This is very important because the genes carry all the information to build and run the organism.

A set of chromosomes contains all the information needed for a cell to survive and reproduce. If a nucleus, which contains the genetic information, is removed from the cell, the cell dies.

During reproduction, the chromosomes are duplicated and passed along to the next generation. This means that when a cell divides, both resulting cells have exactly the same genetic material.

This is why a lizard always looks like a lizard and a cat looks like a cat. One of the most important things for living organisms to do is to pass along their genetic information to their offspring.

Question 8:

DNA stands for

      a. deoxyribonucleic acid.
      b. dextrose near arrangement.
      c. doesn't need alcohol.
      d. denatured alcohol.

Question 9:

Which of the following is not true?

     a. Chromosomes are duplicated during cell reproduction.
     b. Animal cells have chromosomes.
     c. Plant cells have chromosomes.
     d. Chromosomes grow continuously

Chromosomes are genes that are joined together. Genes are made up of set combinations of DNA molecules. These set combinations are the cell's genetic information.

A DNA molecule's shape looks like a twisted ladder. The following diagram should give you a better idea of what it looks like.

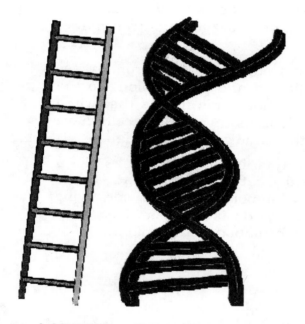

This formation in a molecule is called a **double helix**. The outside supports are made of sugars and phosphates, while the rungs (stem) are made of nucleic bases.

LADDER   TWISTED LADDER

Question 10:

The rungs of the ladder in a DNA molecule are

     a. made of sugars.
     b. made of nucleic bases.
     c. broken.
     d. made of phosphates.

QUESTION 11:

Genes

       a. make up molecules.
       b. float freely in the cytoplasm.
       c. are linked on chromosomes.
       d. make proteins.

The four types of bases are:

       1. cytosine
       2. guanine
       3. adenine
       4. thymine

 Cytosine (1) always pairs with guanine (2) and adenine (3) with thymine (4) in a DNA molecule. These base pairs are held together by weak hydrogen (H••H) bonds. The sequence of the bases forms the genetic code.

Question 12:

In a DNA molecule, which of the following is found in the same quantity as adenine?

       a. cytosine
       b. guanine
       c. uracil
       d. thymine

G-
C-
U-
A-
A-
G-
U-
C-
C-
A-
U-

RNA (RNA - ribonucleic acid) is patterned after DNA. Actually, it is copied from the DNA. Just as many people backup important computer files to protect them, the cell copies the DNA molecule so there is less chance of it getting damaged. The chemical difference between RNA and DNA is the **uracil**, which replaces the base thymine.

RNA can pass through the nuclear membrane and enter the main part of the cell, DNA cannot.

Question 13:

What can RNA do that DNA can't?

     a. duplicate itself
     b. leave the nucleus
     c. form a double helix
     d. store genes

In the following example we will follow the transfer of information from the nucleus (chromatin/gene matter) to somewhere inside the cell body.

How The Nucleus Talks To The Cell

MESSAGE: forms a special enzyme (protein) for energy production

STEP I: DNA in the nucleus contains the original genetic message.

Straightened DNA Chain

```
C ·· G
G ·· C
A ·· T
T ·· A
T ·· A
C ·· G
A ·· T
G ·· C
G ·· C
T ·· A
A ·· T
```

·· Hydrogen Bonds

STEP 2: The molecule begins to separate at the Hydrogen bonds.

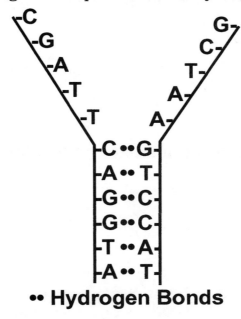

•• Hydrogen Bonds

STEP 3: As the separation occurs, RNA bases begin to link with the "message" base combination.

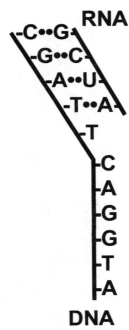

Notice cytosine, guanine, and thymine of the DNA strand all match with their complementary base, while adenine matches with a new base-uracil.

Question 14:

Where is the RNA message formed?

        a. In the cytoplasm.
        b. In the nucleus.
        c. In the ribosome.
        d. In the centriole.

Question 15:

Which base in the DNA strand matches with a different base in the RNA strand?

        a. adenine
        b. thymine
        c. guanine
        d. uracil

STEP 4:   The RNA strand now has the "message" and leaves the nucleus for the cell body. The DNA continues to make these RNAs until stopped by some chemical stimulus. These RNAs are called **Messenger RNA** or **m-RNA**.

STEP 5:   m-RNAs eventually end in the area of the ribosomes. Ribosomes contain ribosomal RNA (r-RNA) and a sort of mutual attraction between it and the m-RNA occurs.

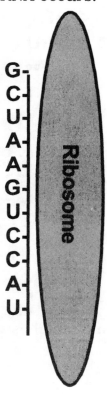

Question 16:

When the m-RNA leaves the nucleus, where does it end up?

      a. It continues out of the cell.
      b. It goes to the mitochondria.
      c. It goes to the ribosome.
      d. It goes to vacuole.

Question 17:

What stops the DNA from making more m-RNA?

      a. the nucleus
      b. the ribosome
      c. the ribosomal RNA
      d. a chemical stimulus

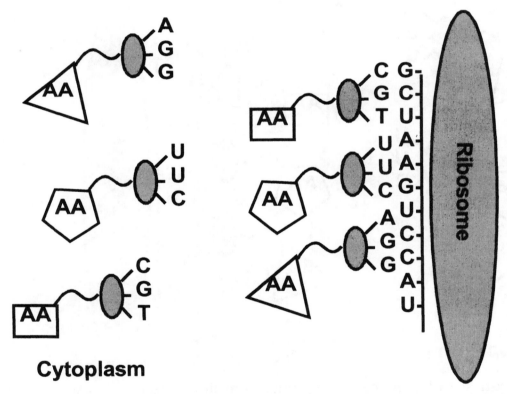

Cytoplasm

Floating out in the cytoplasm are nucleic acids, some of these nucleic acids are transfer RNAs with amino acids, AA in the diagram (amino acids make up proteins) attached to them. There are twenty different types of amino acids.

STEP 6:   The **Transfer RNAs** (t-RNA) come in contact with the m-RNAs attached to the ribosome. When the right combination matches the m-RNA, they "stick" together for a while until the process completes itself.

Question 18:

How many different amino acids are there?

     a. 5
     b. 7
     c. 13
     d. 20

Question 19:

What type of RNA has amino acids attached to it?

     a. messenger
     b. amino acid
     c. transfer
     d. chromosomal

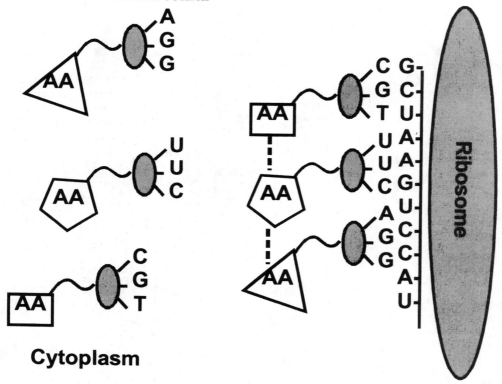

Cytoplasm

As you can see above, there are many combinations of t-RNAs - all carrying a specific amino acid.

The t-RNAs attach to the m-RNA. The amino acids combine together to form an enzyme (protein).

The enzyme will eventually encounter an energy-making situation and do its job. The t-RNA, now minus their specific amino acids, are released back into general circulation in the cytoplasm where they will eventually find their complementary amino acids. The m-RNA continues to attract t-RNAs until it is chemically shut down.

Question 20:

The t-RNA can

> a. attach to any amino acid.
> b. attach to any point on the m-RNA.
> c. attach to a specific amino acid.
> d. form a protein.

Section 4: Energy Production In The Cell

Energy production in the cell occurs mainly in the mitochondria. This is the site where the cell converts food to the energy it can use. The cell must convert the energy, because food molecules have too much energy in them. Just as we convert nuclear energy into electricity, the cell takes the food and makes a chemical known as **ATP** (adenosine triphosphate).

Question 21:

Where does energy production occur?

> a. In the mitochondria.
> b. At the ATP.
> c. At the ribosome.
> d. In the nucleus.

Below is a chemical reaction. It shows how a sugar molecule is broken down. Notice that it is exactly the opposite reaction we saw in photosynthesis. Here energy is being released instead of being stored in the sugar molecule.

Oxidation Or Cellular Respiration

$$C_6H_{12}O_6 + 6O_2 \quad \xrightarrow{\text{ENZYMES}} \quad 6CO_2 + 6H_2O + \text{energy}$$

Question 22:

Oxidation is the opposite of what other reaction?

       a. enzymea
       b. photosynthesis
       c. electrolysis
       d. hydrolysis

In hydrolysis, water combines with a fat to break the fat down into fatty acid and glycerol. The reaction releases a small amount of energy. However, the glycerol can then enter the oxidation pathway that the sugar molecule followed. This allows the cell to get more energy from the fat.

Hydrolysis

H$_2$O + fat → fatty acid + glycerol + small amount of energy

Question 23:

What two chemicals react in hydrolysis?

       a. fat and fatty acid
       b. fat and water
       c. water and fatty acid
       d. fatty acid and glycerol

Now, let's take a look at how the cell uses the energy given off in these reactions. Remember the cell must be able to convert this energy to small units that it is able to use. There are two main chemicals involved.

ATP - adenosine triphosphate (carries three phosphate molecules)

ADP - adenosine diphosphate (carries two phosphate molecules)

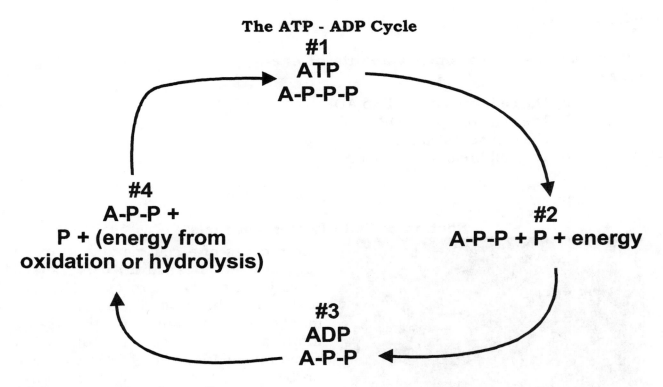

The ATP - ADP Cycle

#1
ATP
A-P-P-P

#4
A-P-P +
P + (energy from oxidation or hydrolysis)

#2
A-P-P + P + energy

#3
ADP
A-P-P

Let's go over the above diagram.

STEP 1: This is an ATP molecule. It has energy stored in it for the cell. When the cell does not need energy it just floats around.

STEP 2: The cell now needs energy. It takes the ATP molecule and breaks off one of the phosphates. This releases energy for the cell to use.

STEP 3: The cell has used the ATP molecule for energy, but has enough other ATP molecules around so it does not have to make more by breaking down food molecules.

STEP 4: The cell supply of ATP is getting low. It is time for it to make more. It breaks down food to release energy. It then takes that energy to attach a phosphate to an ADP molecule. We are now back at the ATP molecule in Step 1.

Question 24:

When the cell's supply of ATP is high, which of the following is true?

        a. The cell converts ATP to ADP.
        b. The cell converts ADP to ATP.
        c. The cell stops converting ADP to ATP.
        d. The cell breaks down food.

Question 25:

When the cell needs small amounts of energy, which of the following is true?

      a. The cell converts ATP to ADP.
      b. The cell converts ADP to ATP.
      c. The cell stops converting ADP to ATP.
      d. The cell breaks down food.

Section 5: Cell Division - Mitosis

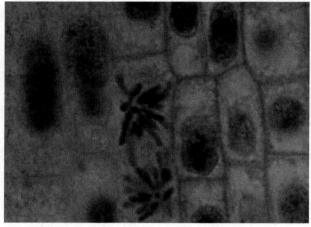

The process of a cell making an <u>exact copy</u> of itself is called **mitosis**. This is a very important process, because both cells (the original and the copy) must end up having the <u>same</u> information. If the cells do not get the same information, one of the cells will probably die because it does not have everything it needs.

Plant cell undergoing mitosis

Question 26:

Why must the cells end up with the same information?

      a. because they are supposed to
      b. because they must reproduce
      c. because they do not need to get the same material
      d. because one cell would likely die if it did not get the right material
      e. because every cell has different genetic material

The following are the basic steps in mitosis, identical cell reproduction:

Animal Cell

STEP 1: **Interphase**

<u>INTERPHASE</u>

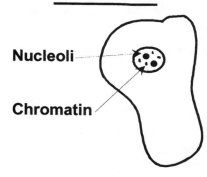

Nucleoli

Chromatin

This is the time between the last cell division and immediately before mitosis is ready to begin again. The cell must grow. After the last division, the cell became half its original size. Now it is growing. The **chromosomes**, with all the cell's genetic material in the form of DNA, are unwound and are spread throughout the nucleus. In this form they are simply called **chromatin** because individual chromosomes are not visible. It is necessary for the chromosomes to unwind for them to be able to make RNA. The final step in this phase is when the DNA makes a copy of itself. The cell now has two copies of the DNA so it can divide and give a set to each cell.

Question 27:

Which of the following does not occur during interphase?

    a. the cell divides
    b. the cell duplicates its DNA
    c. the cell grows
    d. the cell chromosomes unravel

STEP 2:   Mitosis Begins Prophase (Animal Cell)

PROPHASE

Centromere

Centriole

Chromatids

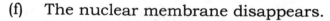

(a) The centriole divides. Each half then migrates to a different half of the cell.

(b) Fibers start to radiate from the centriole halves. They are called **aster** fibers.

(c) The chromatin in the nucleus starts to coil up into its chromosome phase.

(d) The nucleoli, one of the structures in the nucleus, disappear.

(e) The chromosomes continue to coil. They are now called **chromatids**. The identical chromosomes formed during interphase join so you have pairs of chromosomes. The pairs are joined together at their center by a **centromere**.

(f) The nuclear membrane disappears.

(g) The chromatid pairs migrate toward the equator and line up down the middle of the cell. The **aster** fibers have gotten longer and they are now called the **spindle**. One spindle fiber from each half of the cell attaches to one of the chromatids in each pairing of chromosomes.

Question 28:

Which of the following does <u>not</u> occur during prophase?

>   a. The chromosomes coil.
>   b. The nuclear membrane disappears.
>   c. The centriole splits.
>   d. The cell membrane disappears.

Question 29:

What do the aster fibers attach to?

>   a. the nuclear membrane
>   b. the cell membrane
>   c. the chromosomes
>   d. the nucleoli

STEP 3: Metaphase

METAPHASE

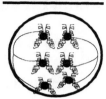

During metaphase the **chromatids** continue to shorten and get fatter. They are now in a line down the center of the equator.

STEP 4: Anaphase

ANAPHASE

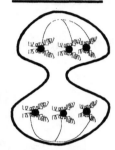

(a) The chromosome pairs break apart and the spindle fibers pull one chromosome from each pair to each pole of the cell.

ANIMAL 1. ANIMAL CELL - A cleavage furrow pushes in at the middle of the cell and slowly divides the daughter cells.

PLANT 2. PLANT CELL - A cell plate forms down the middle of the cell and it divides the daughter cells.

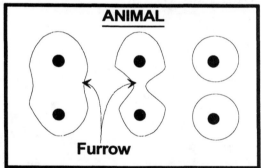

ANIMAL

Furrow

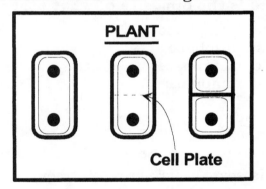

PLANT

Cell Plate

Question 30:

What is the difference between plant cell division and animal cell division?

        a. A plant cell develops a cleavage furrow.
        b. There are no differences.
        c. A plant cell forms a cell plate.
        d. Plant cells end up with eight cells.

STEP 5: Telophase

Telophase is the opposite of prophase in that the fibers disappear and the nucleus reforms. It contains both nucleoli and chromatin.

Cell division is the same for plant cells, except plants do not have centromeres. The spindle fibers form without them.

Question 31:

Telophase is the opposite of what other stage of mitosis?

        a. interphase
        b. prophase
        c. metaphase
        d. anaphase

Section 6: Cell Division - Meiosis

Meiosis is sex cell formation. In meiosis, cell division occurs in two parts. The first part is called the first meiotic division. The cell divides and splits all the genetic information in the same fashion as mitosis. This leaves the cell with two copies of each chromosome.

The second part involves the reduction of the chromosome pairs into single chromosomes. This leaves each cell with only one copy of each chromosome. This is very important because if the organism could not reduce the number of chromosomes in its sex cells, the number of chromosomes would always increase when it mated. To put this another way, if an organism got two of each chromosome from each parent it would end up with four of each chromosome. A cell with only one set of chromosomes is called **haploid**. A cell with two sets of chromosomes is **diploid**.

The resulting cells in a male organism are sperm. Four sperm are produced for each original cell. They all are able to fertilize an egg.

In a female, the resulting cells are the **öotid** (egg) and polar bodies. When the cells in a female divide, all of the cytoplasm goes with one cell. This becomes the egg. The other cells are called polar bodies. They have very little cytoplasm and quickly die.

If fertilization occurs, a sperm containing a haploid number of chromosomes unites with an **ovum** containing a haploid number of chromosomes. The fertilized cell, a **zygote**, contains a diploid number of chromosomes. In the diploid state, regular mitotic division can occur and the zygote becomes the kind of living being dictated by the genes.

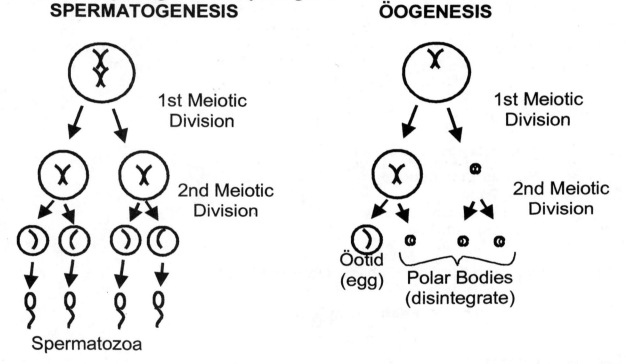

Question 32:

What is a haploid cell?

     a. a cell that is ready to divide
     b. a cell that is in the process of division
     c. a cell that has only one set of chromosomes
     d. a cell that has just finished dividing

Question 33:

Which of the following is true?

  a. four sperm cells are produced in meiosis
  b. four egg cells are produced in meiosis
  c. three of the four sperm cells die quickly
  d. only one sperm cell is viable

Section 7: Genetics

Gregor Mendel is called the "father of genetics". In the early 1900's discoveries and conclusions gathered from his work with garden peas were published.

Question 34:

Another name for Gregor Mendel is?

  a. the father of genetics
  b. Father Time
  c. the father of our country
  d. Father Garden Pea

The following is a summary of the basic laws he discovered.

The Mendelian Laws Of Inheritance

1. The Law of Dominance Each gene has two copies, one from the mother and one from the father. One of the copies may be **dominant** and show its characteristic over the other copy. If so, the other copy is considered to be **recessive**.

EXAMPLE: A pure tall pea plant crossed with a pure short pea plant produced seeds that produced only tall pea plants.

CONCLUSION: The "tall" factor (gene) was dominant over the "short" factor (gene).

TALL/DOMINANT

SHORT/RECESSIVE

Question 35:

Which of the following is not true?

    a. One gene is always dominant.
    b. A dominant gene masks a recessive gene.
    c. An organism has a set number of genes.
    d. Genes are found on the chromosomes.

Traits are represented by letters to quickly identify different characteristics. Capitals are employed to note dominance and lower case to show recessiveness.

EXAMPLE: (a) TT Gene pair indicating "tall" dominance

          (b) tt Gene pair indicating "short" recessiveness

          (c) Tt Gene pair indicating that the "tall" gene will dominate the recessive "short" gene

Gene pairs are often referred to as being either **homozygous** (genes with similar traits like (a) and (b) above) or **heterozygous** (genes with different traits, such as (c) above). The letters (TT, tt, or Tt) are referred to as the **genotype,** the genetic composition, of the organism.

Question 36:

What is a heterozygous animal?

       a. an animal with two alike genes
       b. an animal with only one set of chromosomes
       c. an animal with four genes
       d. an animal with unlike genes

The trait, which determines the physical appearance (tall, short), is called the **phenotype**.

EXAMPLE: **A CROSS BETWEEN A PURE TAN MOUSE AND A PURE WHITE MOUSE**

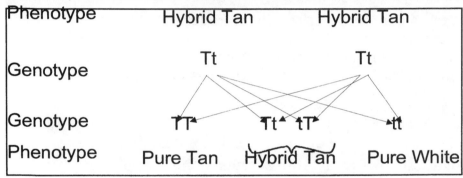

Phenotype	Homozygous Pure Tan	Homozygous Pure White
Genotype	TT	tt
Genotype	Tt Tt Tt Tt	
Phenotype	All hybrid or heterozygous tan	

CONTINUING, A CROSS BETWEEN TWO HYBRID TAN OFFSPRING

Phenotype	Hybrid Tan	Hybrid Tan
Genotype	Tt	Tt
Genotype	TT Tt tT tt	
Phenotype	Pure Tan Hybrid Tan Pure White	

Question 37:

Which of the following is true?

    a. Hybrid tan mice (Tt) will only have white children.
    b. Hybrid tan mice (Tt) will only have tan children.
    c. Hybrid tan mice (Tt) will have white and tan children.
    d. Hybrid tan mice (Tt) will only have children of one phenotype.

2. The Law of Segregation   Mendel concluded the genes were separated during the formation of the sex cells (meiosis) and they (the genes) recombine during fertilization.

3. The Law of Independent Assortment   Mendel concluded one trait might be inherited independently from another trait.

EXAMPLE: Tall pea plants may produce either wrinkled or smooth seeds (peas). Short plants showed the same diversity.

Question 38:

Mendel concluded that

     a. genes can be inherited independently.
     b. all genes are linked.
     c. genes are mixed during mitosis.
     d. genes are separated during mitosis.

Section 8: Living Things

The classification of living things has long been the subject of debate. Previously, living things were classified as being plant or animal. Improvement in microscopes, better chemical analysis of organisms, and the wide diversity of living things, has led most scientists to agree that there are no less than three major divisions, protist, plant, and animal, of living things. Some texts list as many as five major divisions.

Question 39:

What are two ways that organisms can be identified?

     a. microscope and chemical analysis
     b. plant and animal
     c. scientific study and theology
     d. hybrid crossing and cross-sectioning

The following is a list of the major divisions and the organisms contained in them.

The Protist Kingdom

The living organisms in the protist kingdom are generally classified by the following:

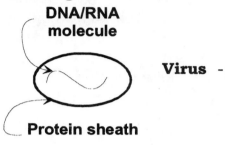

DNA/RNA molecule

Protein sheath

Virus - classified by the host they select. There are bacterial, plant, and animal virus. A virus invades a host and reproduces itself. Sometimes the host will die due to the infection. The common cold and HIV are both viruses.

Bacteria - classified according to shape. The three shapes are spherical ⫮, tubular (cylindrical) ▭ and coiled ⟳ .

Most bacteria depend on living or dead organisms for their food. They are parasites (living off a host) or saprophytes (living off dead organic matter). Some bacteria have the ability to manufacture their food **photosynthetically** or **chemosynthetically** (producing chemical energy by breaking down chemicals—this chemical energy can be used to make sugars and other foods).

Examples of some common bacteria and their environments are:

Live in oxygen (aerobes):	Diphtheria Tuberculoses Cholera
Do not live in oxygen (anaerobes):	Tetanus Botulism

E. coli (Escherichia coli) is a common bacterium that lives in man and survives in both aerobic and anaerobic environments.

Reproduction in bacteria is by fission, cell division forming new organisms.

Protozoa - classified according to their form of locomotion.

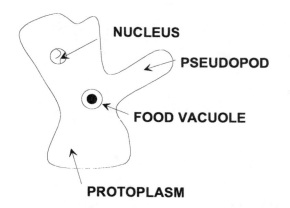

NUCLEUS

PSEUDOPOD

FOOD VACUOLE

PROTOPLASM

Amoeba (Sarcondina) - The amoeba is unique in that it has the ability to change the consistency of its protoplasm from a gel-like substance to a thick, watery solution. This solution flows from one part of the cell toward the direction the amoeba desires to move. This forms a **pseudopod**. The vacated portion of the cell follows along. This action is called protoplasmic streaming. The overall movement of the amoeba is called amoeboid movement.

Amoebas capture their food by enveloping victims with their pseudopods, forming a food vacuole.

Reproduction is by fission.

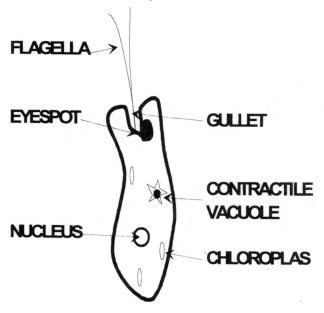

FLAGELLA

EYESPOT

NUCLEUS

GULLET

CONTRACTILE VACUOLE

CHLOROPLAS

Euglena (Mastigophora) -

These organisms have one or two long whip-like threads called **flagellum** (pl. flagella). The flagella are rotated and pull the organisms through the water. **Euglena** is a plant/animal. During the periods of sufficient light, the chloroplasts carry on photosynthesis to make food. However, at night or during periods of darkness, food is absorbed through the cell membrane and eventually digested.

Reproduction is by fission.

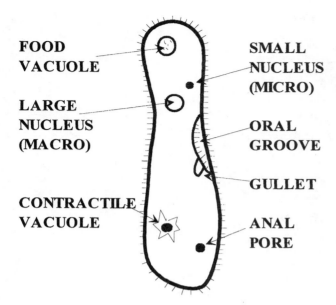

FOOD VACUOLE

LARGE NUCLEUS (MACRO)

CONTRACTILE VACUOLE

SMALL NUCLEUS (MICRO)

ORAL GROOVE

GULLET

ANAL PORE

Paramecium -

These protozoa have short protoplasmic hairs called cilia, which are used to move the organism through the water. The oral groove is a unique feature in the paramecium. Cilia agitate the surrounding water by fanning bits of food into the gullet where food vacuoles are formed.

Reproduction is by fission (mitotic division) and conjugation (two parents exchanging information, see below).

Steps of Conjugation

(1) Two cells join at the oral grooves.

(2) The micronuclei undergo numerous cell divisions and the macronuclei disappear.

(3) Eventually, a large and a small micronucleus exist in each cell. At this time, the small micronuclei are exchanged.

(4) The cells separate and the newly reconstituted micronucleus undergoes more divisions.

(5) Two further mitotic divisions occur forming eight new paramecia.

Malaria - has no form of locomotion. Depends on host for transfer from place to place. Reproduction occurs when the nucleus fragments. The fragments are surrounded by cytoplasm and are called spores. The host cell eventually ruptures, releasing the spores to infect other cells.

Question 40:

How are viruses classified?

    a. by type of host
    b. by type of locomotion
    c. by type of reproduction
    d. by size

Question 41:

Protozoa that move with pseudopods are called

    a. euglena
    b. paramecium
    c. stenator
    d. amoeba

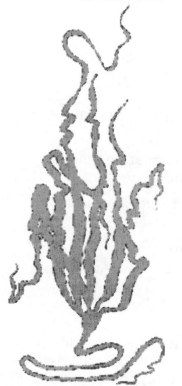

Algae - classified according to color. Most look like plants such as seaweed and kelp. However, the blue-green algae looks like bacteria. Many algae make their food by photosynthesis.

One common use for red algae is the manufacture of **agar**. Agar is the most common medium for growing bacteria in a laboratory. First the agar is warmed up and mixed with nutrients. It is then poured into petri dishes. When it cools it forms a gel. When a scientist wants to grow a particular bacteria or mold, he pokes the sterile gel with it. This infects the gel and a whole colony of the infecting agent grows.

Kelp is a type of brown algae that lives in colonies.

Blue Green Algae

CYANOPHYTA

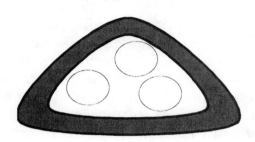

This is the type of algae often associated with scum in ponds and standing water. It is generally found in warmer areas and does not grow well in colder water.

Green Algae (Spirogyra)

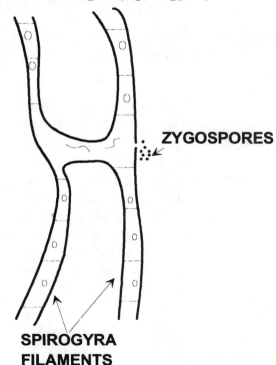

ZYGOSPORES

SPIROGYRA FILAMENTS

This is the type of plant commonly found in fish tanks. Spirogyra are different because they reproduce by both fission and conjugation.

Steps of Conjugation

1) A connecting tube forms between two spirogyra filaments.

2) The interior of one cell flows through the tube into the other cell.

3) New algae cells **(Zygospores)** are formed by the combination of two similar gametes.

4) Zygospores fall from the cell.

5) The zygospores form new spirogyra filaments if conditions are suitable.

Golden Brown Algae

DIFFERENT SHAPES SIZES AND DESIGNS OF DIATOMS

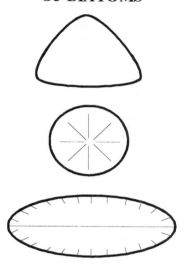

Diatoms are very abundant in the oceans. They are different from other algae because of the shell they build around themselves. This shell is made from **silica** extracted from seawater. The shells vary in size, shape, and design, but they all must be thin enough so that the algae is able to carry on photosynthesis. If they were too thick, light would not be able to penetrate the shell and photosynthesis would not occur. After the algae produces sugar through photosynthesis it quickly converts most of it to oils for storage. Many scientists believe that prehistoric diatoms, not dinosaurs, are the source of the petroleum oil we use.

Fungi - classified by shape. All fungi are parasitic or saprophytic - that is, they depend on other living or dead things for their food.

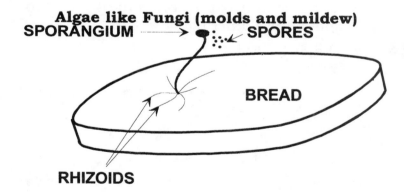

Algae like Fungi (molds and mildew)

SPORANGIUM → SPORES

BREAD

RHIZOIDS

Molds have structures that are similar to roots (**hyphae** rhizoids), but they are not true roots. Instead they penetrate the source of food and secrete enzymes. The enzymes break down the food into usable nutrients. The nutrients must be small enough to be absorbed by the hyphae.

Molds create spores for reproduction. The mold creates a shoot called a sporangium. When it matures, it releases a large amount of spores, which will form new fungi if they land in a moist environment.

Sac-Shaped Fungi

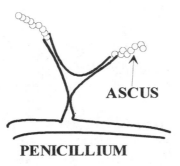

YEAST

ASCUS

PENICILLIUM

These fungi also reproduce by spores. The spores are formed in an oval sac called the **ascus**. These fungi are responsible for much of the damage done to human food supplies.

Yeast is also responsible for fermentation. We use it to make alcohol (beer, wine and distilled spirits). It is also commonly used in baking. Breads that need to rise before baking use yeast. The yeast gives off carbon dioxide in the process of making energy. The carbon dioxide forms air pockets, causing the bread to rise.

Club Fungi (Mushrooms)

This type of fungi also reproduces by using spores. The spores are produced in a club shaped (mushroom shaped) structure. The top of a mushroom is called the cap. They also have root-like structures called **hyphae**. The hyphae are responsible for collecting the food.

Imperfect Fungi - Imperfect fungi reproduce asexually. They do not produce spores. Common types of imperfect fungi are ringworm and athlete's foot.

Slime Molds - Slime molds are similar to fungi, but they are mobile. They are able to move around like an amoeba. Their reproduction also involves making spores in sporangia. Another difference is the fact each of their cells contains many nuclei.

Lichens

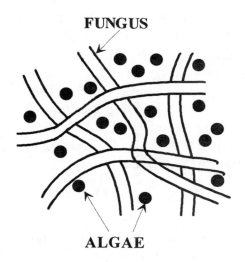

FUNGUS

ALGAE

Lichens are a unique kind of life form where algae and fungi grow together **symbiotically** (to the benefit of both). The algae provide the food and the fungi provide the water. They are able to exist in a much wider environment living together than if they lived separately.

Question 42:

How do most algae get their food?

    a. by eating animals
    b. by eating plants
    c. by eating dead material
    d. they make their own

Question 43:

How do lichens get their food?

    a. by eating animals
    b. by eating plants
    c. by eating dead material
    d. the algae make it

The Plant Kingdom

The different types of plants you should be familiar with are the ferns, the conifers, and the flowering seed plants.

Ferns -   The leafy part of a fern is called a **frond**. The root is called a **rhizome**. Ferns release **spores**, which after dispersal, land on the soil, develop sperm and ova, fertilize, and become the next generation of ferns.

Let's take a closer look at the reproduction process. It occurs in two stages. As the fern matures, reproduction becomes the prime function of the plant. Blister-like **sori** form on the underside of the fronds. These sori contain the sporangium from which spores will be dispersed. The spores fall into a moist environment and germinate. This is the gametophyte stage of reproduction. The spores forms a heart-shaped (♥) **prothallus** where ova (female) and sperm (male) develop. The sperm eventually swim over to the ova and fertilization occurs. The zygote is the first part of the **sporophyte** stage of reproduction. The zygote divides and cells specialize until a new fern is formed. Just remember, ferns have a whole other stage of development that is not visible.

Conifers - These trees produce **cones**, which house the seeds. These plants stay green year-round. EXAMPLES: junipers, pines, spruces, firs, cedars and sequoias.

This type of tree is harvested extensively to make lumber products and also for making paper.

Question 44:

Which type of plant stays green all year round?

> a. flowering seed plants
> b. conifers
> c. ferns
> d. rhizomes

Question 45:

What is the leafy part of a fern called?

> a. a frond
> b. a rhizome
> c. an ovum
> d. a leaf

Flowering Seed Plants - This is the most varied group of plants on earth. Their seeds are equipped with a food supply, which the new plants use for food until they develop their first leaves. The fact the plants start with a supply of food allows them to get established before they have to rely on their own food production. There are two major classifications of flowering seed plants.

The first type of plant is the **monocots.** They have a single (mono) first leaf. EXAMPLES: grasses, corn, and lilies.

The veins in their leaves run in parallel along the length of the leaf.

It is important to know that this variety of plant is responsible for a large part of the human food production. All of the grains (wheat and corn) as well as rice are monocots.

Dicots: have two first leaves. EXAMPLES: sunflowers, mustard, maple trees, oak trees, and tomatoes.

An easy way to tell if a plant is a dicot is to look at the leaves. If the veins in the leaf branch (are netted), then the plant is a dicot. If they run straight without branching, the plant is a monocot.

ENLARGED

Question 46:

A plant with veins that run next to each other is most likely

    a. a dicot.
    b. a conifer.
    c. a rhizome.
    d. a monocot.

Parts of Flowering Seed Plants

Root System - The root systems of flowering seed plants are well established with tiny root hairs used to obtain water and minerals from the soil. They serve to anchor the plant in the soil and keep it from falling over. They are also important for the storage of food and water. Think about how much food a potato stores in its roots.

Question 47:

What two things does a plant get from the soil?

  a. water and oxygen
  b. water and minerals
  c. water and carbon dioxide
  d. carbon dioxide and minerals

It is important to know something about the transport system of plants. There are two types of transport systems.

Phloem - This is the part of the plant that transfers food downward from the leaf to the rest of the plant. It is formed of live cells and it is found near the outer surface of the plant. The food is transferred from cell to cell down the plant. The cells in the phloem tend to be very long because transfer occurs much quicker inside each cell than it does when it has to go between cells.

Xylem - This is the other part of the transport system in a plant. It transfers water and minerals upward in the plant. It is composed of the remains of dead cells. The ends of the cells dissolve and a hollow tube is left. For many years scientists wondered how water was able to go from the roots to the top of a tall tree. It would require an enormous amount of energy to pump the water up, and it would be impossible to suck the water up (The maximum height that a perfect vacuum can raise water is thirty-two feet). The current theory is called the Transpiration Tension Theory. Scientists believe as the leaves use water, new molecules are pulled along to replace them because of the surface tension of water. The water consists of a continuous chain of molecules from the root to the leaves.

Question 48:

What is transferred downward in a plant?

    a. water
    b. minerals
    c. glucose
    d. wastes

Question 49:

What is transferred upward in a plant?

    a. water
    b. minerals
    c. food
    d. both a and b

Stem - The stem consists of bark (outer covering and protection), cambium (phloem), wood (xylem), and pith (the center most part of woody stems).

Question 50:

What is the center of the stem called?

    a. bark
    b. cambium
    c. xylem
    d. pith

Leaf Cross-section

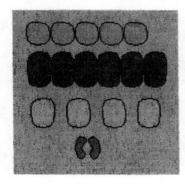

Cuticle

Palisade Layer

Spongy Layer

Stomata

Leaf - Manufactures food for the plant through the photosynthesis process. The cells responsible for photosynthesis are called **paltsadw** cells and are contained in the palisade layer. The **cuticle** is the waxy covering of the leaf. The waxy covering greatly reduces the amount of moisture lost by the leaves. Leaves have holes in them, which are used to regulate the passage of carbon dioxide (CO_2) and water (H_2O). These holes are called **stomata**. The **veins** of the leaf are the xylem and phloem.

Question 51:

If a cell needed a greater concentration of carbon dioxide, which cells would be affected?

    a. paltsadw
    b. cuticle
    c. stomata
    d. xylem

Flowering Plant Reproduction

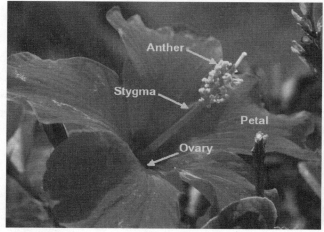 

| **Pistil** | - | The sticky top is called a **stygma**. The tube is called a **style**. The base of the tube is called the **ovary**. This part of the plant is "female". |
| **Stamen** | - | The stalk supports the **anther**, which holds the pollen. This is the "male" part of the plant. Pollen matures into sperm. |

Some plants are able to self-pollinate (can fertilize themselves) while others must cross-fertilize (one plant supplies the pollen and one plant supplies the egg). Once fertilization occurs, a zygote forms and the plant puts all of its energy into seed (fruit) production.

Question 52:

What is the female part of the plant?

    a. the pistil
    b. the stamen
    c. the style
    d. the ovary

The Animal Kingdom

The animal kingdom is split into two major classifications: **Invertebrates** (without backbones) and **vertebrates** (with backbones).

Invertebrates

Porifera - sponges

Sponges are filled with holes. Sponge cells draw water through the holes (called **incurrent pores**) and remove nutrients as well as oxygen. They then return the water to its surroundings through larger holes (called **excurrent pores**).

Cells of a sponge are arranged in two layers. On the outside, there are **epidermal** cells for protection. Inside, there are cells known as **collar cells**.

Each collar cell has a flagellum. The flagellum beat rapidly, which causes a current to flow past the collar cells. Here, food and oxygen are removed and passed along to cells called **amebocytes**, which distribute the nutrients to other cells. The water then continues to flow out the excurrent pores.

Sponges have **spicules**. They make up the skeleton of the sponge. They are what remains after a sponge dies.

Sponges are able to reproduce in three ways. The first is by **budding**, reproduction by breaking off a piece of the original to form two individuals. The second is **regeneration**, or replacing tissue that is lost. They may also reproduce sexually by releasing sperm in the water. The sperm swim around and enter other sponges and fertilize the ova. The zygote eventually develops into a "free swimmer" that will eventually settle to the ocean floor and become a sponge. This allows sponges to spread out to new areas.

EXCURRENT PORE

INCURRENT PORE

SPICULE

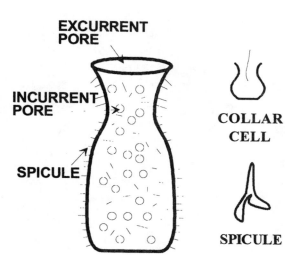

COLLAR CELL

SPICULE

Coelenterates - Jellyfish and Corals

Coelenterates exist in various body shapes during their life span. Some begin life as free-swimming **planula**. Planula are the larva of coelenterates. Some planula develop into a polyp-shaped **hydra** or into a **medusa** (a type of mature coelenterate that lacks means of self-propulsion). Both adult forms of coelenterates are able to reproduce. Other coelenterates have planula and some form alternate generations. Planula develop into polyps, which then produce more planula. They then develop into medusas, which produce more planula in order to complete the cycle.

Coelenterates contain two layers of cells separated by a jelly-like substance called **mesoglea**. The stinging cells located in the **tentacles** are called **nematocysts**. They contain paralyzing poisons. Food is obtained when several stings from the nematocysts paralyze a victim. Slowly, food is drawn into a gastrovascular cavity (in polyps) where it is thoroughly digested. Reproduction may occur through budding, regeneration, or sexual activity.

There are some fish, clown fish for example, which are immune to the poisons in the nematocysts. They live in a symbiotic relationship with the coelenterate. The clown fish swim among the tentacles and when another fish comes to eat it, the predator fish gets stung. The clown fish feeds off the poisoned predator fish.

Worms - There are three distinct types of worms. They show increasing specialization and complexity.

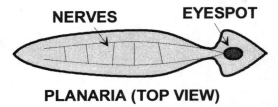

PLANARIA (TOP VIEW)

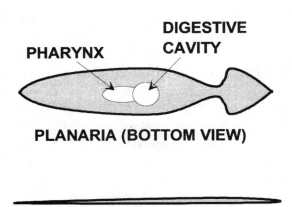

PLANARIA (BOTTOM VIEW)

PLANARIA (SIDE VIEW)

Platyhelminthes - Flatworms (Planaria)

These are the least complex of the worms, but they are much more complex than the organisms that have come before them. They are the first organisms to have three layers of cells: **ectoderm**, **mesoderm** and **endoderm**.

The planarian (flatworm) is a free-swimmer which sucks its food through the pharynx tube.

It may reproduce by asexual (fission) or sexual means. The animal contains both male and female sex organs (**hermaphroditic**) so cross-fertilization is easily accomplished.

The planarian has marvelous powers of regeneration. When it is damaged it can regenerate up to half its body.

Nematodes - Round Worms (Hookworm, Trichina)

These worms are a little more complex than flatworms. The biggest difference is their body shape. They are round instead of being flat, as their names suggest. They are the first animals that have a digestive system with two openings, one for the mouth and one for the anus. Flat worms only have one opening which serves both functions.

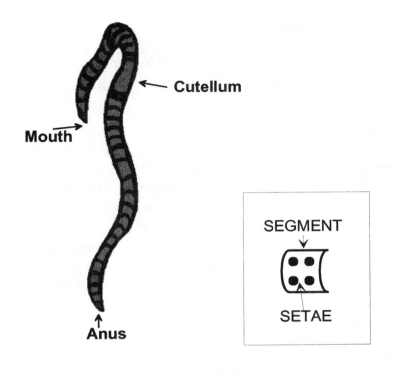

Mouth

Cutellum

Anus

SEGMENT

SETAE

EARTHWORM REPRODUCTION
TESTES   OVARIES

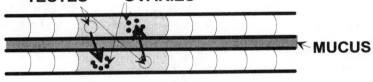

MUCUS

LARGE ARROWS INDICATE THE
DIRECTION OF THE SPERM EXCHANGE

Annelids - Segmented Worms (Earth Worm)

The annelids are much more advanced than the other worms. They have well-developed nervous, digestive, excretory, circulatory, muscular, and reproductive systems.

The digestive system has a **gizzard**, which grinds up the soil the earthworm swallows. Digestive enzymes attack the finely ground up soil, extracting nutrients. No longer is the food simply passing through the body.

After the food is digested, the circulatory system takes over. Annelids have multiple hearts and a circulatory system that distributes food over the length of the body and eliminates waste products.

Earthworms have "grippers" called **setae** on their underside. This allows them to anchor themselves into the ground.

Reproduction is sexual; one worm supplies the sperm and the other the egg. However, one interesting feature is earthworms are hermaphroditic. That is, they have both male and female sex organs. They cannot self fertilize; they must find another worm with which to mate. The two worms are able to simultaneously fertilize each other.

Mollusks - Shellfish (Clams, Oysters, Scallops)

Mollusks have soft bodies and an outer layer of cells called the mantle. There are three major categories of mollusks.

Gastropods - "Stomach Foot" - (Snails)

Most of these mollusks have a shell. (Slugs have none at all!). The shell is in a spiral shape and the animal has its vital organs protected inside the shell.

Gastropods have eyestalks, which are flexible, so that they can move their eyes to look in different directions.

Gastropods "breathe" through the exchange of gases in the **mantle** cavity. Oxygen dissolves in and carbon dioxide dissolves out.

Gastropods are capable of movement, although it tends to be slow. They secrete slime and contract the foot muscle to pull themselves forward. When they are scared, they pull the foot and the rest of their body back into their shell for protection.

Eating is accomplished by scraping its **radula** (made of chitin) against leaves and digesting nutrients in a fully developed digestive system. Some Gastropods eat other mollusks.

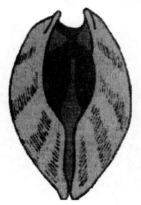

Pelecypods – "Two Shells" - (Clams, Oysters]

As the name suggests these mollusks have two shells. Some bi-valves have symmetrical shells (both are the same); others have one shell that is larger than the other shell. They can vary greatly in size, ranging from under half an inch to the enormity of giant clams, which weigh hundreds of pounds.

Bi-valves contain two **siphon tubes**. One is used to bring nutrients in, logically called the incurrent tube, and one sends waste out, called the excurrent tube. The flow of water through the tube sucks in food. The food is captured by the mouth and then sent to the digestive system. The nutrients from digestion are moved around with a circulatory system while the waste products of digestion are excreted through the anus. The circulating water also flows over the gills. Here, oxygen is removed from the water and carbon dioxide waste is put into the water to be sent out the excurrent tube.

Cephalopods - "Head Foot" - Octopus, Squid

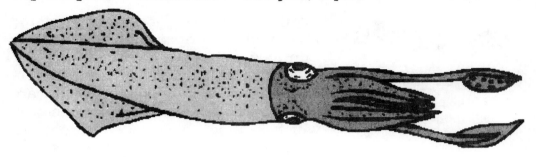

Squid are free-swimmers that use "jet-propulsion" to move around their marine environments. Their tentacles have sucker discs with which squid are able to grab food. Evidence of epic battles between giant squid and sperm whales have been found on the whales where some scars from the sucker disc have been over a foot in diameter. Squid must rely on their speed for protection.

While octopi can move by jet propulsion, their more common mode of movement is by walking along the bottom on their tentacles. Often they are found with their bodies in rock crevasses for protection. When caught in the open, an octopus will excrete a cloud of ink, which hides it while it escapes.

The eyes of cephalopods are more advanced than other mollusks. Their digestive and circulatory systems are also more advanced than the other mollusks.

Arthropods - "Jointed Foot"

This is the largest and most varied phylum of animals on the earth. All arthropods have the following common characteristics:

1. A hard outer body shell called an **exoskeleton**. This exoskeleton is made of a substance called **chitin**.

2. These are the first animals to have **jointed appendages**.

3. There are four classifications of arthropods:

   a. Myriapoda

   b. Insects

   c. Crustaceans

   d. Arachnids

Myriapoda – "Many Feet" - Centipedes, Millipedes

**CENTIPEDE
TWO LEGS PER
SEGMENT**

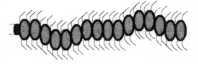

**MILLIPEDE
FOUR LEGS PER
SEGMENT**

There are two major branches of the Myriapoda, centipedes and millipedes. Centipedes have one set of legs per segment, and millipedes have two sets of legs per segment. Centipedes are carnivorous and contain poison claws, which enable them to capture food. Millipedes are mainly herbivorous.

Insects - Mosquitoes, Flies

Insects are responsible for a lot of crop damage, but there are also some insects that are beneficial to humans. Many farmers release Ladybugs to eat aphids and other insects, which would harm crops.

There are some distinct characteristics that separate insects from other arthropods. Insects have three major body parts: head, thorax, and abdomen. They also have six legs; breathing tubes called **spiracles** located in the abdomen; one pair of antenna; and two pairs of wings.

The insect life cycle, coupled with wings and special feeding parts, has allowed insects to inhabit all but the coldest portions of the earth's surface. They are often the first animals to move into a new area such as a newly formed volcanic island.

Most insects undergo a **metamorphosis** (change in body shape) from egg through to adult form.

1.   Egg

2.   Larva (worm-like—caterpillar, etc.)

3.   Pupa (change from worm-like form to adult form)

4.   Adult

Not all insects go through all phases.

Insect eggs that hatch into small adult forms, called **nymphs**, are **bugs**. A good example of a bug is a grasshopper.

Crustaceans - Lobsters, Crabs, and Shrimp

The big difference between crustaceans and insects is that the head and the thorax are joined together in one part the cephalothorax. The abdomen remains the same as in insects. Crustaceans are the largest of the arthropods with lobsters growing to 40 pounds or more. Crustaceans have gills. Even the crabs that live on land must keep their gills moist in order to transfer oxygen and carbon dioxide.

Arachnids - Spiders, Scorpions, Horse-Shoe Crabs, Mites and Ticks

Arachnids have some features that are similar to crustaceans. Arachnids also have only two body parts: the cephalothorax and abdomen.

Spiders have **book lungs** for the transfer of oxygen and carbon dioxide. They also have exactly eight legs: no more, no less.

Another distinguishing feature is they have no antennae.

Echinoderms - Starfish

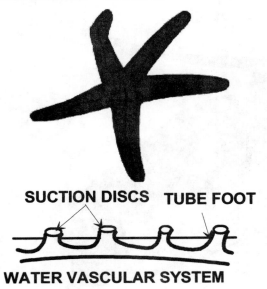

SUCTION DISCS   **TUBE FOOT**

WATER VASCULAR SYSTEM

Starfish have hard, spiny bodies. The underside of each arm has two rows of **tube feet.** These feet are manipulated by the **water vascular system**.

When water is pumped into this system the **suction discs** puff out and release their grip on the surface. When the water is moved back out, the tube feet can attach to something using suction. By rhythmically moving the water through the system, alternating the attachment/release of the discs, the starfish is able to move through the water.

The tube feet are also used to capture oysters or clams for food. The starfish attaches to the clam and starts to pull it apart. At first the clam is strong enough to keep its shell closed. Over time however, the clam tires and its shell opens a little. The starfish then slips its stomach inside the shells and digests the contents.

Starfish reproduce sexually. Male and female starfish release sperm and ova into the water. Fertilization occurs and produces ciliated larva (similar to that of paramecium). The larva are able to move around and often drift long distances with the ocean currents. Eventually they settle to the bottom and start their lives as adults.

Adult echinoderms exhibit radial symmetry. Most other adult animals are bisymmetrical (there is only one way to cut them down the middle and end up with both halves being alike.) Animals with radial symmetry can be cut in more than one way to get identical halves.

Chordates

Chordates are the most advanced form of animals. Chordates contain three prominent features at some time in their lives. Some animals, like humans, only exhibit some of these features while they are developing before they are born. They all have:

1.   **Notochord** - a hard, internal, supporting rod of connective tissue.

2.   **Paired Gill Slits** - become gills in fish and amphibians; disappear in other chordates (including man).

3.   **A Dorsal Nerve Cord** - spinal cord.

The simplest of the chordates are the sharks and rays. While some sharks are very efficient hunters, they are not as evolutionarily advanced as fish. A shark is not a fish. Its skeleton is made of cartilage; it does not have bones. Its notochord also is not enclosed in a backbone for protection.

Vertebrates

The rest of the animals listed will all be vertebrates. Vertebrates have their notochord surrounded by a backbone for protection. They also have bones in their skeleton

Pisces - Fish

These are the simplest of the remaining animals. Their heart only has two chambers, so the blood coming from the gills mixes with the blood coming from the body in the heart.

Fish have scales on the outside of their bodies and rely on gills for breathing.

Many fish have a swim bladder. This cavity can be filled with gas, which allows the fish to adjust its buoyancy to different depths in the water.

Fish reproduce sexually. Often the eggs and the sperm are simply released in the water to float around freely. It is left to chance that they will meet up and fertilize each other.

The fins on a fish serve as stabilizers. They keep the fish from spinning out of control in the water.

Amphibians - Frogs

Adult amphibians tend to live in moist environments. They have lungs, but need to keep their skin moist. Many amphibians go through a juvenile stage and then they go though a metamorphosis to the adult phase. A frog is a good example. When it first hatches out of the egg it still has the yolk sac attached. It has more structure that is similar to fish than it does to adult amphibians. It has a long tail for swimming, gills and a two-chambered heart. It cannot survive on land and it has no legs. After the tadpole lives like this for awhile and stores up enough energy, it will undergo metamorphosis. It uses the energy stored in its tail to change into the adult form. The first thing to appear is the back leg. Slowly it will also develop smaller front legs, lungs and a three-chamber heart. It will now be able to survive on land as long as it keeps its skin moist. It will also be at home in the water as long as it is able to come up for air and breath. It will no longer be able to survive exclusively in the water because it has lost its gills.

In areas where it gets colder in the winter, the frogs will hibernate. They will go down into the mud at the bottom of a pond to hibernate. All of its processes will slow way down. It lives off the food it stored over the summer. Because its metabolism (how fast it is using energy) has slowed way down frogs do not have to breathe air when they hibernate. They are able to transfer enough oxygen and carbon dioxide through their skin.

Amphibians reproduce sexually. The female lays its eggs in water and the male fertilizes them. They can often be found in clumps in ponds.

Reptiles - Turtles, Alligators, and Snakes

Reptiles are even more advanced than amphibians. They have made the transition to true land animals, although some have returned to the water to live. A big advance for reptiles is that they have a four-chambered heart. A four chamber heart allows reptiles to keep the oxygenated blood from their lungs separate from the blood laden with carbon dioxide that is returning from the rest of the body. Reptiles also have four legs, although as snakes have developed their legs have shrunk back into their body and all that is left are the bones. Reptiles are **cold-blooded**; they cannot control their body temperature. This means that they are only able to move very slowly when they are cold. To counteract this you will often see reptiles sunning themselves (laying on a rock in the sun). This raises their body temperature. Reptiles have thick, scaly skin.

Reptiles reproduce sexually. Fertilization occurs internally as the male places the sperm in the female. Most of the time the female then lays eggs, however there are some reptiles whose young are born alive directly from the mother.

Aves - Birds

Birds are the next step up evolutionarily from reptiles. They are the first animals that are **warm-blooded**; they are able to control their body temperature. Their feathers provide them with insulation. When it gets cold, they fluff out their feathers to trap more of the warm air close to their bodies.

Birds, like reptiles, have a four-chambered heart. An interesting feature birds have is their wings. Although not all wings are used for flight, all birds have them. They also have hollow bones. This makes their bones much lighter than other animals. If they had solid bones like other animals they would be too heavy to fly.

Bird reproduction is similar to reptiles. They reproduce sexually and fertilization takes place internally. The eggs are then often laid in a nest. The eggs are covered with a calcium-based shell. In the twentieth century many large birds were having problems. Humans were spraying for insects with DDT. The birds were secreting the DDT in their eggshells, which made them very fragile. When the birds sat on the nest to keep the eggs warm, the shells cracked and the eggs died as a result.

Most birds show many adaptations from their basic structure depending on where they live and what they feed on. A bird's beak will be different depending on if they feed on insects or seeds. Their feet also show adaptations. The long talons of eagles and owls are designed for grabbing their food.

Mammals - Bats, Whales, Porpoises, Platypus, Kangaroos, and Humans

Mammals possess a body covering of hair, four-chambered hearts, a diaphragm to separate the chest cavity from the digestive cavity, a highly developed brain, and **mammary glands** which provide nourishment (milk) for the newborn.

Monotremes – Platypus and Echidna

These are the least advanced of the mammals. They lay eggs like birds. Their mammary glands are not very developed. The milk just sort of oozes out when the young feed. They are found only in Australia and its surrounding islands. Competition with more advances mammals eliminated monotremes from the rest of the world.

Marsupials – Kangaroos and Opossum

While there are a few marsupials found throughout the world, the vast majority are found in Australia and its surrounding islands. Here marsupials have adapted to all of the niches filled by more advanced mammals in the rest of the world.

Marsupial babies are born alive, but very young. They then crawl up to the mother's pouch. Here they feed on a mammary gland and continue to develop. They will spend the first weeks of their lives exclusively in their mother's pouch. Even after they are finally big enough to emerge on their own, they will still return to their mother's pouch for protection.

Placentals - Mice, Bears and Humans

These are the most advanced of the mammals. Their young are generally born fully developed, although some are not fully capable of surviving on their own at the time of birth. The young tend to spend a long time in the **womb** (the place inside the mother where the babies develop) before they are born.

Placentals are the most advanced animals and have a higher survival rate than many other animals because their young have such a long period of development inside the mother. For this reason, the birth rate of placentals tends to be lower than many other animals. Some placentals only give birth every couple of years.

Question 53:

Which of the following are vertebrates?

      a. mollusks
      b. aves
      c. echinoderms
      d. a and b

Classification Rankings

All of the different classifications mentioned can be broken down into different groups. In order of increasing specialization, they are: Kingdom, Phylum, Class, Order, Family, Genus, and Species. Kingdoms are the broadest category (Plant and Animal) and Species are the smallest. All members of a given species are able to interbreed and produce **viable** offspring (young that survive and can reproduce).

If you are asked which group has more members, the order that an organism is in always has more members than its Family, Genus, or Species.

Human Systems

Organ systems are important for maintaining internal balance for the organism. Living things can only continue to exist within a certain range of conditions. Extremes of temperature, for example, can be fatal. This balance is referred to as **homeostasis**.

The Male Human Reproductive System

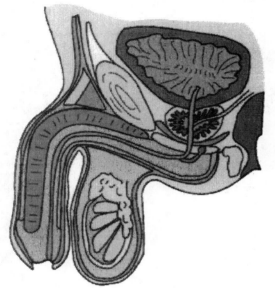

Sex cells are produced in the **testes**. They grow tails (**flagella**) and are called **sperm** or **spermatozoa**. The tail's function is to provide locomotion in the fluid called **semen**.

Testes are held in a sac called the **scrotum**, which is located below, and outside the abdomen. The location is critical because sperm production and storage is best at lower than body temperature (98.6 F).

The duct system from the testes through the penis involves the **epididymis**, the **vas deferens**, the **ejaculatory duct**, and the **urethra**. The sperm travel through this passageway of ducts to exit the male body. The **prostate** and **seminal vesicles** provide semen and chemicals to activate the sperm.

Question 54:

Why must sperm cells develop outside the body?

        a. To keep them warm.
        b. To keep them cool.
        c. To keep them wet.
        d. To keep them dry.

Question 55:

How does sperm move?

  a. with pseudopods
  b. with cilia
  c. with flagella
  d. with legs

The Female Human Reproductive System

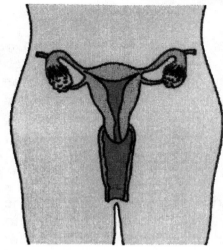

Female sex cells are produced in the **ovaries**. Female sex cells have no means of locomotion. The cells are called **ova** (pl.).

The ovaries are located in the lower abdominal cavity and produce the hormones **estrogen** and **progesterone**.

An egg (ovum) is passed from the ovary to the **fallopian tube** (oviduct) where it is moved along by the ciliated (small hair-like projections that beat back and forth) lining of the tube.

If fertilization has occurred in the fallopian tubes, the **zygote** attaches to the walls of the uterus and grows into a **fetus**.

If fertilization has not occurred, the female experiences **menstruation**, and the inner layers of the uterus are discharged.

The **vagina** is the cavity that receives semen from the male. It also discharges menstrual flow and is the passageway for birth.

External features include the **vulva** (labia majora, labia minora), which encloses the vagina, and the **clitoris**, which is a small erectile, sensitive tissue.

Question 56:

Which of the following is true if menstruation occurs?

       a. implantation occurred
       b. the egg was not fertilized
       c. menopause
       d. a zygote is formed

Question 57:

Where does the egg implant if it is fertilized?

       a. in the uterus
       b. in the fallopian tubes
       c. in the vulva
       d. in the vagina

The Circulatory System

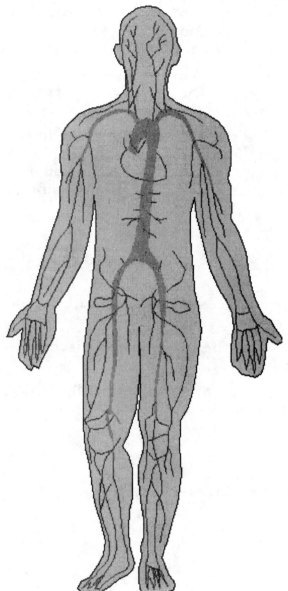

The function of the circulatory system is to provide the flow of materials through the body. Circulation provides for the exchange of gases (O_2-CO_2), removal of wastes, regulation of body temperature, nutrition, H_2O regulation, proper pH maintenance, and immune protection (white blood cells and antibodies).

Blood is divided into two parts, the plasma (fluid) and the cells. The **plasma** contains water, carbonates, chlorides, phosphates, urea, hormones, vitamins, digested food, albumin, globulin, fibrinogen, and prothrombin.

There are three different types of blood cells.

1) **Red blood corpuscles (erythrocytes)-**

The main function of this type of cell is to transport oxygen. The cells contain a lot of hemoglobin. It can readily combine with and disassociate from oxygen. It all depends on the surrounding concentrations of oxygen. When there is a low surrounding concentration it releases oxygen. When the surrounding concentration is high, it accepts oxygen. Therefore, red blood cells pick up oxygen in the lungs and distribute it to the rest of the body. Mature red blood cells have no nucleus (so they can carry more hemoglobin) and are shaped like a donut without the hole (to increase their surface area). More surface area means quicker transport of oxygen.

2) **White blood corpuscles (leukocytes)** - White blood cells are the second type of blood cell. They contain no hemoglobin. Their job is not the transfer of oxygen. Their job is in fighting infections. They are **amoeboid** in shape and method of locomotion. They roam around the blood stream looking for invaders (bacteria and viruses). When they find them they eat them. They work closely with antibodies. When the body gets an infection it produces antibodies. Antibodies cause viruses and bacteria to group together. This makes it easier for the white blood cell to catch and eat the infecting organism.

White blood cells are not confined to the blood stream (arteries, veins, and capillaries). They are able to squeeze out through the walls and go out among the cells to where the infection is.

3) **Platelets (thrombocytes)** – Platelets are important in **clotting**. If we did not have platelets, the simplest cut would cause us to bleed to death. When we are cut platelets rupture at the site. This starts the clotting process. A net is made of thrombin and fibrinogen fiber, which traps red blood cells. These cells then dry into a clot.

All of the blood cells are produced in the **bone marrow** with the exception of leukocytes, which may also form in the **spleen**.

Question 58:

Which type of blood cells protects you from bleeding to death when you cut your finger?

    a. red
    b. white
    c. platelets
    d. protectors

Vessels carrying blood include:

1) from heart to body - **aorta, arteries, arterioles** (the smallest arteries)

2) **capillaries** - small blood vessels connecting arterioles to veinules

3) from body to heart - **veinules** (the smallest veins)**, veins, vena cava**

Capillaries - the site where nutrients are exchanged.

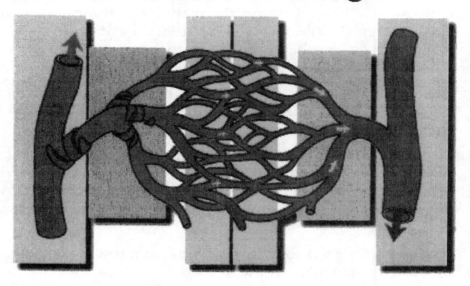

Arteries have thick walls and are under pressure from the heart pushing blood through the body. The capillaries connect the **arterial** system to the **venous** system. Veins have thin walls and low pressure. The blood is moved along veins when muscles contract. Valves prevent the blood from flowing backward.

The **heart** is a muscular pump, which causes the blood to circulate through the body. It is **cone-shaped** and has walls, which have three layers of muscle tissue: **endocardium, myocardium,** and **pericardium.**

Blood flows back to the heart from all parts of the body. The **venae cavae** empty into the **right atrium** of the heart. Blood flows to the **right ventricle** and then out to the lungs through the **pulmonary arteries** (the only non-oxygenated arterial blood in the body). After the exchange of gases in the lungs, blood returns through the **pulmonary vein** (oxygenated blood) to the **left atrium,** then to the **left ventricle** and out to the body through the **aorta.**

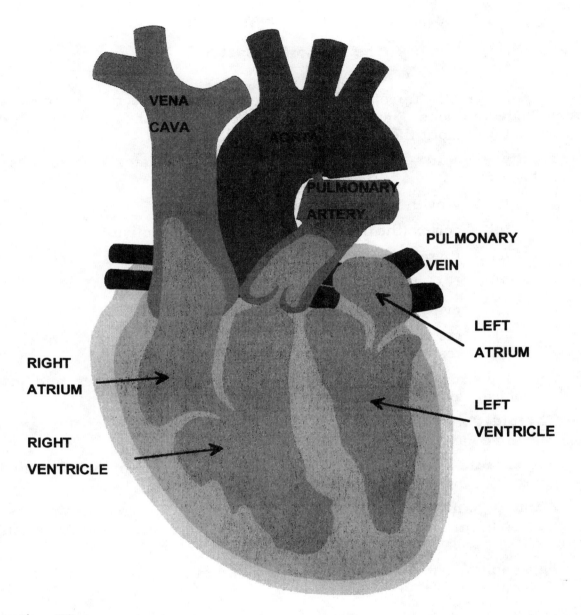

Question 59:

Which of the following is not true?

    a. The left ventricle pumps blood to the body.
    b. The veins only carry deoxygenated blood.
    c. Most of the transfer occurs in the capillaries.
    d. The pulmonary artery carries blood with a lower oxygen content than the aorta.

The Endocrine System

This system is made up of glands in the body that secrete **hormones** to regulate body functions. The hormones are released into the circulatory system and carried throughout the body.

1. **Pituitary gland** - located in the brain. It regulates or activates the following:

   (a) growth

   (b) cortex (the outer portion of the brain) activity

   (c) thyroid activity

   (d) H_2O in the blood

   (e) ovary or sperm development

   (f) corpus luteum (a ductless gland in the ovary) and testosterone

2. **Pineal gland** - located in the brain. It regulates ovaries and is the "biological clock" of the body.

3. **Thyroid gland** - located in the neck. It regulates metabolic rate and calcium concentration in the blood.

4. **Parathyroid gland** - located on the backside of the thyroid. It regulates calcium in the blood.

5. **Adrenal gland** - located on the top of the kidneys. It regulates potassium and sodium in the blood, heartbeat, blood pressure, and blood sugar level.

6. **Pancreas** - located below the stomach. It regulates passage of sugar into the cells.

7. **Ovaries** - located in the pelvis of the female. It regulates the development of sex organs and characteristics.

8. **Testes** - located below the pelvis in the male.

9. **Thymus** - located in chest. Its function is unknown.

Question 60:

Which does a gland in the brain not control?

    a. Sugar
    b. Growth
    c. Ovaries
    d. Thyroid

The Nervous System

This system consists of the **brain**, **spinal cord** and **nerves**. The function of this system is to regulate and coordinate body activities.

There are two main divisions in this system:

1.   **central nervous system** - which causes voluntary movement.

2.   **autonomic nervous system** - which regulates heartbeat, glands, and smooth muscles.

When the brain has a message to send to the rest of the body, it travels along the nerves. The junction between two nerves is called a synapse. The axon of one nerve meets the dendrite of the other. Chemicals pass across the space in between to tell the second nerve to carry on the signal.

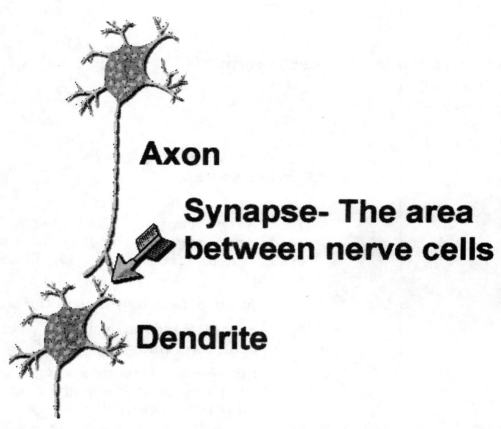

Axon

Synapse- The area between nerve cells

Dendrite

Some nerves are able to regenerate, but the nerves of the brain and spinal cord cannot.

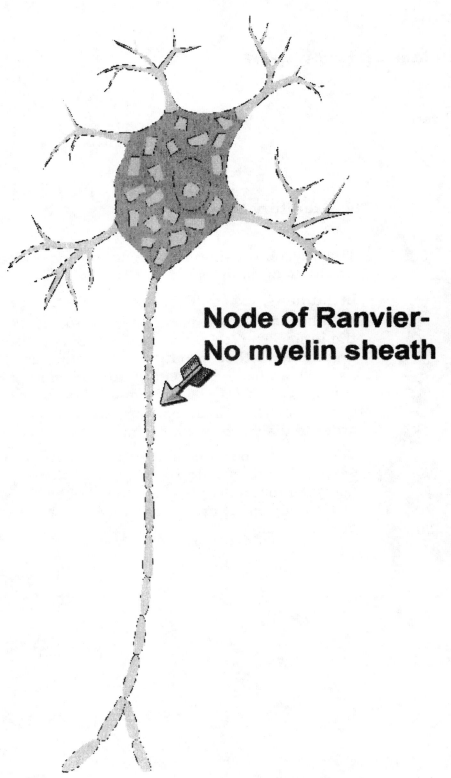

**Node of Ranvier-
No myelin sheath**

Most nerves are covered with a **myelin** sheath. It greatly speeds up the movement of the signal through the nerve. The signal jumps from one **node of Ranvier** (site of no myelin) to the next node of Ranvier

Question 61:

Which is not part of the nervous system?

    a. Glands
    b. Brain
    c. Spinal cord
    d. Nerves

Kidney

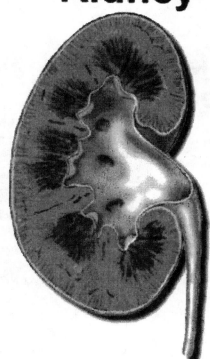

The Excretory System

This system eliminates toxic or excessive by-products of metabolism.

In humans, excess CO_2 that builds up from the metabolism of food is removed from the body by the lungs. The **kidneys** are the primary excretory organs for other products of metabolism. The kidneys remove the end products of digestion, some excess H_2O, vitamins, hormones and enzymes. They also convert **urea** to **urine** in order to discharge waste from the body.

The kidneys perform a very important function: when the kidneys stop working the blood quickly becomes toxic. People with this problem must go in for dialysis. There, a machine takes the toxins out of the blood.

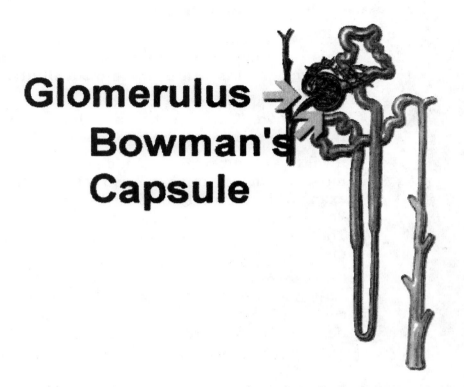

Glomerulus
Bowman's
Capsule

The kidneys are composed of many individual **nephrons**. Blood enters the nephron at the **glomerulus**. The glomerulus is composed of a ball of twisting capillaries. The blood enters under pressure, which forces fluid out into the **Bowman's capsule**. From the Bowman's capsule, the fluid flows down a long loop (the **Loop of Henle**) and the water is reabsorbed. The fluid left is urea. It is collected and stored in the bladder until it is excreted through the urinary tract.

Question 62:

Kidneys are one of the most common organs to be transplanted and the waiting list is long. Many people wait for years before they are chosen as recipients. What is one of the main reasons people can wait on the list for a new kidney longer than for some other organs?

    a. There is no need to rush out and get a new kidney.
    b. Kidney failure is not life threatening
    c. People in kidney failure can be kept alive by dialysis while failure of other organs will kill them.
    d. There are more hearts available for transplant than kidneys.

The Muscular System

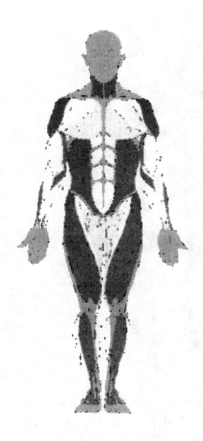

This is the system that causes movement. This system contains **voluntary** and **involuntary** muscles.

Voluntary muscles are **striated** and are used for fast contraction. They are the ones that are connected to the bones and cause them to move.

Involuntary muscles include **smooth** and **cardiac** muscle. Smooth muscle contraction is slow. A good example is the muscles that line the digestive tract. You have no conscious control over these muscles. They move the food along in a slow deliberate manner.

Cardiac muscle contracts in a regular fashion and does not tire easily. It is the only type of muscle that can contract on its own without any stimulus from nerves. If living cardiac cells are put in a beaker with a nutrient broth they will continue to contract on their own.

Question 63:

What are the two types of muscle?

    a. Voluntary and striated
    b. Involuntary and voluntary
    c. Involuntary and smooth
    d. Involuntary and cardiac

The Respiratory System

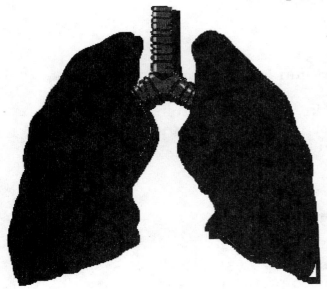

This is the process by which cells receive O_2 and give off CO_2. The steps involved in respiration are:

1. **Breathing** – the movement of air in and out of the lungs.

2. **External Respiration** – the exchange of gases (O_2 - CO_2) in the lungs.

3. **Transpiration** – the movement of O_2 - CO_2 by blood to and from cells.

4. **Internal Respiration** – the exchange of gases between the cells and the blood.

Oxygen is used with nutrients in the cell to produce usable energy.

Alveoli

Let's take a closer look at an **alveoli**. Alveoli are the functional unit of the lungs. They look like a tiny balloon. When we breathe in air inflates these little sacs. Many capillaries surround the sacs. These capillaries are carrying deoxygenated blood from the pulmonary artery. Carbon dioxide dissolves out of the blood and into the air sac. Oxygen from the sac dissolves into the blood creating oxygen rich blood. The oxygen rich blood then flows back down the pulmonary vein to the left atrium of the heart. When the carbon dioxide level in the sac reaches a certain point, nerves send a message to the brain and we exhale.

Question 64:

Which of the following is true?

    a. Oxygen is in a higher concentration in the blood than in the alveoli.
    b. CO_2 concentration is higher in the alveoli than in the blood.
    c. The oxygen level in the alveoli makes you breath.
    d. CO_2 dissolves from the blood to the alveoli.

The Integumentary System

The **skin** provides an outer protective covering for the body. It keeps viruses and bacteria from infecting the body. It also protects us from the harmful rays of the sun. When we are exposed to a lot of sunlight our skin produces extra melanin and it gets darker.

The Digestive System

Digestive Tract

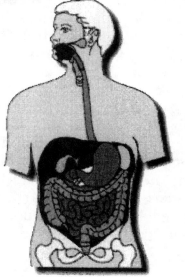

This is the process that changes large organic molecules into smaller organic molecules that can pass through cell membranes. **Enzymes** are responsible for this process.

1. **Mouth** - contains **teeth** and the **tongue**. Secretes **mucus** and **saliva** and begins the breakdown of food by enzymes.

2. **Esophagus** - moves food to the stomach area.

3. **Stomach** - churns food and mixes in **gastric juices** and **hydrochloric acid** to further break down food. Here the digestion of fats begins.

4. **Small Intestine**—more secretions are added here. They include **pancreatic juice**, **bile**, and **intestinal juices**. Food is broken into usable molecules and taken away by the blood. The small intestines contain many **villi** (small projections) which increase the surface area and allow for greater absorption.

5. **Large Intestine** (colon)—undigested food and unusable solids (feces) are compacted and water is removed. The excess waste is then removed from the body through the anus.

Question 65:

Which of the following is the path food takes through the digestive system?

    a. mouth, esophagus, stomach, small intestine, large intestine
    b. mouth, esophagus, stomach, large intestine, small intestine
    c. mouth, stomach, esophagus, small intestine, large intestine
    d. mouth, stomach, esophagus, large intestine, small intestine

This completes our biology review. Before you take the chapter test, be sure to check your answers to the questions appearing throughout the chapter.

ANSWERS – BIOLOGY CHAPTER QUESTIONS

If you have answered a question incorrectly, refer to the page where the question appears and review the information given there.

1. d. The mitochondria organelles are where energy production takes place.

2. b. The main function of the cell membrane is to control what enters and leaves the cell. It is the cell's first line of defense against disease.

3. c. The cell wall is non-living (dead) and made of cellulose. The first three answers can be ruled out because they say it is living. The last answer indicates that it has chlorophyll.

4. a. Plant cells lack mobility and need the protection they get from their cell walls. The other answers are functions carried out by the living parts of the plant.

5. c. Water and carbon dioxide combine to form sugar. All of the incorrect answers contain at least one of the products.

6. d. Since photosynthesis is the process that plants use to make food, they would eventually die if they could no longer do it. Animals either feed on plants or on animals that eat plants. If all plants die, animals would also eventually die.

7. d. Some plants live off other plants, and some live off of dead plants and animals. The other answers are all false. Animals and fish do not make their own food. Not every plant can make its own food, and all organisms are able to change molecules.

8. a. DNA stands for deoxyribonucleic acid.

9. d. The first three answers are all true. The fourth answer says that chromosomes grow continuously. This is not true. Chromosomes do not get longer all the time. When a cell divides it makes new chromosomes of exactly the same size.

10. b. The rungs are made of nucleic bases. The outside is made of sugars and phosphates. That means that they are not in the rungs. The paragraph says nothing about whether the rungs shift or are broken.

11. c. Genes are joined together to make chromosomes. This is the best answer. A chromosome is a type of molecule, but c is a better answer than a. Genes are not found outside the cell and do not float freely in the cytoplasm.

12. d. Adenine pairs with thymine. Cytosine and guanine would be paired together.

13. b. RNA is able to leave the nucleus. The other answers are all wrong. DNA is able to duplicate itself and form a double helix. It also stores the genes. Neither DNA nor RNA divides the cell.

14. b. Since the DNA starts out in the nucleus and cannot leave RNA must be produced in the nucleus. All of the other choices are outside the nucleus.

15. a. In an RNA strand, thymine is replaced by uracil. Adenine bonds with thymine in DNA, so it would have a different base in RNA. Cytosine and guanine always pair together in both DNA and RNA

16. c. m-RNA ends in the area of a ribosome where a mutual attraction occurs.

17. d. DNA continues to make m-RNA until it is stopped by a chemical stimulus.

18. d. There are twenty amino acids.

19. c. Transfer RNAs have amino acids attached to them. The only other type of RNA that we have talked about is messenger RNA. It is produced in the nucleus and has no amino acids.

20. c. This is a tricky question. The first answer appears correct. "t-RNA can attach to any amino acid." The key word to watch out for is "any." Each t-RNA attaches only to a specific amino acid. The same is true for answer b. t-RNA can only attach to a specific point on the messenger RNA. The last answer is wrong because it is the amino acids that form the protein not the transfer RNA.

21. a. Energy production occurs mainly in the mitochondria.

22. b. Oxidation is the opposite of photosynthesis because the products and the reactants switch. Energy is given off instead of being stored.

23. b. Looking at a formula, the reactants would be on the left-hand side of the arrow. The chemicals on the left-hand side of the formula in question are water and fat.

24. c. This is the state of the cell when it goes from step four to step one. In this phase the cell stops converting ADP to ATP.

25. a. The key words here is "small amounts" of energy. If the cell needed large amounts of energy, it would start breaking down food. When the cell only needs small amounts of energy, it converts ATP to ADP.

26. d. It is important for cells to get the same material because they would probably die if they did not get the correct materials.

27. a. Interphase is the period between cell divisions. It would be impossible for the cell to divide during interphase.

28. d. The first three choices are all said to occur during prophase. Only the last choice is not talked about. It would be very bad if the cell membrane did disappear because all of the cellular material would then scatter.

29. c. The spindle fibers form from the aster. The fibers attach to the chromosomes.

30. c. The last two paragraphs list some of the differences between plant and animal cell division. There is no mention of an animal cell making a cell plate, but it is stated that plant cells make one.

31. b. Telophase is the opposite of prophase.

32. c. A cell must get only one set of chromosomes from each parent to keep the number of chromosomes from doubling in each generation. A cell with only one set of chromosomes is said to be haploid.

33. a. Only the first choice is true. Only one egg cell is produced in meiosis and it is haploid. All four of the sperm cells produced are capable of fertilizing the egg.

34. a. The paragraph states that Gregor Mendel is also called the "father of genetics".

35. a. A dominant trait is one that shows itself even when another trait is also present. In the case shown, the tall gene shows up even though the short gene is present.

36. d. A heterozygous animal is one that has unlike alleles for a particular gene. Animals with like alleles are called homozygous.

37. c. From the diagram it is easy to see that hybrid tan mice will have both white and tan babies. Since the babies are both colors (white and tan) the babies must have more than one phenotype and genotype.

38. a. You must be very careful when you answer this question. At first glance c and d both appear as good choices. Upon closer examination, you can see that the answers say mitosis instead of meiosis. That leaves us with answer a: genes can be inherited independently.

39. a. The paragraph states that because of improvements in microscopes and chemical analysis, there are at least three major classifications of organisms. Going one step further from there, it would be safe to assume that microscopes and chemical analysis are used to identify organisms.

40. a. Viruses are classified by the type of host they infect.

41. d. Amoeba move by pseudopods.

42. d. Algae make their own food by photosynthesis.

43. d. Lichens maintain a symbiotic relationship with algae, which supply the food.

44. b. Conifers stay green year round.

45. a. The leafy part of a fern is called a frond.

46. d. Looking back at the photo of plant leaves, we can see that the monocot leaf has veins that run next to each other while the dicot has netted leaves.

47. b. Plants get water and minerals from the soil.

48. c. Phloem transports materials downward in the plant. One of the main things it transports is food. Glucose is a type of food that is produced in the leaves.

49. d. This is a trick question because both water and minerals are transferred upward in a plant. Therefore, you must choose both and not pick a or b. Remember to always pick the best answer.

50. d. The pith comprises the centermost part of woody stems.

51. c. The regulation of the flow of water and carbon dioxide is controlled by holes in the leaves called stomata.

52. a. The pistil is the female part of the plant. The ovary and the style are both parts of the pistil.

53. b. Aves, or birds, are the only vertebrate listed. The other two choices, mollusks and echinoderms, are both invertebrate.

54. b. Sperm develop best at temperatures lower than body temperature. Therefore they develop outside the body to keep cool.

55. c. Sperms grow tails called flagella for propulsion.

56. b. If an egg is not fertilized menstruation will occur.

57. a. A fertilized egg is called a zygote. It implants itself in the uterus.

58. c. The best answer here is platelets. When you cut yourself the platelets rupture to start the clotting process. They cause a fibrous net to form, which traps the red blood cells. When the red blood cells dry a clot is formed. Even though red blood cells make up part of the clot, if there are no platelets to form the net, they will simply flow freely from the wound.

59. b. While most veins carry deoxygenated blood back to the heart, the pulmonary vein carries blood from the lungs to the heart, which has a high oxygen concentration.

60 a. The other choices are all controlled in part by the pituitary gland, which is found in the brain. The pancreas controls sugar. The pancreas produces insulin, which controls the level of sugar in the

blood. People who cannot produce insulin are called diabetics. People with a low insulin production level can control the disease by changing their diet. However, people with more severe cases must get insulin through shots.

61. a. While glands can secrete chemicals, which have an effect on the nerves, they are not part of the nervous system.

62. c. Even though the failure of any organ is bad, many people live for a long time even when they are in total kidney failure. They must go in for dialysis on a regular basis. The machines take over the functions of the kidneys. Therefore people are able to stay on the waiting list a longer time for a kidney. While they are waiting they are capable of leading semi-normal lives.

63. b. This is the only choice that lists both major types of muscle. Choices a, c, and d all list the one kind of muscle found in a particular type.

64. d. Answers a and b are all backwards. Choice c is incorrect because it is the level of carbon dioxide that causes you to breathe, not the level of oxygen.

65. a. The correct flow of food is from the mouth, down the esophagus, to the stomach. From the stomach it flows into the small intestines where most of the nutrients are absorbed. Finally the food enters the large intestine where water is reabsorbed before the rest of the wastes are eliminated.

After you have checked your answers to the questions found throughout the chapter, you are ready to take the chapter test.

CHAPTER TEST - BIOLOGY

Questions 1-3 refer to the following chart:

VITAMIN	NAME	PREVENTS	FOOD FOUND IN
A	CAROTENE	NIGHT BLINDNESS DRY SKIN	YELLOW FRUITS AND VEGETABLES, EGG YOLKS AND LIVER
B-1	THIAMINE	BERI BERI, MENTAL DISORDERS	BRAIN, LIVER, WHOLE GRAINS
B-2	RIBOFLAVIN	SKIN DISORDERS	GRAIN, EGGS, MILK, LIVER
B-6	PYRIDOXINE	SKIN DISORDERS, DERMATITIS	GRAIN, LIVER, FISH, KIDNEY
B-3	NIACIN	PELLAGRA, DIGESTIVE DISORDERS	GRAIN, LIVER, MEAT YEAST
	BIOTIN	MUSCLE PAINS WEAKNESS	EGG YOLK, PRODUCED BY BACTERIA IN THE INTESTINES
	FOLIC ACID	ANEMIA	LIVER AND LEAFY VEGETABLES
	PANTOTHENIC ACID	CARDIOVASCULAR NEURAL DISORDERS	MANY FOODS
B-12	CYANOCOBALAMIN	ANEMIA	LIVER, EGGS, FISH, AND MILK
C	ASCORBIC ACID	SCURVY	CITRUS FRUITS, TOMATOES
D	CALCIFEROL	RICKETS	FISH OIL, MILK, SUN ON THE SKIN
E	TOCOPHEROL	ANEMIA	GREEN VEGETABLES, FISH OIL
K	PHYLLOQUINONE	LACK OF BLOOD CLOTTING	GREEN VEGETABLES

Question 1:

Which of the following vitamins if absent would cause you to bleed to death from a small wound?

  a. vitamin C
  b. vitamin K
  c. vitamin B-12
  d. vitamin D

Question 2:

Which of the following foods is not a source of vitamin B-2?

  a. fish
  b. grain
  c. milk
  d. liver

Question 3:

Which is another name for vitamin D?

  a. Tocopherol
  b. Pantothenic Acid
  c. Niacin
  d. Calciferol

Question 4:

Trees are always making new xylem. It is composed of dead cells that form hollow tubes. It is responsible for bringing the water from the roots to the leaves. The rate at which new xylem is formed depends on the growing conditions. During the winter when growth is slow rings are formed. Which of the following is true?

  a. The thickest tree is always the oldest.
  b. The tallest tree is always the oldest.
  c. Trees in good growing conditions get thicker faster.
  d. Xylem brings sugar down to the roots.

Question 5:

The surface of human blood can contain two main antigens, proteins that antibodies attack. They are called A and B. If both antigens are missing the blood is labeled O. Both antigens are controlled by a single gene. Neither one is dominant over the other, so if both alleles (possible traits of the gene) are present the blood would test AB. If a child has a father with an AB blood type, which of the following blood types could the child not have?

      a.   O
      b.   B
      c.   A
      d.   AB

Question 6:

All cells in an organism have the same genetic information. Cells look and act differently depending on the information they use. Which of the following is true?

      a.   Only cells in the pancreas contain the genetic information to make insulin.
      b.   A heart cell has the information to make insulin.
      c.   Brain cells contain the most genetic information.
      d.   Skin cells contain the most genetic information.

Question 7:

Organisms in a similar niche (place in the environment) develop similar structures. These structures can develop from parts that are vastly different in an organism's close relatives. For example, the wings of a fly and the wings of a bat have very different evolutionary origins. The structure of a bat wing is analogous in humans, a much closer relative than the fly, to the hand. Which of the following is most likely another example of this type of development?

      a.   bat wings and bird wings
      b.   duck feet and frog feet
      c.   human hair and animal fur
      d.   dolphin fins and fish fins

Question 8:

Wine is made when juice is fermented. Yeast is added to the juice and it breaks down the sugar in the juice to form alcohol. In a dry wine the yeast converts all the sugar to alcohol, but in a sweet wine the alcohol level reaches a level high enough to kill the yeast before it has used up all the sugar. Choose the best answer to explain the yeast population in the following graph for a dry wine.

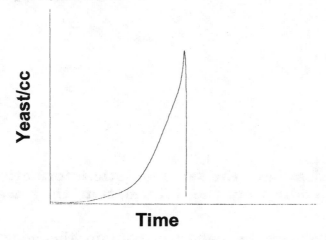

a. The yeast population grew quickly and then died off because the alcohol concentration got too high.
b. The yeast population grew quickly and then leveled off.
c. The yeast population stayed the same the whole time.
d. The yeast population grew and then died off when the sugar ran out.

Question 9:

Which of the following is not true about wine?

a. Yeast converts sugar into alcohol.
b. Dry wines contain excess sugar.
c. The sugar content is a factor in determining if a wine is sweet or dry
d. Alcohol in certain concentrations kills yeast

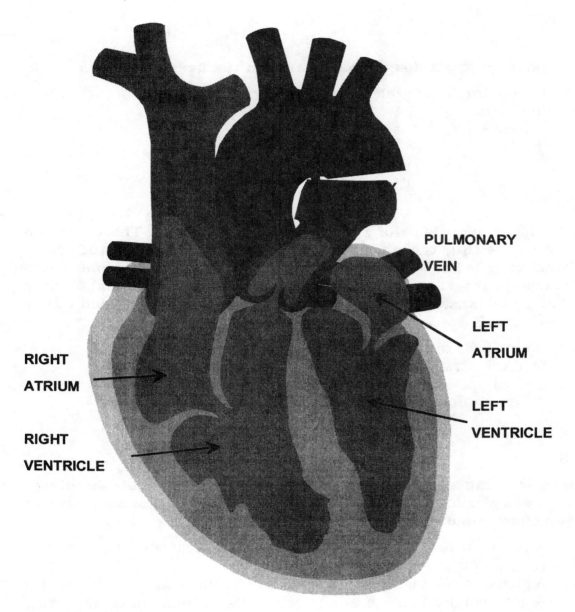

PULMONARY VEIN

LEFT ATRIUM

LEFT VENTRICLE

RIGHT ATRIUM

RIGHT VENTRICLE

Question 10:

What are the two major arteries leaving the heart?

    a.   pulmonary artery and aorta
    b.   aorta and pulmonary vein
    c.   left ventricle and right atrium
    d.   vena cava and pulmonary artery

Question 11:

What keeps the blood from flowing backwards in the heart?

    a.   the contraction of the other chambers
    b.   the aorta
    c.   valves
    d.   doors

Question 12:

Animals with spinal chords belong in the phylum chordata. There are two major subphylum within the chordates, those with backbones and those without backbones. The vertebrates, animals with backbones, are composed of some of the most recognizable classes of animals. They include fish, amphibians, reptiles, aves (birds) and mammals. Which of the following is not true?

    a.   the mallard duck is a member of the vertebrates
    b.   fish are a type of invertebrate
    c.   all mammals are also vertebrates
    d.   all vertebrates are chordates

Question 13:

XYZ company is doing an experiment to find out which of their fertilizers works best on pea plants. Which of the following would be the best control group for the experiment?

    a.   A group of pea plants that gets the same light and water as the rest, which gets no fertilizer at all.
    b.   A group of pea plants, which gets double the amount of fertilizer.
    c.   A group of bean plants, which gets the same amount of water and fertilizer as the rest.
    d.   A group of pea plants, which gets fertilizer but no water.

	Week 1	Week 2	Week 3	Week 4
No fertilizer	4"	5"	6"	8"
Fertilizer 1	4"	6"	9"	12"
Fertilizer 2	4"	5"	6"	8"
Fertilizer 3	4"	6"	8"	10"

Question 14:

Which fertilizer is a waste of money?

      a.   fertilizer 1
      b.   fertilizer 2
      c.   fertilizer 3
      d.   all of them work well

Question 15:

If all the fertilizers cost the same amount, which fertilizer is the best value for the dollar?

      a. fertilizer 1
      b. fertilizer 2
      c. fertilizer 3
      d. all of them would have the same value

The following data was obtained in an experiment to determine the dominant and recessive alleles in a flower. Each tally mark represents one offspring with that genotype.

	RR	Rr	rr
Tally marks	~~1111~~ ~~1111~~ ~~1111~~ ~~1111~~ 1111	~~1111~~ ~~1111~~ ~~1111~~ ~~1111~~ ~~1111~~ ~~1111~~ ~~1111~~ ~~1111~~ ~~1111~~ ~~1111~~	~~1111~~ ~~1111~~ ~~1111~~ ~~1111~~ ~~1111~~ 1
Totals	24	50	26

Genotype = RR : Rr : rr   Phenotype= Red : White
         24 : 50 :26   74 : 26

Question 16:

What percentage of 100 offspring may be predicted to show the dominant trait?

        a.   24%
        b.   50%
        c.   74%
        d.   26%

Question 17:

What are the chances of getting a white trait from the cross of Rr and Rr?

        a.   3 to 1
        b.   1 to 4
        c.   2 to 5
        d.   1 to 3
        e.   1 to 1

Question 18:

If additional data were collected, what may be predicted?

        a.   The genotype ratio would be the same.
        b.   The majority selection would be "rr".
        c.   The majority selection would be "RR".
        d.   The results would be totally unpredictable.

Question 19:

A common form of reproduction in animals is sexual reproduction. The parents of the offspring are both diploid (have two copies of each chromosome) and they produce some special cells that are haploid. One haploid cell from the mother combines with one haploid cell from the father. This forms a new diploid offspring. Which of the following is not true?

        a.   Diploid animals only have one copy of each gene.
        b.   Offspring get information from both parents.
        c.   Offspring have the same number of chromosomes as the parents.
        d.   Both parents have the same number of chromosomes.

Question 20:

In Darwin's theory of evolution, he stated that organisms evolve based on their fitness to produce viable (young that are able to reproduce) offspring. Animals that produce more viable offspring than other members of their species will cause their characteristics to show up in future generations. Those that do not produce viable offspring do not pass along their characteristics. Which of the following is not an example of "survival of the fittest?"

    a.   Antelope A is faster than antelope B. Antelope B gets caught and eaten by a lion before it has offspring while antelope A dies of old age after having many offspring.

    b.   Reindeer A has a thicker coat than reindeer B. During the winter (when they are young) it is especially cold and reindeer B dies before mating. Reindeer A grows to be the leader of the herd and has many offspring.

    c.   Bat B has a slight refinement in its echolocation. It is able to catch many more bugs than the average bat. Its children also are able to catch more bugs and have a 75% higher survival rate.

    d.   In an area, red tail hawks and peregrine falcons compete for the same food source. The falcons being smaller and quicker are able to catch more food and finally the hawks die off.

Question 21:

Photosynthesis is the process by which plants store energy. Plants take the energy contained in sunlight and by using chlorophyll and other enzymes make sugar. Sugar is the basic building block of all food. Multiple sugars can be joined together to make starch. If glycerol (formed by breaking down sugar) is joined with a fatty acid it makes a fat. Finally if sugar is joined to an amine group an amino acid is formed. Which of the following can plants do that animals cannot?

    a.   convert starch to sugar
    b.   convert sugar to amino acids
    c.   produce sugar
    d.   convert sugar to fat

Question 22:

Where do plants get the energy to make sugar?

      a.   from starch
      b.   from sunlight
      c.   from chlorophyll
      d.   from enzymes

Question 23:

Many scientists believe that when the Earth first formed it was lifeless. The first life to form was found in the oceans. Slowly life became more complicated and multi-cellular organisms formed. The next great age was the age of invertebrates, followed by the age of fish. The next age is the first animals to live at least part-time on land, amphibians. Following the amphibians were the reptiles. Finally, along came the mammals. Which of the following places the great ages from youngest (most recent) to oldest?

      a.   amphibians, fish, reptiles
      b.   mammals, fish, no life
      c.   fish, amphibians, reptiles
      d.   amphibians, reptiles, mammals

ANSWERS - CHAPTER TEST BIOLOGY

1. b. In this type of question you must simply look down the columns listing the things the vitamins prevent and chose the vitamin important in blood clotting. Vitamin K is important in blood clotting. Without it, even small cuts can be very dangerous.

2. a. Here you are required to find vitamin B-2 and then follow the row over to find in which foods it is found. The only choice not listed is fish.

3. d. Here you must first find vitamin D and then follow the row over to the vitamin names. Calciferol is the name of vitamin D.

4. c. This question is a little tougher than simple chart reading; you must do some analysis. The first answer looks correct; however, the paragraph states trees form new xylem at different rates, based on growing conditions. Therefore, a younger tree in good growing conditions might soon grow bigger than an older one in poorer growing conditions. Likewise, the tallest tree is not always the oldest. Answer d, states the opposite of what is in the paragraph. The paragraph states xylem takes the water from the roots to the leaves. When you take the test always make sure you eliminate answers you know are wrong before you make your best guess at the correct answer. Finally, answer c is supported by the paragraph. It states new xylem is formed faster when the tree is in good growing conditions, which means the trees will get thicker, faster.

5. a. Again, you would need to do a little analysis for this problem. If the father is AB, he would need to pass on either an A or B gene to his children. If a person has at least one A or B gene, he cannot have an O blood type.

6. b. The paragraph states all cells in an organism contain the same information. If this is true, heart cells must contain the information to produce insulin, but do not use it.

7. d. Here you are required to first understand the presented concept and then apply it to come up with another example. First you have to look at the animals and find ones which are not very close evolutionarily. Human hair and animal fur are too similar for what we are trying to find out. Likewise, bat wings and bird wings derive from the same evolutionary origins. The same goes for duck feet and frog feet. Choice e is definitely wrong because it compares an animal with an inanimate object. This leaves us with our correct answer: dolphin fins and fish fins. If you were to cut open a dolphin fin, you would find a bond structure similar to the human hand.

8. d. There are two reasons why the yeast population could die off. The first is because the alcohol concentration went too high. The second is the yeast used up all the sugar. In the case of a dry wine, all the sugar is used up.

9. b. This is the opposite of what the paragraph states. Wines with excess sugar are sweet.

10. a. If you are unsure of the correct answer, look at the valves in the heart. If blood were to try and flow from the heart into the pulmonary vein or into the vena cava, the valves would close and cut the blood flow off.

11. c. Valves keep the blood from flowing backward in the heart.

12. b. Fish are listed as members of the vertebrates.

13. a. A good control group gets everything the other groups get, except for the product you are testing. Therefore, choice a is the best.

14. b. A fertilizer that is a waste of money would show the same or worse results than the control group. Fertilizer 2 has the same results as the control group, so the best answer is b.

15. a. If all the fertilizers cost the same amount of money, the fertilizer getting the best results would return the most value. The best answer is Fertilizer 1, or answer a.

16. c. An offspring that shows the dominant trait would have to have at least one copy of the dominant gene. The results show there are twenty-four with both dominant genes and fifty others with just one dominant gene. Adding the two together, the total is seventy-four. There were a total of one hundred offspring, so 74% of the offspring received at least one dominant trait.

17. d. This is very easy to see if you use a Punnett square.

	R	r
R	RR	Rr
r	rR	rr

The only flowers which will have white flowers are the ones with both little r's from the cross. Therefore, you would expect to get only one white flower for every three red flowers.

18. a. The genotype of the cross would be expected to remain the same, no matter how many offspring are produced. The larger the sample, the closer to the expected results you would get.

19 a. The paragraph states diploid animals have two copies of each gene. The other answers are all true.

20. d. Example d compares two different species. Survival of the fittest compares animals within the same species and their ability to pass on their genes to their offspring.

21. c. Animals cannot produce their own food, they must eat it. Animals can convert sugar to fats and amino acids, as well as convert amino acids and fats back to sugar.

22. b. Plants get the energy to make sugar from sunlight.

23. b. Answer b is the only choice listing the ages from youngest to oldest. Answer d lists the ages from oldest to youngest. Always make sure you answer the question being asked.

Section 1: The Universe

The universe is thought to have begun about twenty billion years ago. Because the matter in the universe is expanding (that is, moving outward at fantastic speeds), scientists today favor the **Big Bang** theory to explain how it came into being and evolved into what it is today.

The Big Bang theory states that all the matter was in the same place at one time and a huge explosion took place. The explosion propelled matter outward in all directions. Eventually, the matter developed into millions of billions of galaxies containing millions and billions of stars.

At present, the edge of the universe is thought to be twenty billion light years from earth. (A light year is the **distance** light travels in one year - approximately six trillion miles).

Try a sample question. Treat the material you have just read as a reading passage.

Question 1:

Traveling at the speed of light, how long would it take you to reach the present edge of the universe?

   d. 600 trillion miles
   b. 20 billion miles
   c. 20 billion years
   d. 6 trillion light years

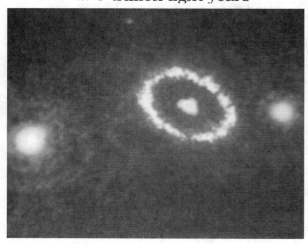

Galaxies

There are many galaxies in the universe. They vary as to size, shape, and density (amount of matter). Our own galaxy, the **Milky Way**, is between 80,000 to 100,000 light years in diameter and is a two-armed spiral galaxy. It is thickest at its core and thinner in the arms - perhaps having a ten light year thickness.

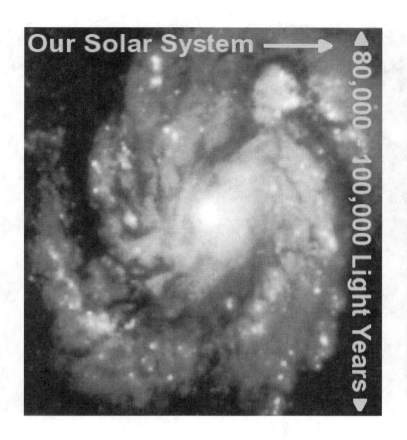

Our Solar System ⟶

▲ 80,000 - 100,000 Light Years ▼

Our solar system is located approximately 2/3 to 3/4 out on one of the arms. It is truly only a "speck of dust" in the total galaxy.

Question 2:

What is the distance across the Milky Way galaxy?

      a. 10 light years
      b. 100,000 light years
      c. 100,000 miles
      d. 6 trillion miles

The Solar System

The sun is our solar system's star. It is an average-sized star approximately five billion years old. It may have come into existence through the collapse of a huge gas and dust cloud called a **nebula**. Compression of the matter, largely hydrogen gas, caused the temperature to rise to a point where fusion could begin. The fusion of hydrogen into helium (and perhaps other types of fusion reactions) creates energy in the form of heat and light. Other forms of electromagnetic energy are created as well. Some of these are radio waves, infra-red rays, ultraviolet rays, x-rays, gamma rays, and maybe cosmic rays.

Not all of the gas was consumed creating the sun. Some gas formed eddies (whirlpools) in orbit around the sun. These later became the planets, moons (natural satellites), asteroids, and comets.

NEBULA
(GAS AND DUST
CLOUD)

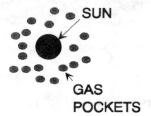

SUN

GAS
POCKETS

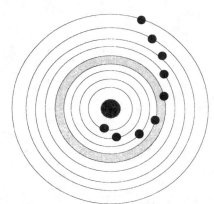

SHRINKING POCKETS
OF GAS BECOME MEMBERS
OF OUR SOLAR SYSTEM

The solar system is thought to have existed, basically as it is today, about 4.6 billion years ago - that's the age of the earth.

Question 3:

What is not formed from eddies?

      a. planets
      b. moons
      c. comets
      d. stars

Terrestrial (Solid)

Inner Planets

The Planets

MERCURY

- The smallest planet.
- Has no atmosphere.
- The surface is marred by meteorite impacts.
- Closest to the sun.
- Has no moons.
- Has a very slow rotation.

VENUS

- Earth's twin (almost the same size).
- Atmosphere is largely CO_2
- Surface is obscured by clouds.
- Rotates east to west, which is the opposite of most planets (retrograde rotation).
- Has a very hot surface temperature ($900°$ hot enough to melt lead).
- The third brightest object in the sky after the sun and moon.

Venus's very dense atmosphere is what keeps the planet's surface so warm. The cloud cover warms the surface through the **"greenhouse effect"**.

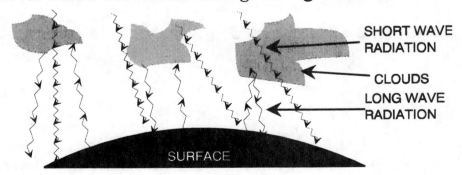

SHORT WAVE RADIATION

CLOUDS

LONG WAVE RADIATION

SURFACE

The radiation from the sun has a shorter wavelength, and it is able to pass through the cloud layer. However, after it strikes and warms the surface it is converted to heat. Heat has a longer wavelength and it cannot pass through the clouds as easily as the shorter wavelength radiation. A large portion of the heat is reflected back to the surface by the clouds. The net effect is a warmer surface similar to the way the glass roof warms a greenhouse.

EARTH

- Located just the right distance from the sun for water to exist in all three states of matter (solid, liquid, and gas).
- The only planet with an abundance of water.
- A "live" planet in that it is constantly renewing its crustal material; has weather.
- Has one satellite: the moon. The moon is located 243,000 miles from the earth.
- The moon is the main cause of tides.

MARS

- The "Red Planet"
- Half the size of the Earth.
- Has polar ice caps.
- Has weather (dust storms).
- Shows seasonal changes.
- Has two large moons: Deimos and Phobos.

Question 4:

Which planet is about the same size as the earth?

        a. Mercury
        b. Venus
        c. Mars
        d. Jupiter

Question 5:

Which planet is seen first in the evening sky?

        a. Mercury
        b. Venus
        c. Mars
        d. Jupiter

The Asteroid Belt

The asteroid belt is located between Mars and Jupiter. The asteroids range in size from a grain of sand to 250 miles across (the largest Ceres). There are at least three theories for the formation or the asteroids. The first is that a large planet may have broken apart due to tidal forces. Another theory is that the asteroids are eddies that never combined to form a planet. The last is that they are the remains of two planets that collided and broke apart.

Gas Giant

Outer Planets

Jupiter

- The largest planet.
- Has a gigantic red spot in its atmosphere.
- Rotates the fastest of all planets.
- Fast rotation causes the equator to bulge.

Saturn

- Known for its rings
- Second in size.
- Has a large number of satellites.

Uranus And Neptune

- Very similar in size - third and fourth, respectively.
- Neptune has rings like Saturn.
- Neptune for brief periods of time is the outermost planet.

Question 6:

What is the second largest planet?

 a. Saturn
 b. Uranus
 c. Neptune
 d. Pluto

Terrestrial Solid

PLUTO

- The smallest planet.
- Orbits off the plane of orbit of other planets by 17^0.
- May be a captured planet.
- Usually the farthest planet from the sun.

Section 2: The Earth

The earth is ninety-three million miles from the sun. After forming, the earth probably underwent changes to produce the earth we know today.

Structure And Composition

Scientists who study earthquakes and meteorites have given us the picture of the interior of the earth. Because the outer core of the earth is liquid, rotational forces produce a magnetic field around the earth. The magnetic poles of the earth wander. At the present time, the magnetic poles are not located where the geographic poles are. They could line up when the magnetic poles wander.

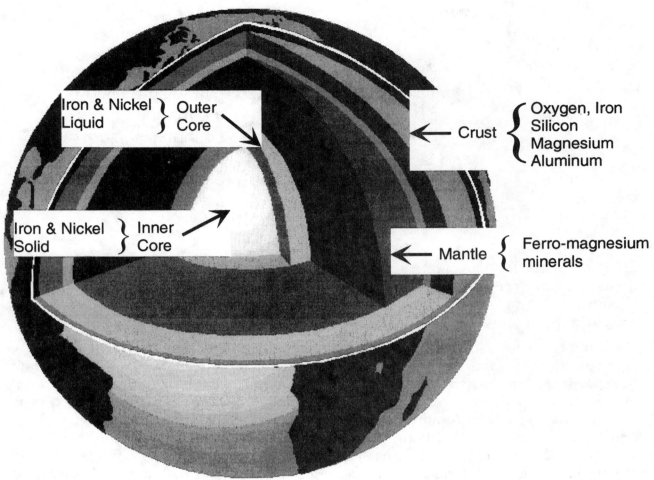

Iron & Nickel Liquid } Outer Core

Oxygen, Iron Silicon Magnesium Aluminum } Crust

Iron & Nickel Solid } Inner Core

Mantle { Ferro-magnesium minerals

Question 7:

What causes the magnetic field of the earth?

        a. magnets in the crust
        b. iron in the crust
        c. the moon
        d. the rotation of the core of the earth

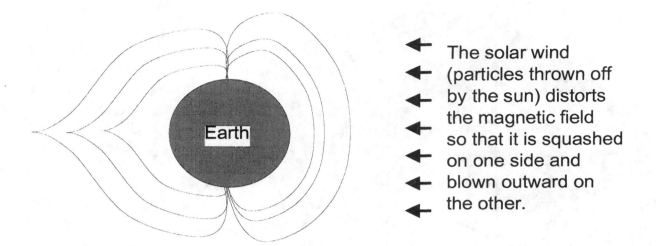

The solar wind (particles thrown off by the sun) distorts the magnetic field so that it is squashed on one side and blown outward on the other.

This magnetic field protects the earth from these solar particles by trapping them in areas around the earth called the **Van Allen Radiation Belts**. These particles are the cause of the northern or southern lights, called the **Aurora Borealis** (N) or the **Aurora Australis** (S).

The energy needed to sustain life is derived from the sun. Parts of the globe receive different amounts of solar energy, depending on the time of year. This is because the earth's axis is slightly tilted relative to the sun, so that when the northern hemisphere is experiencing summer, the southern hemisphere is in winter. The key turning points for the seasons are: about March 21, when both hemispheres are equally facing the sun, is the beginning of spring for the north (the **vernal equinox**) and the start of autumn for the south (**autumnal equinox**). June 21 is the summer solstice for the north and, simultaneously, the winter solstice for the south, as at this time, the north is tilted toward the sun and the south away from it. September 21 is the beginning of autumn for the north and the beginning of spring for the south. December 21 marks the start of the north's winter and the south's summer.

The earth does not orbit the sun in a perfect circle but rather in an **ellipse**, so at some points in its orbit, the earth is closer to the sun. The moon also circles the earth in an elliptical orbit and it takes approximately twenty-eight days for the moon to complete one cycle. The new moon refers to the point where the moon is between the earth and the sun, and its lighted face is not visible from earth. The full moon is when the earth is between the moon and the sun. In the first and last quarters, the moon is at a right angle with the earth-sun axis and is only half visible from earth. When the lighted surface of the moon when viewed from the Earth is going from new to full is is called waxing, and when the lighted surface is getting smaller it is waning.

The Crust

The crust is made largely of silicate minerals (over 90%). The composition of the crust may be summarized in the following diagram:

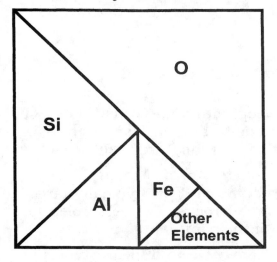

APPROXIMATELY

O = 50%

Si = 25%

Al = 12.5%

Fe = 6.25%

Oxygen and silicon combine to form silica. Under the right circumstances it combines with other metals to form the many silicate minerals that make up the crust. Quartz and feldspar are very common silicate minerals.

Other minerals include:

1) iron ores such as limonite, hematite, and magnetite

2) carbonates such as calcite and dolomite.

Question 8:

Which of the following are the most common?

    a. limonite and hematite
    b. hematite and magnetite
    c. calcite and dolomite
    d. feldspar and quartz

Under the right conditions, minerals combine to form rocks. Rocks may form in one of three ways:

1) from melted rock (magma/lava)

2) from cementing together

3) under the influence of heat and pressure.

Question 9:

Which of the following is not a way rocks form?

> a. from melted rock
> b. from crystallization
> c. from cementing
> d. from heat and pressure

Igneous Rock

Igneous rock forms from melted rock material deep within the crust or upper mantle. If the melted rock reaches the surface via a volcano or fissure (crack in crust at surface) it is called **lava**. While below the surface the melt is called **magma** because it is chemically different from lava.

Rocks formed below the surface are called **intrusions** and are typically large-grained because of slow cooling. Granite family rocks are examples of intrusives. Granite type rocks make up the bulk of the continental crust.

Rocks formed on or near the surface are called **extrusions** and are typically very fine-grained or glassy in texture because of rapid cooling. Basaltic family rocks are examples of extrusives. Basalts make up the bulk of the seafloor crust.

Question 10:

Which of the following is true?

> a. extrusives form below the crust
> b. lava and magma are exactly alike
> c. intrusives are small grained
> d. rocks formed by volcanoes are short-grained

Sedimentary Rocks

Sedimentary rocks form from sediments. They are classified as to their composition as well as to how they form.

Clastics - form from particles of other rocks. Typically, a river washes sand, silt, and clay into the ocean where these particles settle to the bottom of the ocean floor. As more particles are deposited on top, water is squeezed out leaving rock "glue" (silica, iron, calcite) holding the particles together and forming a rock. Examples: **conglomerate**, **sandstone**, and **shale**.

Organics -   form from the remains of living things. Typically, shells from shellfish deposited in mud (clay) get buried and become fossils. **Chalk**, **fossiliferous limestone**, and **soft coal** (bituminous coal), are examples of organic sedimentary rocks.

Question 11:

Which of the following was never part of a living organism?

    a. shale
    b. coal
    c. diamond
    d. limestone

Chemicals -   form when physical or chemical changes occur in water. There are two ways chemical sedimentary rocks can form:

1) as precipitates - chemical limestone forms this way when temperature changes occur along the ocean landmass interface. CO_2 is given up to the atmosphere as the temperature rises. This allows limestone $(CaCO_3)$[same as calcite] to deposit molecularly on the ocean floor.

2) as evaporates - salt (halite) and gypsum form when bodies of water containing these minerals evaporate, leaving the chemical deposits behind.

Question 12:

How does gypsum form?

    a. by temperature changes
    b. by carbon dioxide being given off
    c. by reaction with the atmosphere
    d. by evaporation

Metamorphic Rocks

Metamorphic rocks form when rocks (any kind) come in contact with extreme heat (such as liquid rock) or experience tremendous pressures within the crust. Examples of rocks that have changed metamorphically are:

METAMORPHIC

sed. limestone ➜ marble

sed. shale ➜ slate

sed. sandstone ➜ quartzite

ign. granite ➜ gneiss

meta. slate ➜ phyllite ➜ schist

The Rock Cycle

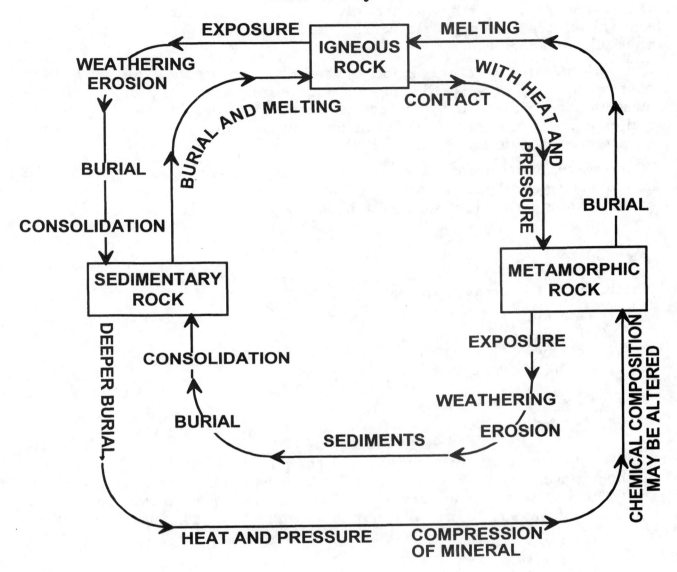

Question 13:

What would have been found in an area before you find marble?

     a. quartzite
     b. limestone
     c. phyllite
     d. slate

Weathering And Erosion

The surface of the Earth is constantly changing due to the breakdown and removal of rock material. Weathering, the breakdown of rocks, occurs both physically and chemically.

The work of water in both its liquid and frozen states accounts for most of the physical breakup of rock. Chemically, acids (rain), water, and oxygen do the most damage. Simply, the chemicals combine with rock minerals to corrode and expand the number of cracks or total surface area thereby exposing the rock to more weathering.

Wind, water, and ice are the agents of erosion. Billions of tons of rocks are moved each year by these agents. Glaciers carry all sizes of rocks, while running water carries less, and wind the least.

Question 14:

Which has to be removed to prevent erosion?

a. wind
b. rain
c. oxygen
d. all of the above

Section 3: Plate Tectonics

After 4.6 billion years of weathering and erosion, the earth should be smooth on the surface. It isn't. Why? Years back, A. Wegener proposed the Continental Drift Theory. He said continents were shaped like jigsaw puzzle pieces and could be fit together. He used South America and Africa as his prime examples.

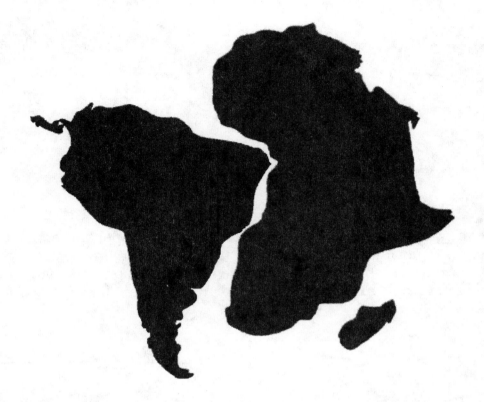

Today, we are almost sure Wegener's Theory is not true. However, the continents do move - as part of the Earth called the **lithosphere** (a 70-km thick piece of rock - part of which is crust and part upper mantle). The surface is made up of large blocks of rock called **plates**. The blocks are in motion because of the activity of heat and melted rock below the lithosphere in a place we call the **asthenosphere**. Here, partly melted rock moves because of convection, forcing the plates to move away from the mid-ocean ridge area.

Question 15:

What are the large blocks of rock making up the crust float on the mantle commonly called?

    a. plates
    b. continents
    c. blocks
    d. lithosphere

Mid-Ocean Ridge

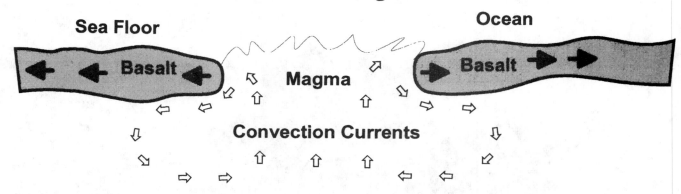

As the plates move <u>away</u> from the mid-ocean ridge, they propel the continents in the direction of movement. We know they are moving because of earthquakes; also, we know there must be some convection because volcanoes are part of the ridge system; in addition sea floor rock is basaltic, formed from lava (melted rock).

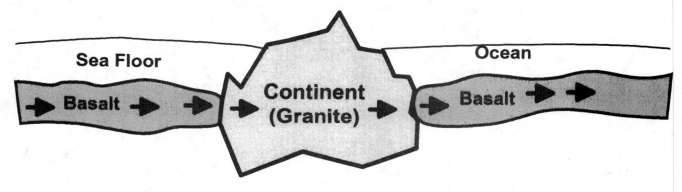

Question 16:

Which of the following are not natural disasters that are caused by moving plates?

    a. volcanoes at the mid ocean ridge
    b. tidal waves
    c. earthquakes
    d. tornadoes

Plates may do one of the following three actions:

1) collide

2) separate

3) move beside each other.

Colliding Plates Without Continents

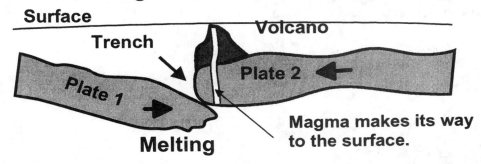

Colliding Plates With a Continent

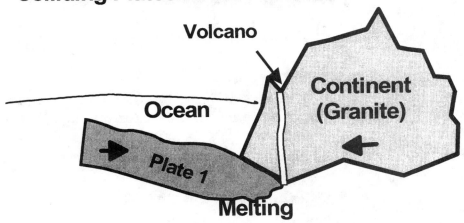

Japan and China are good examples of the above illustration. Japan is volcanic with frequent earthquakes (shallow).

China experiences deep and devastating earthquakes.

Colliding Plates With Two Continents

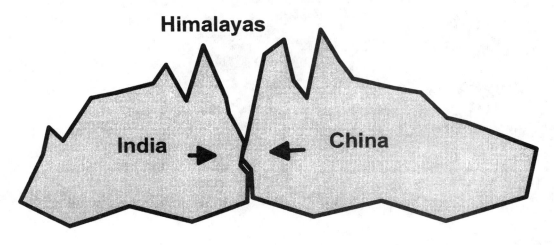

Here, the continents collide, scraping the sea floor up between them and forming very high mountains. Some of the world's large mountain chains are formed in this manner.

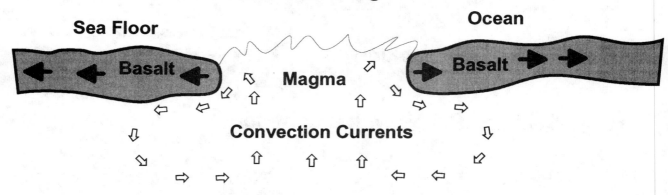

Separating Plates
Mid-Ocean Ridge

Sea Floor

Ocean

Basalt

Basalt

Magma

Convection Currents

Plates Moving Beside Each Other

The Pacific Plate and the North American Plate are a good example of this phenomenon. There, most of California (part of North American Plate) and the Southwest part of California (part of the Pacific Plate) slide past each other causing frequent earthquakes.

San Francisco

San Andreas Fault
(One of many in Southern California)

San Diego

Baja California Mexico

It is in this way that the earth's surface is constantly renewing itself as crustal rocks are formed at ridges and destroyed at trenches or other subduction (wherever crust moves downward toward the mantle) zones.

Question 17:

What two plates are on either side of the San Andreas Fault?

        a. Mexican and North American
        b. Mexican and Pacific
        c. Pacific and North American
        d. Californian and North American

Section 4: The Oceans

The oceans cover 71% or three-fourths of the Earth's surface. They average two-and-a-half to three miles in depth and have a salinity (saltiness) of 3.5%. Being liquid, the oceans are always in motion, aiding in the distribution of heat from equatorial regions towards the poles. In fact, the oceans are regarded as the earth's thermostat. Wherever it gets too warm, hurricanes form in tropical waters to provide a quick release of heat energy from that area.

Question 18:

What percentage of the earth's surface is covered by land?

    a. 17
    b. 29
    c. 71
    d. 83

Section 5: The Atmosphere

The earth's atmosphere is roughly 600 miles thick. It is composed largely of the free gases, oxygen 21% and nitrogen 78%. Most of these gases are concentrated into the bottom most layer of the atmosphere called the troposphere.

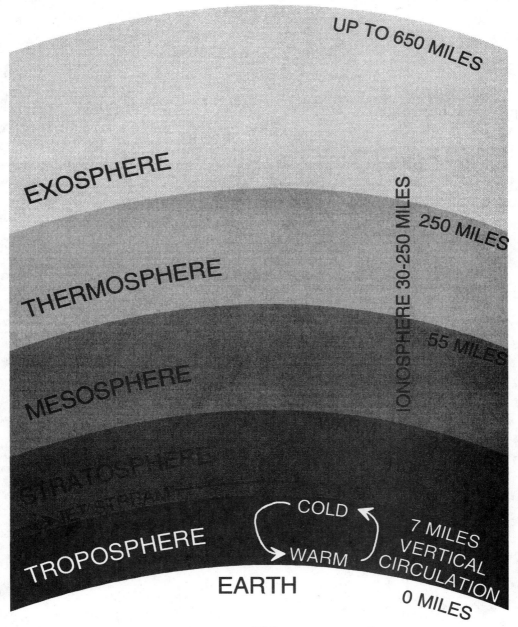

Weather occurs in the troposphere. This layer is warmed as the surface of the earth, rises, cools, and sinks again to replace air that is rising. In other words, convection is operating in the lower atmosphere.

As air rises, it may take water molecules off of the surface. This is called **evaporation**. The water molecules and air move upward and cool. Cooler air cannot hold as much moisture as warmer air. As the gaseous water cools it **condenses** to form clouds. If enough water condenses, the clouds may give up the water again as **precipitation**.

Evaporation, condensation, and precipitation form a cycle known as the **water cycle** or **hydrologic cycle**. This cycle is responsible for the transfer of a large amounts of energy from the surface the atmosphere. Water needs energy just to change from a liquid to a gas - with <u>NO</u> <u>CHANGE</u> <u>IN</u> <u>TEMPERATURE</u>. When the water evaporates, it carries this extra energy up into the atmosphere. When the water condenses, it gives up the energy to the atmosphere. This energy may cause storms to occur.

Humidity is an index of the amount of water vapor suspended in the air. Since the air's capacity to hold water vapor increases as temperature increases, a useful measure of humidity is relative humidity, which is the quantity of water vapor *as a percentage* of how much vapor the air can actually hold *at a specified temperature*. Saturation refers to the situation where the air is holding all the vapor it can handle, 100% relative humidity.

Question 19:

Which of the following, if stopped, would not break the hydrologic cycle?

    a. rain
    b. evaporation
    c. ice
    d. snow

Weather is formed both locally and on a broad scale. Locally, thunderstorms are a good example - even monsoon-type weather, although wider in scale, is more dependent upon local geography than, say, polar-front weather systems. Polar fronts are formed when cold, dry air meets warm, moist tropical air. The result is usually precipitation (rain, snow). Temperature, humidity, pressure, and the location of the jet stream may determine the position of polar fronts.

In addition to weather, our atmosphere provides us with a protective layer of poisonous ozone that absorbs ultra-violet light. Ultra-violet light is responsible for sunburn. The ionosphere also reflects certain wavelengths of radio waves allowing for long distance radio communication.

Question 20:

What does ozone protect us from?

    a. poisons
    b. sunburn
    c. radio waves
    d. poisons and sunburn

Section 6: Ages In Earth's History

Based on the rates of decay of certain radioactive isotopes, the Earth is estimated to be about 4.5 billion years old. On the geologic time scale, this vast stretch of time is usually divided into **eons**, which are further divided into **eras**, **periods**, and **epochs**.

In the **Pre-Cambrian** eon (before about 600 million years ago) the forms of life were mainly bacteria, algae, and fungi, but the fossil remains are scarce. About 88% of the earth's history is taken up by the Pre-Cambrian eon, after which begins the current eon, the **Phanerozoic**.

The Paleozoic Era

- The early part of the **Paleozoic** era (from 600 million to 350 million years ago) was dominated by simple marine life.

- The Middle part of the Paleozoic era is called the age of fishes.

- The later Paleozoic era (until 220 million years ago) saw insects and amphibians

- This era accounts for about 6% of total geologic time.

The Mesozoic

- The **Mesozoic** era (from 220 million to 70 million years ago) is dominated by the rise and extinction of dinosaurs.

- Flowering plants (angiosperms) appeared in the later part of this era in what is known as the Cretaceous period.

- This era represents about 4% of geologic time.

The Cenozoic

- The **Cenozoic** era covers from 70 million years ago to the present

- Birds appeared in the Paleocene epoch (70-60 million years ago).

- Mammals followed in the Eocene epoch (60-40 million years ago).

- The "ice age" occurred in the Pleistocene epoch (1 million-10 thousand years ago), which falls under the Quaternary period (the last million years).

- Human history begins with the Stone, Bronze, and Iron Ages, which will be covered in the Social Studies section.

- This era accounts for only about 2% of total geologic time.

This completes our review of Earth Science. Before you take the Chapter Test, check your answers for the questions that were found throughout the chapter.

1. c. The last paragraph states that the edge of the universe is thought to be 20 billion light years from the earth. Therefore if you traveled at the speed of light it would take 20 billion years.

2. b. Be careful when answering this question; the paragraphs state that the galaxy is 100,000 light years across. Make sure you don't pick 100,000 miles.

3. d. The second paragraph states that not all of the gas ended up in the sun. Eddies were formed and when they cooled they formed planets, moons, comets, and asteroids. Stars take the largest percentage of the gas cloud and are therefore not formed from eddies.

4. b. For the answer to this question you must read the paragraphs about the planets. The paragraph about Venus says that it is Earth's <u>twin</u> in size.

5. b. Again you would have to read the paragraphs about the planets. In the paragraph about Venus it says that it is the third brightest object in the sky, behind the sun and the moon. From this information you must make the connection that it would be the first to appear in the evening sky after the moon.

6. a. Reading over the descriptions of the planets, we see that in the paragraph about Saturn it says that it is second in size.

7. d. The paragraph states the rotation of the liquid outer core of the earth causes a magnetic field.

8. d. This question requires you to think a little. Looking at the diagram you can see the silicates are the most common. You must then read to find out which minerals are silicates. This then gives you the most common minerals.

9. b. Crystallization is the one choice that is not listed in the paragraph as a way for rocks to form. Crystallization is how minerals form and then multiple minerals will join together and form a rock.

10. d. The only correct answer is rocks formed by volcanoes are short grained. The second paragraph states that granite is a type of intrusive, and that intrusives are large grained. The first paragraph states that lava and magma are chemically different. The third paragraph states that extrusives form at or near the surface. Rocks formed by volcanoes would form at or near the surface and would consequently be short grained.

11. a. Looking at the paragraph on clastics, we see that shale is the only choice listed. Coal, limestone, and chalk are all listed as organics. Diamond is not listed in either paragraph. Diamond is in fact formed from coal under the influence of heat and pressure. To answer the question you really just had to find a clastic, shale, and since it was never alive it is the correct answer.

12. d. In the paragraph on evaporation, gypsum and salt are the two things listed as examples. Therefore gypsum forms by evaporation.

13. b. Looking at the table of metamorphic rocks, you can see that sedimentary limestone is across from marble. Under the effects of heat and pressure, limestone will turn into marble. Therefore limestone must be found in an area before it can be turned into marble.

14. d. All of the choices: wind, rain, and oxygen, are listed in the paragraphs as being causes of erosion. Wind, rain, and ice are listed as physical erosive agents. Oxygen is listed in the paragraph about chemical agents.

15. a. The last paragraph states the large blocks of rock floating on the mantle are called plates. Always read carefully, many people will mistakenly choose continents for this question.

16. d. Volcanoes and earthquakes are all listed as proof of the plates' movement. Tornadoes, being above ground, would not be affected by plate movement. Looking closer at answer b, tidal waves occur when an earthquake happens underwater.

17. c. For this question you have to read the paragraphs until you find a reference to the San Andreas Fault. It is found in the last paragraph. It states the San Andreas Fault is caused by the collision of the Pacific and North American plates.

18. b. This is a trick question. The paragraph states that 71% of the Earth's surface is covered by water. If you answer 71% you are wrong because the question asks for how much of the Earth is covered by land. The amount covered by land would be whatever is not covered by water, or 29%.

19. c. Rain and snow are both types of precipitation and would be part of the hydrologic cycle. Evaporation and condensation are both listed as parts of the hydrologic cycle. The only choice left, ice, is not part of the hydrologic cycle. The formation of ice on lakes is separate from the cycle that forms the weather.

20. b. The second paragraph states ozone absorbs sunburn-causing ultra-violet light. It also says ozone is poisonous; it does not say it protects us from poison.

After you have reviewed the areas where you had difficulty, you will be ready to take the Earth Science Chapter Test that begins on the next page.

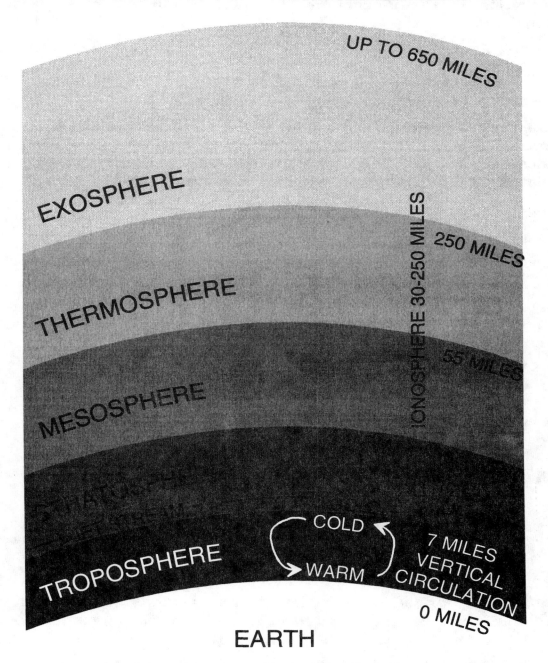

UP TO 650 MILES

EXOSPHERE

THERMOSPHERE

250 MILES

IONOSPHERE 30-250 MILES

55 MILES

MESOSPHERE

TROPOSPHERE

COLD
WARM

7 MILES
VERTICAL
CIRCULATION

0 MILES

EARTH

1. **The bottom layer of the atmosphere is called the**

   a. tropospanse
   b. troposphere
   c. ionosphere
   d. exosphere

2. You call a radio station to complain about the poor reception you have been getting, and they respond that there has been a big disruption in the ionosphere. At what height did this disruption occur?

    a. between 1 and 7 miles
    b. between 7 and 15 miles
    c. between 7 and 30 miles
    d. over 30 miles

3. Limestone is formed when millions of sea animals die and their shells get compressed into a rock. You believe that marble then forms when limestone is under high temperature and pressure. Which of the following if true would help back up your assumption?

    a. volcanoes at the mid-ocean ridge.
    b. marble is often found at the site of ancient seabeds.
    c. when you dig marble at the quarry it is warm.
    d. marble is found at the site of an ancient glacial deposit.

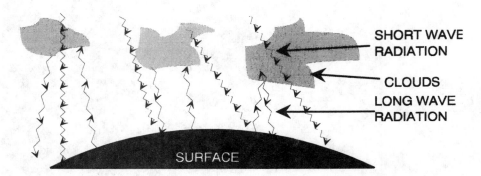

4. What is a contributing factor to the greenhouse effect?

    a. the surface of the planet warms up
    b. the changes in solar radiation
    c. short-wave radiation passes through clouds easier than long-wave radiation.
    d. evaporation

5. Planets are formed when eddies around a newly formed star cool. Which of the following would have formed from the largest eddy?

    a. Pluto
    b. Jupiter
    c. Mars
    d. Earth

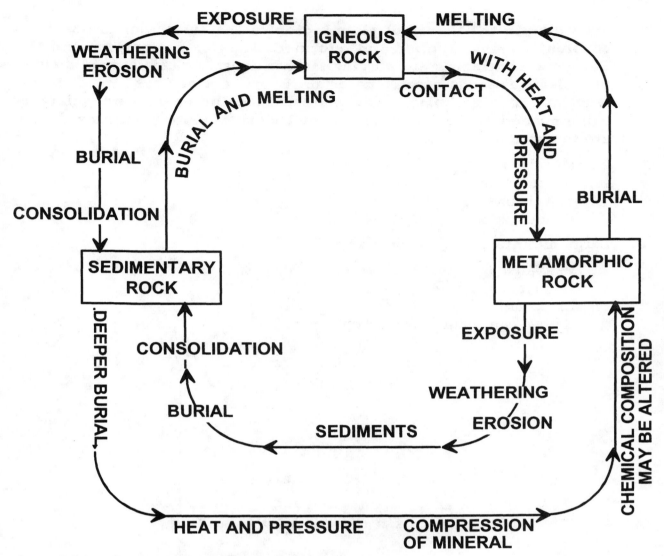

6. Metamorphosis occurs because of

    a. melting and cooling
    b. erosion and weathering
    c. erosion and deposition
    d. extreme heat and pressure short of total melting

7. According to the theory of plate tectonics the surface of the earth is constantly being renewed and reformed. The North American and the European continents are moving farther apart. At this spread a ridge of volcanoes adds extra material. Every action has an opposite reaction. In other places the plates are colliding and one plate is being pushed under the other. In the theory of Plate Tectonics, plates are renewed at

    a. ridge areas
    b. trenches
    c. volcanoes
    d. fault zones

8. **Large mountain chains form when**

    a. plates slide past each other
    b. plates separate
    c. oceanic plates collide
    d. two continents riding on plates collide

9. **Of the following, which one is part of the hydrologic cycle?**

    a. maturation
    b. inebriation
    c. condensation
    d. saturation

10. **Halite is found in the remains of old seabeds. Over time the seas dried up and halite was left behind. Which of the following best describe halite.**

    a. metamorphic rock
    b. sedimentary clastic rock
    c. sedimentary chemical evaporite rock
    d. sedimentary organic rock

11. **The moon or sun pulling on the ocean causes tides. Though the sun is much larger than the moon, because the moon is so much closer, the moon has more of an effect on the tides. What do you think would cause the largest tides?**

    a. The sun and the moon pulling in the same direction
    b. The sun pulling directly opposite the moon
    c. The sun pulling at a 90⁰ angle from the moon
    d. The moon pulling on a small body of water.

ANSWERS - CHAPTER TEST EARTH SCIENCE

1) b Looking at the diagram, you need to find the lowest level. This level is the troposphere and it goes from zero to seven miles in height. This is the level where our weather occurs.

2) d The ionosphere goes from thirty to 250 miles in height.

3) b If marble is found in areas where ancient seas were found, this would back up your assumption. Volcanoes would have nothing to do with your assumption. Whether marble is warm when you dig it would not prove or disprove your theory because the heat and pressure transformation take place over time.

4) c Choice a is the net result of the greenhouse effect. The best choice is c because it gives the exact reason why the radiation comes in through the clouds, but has a harder time getting back out.

5) b To answer this question you will need a small amount of previous knowledge, that Jupiter is the largest planet. The largest planet would have the largest eddy.

6) d Metamorphosis occurs when rock under high heat and temperature changes to a different form. However, the temperature must remain lower than the melting point, or the rock will melt instead of going through metamorphosis. Erosion does not change the type of rock; it simply breaks it into smaller pieces.

7) a The plates are renewed at the ridge areas. Ridges are a long series of volcanoes that spew out new material. The answer is not simply volcanoes because the question asks for a location (ridge areas) not how (volcanoes).

8) d Let's look at each answer individually. Plates sliding past each other do not make huge mountains because most of the force is spent overcoming friction. When plates separate, there is, again, no force to create a mountain. When oceanic plate collide, one can slide under the other forming a trench or they can crumple up for islands. However, they started so low below the surface the do not appear as a large mountain chain. Two continents colliding is the best answer. Here the force has nowhere to go but into forming mountains. The plates crumple up as they crash into each other.

9) c The hydrologic cycle starts with water evaporation from the surface. The water then condenses in clouds and finally it precipitates back to the Earth.

10) c The key here is to notice the words "dried up." This lets you know that evaporation is occurring. There is no mention whether halite is able to undergo metamorphosis or that it is made from living material.

11) a The best choice is clearly when the sun and moon are pulling in the same direction. Here their forces will be added together. When you take a look at tides, the moon (and the sun) not only pull the ocean close to them up away from the earth, but they also pull the earth away from the ocean on the other side. This causes the tide to rise on the side of the earth opposite the moon (or sun). When the sun and moon pull in opposite directions there will also be large tides but some of their forces will cancel each other out. When the sun and moon pull at 90^0 the tides are smaller because the sun and moon are canceling each other out.

Chapter 7: PHYSICS

Physics may be divided into three very broad areas: mechanics, thermodynamics, and electromagnetism. **Mechanics** studies the forces that exist among physical objects. **Thermodynamics** studies the movements of heat energy, and **electromagnetism** studies the movements of energy in forms such as light, electricity, and magnetism.

Much of physics involves measurement. Physicists make a distinction between two types of quantities: scalars and vectors. A **scalar** is a quantity and unit of measurement, such as thirty-two degrees Fahrenheit, 100 kilograms or fifty-five miles per hour. A **vector** has quantity, a unit, and a specific direction (for example fifty-five miles per hour, northwest). Vectors are graphically represented by arrows pointing in the specified direction. Greater quantities are represented by drawing longer vectors.

As an example of a vector diagram, suppose an object traveled a distance of six miles east and then traveled eight miles north:

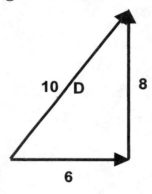

The vector labeled D represents the overall displacement (change in position) of the object. By using the Pythagorean Theorem, it can be seen that the length of the displacement is ten. (This theorem is covered in the Mathematics section.)

Section 1: Motion

Sir Isaac Newton formulated the laws of motion. Motion is the result of a force acting on a mass.

First Law of Motion: The two parts of the First Law of Motion are:

1) A body at rest tends to stay at rest

2) A body in motion tends to stay in motion unless acted upon by an outside force.

EXAMPLES:

1) A book on a table will stay there forever unless someone or something applies a force to it, causing it to move.

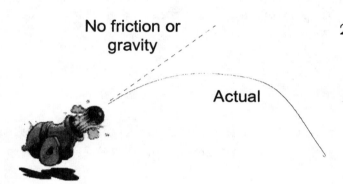

No friction or gravity

Actual

2) A cannon shot would travel in a straight line forever if it wasn't for the friction of the air slowing it down and the force of gravity pulling it to the surface of the Earth.

Question 1:

What is the flight path of a bullet?

     a. A straight line.
     b. A line that curves with the earth.
     c. A line that points out into outer space.
     d. A line that is curved due to gravity.

Question 2:

What happens to a marble that is set on a level desk?

     a. It rolls off.
     b. It rolls in a circle.
     c. It stays where it is placed.
     d. It would follow a curved path off the table.

Second Law of Motion: Force = mass x acceleration, or F = ma

EXAMPLE:

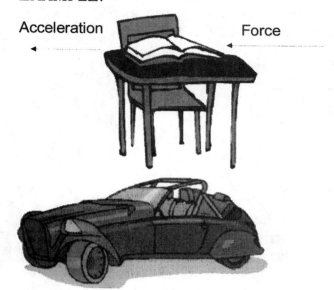

Acceleration

Force

The book on the table in the example has a mass of 1 kg. Some force is applied causing the book to move from its original position. The change from an initial velocity to a new velocity represents acceleration (Ex.: changing speeds in a car from 40 mph to 55 mph. That change is referred to as acceleration). Let us say the acceleration was 2 m/sec. By applying the numbers to the formula we get

$$F = 1 \text{ kg} \times 2 \text{ m/sec}$$

$$F = \frac{2 \text{ kg-m}}{\text{sec}} \text{ or 2 nt (Newtons)}$$

The book only moves because a force causes it to accelerate. Obviously, this force would be very negligible if one were to attempt to use it to stop a speeding car.

Question 3:

What would be the acceleration of a 3 kg object if a 9 (kg x m/sec) force is applied to it?

        a. 1/3 (m/sec^2)
        b. 3 (m/sec^2)
        c. 9 (m/sec^2)
        d. 27 (m/sec^2)

Third Law of Motion: For every action there is an equal and opposite reaction.

EXAMPLE:

Balloon's Motion

Escaping Air

A balloon is a good example of action-reaction. When releasing a balloon filled with air, the air escapes out the blow hole while the balloon is propelled forward.

Question 4:

If you throw a baseball while you are standing in a row boat, what happens?

        a.   The ball moves, but the boat does not.
        b.   The boat moves, but the ball does not.
        c.   The boat and the ball move the same amount.
        d.   The boat moves away from the ball but not as much as the ball moves.

Newton is also responsible for our understanding of gravity. The formula for gravity is derived from F = ma. It is:

$$\text{Force of gravity} = \frac{(\text{Gravity constant})(\text{mass})(\text{mass})}{(\text{Distance})^2} \quad \text{to simplify,}$$

$$F = \frac{G M_1 M_2}{D^2}$$

Examples: 1) Two large masses near each other:

Mass = 2

Mass = 4

distance = 2

M_1 M_2

$$F = \frac{M_1 M_2}{d^2} = \frac{(2)(4)}{2^2} = 2 \text{ gravity units}$$

2) Two small masses near each other:

Mass = 1

Mass = 2

distance = 2

M_1 M_2

$$F = \frac{M_1 M_2}{d^2} = \frac{(1)(2)}{2^2} = \frac{1}{2} \text{ gravity units}$$

To summarize: the greater the distance between the masses, the less gravitational attraction.

By the way, the acceleration due to the force of gravity on earth is 9.8 m/sec^2 or 32 ft./sec^2.

If an object travels in a circular path at a constant velocity, the object is being accelerated toward the center of the circle. This type of acceleration is called centripetal acceleration. The opposite of a **centripetal force** is called a **centrifugal force**.

Question 5:

The moon is closer to the Earth than the sun is to the Earth. The moon has a greater impact on the tides through its gravitational pull than the sun has. Which of the following is true?

   a. The moon has a stronger gravitational attraction to the earth than the sun.
   b. The moon is bigger than the earth.
   c. The moon is bigger than the sun.
   d. The moon and the sun are the same size.

Section 2: The Lever

A lever is a bar that is balanced at a point called the fulcrum. There are three classes of levers - First, Second, and Third.

Resistance Force   Effort Force

Remember the seesaw when you were young? The lever seen above is that kind of machine. You know that the heavier person always had to sit closer to the middle of the board and the lighter person could balance the heavier person. That's what this lever does.

EFFORT FORCE   **RESISTANT FORCE**

Other examples of first class levers are the juice can opener, crow bar and scissors.

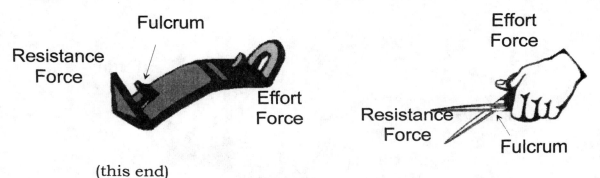

(this end)

Question 6:

Where does the lighter person have to sit to balance a heavier person on a seesaw?

  a.   At the same distance from the fulcrum as the heavier person.
  b.   Farther from the fulcrum than the heavier person.
  c.   Closer to the fulcrum than the heavier person.
  d.   On the same side as the heavier person.

Second class lever:

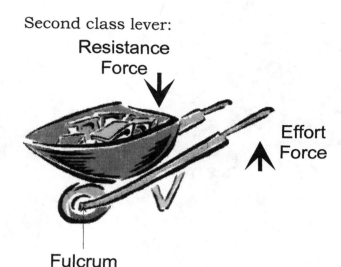

Resistance Force

Effort Force

Fulcrum

A wheelbarrow is a good example of a second class lever.

Here, the load in the wheelbarrow is effort balanced between the wheel (fulcrum) and the force (handlebars).

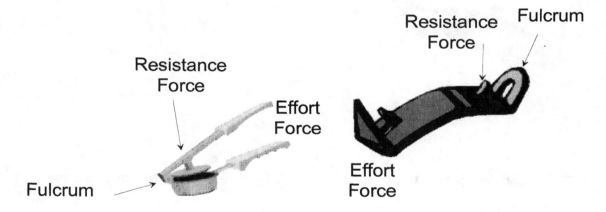

Resistance Force

Effort Force

Fulcrum

Resistance Force

Fulcrum

Effort Force

Other examples are the garlic press and the bottle opener.

Question 7:

Where is the resistance force in a second class lever?

    a.   Between the effort force and the fulcrum.

    b.   Farther out from the fulcrum than the effort force on the same side.

    c.   Farther out from the fulcrum than the effort force on the opposite side.

    d.   Closer to the fulcrum on the opposite side than the effort force.

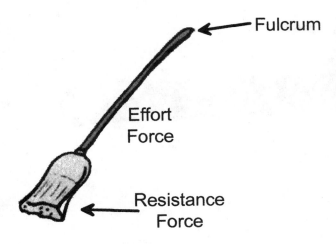

Fulcrum

Effort
Force

Resistance
Force

In a third class lever, the effort force is between the resistance force and the fulcrum. The most common example of a third class lever is a broom.

Question 8:

Which of the following is an example of a third class lever?

    a. a pull tab on a soda can
    b. a seesaw
    c. a rolling pin
    d. a revolving door

SECTION 3: Machines

Machines simplify work to be done. For example, imagine trying to open a can of corn without using a can opener.

The simple machines you should know are: lever, pulley, wedge, inclined plane, screw, and wheel & axle. Some of these machines are related to others, but are used in a different way. Combinations of these machines are called compound machines. (Scissors, wheelbarrows, and cranes are all examples of compound machines.)

Machines usually increase the distance through which a force must act in order to get work done, or they change the direction the force may act.

    Work = force x distance.

Therefore if you increase the distance, you decrease the amount of force you must apply.

EXAMPLE:

Applying ten force units through five distance units equals fifty work units. If the distance is increased to ten, the amount of force needed to do the same amount of work would only be five units.

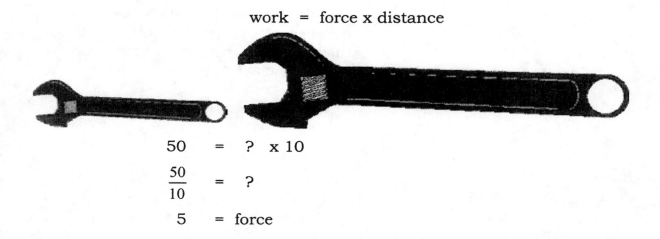

$$\text{work} = \text{force} \times \text{distance}$$

$$50 \ = \ ? \times 10$$

$$\frac{50}{10} \ = \ ?$$

$$5 \ = \ \text{force}$$

Question 9:

If you triple the force through the same distance, how much work would you do?

    a. $\frac{1}{3}$ the work

    b. $\frac{1}{2}$ the work

    c. the same amount of work

    d. 3 times the amount of work

- **Potential energy** is the energy that an object has by virtue of its *position.* An object higher off the ground has greater gravitational potential energy than when it is closer to the ground. A stretched elastic band has greater elastic potential energy than if the elastic band were in its original non-stretched state.

- **Kinetic energy** is the energy that an object has because of its *motion.* When the stationary skier at the top of a hill starts to ski down, kinetic energy increases while potential energy decreases.

Section 4: The Pulley

A pulley is a bearing to which a belt is attached. It can be used to change the direction of the belt, or to turn a shaft.

Points to remember:

    1) All pulleys on the same shaft turn in the same direction.

    2) All pulleys on the same shaft turn at the same speed.

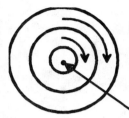

Both pulleys on the shaft will make the same number of revolutions in a given amout of time.

Shaft

3) Different sized pulleys attached to different shafts by a "belt" (or other drive device) turn at different speeds. Comparison of speed is the inverse of the ratio of their diameter size.

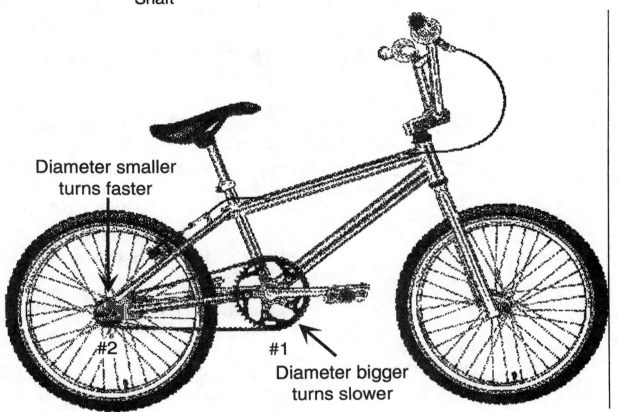

Diameter smaller turns faster

#2

#1

Diameter bigger turns slower

#2 pulley is half the diameter of pulley #1. The inverse is $\frac{2}{1}$ or 2. Therefore pulley #2 turns two times for every turn pulley #1 makes. The speed is twice as fast.

Question 10:

Which of the following is true of pulleys?

    a. different sized pulleys attached by a belt turn at different speeds
    b. pulleys on the same shaft turn at the same speed
    c. pulleys on the same shaft turn the same direction
    d. all of the above

The main purpose of creating pulley systems is to:

1) Change the direction of the force.

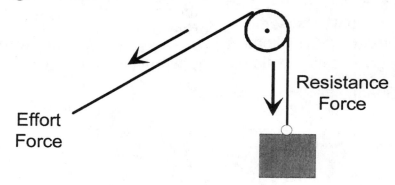

Effort
Force

Resistance
Force

2) Decrease the effort force needed to lift objects at the expense of adding distance through which the effort force must act.

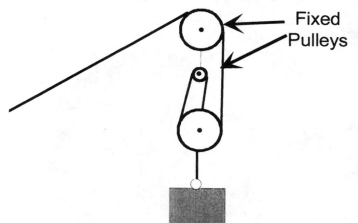

Fixed
Pulleys

The greater the number of ropes connecting the pulleys, the easier it is to lift the resistance force.

Complex pulley systems are used on sailboats, cranes, and elevators. A very simple pulley arrangement is used on clothes dryers and car fans.

Question 11:

Which of the following does not have a pulley system?

    a. a car fan
    b. a can opener
    c. an elevator
    d. a sailboat

Section 5: Gears

Gears are similar to pulleys except that they have teeth to engage other gears instead of using belts.

Points to remember:

1)   One gear engaging another gear causes it to turn in the opposite direction.

2)   An odd number of gears engaging each other in a loop will not turn.

3) Different sized gears turn at different speeds. Comparison of speed is the inverse of the ratio of the number of teeth (cogs) on each gear.

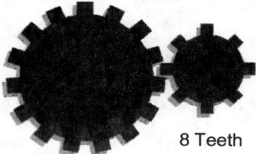

The small gear makes 15 revolutions for every 8 revolutions of the big gear.

8 Teeth

15 Teeth

Question 12:

How would the seventh gear in a straight line series turn?

    a. In the same direction as the first gear.
    b. In the opposite direction as the first gear.
    c. Faster than the first gear.
    d. Slower than the first gear.

Cars use gears in their transmissions to change the amount of output work the motor produces and the number of times the wheels of the car turn.

Another example of gears is on a multi-speed bicycle. The gears are connected by a chain. By changing the gear ratio, the cyclist can bike up a hill using lots less effort than he/she would if using a bicycle without a gear system.

Question 13:

Why does the bicyclist change gears when going up a hill?

    a. to do more work
    b. to do less work
    c. to increase the effort force
    d. to decrease the effort force

Section 6: Inclined Planes

A wedge is a simple machine that employs a large effort force to act through a very short distance. An ax, maul, chisel, nail, and knife are all wedges.

Question 14:

What is the purpose of a wedge?

    a. to increase the effort force
    b. to increase the resistance force
    c. to concentrate the effort force
    d. to absorb the effort force

Inclined Plane

It takes less effort force to move a resistance force up a ramp (inclined plane) than it would to lift that same force straight up to the desired height.

Effort Force

Resistance
Force

Adding distance allows the use of less effort to accomplish the same amount of work.

EXAMPLE: Roads (going over hills) and ramps for wheelchairs.

Question 15:

Which of the following is not an inclined plane?

    a. a wheelchair ramp
    b. a ramp in a parking garage
    c. an escape chute on an airplane
    d. an elevator in a hotel

A screw is a curved incline plane. The incline wraps around the central post.

Other examples are drill bits, light bulbs, and clamps.

Question 16:

Which of the following is not a curved incline plane?

    a. a screw
    b. a twist off bottle cap
    c. a driveway
    d. a spiraling parking garage ramp
    e. a drill bit

Section 7: Wheel And Axle

Just remember this, a wheel and axle <u>reduces</u> friction. In many instances a lot of energy is wasted overcoming friction. Any wheel on an axle reduces the energy wasted. This means more work can be done for the same amount of effort. A machine employing wheel and axle mechanisms is more efficient.

Question 17:

What is the purpose of a wheel and axle?

    a. to make a car go faster
    b. to reduce friction
    c. to increase the resistance force
    d. to waste energy

Section 8: Heat And Energy Transfer

Heat is the total energy of motion of all the molecules in an object. A measure of the speed the molecules are moving is called temperature.

Heat is transferred from areas of greater concentrations to areas of lesser concentrations - that is, from where it is hot to where it is cool. A melting ice cube in your hand is warming from the heat of your body.

Question 18:

Which of the following is not the way heat would flow?

        a. from ice to water
        b. from fire to water
        c. from your body to ice
        d. from boiling water to you

Heat may travel from one place to another by the following ways:

    1) **conduction** - direct contact between the heat source and the object.

    2) **convection** - heat is moved from one point to another by the movement of a liquid or a gas, usually water or the air.

    3) **radiation** - here, heat travels through any medium by wave motion (like the heat of the sun).

Heat travels best through conductors. Good conductors are usually metals - gold, silver, copper, aluminum, and steel are conductors of heat energy. Gold, silver and copper are perhaps the best.

Anything that does not conduct heat well is said to be a non-conductor, or insulator.

Question 19:

Which of the following is not a good conductor?

        a. copper
        b. silver
        c. gold
        d. wood

Section 9: Reflection And Refraction

When you look in a mirror you see your reflection. Reflection is the bouncing back of energy waves off a surface. Sunlight reflects off glass, the ocean, and even the moon.

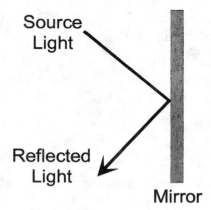

Light reflects off a flat mirror at the same angle it strikes that mirror.

Question 20:

Which of the following does light bounce off of?

        a. mirrors
        b. water
        c. the moon
        d. all of the above

Another event that may occur when a form of wave energy enters into a different medium (example: light entering water), is refraction. Refraction may be described as the bending of the energy wave.

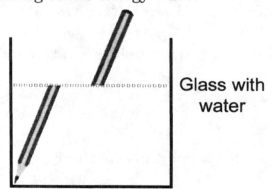

The pencil is not broken. What has happened here is that light waves have been bent (refracted) because they move faster upon entering the water.

Question 21:

What happens to light when it enters a different medium?

      a. it glows
      b. it breaks
      c. it bends
      d. it twists

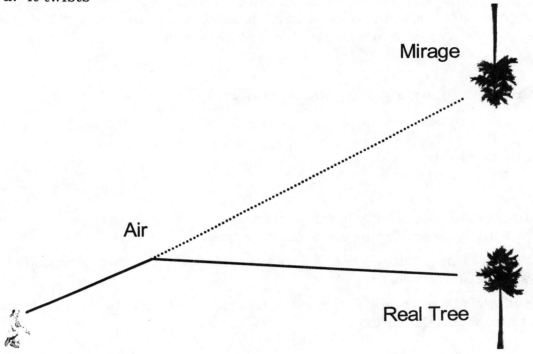

A mirage is an example of the bending of light waves.

- Wavelength is the distance it takes a wave to go through one full cycle.
- Frequency is how quickly a wave goes through one full cycle.
- The shorter the wavelength, the higher the frequency
- In the visible spectrum, red has a longer wavelength than violet
- Infrared has a longer wavelength than red
- Ultraviolet has a shorter wavelength than violet
- X-rays have a shorter wavelength than ultraviolet

Section 10: Electricity And Magnetism

Electricity is the movement of electrons from one place to another. Lightning is a form of static electricity. So is the shock you receive when you touch a doorknob after dragging your feet across a rug on a dry day. As long as a large enough potential (difference) exists between one point and another, electricity will flow.

Electricity flows best through a conductor. The best conductors are gold, silver and copper. Things that do not conduct electricity well are called insulators. Glass, plastic, ceramic, and wood are all insulators.

Question 22:

Which of the following are good insulators?

       a. copper
       b. wood
       c. silver
       d. a and c only

The amount of electricity that flows through a wire is known as the current. The current is measured in units called **amperes** or **amps**.

The electrical push through the wires is the electromotive force called **voltage** and is measured in **volts**.

There is always resistance to the flow of electricity. This is called **resistance** and is measured in **ohms** (Ω).

Question 23:

Match the word in column A with the measurement in B.

A	B
1. resistance	a. volts
2. current	b. amps
3. voltage	c. ohms

The relationship of the current (I), voltage (E), and resistance (R) is shown in Ohm's Law:

Voltage (E) = current (I) x Resistance (R)   E = IR

A good way of remembering this formula is to use the following diagram:

In order to solve problems using Ohm's Law, just cover what you don't know and solve. For example: How much voltage is required to provide 50 Amps passing through 10Ω resistance?

50 x 10 = 500 volts

EXAMPLE: What is the resistance of a T.V. set if the voltage is 120V and the current is 6 amps?

$$\frac{E}{I} = \frac{120V}{6\,amps} = 20\Omega$$

Question 24:

What is the resistance if the current is 60 amps and the voltage is 120 volts?

      a. 1/2 ohm
      b. 2 ohms
      c. 30 ohms
      d. 7200 ohms

Power is the amount of work done by the electricity. It is measured in **watts**. We have the same kind of formula as above:

Power (P) = current (I) x voltage (E) or, P = I x E.

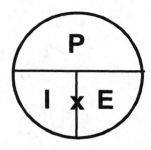

Solve any problems as you would using Ohm's Law.

Question 25:

What is the power if the current is ten amps and the voltage is 120 volts?

    a. 1/12
    b. 1.2
    c. 12
    d. 1200

Electricity flows through a circuit unless we're dealing with static electricity.. A circuit is an unbroken path in which electricity flows to and from the source.

There are two types of circuits: **Series** and **Parallel**.

Series Circuit

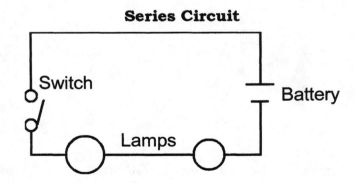

Pictured above is an open circuit. No electricity will flow until the path is completed by closing the switch.

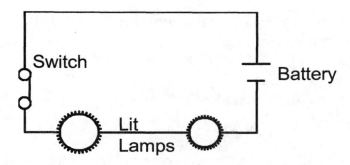

If we were to disconnect a lamp, the circuit would be broken and the other lamp would go out.

Electricity entering our homes must pass through a fuse box or circuit breaker box. This is wired in a series to protect us from electrical overloads, which can cause a fire. Lights on a single switch are also series wired. Any appliance operated with a switch is series wired. However, the circuit wiring in a house is parallel, not series.

Question 26:

Why is the circuit breaker wired in series?

      a. That is just the way it is done.
      b. To protect against overloads.
      c. To save energy.
      d. So switches can be run.

Parallel Circuits

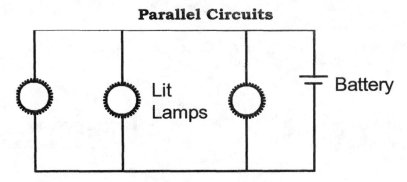

In a parallel circuit, electricity may follow different paths to return to the source. Remember, the circuit must be complete or else no electricity will flow. In the above diagram, the electricity follows three different paths: through each lamp (3) and back to the source. Here, if a lamp burns out disconnecting that part of the circuit, the electricity continues to flow through the other two lamps back to the source.

This is similar to your own home, where when a light bulb burns out the entire house is not thrown into darkness.

Question 27:

Why are some circuts run in parallel?

      a.   to keep lights from burning out

      b.   to prevent circut overloads

      c.   so you don't lose all your power if one electrical appliance burns out

      d.   to save energy

Section 11: Magnetism

A natural magnet is called a lodestone. It is a rock that has a high percentage of iron (called magnetite) in its chemical make-up.

Magnets have two poles: north and south. Emanating from these poles are invisible magnetic lines of force. If we sprinkle iron filings on top of a piece of paper covering a magnet, the iron filings line up on the lines of force.

Notice, N and S attract. This conforms to opposites attract and likes repel. Two N/N or S/S would show a pattern like.

Question 28:

What are the poles of a magnet called?

      a. east and west

      b. east and north

      c. east and south

      d. north and south

Magnetism and electricity are related. If we were to pass a magnet through a coil of wire connected to a galvanometer, the needle would move as long as the magnet were in motion.

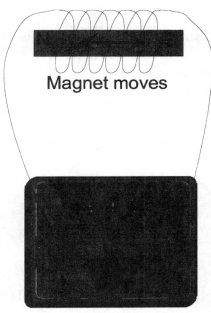

Magnet moves

What is happening is the magnetic lines of force are causing electrons to move back and forth in the wire (alternating current).

This "induction" effect is used to generate electricity. Atomic energy, running water (rivers, waterfalls, dams), gas or coal fuel provide the power to turn large turbines which have huge magnets and wire coils turning in a field of magnetic lines of force. This generates huge amounts of electricity, which eventually is divided and dealt out to all the electric company's consumers.

Question 29:

What is the induction effect?

> a. An alternating current.
> b. Wire coils and magnets.
> c. The burning of coal.
> d. The flow of electrons due to a magnetic field.

Section 12: Fission And Fusion

Fission

Atomic energy has been with us, in usable form, for the past fifty years. This type of energy is best understood as the **radioactive decay process**.

Unstable atoms are always undergoing the decay process. In a given amount of time, half of the radioactive substance will have decayed into daughter elements. Scientists can determine the half-life of radioactive substances.

EXAMPLE: ^{238}U (Uranium with an atomic weight of 238) has a half-life of 4,500,000,000 years (4.5 billion years). This means that one pound of ^{238}U existing 4.5 billion years ago is only a half pound of ^{238}U today. The other half pound is now converted into **daughter elements** such as Radon (Rn), Thorium (Th), Radium (Ra), and Lead (Pb).

$$X = {}^{238}U \text{ atoms}$$

$$Y = \text{decayed } {}^{238}U \text{ atoms}$$

1 lb. ^{238}U
4.5 billion years ago

Now 1/2 lb. ^{238}U
1/2 lb. daughter elements

Question 30:

Into which of the following does uranium not decay?

      a. thorium
      b. radon
      c. lead
      d. none of these

In order to calculate the amount of original radioactive elements remaining after a number of half-lives, one must use the formula:

$$\left(\frac{1}{2}\right)^n$$

EXAMPLE:

A substance passed through four half-lives. How much of the original substance remains? How much has decayed?

$$\left(\frac{1}{2}\right)^n = \left(\frac{1}{2}\right)^4 = \left(\frac{1}{2}\right)\left(\frac{1}{2}\right)\left(\frac{1}{2}\right)\left(\frac{1}{2}\right) = \frac{1}{16}$$

Only $\frac{1}{16}$ of the original radioactive substance remains, and $\frac{15}{16}$ has decayed.

$$\frac{1}{16} + \frac{15}{16} = \frac{16}{16} = 1$$

EXAMPLE:

A radioactive substance has a half-life of twenty-five years and passes through five half-lives.

    a)   How many years does it take to pass through five half-lives?

    b)   How much of the original material remains?

    c)   How many years will it be before 99% of the original substance decays?

    a) $\left(\dfrac{25 \text{ years}}{\text{half life}}\right)(5 \text{ half lives}) = 125 \text{ years}$

    b) $\left(\dfrac{1}{2}\right)^n = \left(\dfrac{1}{2}\right)^5 = \left(\dfrac{1}{2}\right)\left(\dfrac{1}{2}\right)\left(\dfrac{1}{2}\right)\left(\dfrac{1}{2}\right)\left(\dfrac{1}{2}\right) = \dfrac{1}{32}$ of the original substance remains.

    (c) $\left(\dfrac{1}{2}\right)^n = \left(\dfrac{1}{2}\right)^2 = \dfrac{1}{4}$

          $\left(\dfrac{1}{2}\right)^n = \left(\dfrac{1}{2}\right)^3 = \dfrac{1}{8}$

          $\left(\dfrac{1}{2}\right)^n = \left(\dfrac{1}{2}\right)^4 = \dfrac{1}{16}$

          $\left(\dfrac{1}{2}\right)^n = \left(\dfrac{1}{2}\right)^5 = \dfrac{1}{32}$

          $\left(\dfrac{1}{2}\right)^n = \left(\dfrac{1}{2}\right)^6 = \dfrac{1}{64}$

          $\left(\dfrac{1}{2}\right)^n = \left(\dfrac{1}{2}\right)^7 = \dfrac{1}{128}$

After seven half-lives less than 1% of the original substance remains.

$$7 \times 25 \text{ years} = 175 \text{ years}$$

Question 31:

How much of the original material is left if the material has a half-life of twenty years and the time elapsed is 100 years?

 a. $\dfrac{1}{64}$

 b. $\dfrac{1}{32}$

 c. $\dfrac{1}{16}$

 d. $\dfrac{31}{32}$

The reason for decay is instability. This probably has something to do with the amount of neutrons in the nucleus of the atom; protons do not seem to decay.

Two kinds of particles are thrown off during decay:

Alpha (α) and Beta (β)

An alpha particle is comparable to a helium nucleus:

$$\alpha = {}^{4}_{2}He$$

A beta particle is comparable to an electron. Now I know you're saying that electrons don't exist in the nucleus - true! Scientists believe a neutron decays (breaks-up) into a proton (+), electron (-), and a neutrino. ($n^0 = p^+ + e^- +$ neutrino). The neutrino goes somewhere. It's a very elusive particle. The electron leaves the nucleus, and the proton stays behind.

Question 32:

What is a beta particle like?

 a. an electron
 b. a proton
 c. two protons and two neutrons
 d. gamma rays

Also leaving the nucleus during decay are gamma rays (γ).

During the decay of ${}^{238}U$, both α and β particles are thrown off until a stable form of Pb is produced.

$$^{238}_{92}U \xrightarrow[\alpha \text{ decay}]{} ^{234}_{90}Th \xrightarrow[\beta \text{ decay}]{} ^{234}_{91}Pa$$

$$-\frac{4}{2}He \qquad -1n^{\phi} + 1p^{+}$$

α decay = loss of 2 p^{+} (at. no. [92 to 90]) and

loss of 4 particles ($2p^{+}$ & $2n^{\phi}$) from atomic weight.

β Decay = loss of 1 neutron, gain of 1 proton

= no loss at. wt., gain of 1 p^{+} = gain in at. no. (90 to 91).

Decay of ^{238}U

$$^{238}_{92}U \xrightarrow{\alpha} ^{234}_{90}Th \xrightarrow{\beta} ^{234}_{91}Pa \xrightarrow{\beta} ^{234}_{92}U \xrightarrow{\alpha} ^{230}_{90}Th \xrightarrow{\alpha} ^{226}_{88}Ra \xrightarrow{\alpha} ^{222}_{86}Rn$$

$$^{222}_{86}Rn \xrightarrow{\alpha} ^{218}_{84}Po \xrightarrow{\alpha} ^{214}_{82}Pb \xrightarrow{\beta} ^{214}_{83}Bi \begin{array}{c} \xrightarrow{\alpha} ^{210}_{81}Ti \xrightarrow{\beta} \\ \xrightarrow{\beta} ^{214}_{84}Po \xrightarrow{\alpha} \end{array} ^{210}_{82}Pb \xrightarrow{\beta} ^{210}_{83}Bi$$

$$^{210}_{83}Bi \xrightarrow{\beta} ^{210}_{84}Po \xrightarrow{\alpha} ^{206}_{82}Pb$$

Fusion

Whereas fission is the decay of elements, fusion is the building of elements. Scientists believe the sun produces its energy by the fusion process. Simply, that hydrogen nuclei combine to form helium nuclei.

$$4 H \rightarrow He$$

The energy produced in this reaction is tremendous - more than fission. Einstein's equation, $E = MC^2$ explains the energy production.

Remember, the sun consumes four tons of H per second.

Now applying numbers to illustrate energy production:

$E = MC^2$

energy = matter "lost" x (speed of light)

ENERGY = 4 tons x (186,000 mi/sec)^2

large number = 4 x 186,000 x 186,000

The reaction is:

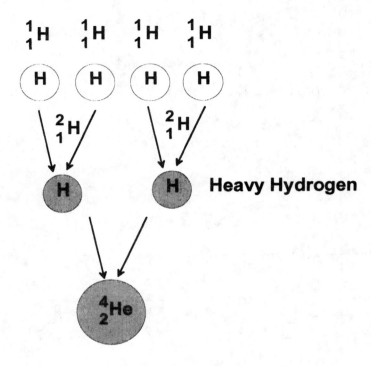

Question 33:

Which of the following is true?

    a. Fusion creates matter.
    b. Fusion releases more energy than fission.
    c. Coal burning produces more energy than fission.
    d. Fission products are always radioactive.

Section 13: Gas Laws

Charles' Law

The volume of a gas is directly proportional to its temperature (when the pressure remains constant).

Temperature & Volume

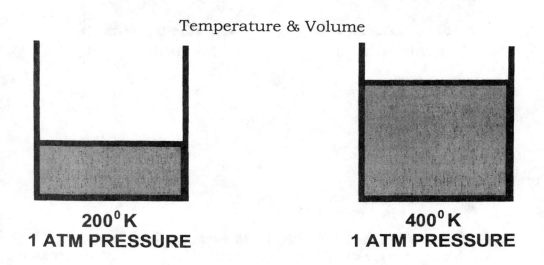

200^{0}K
1 ATM PRESSURE

400^{0}K
1 ATM PRESSURE

If the Temperature rises from 200^0 K to 400^0 K , the volume will also increase.

Question 34:

In the example above how much would the volume increase?

    a. 50%
    b. 100%
    c. 150%
    d. 200%

Boyle's Law

Volume of a gas varies inversely with its pressure.

$$p \, \alpha \, \frac{1}{V}$$

As pressure increases, volume decreases.

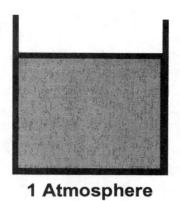 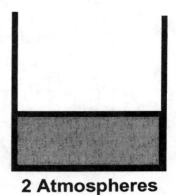

1 Atmosphere   **2 Atmospheres**

$$V = \frac{1}{2}$$

Question 35:

Which of the following is not true?

       a. As pressure increases, volume decreases.
       b. The volume at a given pressure only depends on the pressure.
       c. Pressure and volume are dependent on each other.
       d. a and b only.

ANSWERS - CHAPTER QUESTIONS

1. d. The flight path of a bullet would be similar to that of a cannon. The last paragraph says that the path of a cannon is curved because of the friction of the air and the force of gravity pulls it down.

2. c. This is the first case, where an object at rest stays at rest. The marble stays where it is put the same way that the book stayed where it was placed.

3. b. From the paragraphs, we know that F = M x A.   Since we are given the force and the mass, if we divide the force by the mass we will get acceleration. Nine divided by three equals three.

4. d. When the ball is thrown, the third law of motion states that the boat must move also in the opposite direction. Because the boat is so much more massive, it would not move as far as the baseball.

5. a. The question states that the moon has a greater impact on the tides than the sun due to its gravitational pull. This means that the moon has a greater attraction to the Earth than the sun.

6. b. The example of the seesaw says that a lighter person can balance a heavier person if the heavier person is sitting closer to the fulcrum. This means the lighter person must be sitting farther away.

7. a. The example of the wheelbarrow shows that the resistance force is between the effort force and the fulcrum.

8. d. The best example of a third class lever given is the revolving door. You push on the door in the middle of a side. The resistance is at the edge of a door and the fulcrum is in the center.

9. d. The example says that work is equal to force times distance. If the distance is the same and the force is tripled, the work must also be tripled.

10. d. All of the statements about pulleys are true. Different sized pulleys attached to different shafts turn at different speeds. Pulleys on the same shaft rotate at the same speed and turn in the same direction.

11. b. A can opener does not use a pulley system because a pulley system cannot generate enough force in a small area. It uses a gear system instead. The clothes dryer and car fan are given as examples of simple pulley systems. The elevator and sailboat are complex systems.

12. a. No information is given on the size of the gears so there is no way to say how fast any of the gears are turning. The paragraph does say that touching gears turn in opposite directions. The second gear turns opposite the first. The third turns opposite the second, or the

same way as the first. The fourth turns opposite the first and the fifth the same as the first. The sixth turns the opposite of the first. Finally, the seventh is the same as the first.

13. d. The amount of work being done would remain the same. Shifting gears allows the bicyclist to reduce the amount of effort force while he is going up the hill.

14. c. The paragraph says that a wedge takes a large effort force and makes it act through a small distance. This is the same as saying that a wedge is used to concentrate your force to a specific spot.

15. d. The elevator is the only choice that goes straight up and down, and is therefore not an inclined plane. An escape slopes down to the ground. A wheelchair ramp and a parking garage ramp are both sloped upwards.

16. c. The screw and the drill bit are given as examples of curved inclined planes. A twist off bottle cap has curved grooves to make it a curved incline plane. The spiraling parking garage ramp could also be a curved incline plane. A straight driveway does not fit the curved inclined plane definition.

17. b. The main focus of the paragraph is a wheel and axle reduces friction.

18. a. The last paragraph states that heat flows from areas of high concentrations to areas of low concentrations. The only choice that has heat going from cool to hot is from ice to water.

19. d. Gold, silver, copper, and aluminum are all listed as good conductors. That leaves you with wood, which is a poor conductor.

20. d. The paragraphs state light bounces off all of the choices given.

21. c. The paragraph states light bends when it enters the water and that causes the pencil to look bent.

22. b. The paragraph states that gold, silver, and copper are all good conductors. Therefore answers c, silver, and a, copper, are not correct. Answer b, wood is an insulator.

23. 1-c

    2-b

    3-a

24. b. $\dfrac{E}{I \times R}$ $R = \dfrac{E}{I}$ $R = \dfrac{120}{60}$ $R = 2$

25. d. $P = I \times E = 10 \times 120 = 1200$

26. b. The paragraph states the circuit breaker is wired in series to protect us against overloads.

27. c. The section on parallel circuits said if one section of the circuit broke, the other sections would still function. This is why circuits are run in parallel.

28. d. The last paragraph states the poles of a magnet are called the north and south.

29. d. The induction effect is the flow of electrons due to movement in a magnetic field. Wire coils, magnets and coal are used to produce the effect. Alternating current can be a result of the effect.

30. d. All three of the choices were listed as daughter elements from the decaying of uranium.

31. b. In 100 years the material would go through five half lives.

$$100/20 = 5$$

$(1/2) \times (1/2) = 1/4$ 2 lives

$(1/4) \times (1/2) = 1/8$ 3 lives

$(1/8) \times (1/2) = 1/16$ 4 lives

$(1/16) \times (1/2) = 1/32$ 5 lives

32. a. The paragraph states a beta particle is the same as an electron.

33. b. The first paragraph states fusion releases more energy than fission.

34. b. In the example, the temperature doubles. You are also told that volume increases at the same rate temperature increases. Therefore it would double also. In order for the volume to double it must increase 100%.

35. b. Taking the choices one at a time, we have:

a. As pressure increases, the volume decreases. This is a true statement. Things get smaller when placed under pressure.

b. The volume at a given pressure depends only on the pressure. What this is saying is if you know the pressure, you also know the volume. This is false. You also need to know the temperature of the object.

c. Pressure and volume are dependent on each other. What this is saying is if you change one, the other one will also change. This is a true statement.

Therefore, only b is a false answer.

Question 1:

The second law of motion states that force is equal to mass times acceleration. How much more force would be required to accelerate a fifty-ton ship at the same rate as a ten-ton ship?

      a. The same
      b. Two times
      c. Five times
      d. Ten times

Question 2:

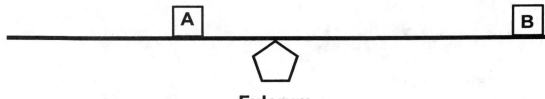

Fulcrum

Work is equal to force times the distance. This means that to do the same amount of work, a greater distance requires less force. Which block in this diagram weighs more?

      a. Block A
      b. Block B
      c. They both weigh the same
      d. It depends on how strong gravity is.

Question 3:

Pulleys are used in two cases. The first instance where pulleys are used is to change the direction of a force. If you were trying to raise a bale of hay to the loft in a barn, it would be impractical to climb on the roof and pull the bale straight up. Instead, it is much easier to run the rope through a pulley above the loft. Then you can pull the bale up while standing on the ground.

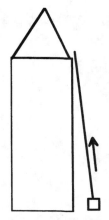 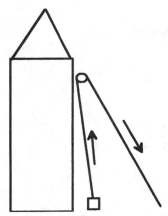

Which of the following uses a single pulley to change the direction of the force?

    a. A flagpole
    b. A chainsaw
    c. An automobile engine
    d. An elevator

Question 4:

The second way pulleys are used is to increase the distance through which a force acts. This means that more work can be done for the same amount of force. At least two pulleys must be used, and one pulley must be able to move.

Diagram A

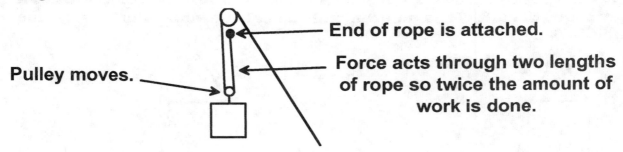

End of rope is attached.

Pulley moves.

Force acts through two lengths of rope so twice the amount of work is done.

Diagram B

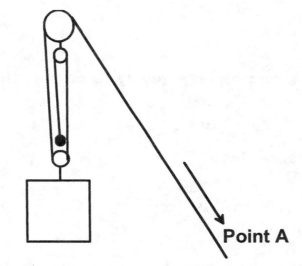

Point A

If the block in diagram B weighs six hundred pounds, how much force must be applied at point A to lift it?

      a. 1800 pounds
      b. 600 pounds
      c. 300 pounds
      d. 200 pounds

Question 5:

The first law of motion states a body at rest stays at rest and a body in motion stays in motion. Which of the following is not an example of this law?

    a. A marble on a flat desk remains in one place.
    b. A marble on a flat desk gets bumped and slowly rolls completely off the desk.
    c. A car traveling down the road continues to move forward even after the foot is taken off the accelerator
    d. All are examples

Question 6:

Ohm's law states voltage = current x resistance. This is more commonly written as $E = I \times R$. If the resistance is cut in half and the voltage is doubled, what happens to the current?

    a. It doubles.
    b. It is cut in half.
    c. It quadruples.
    d. It is cut to on fourth the original.

Question 7:

The volume of a gas decreases as the pressure on it increases. What happens to the volume of a scuba tank as a diver dives into deeper water?

    a. The volume stays the same.
    b. The volume gets bigger.
    c. The volume gets smaller.
    d. It depends on whether the diver is diving in the ocean or a lake.

Question 8:

The ratio by which a set of gears spins is inversely proportional to the ratio of the number of teeth on each gear.

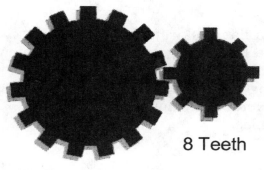

8 Teeth

15 Teeth

If the larger gear makes one hundred and twenty revolutions, how many revolutions will the smaller gear make?

    a. 120
    b. 240
    c. 225
    d. It depends on the size of the gears.

Question 9:

The force, due to gravity, depends on the mass of the two objects and the distance they are separated. Which of the following is true about the attraction between a person and the Earth?

    a. It increases as he moves up and away from the surface.
    b. It decreases as he moves up and away from the surface.
    c. It increases as he moves towards the equator.
    d. It remains the same regardless of where you go.

ANSWERS PHYSICS CHAPTER TEST

1.   c.   Force equals mass times acceleration. The new mass is five times greater than the old mass. Therefore, the force must be five times as great to have the same acceleration.

2.   a.   The two blocks are in balance. Therefore, the block closer to the pivot is the heavier block.

3.   a.   A pulley is placed at the top of a flagpole. This allows the flag to be easily pulled to the top of the pole while the puller stays on the ground.

4.   d.   There are three lengths of rope supporting the block. Therefore, the force needed to lift the block would be one-third of its weight. One-third times six hundred pounds equals two hundred pounds.

$$\frac{1}{3} \times 600 = 200$$

5.   d.   All are examples of this law. Answer a is an example of staying at rest. Answers b and c are examples of bodies staying in motion.

6.   c.   Two times the old voltage divided by one half the old resistance would give you four times the old current.

7.   a.   A scuba tank is rigid, so it would not change with the increase in pressure. If it had been a balloon, it would have gotten smaller as the diver went down deeper.

8.   c.   The smaller gear makes fifteen rotations for every eight the large gear makes. One hundred and twenty divided by eight equals fifteen. Fifteen times fifteen equals two hundred and twenty-five.

$$\frac{120}{8} = 15 \qquad\qquad 15 \times 15 = 225$$

9.   b.   Climbing up on the surface of the Earth means the person is moving farther from the center of the Earth. The farther two objects are separated, the less their gravitational attraction.

ABSOLUTE VALUE: the magnitude of a quantity, irrespective of sign.

ACID: having a pH level of less than 7.

ACOELOMATE: any organism that lacks a cavity through the body for a digestive tract.

ACUTE: an angle less than 90°.

ADP: adenosine diphosphate: a nucleotide that cells use in the energy cycle. Formed when a phosphate removed from adenosine triphosphate (ATP) which releases energy.

AEROBIC: requires the presence of air or free oxygen.

ALKALI METAL: the group of univalent metals including potassium, sodium, lithium, rubidium, cesium, and francium. The first column in the periodic table.

ALLELE: one of two or more alternate forms of a gene. An individual normally has two alleles for each trait, one from either parent.

AMMONIFY: to combine or impregnate with ammonia.

ANAEROBIC: the absence of air or free oxygen.

ANIMALIA: the taxonomic kingdom comprising all animals.

ARTHROPODS: an invertebrate of the phylum Arthropoda. They have a segmented body, jointed limbs, and a mineralized chitinous shell covering. They are the most numerous animals including insects, spiders, crustaceans, and myriapoda.

ATOM: the smallest component of an element consisting of a positively charged nucleus of neutrons and protons that exerts an electrical attraction on one or more electrons in motion around it.

ATOMIC NUMBER: the number of protons in the nucleus of an atom of a given element.

ATOMIC WEIGHT: the number of protons and neutrons in an atom.

ATP: adenosine triphosphate: a nucleotide that is the primary source of energy in all living cells. When converted to ADP it releases energy.

AUTUMNAL EQUINOX: the start of autumn. When the sun is directly over the equator in the fall.

BASE: a chemical compound that reacts with an acid to form a salt; having a pH level of more than 7.

BIOSPHERE: the ecosystem comprising the entire earth and the living organisms that inhabit it.

BLACK HOLE: formed by the gravitational collapse of a star exploding as a supernova, whose gravitational field is so intense that no electromagnetic radiation can escape.

CARNIVORE: an animal that eats flesh.

CAUSATION: the act of causing.

CELL MEMBRANE: the semi-permeable membrane enclosing the cytoplasm of a cell.

CENOZOIC: pertaining to the present era, beginning 65 million years ago. The age of mammals.

CENTRIFUGAL FORCE: the force, equal and opposite to the centripetal force. It appears to propel an object outward.

CENTRIPETAL FORCE: the force, acting upon a body moving along a curved path. It is directed toward the center of the path and constrains the body to the path.

CHLOROPHYLL: the green pigment of plant leaves and algae, which is needed for photosynthesis.

COELOMATE: any organism that has a cavity through the body for a digestive tract.

COMBUSTIBILITY: ability to catch fire and burn.

COMPOUND: composed of two or more parts.

CONDUCTION: the transfer of heat between objects.

CONTROL GROUP: a group for which a variable is not changed. It is used as a baseline for the other groups being tested.

CONVECTION: the transfer of heat by the circulation of a liquid or gas.

CORONA: a white or colored circle or set of concentric circles of light seen around a luminous body, especially around the sun or moon.

CORRELATION: mutual relation of two or more things, parts, etc.

COVALENT BOND:	the bond formed by the sharing of a pair of electrons by two atoms.
CYTOPLASM:	the cell substance between the cell membrane and the nucleus.
DENSITY:	mass per unit volume.
DEOXYRIBONUCLEIC ACID (DNA):	a nucleic acid molecule arranged as a double helix that is the main constituent of the chromosome and that carries the genes.
DEPENDENT VARIABLE:	a variable in a functional relation whose value is determined by the values assumed by other variables in the relation.
DIATOMIC MOLECULE:	a molecule containing just two atoms.
DIFFRACTION:	the bending of light waves, often causing light to break into its component spectrum.
ECOSYSTEM:	the interaction of a community of organisms with its environment.
ELECTROMAGNETIC SPECTRUM:	the entire continuous spectrum of all forms of electromagnetic radiation, from gamma rays to long radio waves.
ELECTROMAGNETISM:	the phenomena associated with electric and magnetic fields and their interactions with each other.
ELEMENT:	substances that cannot be separated into simpler substances by chemical means.
ELLIPSE:	a plane curve such that the sums of the distances of each point in its periphery from two fixed points, the foci, are equal.
EMPIRICAL:	from experience or experiment.
ENTROPY:	a measure of the energy that is not available for work in a thermodynamic process.
EON:	the largest division of geologic time, comprising two or more eras.
EPOCH:	any of several divisions of a geologic period during which a geologic series is formed.
ERA:	a major division of geologic time composed of a number of periods.
EUKARYOTE:	a cell with a distinct membrane-bound nucleus.

FISSION: the splitting of the nucleus of an atom into nuclei of lighter atoms accompanied by the release of energy. Reproduction by mitosis.

FUNGI: a taxonomic kingdom, or in some classification schemes a division of the kingdom Plantae, comprising all the fungus groups and sometimes also the slime molds. Also called Mycota.

FUSION: the joining of atomic nuclei in a reaction to form nuclei of heavier atoms, as in the combination of deuterium atoms to form helium atoms.

GALAXY: a large system of stars held together by mutual gravitation and isolated from similar systems by vast regions of space.

GENOTYPE: the genetic makeup of an organism with reference to a single trait or set of traits.

GLYCOLYSIS: the breaking down of carbohydrates by enzymes, with the release of energy and the production of lactic or pyruvic acid.

HALF-LIFE: the time required for one-half the atoms of a given amount of a radioactive substance to decay.

HALOGEN: any of the electronegative elements, fluorine, chlorine, iodine, bromine, and astatine, that form binary salts by direct union with metals. The second column from the right in the periodic table.

HERBIVORE: an animal that feeds on plants.

HOMEOSTASIS: the tendency of a system to maintain the status quo.

HYDROLOGIC CYCLE: the natural sequence through which water passes into the atmosphere as water vapor, precipitates to earth, and returns to the atmosphere through evaporation.

HYPHAE: one of the threadlike elements of the mycelium in a fungus.

HYPOTHESIS: a theory to explain a phenomena as a guide for future investigation.

IDEAL GAS LAW: if the temperature of the gas increases, the volume of the gas will also increase, if the pressure remains the same.

IGNEOUS: rocks of volcanic origin or rocks crystallized from molten magma.

INDEPENDENT VARIABLE: a variable in a functional relation whose value is not determined by the value of other variables.

INERTIA: the property of matter by which it resists changes in velocity.

INFILTRATION: to pass into or through a substance.

INFRARED: the part of the invisible spectrum that is next to the red end of the visible spectrum. Wavelengths from 800nm to 1mm.

ION: an atom electrically charged by the loss or gain of electrons.

IONIC BOND: the electrostatic bond between two ions.

ISOTOPE: different forms of an element having the same number of protons, but with different numbers of neutrons and atomic weights.

KINEMATICS: the branch of mechanics that deals with pure motion, without reference to the masses or forces involved in it.

KINETIC ENERGY: the energy of a body with respect to its motion.

LAW OF INDIVIDUAL ASSORTMENT: the principle stating that the laws of chance govern which alleles for a gene a parent will give to its offspring.

LIGHT-YEAR: the distance light travels in one year, about 5.88 trillion miles; used as a unit in measuring stellar distances.

LITHOSPHERE: the crust and upper mantle of the earth.

MAMMAL: characterized by a covering of hair on some or most of the body, a four-chambered heart, and nourishment of the newborn with milk from maternal mammary glands.

MATTER: the substance of which any physical object consists.

MEIOSIS: the process of gamete formation in sexual reproduction. It reduces the number of chromosomes by half.

MESOZOIC: the geologic era occurring between 230 million and 65 million years ago. Flowering plants and dinosaurs appeared.

METAMORPHIC: rocks that change to other forms of rock under heat and pressure.

MITOSIS: the type of cell division which results in the same number of chromosomes in each daughter cell.

MOLE: the quantity of a substance, the weight of which equals the substance's molecular weight expressed in grams, and which contains 6.02×10^{23} molecules of the substance.

MONERA: the kingdom of prokaryotic organisms that typically reproduce by asexual budding or fission, comprising the bacteria, blue-green algae, and various primitive pathogens.

NATURAL SELECTION: Animals with superior traits have larger numbers of offspring in subsequent generations.

NEWTON: the unit of force, which produces an acceleration of one meter per second squared on a mass of one kilogram.

NITROGEN CYCLE: the cycle which nitrogen passes through. From the atmosphere, to fixation by plants in the soil, to denitrification releasing the nitrogen back to the atmosphere.

NOBLE GAS: chemically inert gaseous elements of the farthest right group on the periodic table: helium, neon, argon, krypton, xenon, and radon. Also called *inert gas*.

NUCLEUS: found in eukaryotic cells, directs their growth, metabolism, and reproduction, and contains most of the genetic material.

OMNIVORE: something that feeds on both animals and plants.

ORGANELLE: a cell organ.

ORGANIC: chemical compounds derived from plants or animals

OSMOSIS: the tendency of water, to pass through a semi-permeable membrane into a solution with the materials on either side of the membrane, to bring concentrations into balance.

OXIDATION: the deposit that forms on the surface of a metal as it oxidizes.

OZONE: a form of oxygen, O_3, produced when an electric spark or ultraviolet light passes through air or oxygen. In the upper atmosphere it absorbs ultraviolet rays, thereby preventing them from reaching the earth's surface, but near the earth's surface it is a harmful irritant and pollutant.

PALEOZOIC: the geologic era occurring between 570 million and 230 million years ago, when fish, insects, and reptiles first appeared.

PARADIGM: a model.

PARALLAX: the apparent angular displacement of a celestial body due to its being observed from the surface instead of from the center of the earth or due to its being observed from the earth instead of from the sun.

PHANEROZOIC: the current era.

PHENOTYPE: the observable traits of an organism.

PHOTOELECTRIC: electronic effects produced by light, especially the phenomenon whereby a surface emits electrons when exposed to light.

PHOTON: a unit of light energy.

PHOTOSYNTHESIS: the production of carbohydrates, from carbon dioxide, and water using sunlight as the source of energy.

PLANTAE: The kingdom comprising all plants.

POTENTIAL ENERGY: The energy of a body with respect to its position.

PRE-CAMBRIAN: the earliest era of earth's history, ending 570 million years ago, during which the earth's crust formed and life first appeared in the seas.

PROKARYOTE: cells that lacks a distinct membrane-bound nucleus.

PROTISTA: the kingdom comprising the protozoans and slime molds.

PULSAR: rapidly rotating neutron stars, that emit pulses of radiation, especially radio waves, with a high degree of regularity.

QUASAR: starlike objects that may be the most distant and brightest objects in the universe.

RADIATION:	energy which is emitted as particles or waves.
RADIOACTIVITY:	spontaneously emitting radiation resulting from changes in the nuclei of certain atoms.
RED GIANT:	stars in an intermediate stage of evolution, characterized by a large volume, low surface temperature, and reddish hue.
REDUCTION:	the first meiotic cell division in meiosis where the chromosome number is reduced by half. Also the opposite of oxidation.
REFRACTION:	the change of direction of a wave when it passes from one medium into another.
RIBONUCLEIC ACID (RNA):	single-stranded nucleic acid molecules. Differ from DNA due to their single strand and the presence of uracil instead of thymine.
SCALAR:	a quantity with magnitude but no direction.
SCIENTIFIC METHOD:	research in which a problem is identified, relevant data is gathered, a hypothesis is formulated, and the hypothesis is tested.
SEDIMENTARY:	rocks formed by the deposit of sediment.
STRATOSPHERE:	the upper atmosphere above the troposphere up to about 30 miles (50km) above the earth, which has little vertical variation in temperature.
SUBDUCTION:	one earth's crust plate being overridden by another.
SYMBIOSIS:	two dissimilar organisms living together as one unit.
TAXON:	a category, as a species or genus.
TECTONICS:	the branch of geology that studies structural features of the plates in the earth's crust.
THEORY:	an explanation, which has neither been proved, nor disproved. For example, the Theory of Evolution.
THERMODYNAMICS:	the branch of science chiefly concerned with heat transfer.
TRANSPIRATION:	the passage of water through a plant from the roots through the vascular system to the atmosphere.
ULTRAVIOLET:	Electromagnetic radiation having wavelengths in the range of approximately 5-400nm, shorter than visible light but longer than x-rays.
VECTOR:	a quantity possessing both magnitude and direction.

VELOCITY: the rate of change in the position of an object.

VERNAL EQUINOX: the spring equinox when the length of day is the same all over the earth due to the sun's crossing the equator.

VERTEBRATE: animals with a segmented backbone.

WAVELENGTH: the distance between two successive peaks in a wave.

WHITE DWARF: a star that has undergone gravitational collapse and is in the final stage of its life cycle.

WORK: the product of a force and the distance through which it acts.

PART V
SAMPLE TEST

LANGUAGE ARTS SAMPLE TEST (30 questions)

Understanding Literature (9 questions)
Reading Instruction (9 questions)
Language in Writing (7-8 questions)
Communication Skills (3 questions)
Text Structures and Organization (1-2 questions)

Directions: For each question, select the best answer out of the four given choices.

1. *Pilgrim's Progress* by Bunyan is an example of a

   (A) play
   (B) novel
   (C) lyric poem
   (D) journal

2. "April is the cruellest month..." is an example of

   (A) simile
   (B) kenning
   (C) personification
   (D) litotes

3. Which of the following periods of English literature is associated with the early 19th century?

   (A) Elizabethan
   (B) Augustan
   (C) Romantic
   (D) Victorian

4. In Greek tragedy, the tragic hero's flaw is usually identified as

   (A) gluttony
   (B) sloth
   (C) envy
   (D) pride

5. A line of accentual verse is characterized by the number of

   (A) syllables
   (B) stresses
   (C) letters
   (D) words

6. A novel in which the narrator has knowledge of the innermost thoughts of all the characters is probably written from which of the following points of view?

    (A) first person
    (B) limited
    (C) omniscient
    (D) unreliable

7. Compared to non-fiction writing, literary language is apt to be more

    (A) literal
    (B) linear
    (C) suggestive
    (D) denotative

8. The sound similarity between the words "shutter" and "lover" is an example of

    (A) alliteration
    (B) assonance
    (C) dissonance
    (D) cacophony

9. If a fictional narrative focuses on one main character, this character is referred to as a

    (A) protagonist
    (B) antagonist
    (C) deuteragonist
    (D) nemesis

10. The consonant sound of the letter *p* in *plant* is best described as a

    (A) glottal
    (B) plosive
    (C) liquid
    (D) semivowel

11. Which of the following units represents an *intrinsically* meaningless sound?

    (A) morpheme
    (B) lexeme
    (C) phoneme
    (D) sememe

12. **A person who studies the historical derivations of words would be called a**

   (A) grammarian
   (B) rhetorician
   (C) etymologist
   (D) lexicographer

13. **Which of the following pairs of words would be considered homonyms?**

   (A) discrete and discreet
   (B) cow and bovine
   (C) number and numeral
   (D) maximum and minimum

14. **Which of the following words contains a vowel digraph?**

   (A) said
   (B) sour
   (C) sire
   (D) soil

15. **Which of the following activities would most likely be used in a meaning-based approach to reading instruction?**

   (A) phonemic segmentation
   (B) phonemic substitution
   (C) rhyme words
   (D) whole-word methodology

16. **Which of the following activities involves filling in missing words?**

   (A) cloze
   (B) webbing
   (C) rebus
   (D) morphemic identification

17. **The vowel sound in the word *feet* is best described as**

   (A) a dipthong
   (B) a front vowel
   (C) a back vowel
   (D) the schwa sound

18. **The difference between a voiced and a voiceless consonant involves**

   (A) aspiration
   (B) rounding of the lips
   (C) vibration of the vocal cords
   (D) position of the tongue

19. **An adverb may modify all of the following EXCEPT**

(A) a noun
(B) a verb
(C) an adverb
(D) an adjective

20. **Indicative, imperative, and subjunctive are three types of**

(A) case
(B) tense
(C) aspect
(D) mood

21. **In the sentence "There is a book on the table", the word "there" is functioning as a/an**

(A) direct object
(B) indirect object
(C) subject
(D) predicate

22. **A transitive verb is one that**

(A) has no specific tense
(B) always ends with *–ing*
(C) requires a direct object
(D) requires an indirect object

23. **In the sentence "Reading is necessary for a good life," the word "reading" is an example of which kind of verbal phrase?**

(A) infinitive
(B) participle
(C) gerund
(D) predicate

24. **In the sentence "John is taller than Chuck," which degree of comparison is being used?**

(A) positive
(B) comparative
(C) superlative
(D) double superlative

25. **The sentence "How far does light travel in one second?" is best categorized as**

(A) declarative
(B) counterfactual
(C) interrogative
(D) exclamatory

26. **Which of the following logical fallacies involves "circular reasoning"?**

(A) Tautology
(B) Non sequitur
(C) Ad hominem
(D) Ad populum

27. **The elements of an expository paragraph are best described as being arranged in what kind of logical order?**

(A) general statement to specific evidence
(B) personal memories to universal truths
(C) general truths to detailed prescriptions
(D) rational analysis to general speculation

28. **All of the following are typical methods of the prewriting stage EXCEPT**

(A) freewriting
(B) observation
(C) research
(D) drafting

29. **If one needed information on the dominant religion of the Ukraine, one would consult a/an**

(A) dictionary
(B) glossary
(C) almanac
(D) anthology

30. **Which of the following could be described as the most persuasive or hortatory?**

(A) a treatise on quantum physics
(B) a newpaper report of an earthquake
(C) a film critique
(D) a speech at a political convention

SOCIAL STUDIES SAMPLE TEST (30 questions)

Geography (4-5 questions)

World History (3 questions)

United States History (7-8 questions)

Political Science (6 questions)

Economics (4-5 questions)

Anthropology, Sociology & Psychology (4-5 questions)

Directions: For each question, select the best answer out of the four given choices.

1. The climate of central Africa is best described as

   (A) temperate
   (B) polar
   (C) equatorial
   (D) arid

2. Baja, California is an example of which kind of land mass?

   (A) island
   (B) peninsula
   (C) isthmus
   (D) archipelago

3. Which of the following is an example of a meridian of longitude?

   (A) the Equator
   (B) the Tropic of Capricorn
   (C) the Tropic of Cancer
   (D) the International Date Line

4. The Ganges River is located on which continent?

   (A) Africa
   (B) Asia
   (C) Australia
   (D) Antarctica

5. A topographical map would probably indicate which of the following?

   (A) population density
   (B) capitals of countries
   (C) elevations of land
   (D) sites of military battles

6. **Prehistorical peoples were characterized by all of the following EXCEPT**

   (A) weapons made from stone
   (B) hunting as a means of food acquisition
   (C) writing by means of cuneiform
   (D) a nomadic existence

7. **The economic relations that existed between medieval lords and serfs are known as**

   (A) feudalism
   (B) manorialism
   (C) socialism
   (D) capitalism

8. **All of the following refer to major periods of European history EXCEPT**

   (A) Renaissance
   (B) Reformation
   (C) Enlightenment
   (D) Détente

9. **The explorer who explored Brazil and gave America its name was**

   (A) Columbus
   (B) Vespucci
   (C) Magellan
   (D) Balboa

10. **The French and Indian War was fought between the**

    (A) French and Hurons
    (B) French and Seminoles
    (C) French and Germans
    (D) French and English

11. **Which act(s) of the British Parliament contributed to the decision of the American colonists in favor of revolution?**

    (A) Reform Acts
    (B) Virginia and Kentucky Resolutions
    (C) Alien and Sedition Acts
    (D) Intolerable Acts

12. **The principles upon which the Americans justified their revolt against George III and the British Parliament are spelled out in the**

    (A) Declaration of Independence
    (B) Articles of the Confederation
    (C) Constitution of 1789
    (D) Monroe Doctrine

13. **The "nullification crisis" resulted from**

   (A) British conscription of American sailors
   (B) South Carolina's repeal of a federal tariff
   (C) Jackson's veto of the Second Bank of the U.S.
   (D) the conflict between Texas and Mexico

14. **The guarantee of the "equal protection of the law" to former slaves was granted by the**

   (A) Emancipation Proclamation
   (B) Thirteenth Amendment
   (C) Fourteenth Amendment
   (D) Fifteenth Amendment

15. **The domestic policy of the Truman Administration is usually referred to as the**

   (A) New Deal
   (B) Fair Deal
   (C) New Frontier
   (D) Great Society

16. **The period of détente in American foreign policy involves U.S. relations with**

   (A) China
   (B) the Soviet Union
   (C) France
   (D) Mexico

17. **The structure of the American federal government is best described as**

   (A) bicameral
   (B) tripartite
   (C) quadrilateral
   (D) pentagonal

18. **The approval of what percent of state legislatures is required for a Constitutional amendment?**

   (A) 50%
   (B) 67%
   (C) 75%
   (D) 100%

19. **Senators are chosen by**

   (A) state legislatures
   (B) the Supreme Court
   (C) popular vote
   (D) the president

20. **All of the following are enumerated powers granted to Congress by the Constitution EXCEPT**

(A) levying taxes
(B) declaring war
(C) establishing a church
(D) borrowing money

21. **A federal civil service based on the merit system was established by which legislation?**

(A) the Pendleton Act of 1883
(B) the Sherman Act of 1890
(C) the Clayton Act of 1914
(D) the Taft-Hartley Act of 1947

22. **Rule by the most talented in the interests of the whole nation is best described as**

(A) autocracy
(B) aristocracy
(C) oligarchy
(D) plutocracy

23. **In a market system, the price of a commodity is determined by**

(A) government decree
(B) supply and demand
(C) chambers of commerce
(D) commercial banks

24. **Which of the following refers to the government's taxing and spending policies?**

(A) monetary policy
(B) fiscal policy
(C) stabilization policy
(D) protectionist policy

25. **The Consumer Price Index (CPI) is a measure of**

(A) the level of unemployment
(B) the level of inflation
(C) the level of interest rates
(D) the level of exchange rates

26. **All of the following are international economic institutions EXCEPT**

(A) WTO
(B) IMF
(C) EU
(D) UN

27. **A person who studies the belief systems of a primitive tribe is a/an**

   (A) archaeologist
   (B) cultural anthropologist
   (C) theologian
   (D) sociologist

28. **If an American social scientist were to describe a particular practice of a primitive tribe as "morally reprehensible", the social scientist would be guilty of**

   (A) ethnocentrism
   (B) egocentrism
   (C) reductionism
   (D) functionalism

29. **Which of the following terms used by sociologists involves the division of society into ranks of unequal status?**

   (A) stratification
   (B) division of labor
   (C) secularization
   (D) Gemeinschaft

30. **The division of the mind into id, ego, and superego is primarily associated with which psychologist?**

   (A) Piaget
   (B) Freud
   (C) Jung
   (D) Pavlov

MATHEMATICS SAMPLE TEST

<u>Arithmetic (9 questions)</u>
<u>Algebra (7 questions)</u>
<u>Geometry (8 questions)</u>
<u>Miscellaneous (6 questions)</u>

Directions: For each question, select the best answer out of the four given choices.

1. Which of the following sets is NOT a proper subset of the real numbers?

   (A) the set of counting numbers
   (B) the set of whole numbers
   (C) the set of integers
   (D) the set of complex numbers

2. Which of the following pairs of numbers is NOT a pair of reciprocals?

   (A) 2 and $\frac{1}{2}$
   (B) $-\frac{3}{4}$ and $-\frac{4}{3}$
   (C) $\sqrt{5}$ and $\frac{\sqrt{5}}{5}$
   (D) -7 and $\frac{1}{7}$

3. The expression $7[3 - 5(10 - 8)] - (-2)^3$ reduces to

   (A) 99
   (B) 73
   (C) −41
   (D) −57

4. The symbol "341" in a base 5 system represents which number?

   (A) four hundred and eighty
   (B) ninety eight
   (C) ninety six
   (D) forty

5. What percentage (approximately) of the positive factors of 36 are prime?

   (A) 22%
   (B) 29%
   (C) 33%
   (D) 43%

538

6. **What is the greatest common factor of 198 and 84?**

   (A) 2
   (B) 3
   (C) 4
   (D) 6

7. **If the ratio of women to men on a committee is 2 to 1, then how many women are on the committee given that the committee has 12 members?**

   (A) 2
   (B) 4
   (C) 8
   (D) 10

8. **Which one of the following is equal to $\sqrt[3]{64}$?**

   (A) 2
   (B) 3
   (C) 4
   (D) 5

9. **Given the real number line below, what is the coordinate of the midpoint of points A and B?**

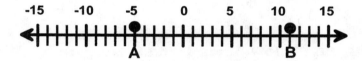

   (A) -1
   (B) 0
   (C) 3
   (D) 5

10. **The expression $5x(2x - 1) + 3x - 8x^3 - 10x^2 + 1$ reduces to**

    (A) $-8x^3 - 10x^2 + 8x + 1$
    (B) $-8x^3 - 10x^2 + 10x$
    (C) $-8x^3 + 3x$
    (D) (D) $-8x^3 - 2x + 1$

11. **Which of the following is $x^4 - 81$ rewritten in factored form?**

    (A) $(x + 9)(x - 9)$
    (B) $(x + 9)(x + 9)$
    (C) $(x^2 + 3)(x^2 - 9)$
    (D) $(x^2 + 9)(x + 3)(x - 3)$

12. Given that $x^2 + 2x - 35 = 0$, what is one possible value of x?

(A) −7
(B) −2
(C) 0
(D) 4

13. If $-\frac{3}{4} x + 2 > 17$, then which of the following is true?

(A) $x > 20$
(B) $x > -20$
(C) $x < -20$
(D) $x > 0$

14. If $|x - 2| + 1 = 8$, then how many different possible values are there for x?

(A) One
(B) Two
(C) Three
(D) Infinitely many

15. If the function $f(x)$ equals $x^2 - 1$ and the function $g(x)$ equals $\frac{1}{4}x$, then what is the value of $f[g(-24)]$?

(A) 35
(B) 24
(C) −24
(D) −35

16. In the diagram below, lines 1 and 2 are parallel. What is the measure of angle C?

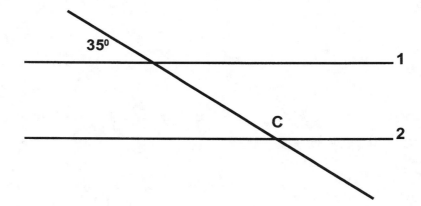

(A) 90°
(B) 105°
(C) 110°
(D) 145°

17. Given the regular octagon below, what is the measure of the exterior angle A?

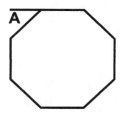

(A) 25°
(B) 35°
(C) 45°
(D) 55°

18. A circle is inscribed in a square. What is the approximate area of the shaded region, given that the circle has a radius of 5 units?

(A) 21.5
(B) 25
(C) 30
(D) 35

19. Square ABCD has a perimeter of 20 units. What is the area of triangle CDE?

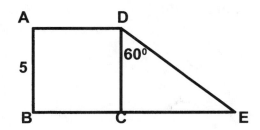

(A) $\dfrac{25\sqrt{3}}{2}$

(B) $25\sqrt{3}$
(C) 50
(D) 75

20. A person starting at point A drives 6 miles east to point B, then drives 12 miles north to point C, and then drives 3 more miles east to point D. How far is it from point A to point D?

    (A) 10 miles
    (B) 15 miles
    (C) 20 miles
    (D) 25 miles

21. If the distance from Town A to Town B is 10 miles and the distance from Town B to Town C is 15 miles, then which of the following is NOT a possible distance from Town A to Town C?

    (A) 15
    (B) 20
    (C) 25
    (D) 30

22. If the volume of the rectangular solid shown below is 150 cubic units, then h equals

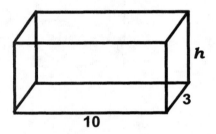

    (A) 5 units
    (B) 5 square units
    (C) 5 cubic units
    (D) it cannot be determined

23. What is the length of arc AB in the circle given below?

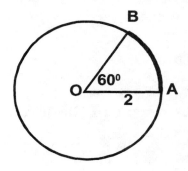

(A) $\dfrac{\pi}{2}$

(B) $\dfrac{2\pi}{3}$

(C) π

(D) 2π

24. Which of the following could be the equation of line A given below?

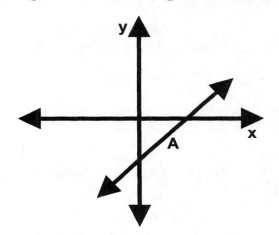

(A) $y = -\tfrac{3}{4}\,x + 5$

(B) $y = \tfrac{3}{4}\,x - 5$

(C) $y = \tfrac{3}{4}\,x + 5$

(D) $y = -\tfrac{3}{4}\,x - 5$

25. The line with the equation $3x - 2y = 10$ passes through which of the following points?

(A) $(-2, 3)$

(B) $(0, -5)$

(C) $(0, 0)$

(D) $(3, -2)$

26. **What is the median of the set of counting numbers less than or equal to 6?**

   (A) 3
   (B) 3.5
   (C) 4
   (D) 4.5

27. **How many different ways can the letters BLOC be ordered?**

   (A) 24
   (B) 64
   (C) 128
   (D) 256

28. **How many different 3-member committees can be formed from a pool of 7 people?**

   (A) 20
   (B) 35
   (C) 75
   (D) 100

29. **If a card is drawn randomly from a standard deck of cards, what is the probability (approximately) that the card drawn will be a red card *or* a queen?**

   (A) 50%
   (B) 54%
   (C) 58%
   (D) 60%

30. **The shaded region in the Venn diagram below represents which operation?**

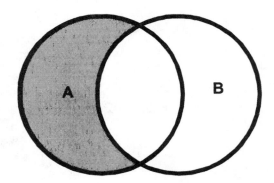

   (A) $A \cup B$
   (B) $A \cap B$
   (C) $A - B$
   (D) $B - A$

Life Science (7 questions)
Earth Science (7 questions)
Physical Science (7 questions)
Chemistry (4 questions)
Methodology (3 questions)
History of Science (2 questions)

Directions: For each question, select the best answer out of the four given choices.

1. **Democritus, Pythagoras, and Hippocrates all belonged to which civilization?**

   (A) Mesopotamian
   (B) Greek
   (C) Babylonian
   (D) Roman

2. **Linnaeus, Darwin and Mendel are names associated with which branch of science?**

   (A) cosmology
   (B) chemistry
   (C) biology
   (D) geology

3. **If a hypothesis is confirmed by experimentation, then it may become a/an**

   (A) axiom
   (B) theory
   (C) conjecture
   (D) syllogism

4. **Inductive reasoning is characterized by which sort of progression?**

   (A) starts with general principles and moves to particular cases
   (B) starts with particular cases and moves to general principles
   (C) starts with moral principles and moves to prescriptions for political action
   (D) starts with abstract ideas and moves to concrete images

5. To say that science is empirical is to say that its characteristic activity is

(A) thinking
(B) observing
(C) expressing
(D) prescribing

6. The fact that oxygen has eight protons is indicated by its

(A) atomic weight
(B) atomic number
(C) atomic mass
(D) molecular formula

7. The isotope Potassium-40 has how many neutrons, given that the atomic number of Potassium is 19?

(A) 20
(B) 21
(C) 22
(D) 23

8. Iodine would fall under which of the following categories?

(A) noble gas
(B) halogen
(C) alkali metal
(D) actinide series

9. Organic chemistry primarily studies compounds that contain

(A) acid
(B) barium
(C) carbon
(D) uranium

10. The components of an animal cell would include all of the following EXCEPT

(A) chlorophyll
(B) cytoplasm
(C) plasma membrane
(D) nucleus

11. The end result of the process of cell division called mitosis is

(A) two identical daughter cells
(B) four gametes
(C) eight zoospores
(D) sixteen mitochondria

12. **The process of photosynthesis could be described by which expression?**

    (A) sodium + chlorine → sodium chloride
    (B) hydrogen + oxygen → water
    (C) chlorine + fluorine + carbon → a chlorofluorocarbon
    (D) photons + chlorophyll + water + carbon dioxide
        → sugar + oxygen

13. **The difference between a prokaryotic and a eukaryotic cell is that**

    (A) prokaryotic cells are found only in fungi
    (B) prokaryotic cells have no means of reproduction
    (C) prokaryotic cells contain chloroplasts
    (D) prokaryotic cells lack a membrane-bound nucleus

14. **Of the following biological kingdoms, which one is comprised of autotrophs?**

    (A) Protista
    (B) Fungi
    (C) Plantae
    (D) Animalia

15. **The process of decomposing nitrogen compounds after the death of an organism is called**

    (A) ammonification
    (B) fixation
    (C) lithification
    (D) sublimation

16. **Which of the following molecules is associated with energy acquisition by a cell?**

    (A) deoxyribonucleic acid (DNA)
    (B) ribonucleic acid (RNA)
    (C) adenosine triphosphate (ATP)
    (D) carbon monoxide (CO)

17. **Which geologic era accounts for the least percentage of the earth's history?**

    (A) Cenozoic
    (B) Mesozoic
    (C) Paleozoic
    (D) Pre-Cambrian

18. **The cooling of magma in a process called crystallization results in which type of rock?**

(A) igneous
(B) sedimentary
(C) metamorphic
(D) silica

19. **Transpiration refers to which of the following processes?**

(A) the release of liquid water by clouds
(B) the transformation of water vapor into liquid water
(C) the seepage of water into the ground
(D) the absorption and release of water by plants

20. **The changing of water from a gaseous state to a solid state is known as**

(A) sublimation
(B) deposition
(C) vaporization
(D) condensation

21. **When the air is holding the maximum amount of water vapor possible at a given temperature, the situtation is referred to as**

(A) absolute zero
(B) saturation
(C) maximum entropy
(D) standard pressure

22. **On or about March 21, the southern hemisphere of the earth experiences its**

(A) vernal equinox
(B) summer solstice
(C) autumnal equinox
(D) winter solstice

23. **All of the following are types of stars EXCEPT**

(A) white dwarf
(B) red giant
(C) nebula
(D) nova

24. **Which of the following variables is considered a vector quantity?**

(A) speed
(B) temperature
(C) acceleration
(D) time

25. **If the mass of one body were to be doubled and the mass of another body were to be quadrupled, then by what factor would the gravitational attraction between the bodies increase (all other things being equal)?**

    (A) 2 times
    (B) 6 times
    (C) 8 times
    (D) 10 times

26. **All other factors being held constant, what would you expect to happen to the volume of an ideal gas if its temperature were to be increased?**

    (A) increase
    (B) decrease
    (C) stay the same
    (D) there is no relation between the two variables

27. **The fact that certain physical events can only happen in one direction and are not reversible is expressed by which law of thermodynamics?**

    (A) Zeroth
    (B) 1st
    (C) 2nd
    (D) 3rd

28. **Which of the following electromagnetic waves has the longest wavelength?**

    (A) Infrared light
    (B) Ultraviolet light
    (C) X-ray
    (D) Gamma ray

29. **Splitting the nucleus of an atom is referred to as**

    (A) fusion
    (B) fission
    (C) diffraction
    (D) refraction

30. In the diagram below, a ball resting at point A is set in motion and travels through points B, C, and D. At which point does the ball have the least amount of gravitational potential energy?

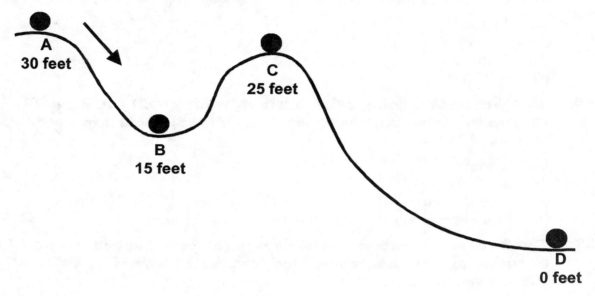

(A) Point A
(B) Point B
(C) Point C
(D) Point D

LANGUAGE ARTS SAMPLE TEST - ANSWERS & EXPLANATIONS

1. (B) Published about 1680, *Pilgrim's Progress* is thought to be the first novel in English. It is an allegory that describes the quest for salvation. It is written in prose, whereas literature in English before that time was written mainly in verse.

2. (C) The line is the opening of T.S. Eliot's *The Waste Land*. It attributes a human quality (cruelty) to an abstract thing (a month).

3. (C) The Romantic period is usually given as the first part of the 19th century. The key writers of this period were Blake (*Songs of Innocence and Experience*), Wordsworth (*Intimations of Immortality from Recollections of Early Childhood*), Coleridge (*Rime of the Ancient Mariner*), Shelley (*Prometheus Unbound*), Byron (*Don Juan*), Keats (*Ode on a Grecian Urn*), and Scott (*Ivanhoe*). The Elizabethan age covered the latter part of the reign of Elizabeth I (the late 16th century) and its key writers were Shakespeare, Marlowe, and Ben Jonson. The Augustan period was roughly in the early and middle 18th century and was dominated by Dryden, Pope, and Swift. The Victorian period was the latter half of the 19th century and included Tennyson, Browning, and Hardy.

4. (D) The tragic hero's flaw is *hubris*, which is roughly translated as pride. All four of the answer choices are examples of the Seven Deadly Sins, which were used in morality plays in the Middle Ages. (The other three are anger, greed, and lust).

5. (B) Accentual verse counts stresses while syllabic verse counts all syllables whether those syllables are stressed or not.

6. (C) An omniscient narrator is not limited by time or place and has knowledge of characters' thoughts, memories, emotions, feelings, etc.

7. (C) Literary language is not merely meant to convey information or formulate theories, so it is apt to be more non-literal and ironic. It will tend not to move in a perfectly straight line from beginning to end and it will tend to rely more on the connotations of words rather than the denotations of words. Ambiguity is common in literary writing whereas it would usually be a defect in non-fiction.

8. (B) Both words have the same stressed vowel sound, which is the definition of assonance. Alliteration is the repetition of an initial consonant sound. Dissonance and cacophony both generally refer to unharmonious or displeasing sounds.

9. (A) The antagonist is the character who stands 'against' the protagonist, impeding the latter's progress. The deuteragonist is the second most important character in a narrative. The nemesis of the protagonist is the agent of retribution.

10. (B) A plosive consonant involves an 'explosion' of breath that you can feel if you hold your hand before your mouth. A glottal such as *h* is formed deep in the throat. The two prime examples of liquids are *r* and *l*. The two semivowels are *y* and *w*.

11. (C) A phoneme has no meaning by itself, but only acquires meaning when sounded with other phonemes. A morpheme, such as the *pro-* in promote or the *de-* in demote, has intrinsic meaning. Lexemes and sememes also carry meaning by themselves.

12. (C) A grammarian studies how words are combined into larger units such as sentences and how different combinations of words produce different meanings. A rhetorician is concerned with effective oratory or public speaking. A lexicographer is a compiler of a dictionary, such as Samuel Johnson and Noah Webster.

13. (A) The pair in answer choice (B) are synonyms, the pair in answer choice (C) look like synonyms but are not (a numeral is used to represent a number) and the pair in answer choice (D) are antonyms (opposite meanings).

14. (A) A vowel digraph is when two (or more) letters represent a single vowel sound. The other three answer choices are best described as dipthongs where there are two discernible vowel sounds in the same syllable.

15. (D) The first three answer choices are common activities in a skills-based approach, where phonemic awareness is emphasized. Phonemic segmentation is the breaking up of a word into its individual sounds, for example breaking up *cat* into /c/ /a/ /t/. Phonemic substitution is creating new meaningful words by replacing one phoneme by another, such as replacing the /c/ in *cat* with /m/ to form the word *mat*. Rhyming involves recognizing common vowel sounds between words. A whole-language approach, in contrast to a skills-based approach, emphasizes meaningful units such as words and tries to teach words as wholes instead of breaking words up into intrinsically meaningless phonemic parts. This approach rests on the premise that even beginning readers have a certain amount of language experience and that new words can be integrated with that prior experience.

16. (A) A cloze procedure involves filling in omitted words from a passage. Webbing is a technique used in pre-writing where diagrams are used to help visualize conceptual relations. A rebus uses pictures to represent some words. Morphemic identification would involve recognizing morphemes in words, such as the *a-* in amoral, the *dis-* in disinformation or the *-ism* in ethnocentrism.

17. (B) The *ee* in *feet* has one distinct sound, so it's not a dipthong. It is a front vowel because the highest part of the tongue is in the front of the mouth when making the sound. It is stressed, whereas the schwa sound is unstressed.

18. (C) Aspiration refers to the explosion of breath as when one pronounces a plosive consonant. Rounding of the lips is important in pronouncing certain vowel sounds. The position of the tongue has nothing to do with whether a consonant is voiced or voiceless.

19. (A) Nouns are modified (or described or limited) by adjectives. The adverbs of a sentence can usually be easily identified by asking questions about the verb (a sentence *must* have a verb).

20. (D) These are the three moods in English, although the use of the subjunctive is optional. Case refers to using different forms of pronouns and placing them in a different spot in a sentence to indicate whether the pronoun is being used as subject, as direct object, as indirect object or in the possessive. The tense of a verb indicates when the action described by the verb took place. The three aspects of verbs are the simple, the perfect, and the progressive.

21. (C) The easiest way to identify the subject is to turn the sentence into a question. This is done by inverting the subject and the verb: "Is there a book on the table?" Since *is* is definitely the verb, *there* must be the subject.

22. (C) A transitive verb is one that requires a direct object, while an intransitive verb does not. Most verbs in English can be used either way.

23. (C) A gerund looks like a verb but functions as a noun. It is formed by attaching *-ing* to the end of a verb: *Reading* is necessary; *Singing* is good; *Smoking* is bad; etc. In all of these sentences, the gerund is the subject. Infinitives function as nouns, adjectives or adverbs. Participles function as adjectives. The predicate of a sentence is everything besides the subject.

24. (B) The positive would be *John is tall*. The superlative would be *John is tallest*. A double superlative is an incorrect construction such as *John is most tallest*. As you can see, the positive involves one object, the comparative at least two objects, and the superlative at least three objects.

25. (C) Interrogative sentences ask questions and end with question marks. Declarative sentences state facts or convey information such as "Light travels 186,000 miles in one second." A counterfactual sentence usually starts with "If I were..." or "If I had..." An exclamatory sentence expresses emotion or feeling: "Gosh, that was the best dinner I've ever eaten!"

26. (A) A non sequitur is an invalid argument where the conclusion does not logically follow from the premises. An ad hominem argument attacks an individual personally. An ad populum argument appeals to what is taken to be popular at the given moment.

27. (A) Personal memories, prescriptions, and speculations are not very important modes of thinking in expository paragraphs.

28. (D) Drafting is the stage after prewriting. Drafting is not merely writing things down (freewriting is also a form of writing but it takes place before drafting). One way to express the difference is to say that prewriting may or may not include putting words on paper, while drafting definitely involves writing (not any type of writing but the composing of words into sentences, and sentences into paragraphs, and paragraphs into a coherent whole).

29. (C) An almanac contains factual information about countries, as would an atlas. Besides the dominant religion, one could find information on dominant languages, currency, population growth rates, etc.

30. (D) All of the first three answer choices may contain persuasive elements, but the main intent is not persuasion.

1. (C) The equator passes through central Africa in the countries of Gabon, Zaire, Uganda, and Kenya. Equatorial regions experience precipitation all year round and high average temperatures. In terms of vegetative features, rain forests occur in equatorial regions. Northern Africa is more arid and receives little or no precipitation. Temperate climates are cooler than equatorial ones but also receive precipitation all year round. Polar climates have the lowest average temperatures.

2. (B) Baja, California is the western part of Mexico just below the American state of California. Other examples of peninsulas would be the Yucatán (also a part of Mexico) and the Iberian Peninsula, which is the western-most extremity of Europe (on which are located the countries of Spain and Portugal).

3. (D) Meridians of longitude are imaginary lines drawn vertically on maps in order to measure east/west distances. The other special meridian of longitude is the prime (or Greenwich) meridian. The other three answer choices are examples of parallels of latitude.

4. (B) The Ganges flows mainly through India, with its source in the Himalayas and its mouth on the Bay of Bengal in of Bangladesh. It has a special religious significance for the Hindus of India.

5. (C) Population density (how many people per square mile or kilometer) would be shown on a demographic map. Capitals would be shown on political maps. Sites of military battles would probably be indicated on a historical map.

6. (C) Lack of writing is one of the things that defines a culture as prehistorical.

7. (B) Feudalism consisted of political rather than economic relations between lords. Socialism and capitalism are both terms used to describe economic relations *after* the end of the medieval period, especially as a result of the Industrial Revolution.

8. (D) The Renaissance began sometime in the 15th century, the Reformation began at the beginning of the 16th, and the Enlightenment is usually identified with the 18th. Détente is the period of less tense relations between the United States and the Soviet Union (USSR) during the early 1970s.

9. (B) Amerigo Vespucci, an Italian, explored the coast of Brazil for the royal court of Portugal in 1501 and Brazil became a Portuguese colony. Portuguese is the official language of Brazil to this day. The other three explorers sailed under the patronage of the Spanish crown.

10. **(D)** The French and Indian War was a war between the French and English for control of North America. Both sides employed the help of Indian allies. The American colonists fought for the British of course, but the taxes imposed on the colonists by the British government to help pay for the war led to the American Revolution.

11. **(D)** The Intolerable Acts (about 1774) closed the port of Boston, required colonists to quarter British soldiers, and revoked the colonial charter of Massachusetts, partly as punishment for the Boston Tea Party. As for the other answer choices, the Reform Acts were a series of electoral reforms in Britain during the 19th century. The Alien and Sedition Acts were a series of measures passed by the new American government in 1798 which gave the government the right to deport aliens considered dangerous. They also outlawed slanderous statements against the U.S. government. The Virginia and Kentucky Resolutions were protests against the Alien and Sedition Acts passed by the legislatures of those two states.

12. **(A)** The Declaration of Independence is described in the main text. The Articles of Confederation formed the first American national government after the end of the Revolutionary War. The Constitution of 1789 replaced the Articles of Confederation. The Monroe Doctrine was the President Monroe's warning to European powers that they should not intervene in the western hemisphere's affairs.

13. **(B)** The nullification crisis between South Carolina and the Federal Government was an example of the conflict between states' rights and federal authority. This conflict would culminate in the Civil War when eleven southern states seceded from the Union and formed the Confederate States of America. South Carolina happened to be the first state to secede in 1860. The other Confederate states were Georgia, Florida, Alabama, Mississippi, Louisiana, Texas, Virginia, North Carolina, Tennessee, and Arkansas.

14. **(C)** The Emancipation Proclamation, issued late in 1862, proclaimed that slaves in Confederate territories would be free as of January 1, 1863. Official abolition of slavery for the whole country came with the Thirteenth Amendment. The Fifteenth Amendment protected the former slaves' right to vote.

15. **(B)** The Fair Deal was Truman's attempt to extend Roosevelt's New Deal. Among its concerns were civil rights and fair employment. The New Frontier was the Kennedy Administration's idealistic program: raising of the minimum wage, improvements in housing, and the Peace Corps. The Great Society was the goal of Lyndon Johnson's administration, where the elimination of poverty and medical care for the elderly (Medicare) were top priorities. Medicare was subsequently extended to younger low-income people as Medicaid.

16. (B) Among the results of better relations with the Soviet Union was the first Strategic Arms Limitation Treaty (SALT I) in 1971. This treaty limited the number of Intercontinental Ballistic Missiles that could be deployed by the U.S. and the Soviet Union.

17. (B) The federal government is tripartite in structure because there are three branches: the legislative, the executive, and the judicial. "Bicameral" refers to the fact that there are two houses of the legislature: the House of Representatives and the Senate.

18. (C) Amendment of the Constitution requires approval of three-quarters or 75% of the state legislatures.

19. (C) Senators used to be chosen by state legislatures but are now directly elected by the people as a result of the 17th Amendment passed in 1913.

20. (C) The federal government is specifically forbidden in establishing a church by the 1st Amendment.

21. (A) The Pendleton Act set up a Civil Service Commission in order to make federal employment less influenced by political patronage and the spoils system and more open to merit and competitive examination.

22. (B) Autocracy is rule by one in the interests of that one. Oligarchy is rule by the few in their own interests. Plutocracy means rule by the wealthy or rich.

23. (B) In a market system, the price is not dictated by any one institution but rather by the decisions of millions of individuals. These millions of decisions go to make up supply and demand, and the interaction of supply and demand determines price.

24. (B) Monetary policy is the government's attempt to regulate the money supply by manipulating interest rates. Stabilization policy refers to the increase in unemployment benefits that occurs during periods of economic recession. A country may or may not have a protectionist policy. If it does, it tries to protect domestic industries by imposing extremely high tariffs (taxes) on imported goods.

25. (B) The CPI is a measure of inflation (a rise in the general level of prices in an economy). It is computed by tracking the prices of a typical 'basket' of goods of a typical household. When the newspaper says that inflation rose last year by a certain percent, it means that the CPI rose by that percent.

26. (D) The United Nations (UN) is generally concerned with political and military relations between nations. The World Trade Organization (WTO) tries to settle trade disputes between nations. The International Monetary Fund (IMF) is concerned with regulating international exchange rates. The European Union (EU) has relaxed border restrictions between western European countries in order to allow labor and capital to flow more freely between those countries.

27. (B) Archaeologists study the physical remains of now extinct cultures. A theologian studies religion. A sociologist tends to study modern (post-Industrial Revolution) societies rather than primitive ones.

28. (A) Ethnocentrism is a cardinal sin in social science because it goes against the idea that social science ought to be value-free, or at least value-neutral. Egocentrism is "self-centeredness" and concerns an individual rather than a whole ethnic group or culture. Reductionism is the tendency to reduce a belief or practice to something more scientifically treatable. For instance, trying to reduce the concept of "mind" to the physical processes of the brain. Functionalism is a type of explanation where a practice is explained by the function it serves for the group (whether the members of the group actually have this intention or not).

29. (A) The usual examples of highly stratified societies are the caste system in India and the class system of Great Britain. Division of labor refers to dividing work into a series of small, specialized tasks in order to increase productivity. Secularization is a long-term historical process whereby social institutions turn away from religious or spiritual matters and concern themselves more with worldly or "temporal" matters. Gemeinschaft is a German term meaning roughly "community."

30. (B) Piaget is known for identifying different stages of learning, Jung posited universal archetypes that underlie seemingly different cultural manifestations, and Pavlov is famous for his observations of salivating dogs.

MATHEMATICS SAMPLE TEST ANSWERS & EXPLANATIONS

1. (D) The set of real numbers is a proper subset of the complex numbers and not the other way around. As for the other answer choices, they are all proper subsets of the real numbers and of the set of complex numbers.

2. (D) The quickest way to test whether a pair of numbers are in fact reciprocals of each other is to multiply them. If you get +1, then the numbers are reciprocals; if you get anything other than +1, then they are not reciprocals. –7 and 1/7 when multiplied give –1, so they are not reciprocals.

3. (C) In simplifying the expression remember PEMDAS, the standard order of operations:

    $7[3 – 5(2)] – (–2)^3$ parentheses

    $7[-7] - (-2)^3$ brackets; multiplication before addition

    $7[-7] - (-8)$ exponent

    $7[-7] + 8$ negative times a negative equals a positive

    $- 49 + 8$ multiplication

    $- 41$ addition

4. (C) The symbol "341" in base 5 means

    $3(5^2) + 4(5^1) + 1(5^0)$

    $3(25) + 4(5) + 1(1)$

    $75 + 20 + 1$

    96

5. (A) 36 has nine positive factors: {1, 2, 3, 4, 6, 9, 12, 18, 36}. Out of these only two are prime: {2, 3}. Two out of nine is approximately 22%.

6. (D) By the Euclidian Algorithm, the GCF of 198 and 84 is the same as the GCF of 84 and 30 (30 is the remainder after dividing 198 by 84). The GCF of 84 and 30 is the same as the GCF of 30 and 24, and the latter is the same as the GCF of 24 and 6, which is 6. An easier way to find the answer without this algorithm is to take the greatest value answer choice, in this case choice D, and divide it into 198 and 84; if it goes into both numbers evenly, then it must be the GCF since it's the greatest value answer.

7. (C) If the ratio of women to men is 2 to 1, then for every group of 3, 2 are women and 1 is a man. Since there are 12 total, we have 4 groups of 3, so there are 4 times 2, or 8, women. Algebraically:

$$\frac{\text{Women}}{\text{total}} = \frac{2}{3} \Rightarrow \frac{W}{12} = \frac{2}{3} \Rightarrow 3W = 24 \Rightarrow W = 8$$

8. (C) The question is asking for the third (or cube) root of 64; in other words, what is the number when multiplied by itself three times that gives you 64? The only answer choice that fits the description is C. As for the other choices, 2^3 is 8 (in other words, the cube root of 8 is 2), 3^3 is 27 (the cube root of 27 is 3) and 5^3 is 125 (the cube root of 125 is 5).

9. (C) The find the coordinate of the midpoint simply average the coordinates of the endpoints (add them and then divide by 2):

$$[11 + (-5)] \div 2 = 6 \div 2 = 3$$

10. (D) Keep PEMDAS in mind when simplifying. Inside the parentheses cannot be added and there are no exponents that can be done, so the first step is multiplication (by distribution).

$10x^2 - 5x + 3x - 8x^3 - 10x^2 + 1$	multiplied $5x(2x - 1)$ by distribution
$- 5x + 3x - 8x^3 + 1$	$10x^2$ and $-10x^2$ add up to zero
$- 2x - 8x^3 + 1$	added $- 5x$ and $3x$
$- 8x^3 - 2x + 1$	no like terms; rewritten in descending order of exponents

11. (D) Factor twice by the difference of two perfect squares method:

$$x^4 - 81 = (x^2)^2 - (9)^2 = (x^2 + 9)(x^2 - 9)$$
$$= (x^2 + 9)(x + 3)(x - 3)$$

12. (A) You can solve the quadratic by factoring the left side:

$$x^2 + 2x - 35 = 0 \qquad \text{given}$$

$$(x + 7)(x - 5) = 0 \qquad \text{factored left side}$$

$(x + 7) = 0$ or $(x - 5) = 0$ since the product equals 0, at least one of the factors must equal 0.

$$x = -7 \text{ or } x = +5$$

You can discard 5 since it's not one of the answer choices. An alternative way of doing the problem is to plug the answer choices into the given equation: if after plugging in and simplifying you get a true statement, then that value is a possible value for x. Plugging in zero (answer choice C) gives:

$$(0)^2 + 2\,(0) - 35 = 0$$

$$+\ 0\ -\ 35 = 0$$

$$-35 = 0$$

This is not a true statement, so 0 is not a possible value for x. Plugging in the correct answer choice, -7, gives:

$$(-7)^2 + 2(-7) - 35 = 0$$

$$49 - 14 - 35 = 0$$

$$49 - 49 = 0$$

$$0 = 0$$

which is a true statement. So, -7 is a possible value for x.

13. (C) Solve the inequality for x, remembering that multiplying or dividing both sides by a negative reverses the direction of the inequality.

$-\frac{3}{4}x + 2 > 17$ given

$-\frac{3}{4}x > 15$ subtracted 2 from both sides

$x < 15\left(-\frac{4}{3}\right)$ multiplied both sides by - 4/3 thereby reversing inequality

$x < -20$ simplified right side by multiplication

14. **(B)** In general, if the absolute value of some quantity is equal to a number other than zero there will be two different solutions. If the absolute value of a quantity is equal to zero, then there will be only one solution. To verify that there are two different solutions in this problem do some algebra:

$\lvert x - 2 \rvert + 1 = 8$	given
$\lvert x - 2 \rvert = 7$	subtracted 1 from both sides
$(x - 2) = 7$ or $(x - 2) = -7$	definition of absolute value
$x = 9$ or $x = -5$	solved for x

15. **(A)** First we have to plug –24 into g and see what comes out; this output then becomes the input for the function f. The output from f is the answer. So, plugging –24 into g gives ¼ (-24) or –6. Taking –6 and plugging into f gives $(-6)^2 - 1$ or 35.

16. **(D)** Since lines 1 and 2 are parallel, angle C and the angle of 35° are supplementary; in other words, they have to add up to 180°. So angle C must be 180° minus 35° or 145°.

17. **(C)** The exterior angles of the octagon must add up to 360° and all 8 of the angles must be equal. So each one must be 45°.

18. **(A)** The usual approach to problems involving "area of the shaded region" is to subtract one area from another. The shaded area in this figure is not a geometric figure for which we have a formula, but we can see that the shaded regions are the difference between the area of the square and the area of the circle. So find the area of the square and then subtract the area of the circle. Since the square has a side equal in length to two radii of the circle, the square has sides of length 10, so the area is $(10)^2$ or 100. The circle has an area of $(5)^2 \pi$ or 25π. 100 – 25 (3.14) = 21.5. The question asks for the approximate area because π is only approximately equal to 3.14.

19. **(A)** The area of triangle CDE is ½ (base)(height) or ½ (DE)(CD). Triangle CDE happens to be a 30°: 60°: 90° triangle which means we can save some time: by the Pythagorean Theorem, if the side opposite the 30° angle is x, then the side opposite the 60° angle is $\sqrt{3}(x)$. The side opposite the 30° angle is the height CD and the side opposite the 60° angle is the base DE. (CD also happens to be one side of the square and we know that it is 5 since the perimeter of the square is given as 20.) Since CD is 5, DE must be

$5\sqrt{3}$. So the area of the triangle is ½ $\left(5\sqrt{3}\right)(5)$ which is answer choice A.

20. (B) The person's driving route could be represented by the following diagram:

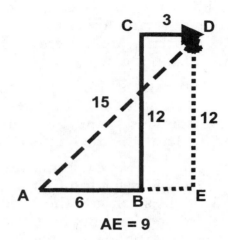

AE = 9

The length AD is the hypotenuse of the right triangle shown in the diagram, so use the Pythagorean Theorem to find AD. You could save time if you recognize that the right triangle is a 9-12-15 (which is a 3-4-5 right triangle multiplied by a factor of 3).

21. (D) The greatest distance from Town A to Town C occurs if the three town all lie on the same line. In this case 25 is the maximum possible distance. If the three towns were in a triangular relation to each other, then the distance from A to C would have to be less than 25 but greater than 5.

22. (A) The height h can be determined by using the definition of volume: length times width times height, so we have $(10)(3)\, h = 150$ or $h = 5$. The length of the height is measured in linear units (or just units), while the volume is expressed in cubic units. Area is expressed in square units.

23. (B) The central angle is given as 60° so the length of the arc ABC must be 60/360 or 1/6 of the entire circumference. Since the radius OA is given as 2, the circumference is $2\pi(2)$ or 4π. ⅙ of $4\pi = \frac{2}{3}\pi$.

24. (B) Without doing any formal algebra, we can see that the slope of the line is positive and that its y-intercept is negative (it crosses the vertical axis below the origin). All of the answer choices are given in slope-intercept form, where the coefficient of x is the value of the slope and the constant term is the y-intercept.

25. (B) The easiest way to determine whether the point is on the given line is to plug the x and y values into the given equation and see if you get a true statement. Plugging in answer choice (A) gives $3(-2) - 2(3) = 10$ or $-12 = 10$, which is not true. Answer choice (C) gives $3(0) - 2(0) = 10$ or $0 = 10$, which is not true. Answer choice (D) gives $3(3) - 2(-2) = 10$ or $13 = 10$, which is also not true.

26. (B) The counting numbers less than or equal to 6 are {1, 2, 3, 4, 5, 6}. Since there is an even number of numbers, there is no single "middle" number so the median is found by averaging the two "middlemost" numbers (3 and 4). Thus the median is (3 + 4)/2 or 3.5.

27. (A) We want to find the number of permutations of the 4 objects B, L, O and C. We have 4 choices for the first spot but once we have chosen we have only 3 choices left for the second spot. Then there are 2 choices for the third spot and finally 1 choice for the final spot. So the total number of permutations of 4 objects is 4! or $4 \times 3 \times 2 \times 1$ or 24.

28. (B) Committee problems like this one usually call for combinations rather than permutations because the order here does not matter. A committee composed of {Alice, Bob} is the same as one composed of {Bob, Alice}, so all of the redundant permutations should be 'divided out':

$$\frac{7 \times 6 \times 5}{3 \times 2 \times 1} = 35$$

29. (B) When doing the computation, remember to deduct the 2 cards that are red *and* queen. The probability of drawing a red card is 26/52 while the probability of drawing a queen is 4/52. Add these and then subtract the 2 red queens:

$$\frac{26}{52} + \frac{4}{52} - \frac{2}{52} = \frac{28}{52} \approx 54\%$$

30. (C) The notation in answer choice (C) and in the Venn diagram both represent the concept of the *difference* between set A and set B, which means the members that are in A but *not* in B. Answer choice (D) represents the members in B but not in A. Answer choice (A) is the union of A and B, while answer choice (B) is the intersection of A and B.

SCIENCE SAMPLE TEST ANSWERS & EXPLANATIONS

1. **(B)** All three were ancient Greeks. The other three civilizations mentioned did not make significant advances in scientific theory.

2. **(C)** All three figures are associated with biology: Linnaeus developed the system of classification that bears his name, Darwin advanced the theory of evolution by natural selection and Mendel is known for his research in genetics.

3. **(B)** An axiom is a self-evident proposition like "two parallel lines never intersect". A conjecture is a reasoned guess and is not that much different from a hypothesis. A syllogism is a logical argument consisting of two premises followed by a conclusion.

4. **(B)** Answer choice (A) describes deductive reasoning. Answer choice (C) describes deductive reasoning in the context of ethics and politics. Answer choice (D) might describe the type of thinking used in poetic or literary writing.

5. **(B)** Science does involve thinking, expressing, and prescribing but its essential activity is careful observation. If a theory does not correspond with observation, the theory is thrown into doubt.

6. **(B)** The atomic number of an element indicates the number of protons, and this is what defines an element as what it is. A different atomic number means a different element. An atomic number of eight means oxygen, an atomic number of seven means nitrogen, an atomic number of six means carbon, etc. Atomic weight and atomic mass are synonymous and they indicate the number of protons plus the number of neutrons. The molecular formula gives the number of atoms of an element in a molecule.

7. **(B)** Potassium-40 must have nineteen protons because that is what defines potassium as an element. Isotopes of an element differ in the number of neutrons, so Potassium-40 has forty minus nineteen, or twenty-one, neutrons.

8. **(B)** Iodine would be an example of a halogen.

9. **(C)** Generally speaking, organic compounds are those that contain carbon. Organic chemistry studies how carbon bonds with other elements, particularly hydrogen, to form hydrocarbons. Inorganic chemistry studies non-hydrocarbon molecules.

10. **(A)** Chlorophyll is a chemical found in plants which aids in photosynthesis and gives plants their characteristically green color. It is composed mainly of carbon and hydrogen.

11. (A) Mitosis results in two identical daughter cells with the diploid number of chromosomes. Gametes are haploid sex cells that result from meiosis. Zoospores are a means of asexual reproduction used by some fungi and protists. Mitochondria function in cellular respiration.

12. (D) Answer choice (A) refers to the formation of the ionic compound sodium chloride (salt). (B) refers to the components of water. (C) refers to a type of compound usually abbreviated CFC. Freon used in air-conditioners is an example of a CFC. When CFCs are released into the atmosphere and then the stratosphere, they may decompose ozone molecules (which are composed of three oxygen atoms) into normal oxygen molecules (which are composed of two oxygen atoms).

13. (D) Answer choices (A), (B) and (C) are all false.

14. (C) Only the plant kingdom is exclusively autotrophic, meaning that all members of the plant kingdom feed themselves through photosynthesis. Some protists, algae for example, may be autotrophic.

15. (A) Fixation is the conversion of atmospheric nitrogen into a form usable by living organisms. Lithification refers to formation of sedimentary rock. Sublimation is the change of water from a solid state to a gaseous state.

16. (C) DNA and RNA are both associated with genetic inheritance and protein synthesis. Carbon monoxide in large amounts is fatal to humans because it has a strong attraction for the iron in human blood and thus prevents blood from performing its oxygen-circulating function.

17. (A) In general, as an era gets more recent, the smaller its slice of total geologic time. The prefixes indicate the order: ceno- means 'new', meso- means 'middle' and paleo- means 'old'. The Pre-Cambrian era, being the least recent, accounts for the biggest percentage of geologic time (about 88%).

18. (A) Sedimentary rock is formed in a process called lithification and will eventually be transformed into metamorphic rock by heat and pressure. Silica is not a type of rock but rather a chemical component of certain types of rock.

19. (D) (A) is called precipitation, (B) is called condensation and (C) is called infiltration.

20. (B) Sublimation is change from a solid to a gas, vaporization is from a liquid to a gas, and condensation is from a gas to a liquid.

21. (B) Absolute zero is the lowest temperature attainable by matter and is expressed as 0 Kelvins (about -273° Celsius and about -460° Fahrenheit). Entropy is a measure of randomness or disorder of atoms in physical systems and is expressed in the second law of thermodynamics.

22. (C) When the Southern Hemisphere is starting autumn, it is the vernal equinox (beginning of spring) for the Northern Hemisphere. At this point both hemispheres are equally facing the sun.

23. (C) A nebula is relatively diffused gas and dust particles. The other three answer choices describe types of stars. A white dwarf is relatively small, dense and not very bright. A red giant is relatively large and bright. A nova is a star that experiences a sudden explosion, becomes very luminous, and quickly fades.

24. (C) Acceleration is the only vector quantity and so it has a direction; the acceleration due to gravity is directed downward toward the earth, centripetal acceleration is directed toward the center of a circular path, etc. Acceleration is defined as the change in velocity with respect to time.

25. (C) According to Newton's Law of Gravitational Attraction, the attraction between two bodies is proportional to their masses and inversely proportional to the square of the distance between them. If we treat the distance as fixed, then the attraction depends entirely on the masses of the bodies: simply multiply the masses to get the total attraction. One mass increases two times while the other increases four times, so the total increase in gravitational attraction is 2 × 4 (=8) times.

26. (A) According to the Ideal Gas Law, if all other factors are held constant and not allowed to change, then as the temperature of the gas is increased, the volume of the gas will also increase.

27. (C) Certain physical events can only happen in one way: a cup can fall from a shelf and shatter. However, shattered cups do not put themselves back together and return to shelves, despite the fact that there is available energy to put it back together. The difference is that the atoms in the pieces of shattered cup are in a state of relatively high disorder while the cup on the shelf has atoms in a relatively highly ordered state. The measure of disorder or randomness of atoms or atomic systems is called entropy.

28. (A) Longer wavelength means less frequency and less energy. The answer choices are arranged from longest to shortest wavelength.

29. (B) Fusion is the opposite of fission. Diffraction and refraction both refer to the change in the direction of light waves.

30. (D) The ball has the greatest amount of gravitational potential energy at point A since at this point it is highest off the ground; it has no kinetic energy since it's at rest. As the ball begins to roll down the slope towards point B, it gains kinetic energy and loses gravitational potential energy. As it rolls back up toward point C, it loses kinetic and gains potential, and then resumes gaining kinetic and losing potential as it rolls down toward point D.